D1486220

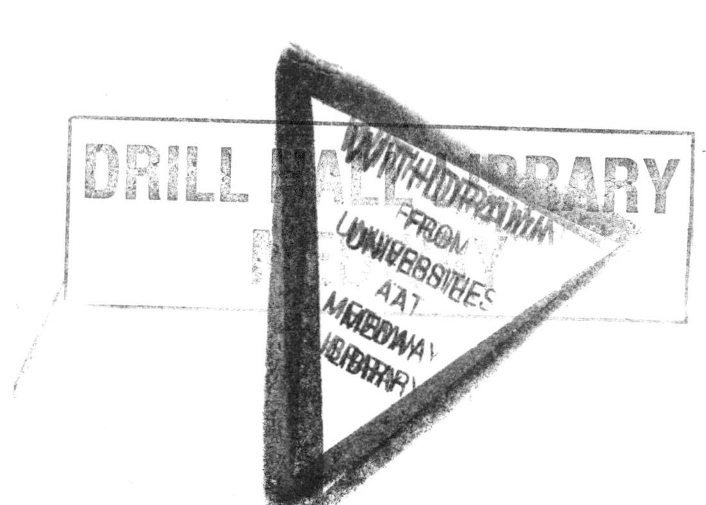

KJOUR

15003518

AFRICA'S LONG ROAD SINCE INDEPENDENCE

3059895

KEITH SOMERVILLE

Africa's Long Road Since Independence

The Many Histories of a Continent

HURST & COMPANY, LONDON

First published in the United Kingdom in 2015 by
C. Hurst & Co. (Publishers) Ltd., 41 Great Russell Street, London, WC1B 3PL
© Keith Somerville, 2015
All rights reserved.
Printed in India

Distributed in the United States, Canada and Latin America by
Oxford University Press, 198 Madison Avenue, New York, NY 10016,
United States of America.

The right of Keith Somerville to be identified as the author of
this publication is asserted by him in accordance with the
Copyright, Designs and Patents Act, 1988.

A Cataloguing-in-Publication data record for this book
is available from the British Library.

ISBN: 978-184904-515-5

This book is printed using paper from registered sustainable
and managed sources.

www.hurstpublishers.com

CONTENTS

ACKNOWLEDGEMENTS

This book has been the product of nearly four decades of the study of Africa, even though it was commissioned and written in 2013–4. There are many people over the years who've encouraged and supported my work as an academic and a journalist. Foremost among these has been Professor Jack Spence—a friend and valued colleague over the years whose advice has always been timely and to the point.

In writing the book I have benefitted from the advice and constructive criticism of a number of academic and former BBC colleagues. Teresa Guerreiro, as always, has been willing to read chapters and suggest improvements and places where I could edit out superfluous text—and has fought hard and usually successfully to stop me starting sentences with *and*. I'm also very grateful to Professor Richard Rathbone and my colleague at the University of Kent, Giacomo Macola, who have read and helped me improve chapters, and given clear and constructive advice.

Others have played an important role in helping me refine my approach to key areas: Mary Harper on Somalia, Martin Plaut on Kenya's role in Somalia, Umaru Fofana, David Keen and Paul Richards on Sierra Leone, Max Bankole Jarrett and Stephen Ellis on Liberia, Fergus Nicoll on Sudan, Alex de Waal on Darfur, Lara Pawson, Isaias Samakuva, and Justin Pearce on Angola, Raymond Suttner on South Africa, Ian Taylor on Botswana, Mathias Muindi on Kenya and Professor Michael Twaddle on Uganda. There have been many others over the years whose input to earlier works has helped enormously with this one. I'd also like to thank Professor Philip Murphy and Sue Onslow at the Institute for Commonwealth Studies, for their support since I became a Senior Research Fellow there.

Michael Dwyer and his team at Hurst and Co have been very supportive and turned this project into a reality for me.

Most of all I need to thank my wife Liz and son Tom for their humour, patience and willingness to criticise, cajole and sometimes just to shut me up! They make sure I don't cross the line in the sand—they know what I mean.

INTRODUCTION

Arriving in Malawi in late September 1981, I was immediately fascinated by Africa, and have never since broken free—or wanted to.

Walking across the tarmac at Lilongwe's tiny airport, which struck me as ludicrously small for a capital city, I was presented with sights, sounds, scents and a type of heat I'd never experienced before. I'd already studied Africa for several years as an undergraduate and postgraduate student, and monitored Ghanaian, Nigerian and South African radio broadcasts from Caversham for the BBC Monitoring Service for 18 months, before being posted to Malawi, but I had much to learn. I was there to monitor more southern African stations and report the news, political and economic information and comment they broadcast.

After my stay in Malawi, I went on to recently independent Zimbabwe to pursue my research on southern African liberation movements and particularly their relations with the Soviet Union, Cuba and China. While there, I met many of the leaders of the liberation movements, including the founder of the Zimbabwe African Union and author of *African Nationalism*,[1] Ndabaningi Sithole. With Sithole I talked not just about Zimbabwe and his own political fortunes, but about the broad thrust of nationalism in Africa.

In the 34 years since that first working trip to Africa I've been back most years and reported on major events such as the first fully democratic elections in South Africa in 1994, the demands for greater democracy in Africa in the early 1990s and the human consequences of the civil war in Angola, to name but a few. In nearly four decades of reporting, documentary-making and research in Africa I've been in the privileged position of witnessing key events at first hand, interviewing major African decision-makers and ordinary people about these events and being able to debate developments and trends with leading analysts and commentators as well as foreign academics and journalists covering the continent's affairs and those of specific states. This has offered me a perspective that is often different from those of academics, and by keeping a foot in the academic and journalistic worlds, I've had the time to dig deeper than deadlines and editors' demands permit many journalists to do.

This background and direct experience has moulded my views on Africa over time and led me to expect the unexpected. Most of all, it has taught me that it's only with the luxury of hindsight and historical analysis that we can begin to identify the circumstances, structures and elements of human agency that combined to produce events that took many by surprise.

An example of this is the peaceful transition in South Africa after the 1994 elections. I had been a close observer of the process of change there as both a journalist and an academic analyst. When I went out in April 1994 to lead the World Service's South Africa news team, I was equipped with a flak jacket and a local minder, both because of the township violence between Nelson Mandela's African National Congress (ANC) and the Zulu leader Mangosuthu Buthelezi's Inkatha Freedom Party (IFP) and because of the threat of violence of far-right Afrikaner nationalist groups. Just after my arrival there were explosions near my hotel in a plush suburb of Johannesburg and in nearby Germiston, set off by these latter groups. But after the elections, reconciliation became the theme of the transition and the feared violence from the far right did not materialise, while Inkatha and Buthelezi were brought into the new ANC-dominated government.

At the same time, the horrific Rwandan genocide was underway, ignored by much of the world's press and by the UN despite the pleas of people on the ground in Kigali. With the luxury of hindsight, analysts and journalists like me can chart the chilling progress towards the genocide, but at the time it took people by surprise, as did the killing of President Juvénal Habyarimana. I was editing the evening edition of the BBC World Service Newshour programme when the news of his death was first reported. I'd been to Rwanda several years before; I was aware of its history and I knew Habyarimana's death would lead to reprisals and the likely resumption of war, but never in my worst nightmares had I foreseen what actually happened.

Constant engagement as a journalist and an academic researcher over this long period has made me wary of great theories that purport to explain Africa's historical development, its political advances and setbacks and its economic development. The journalist in me wants to cover every major event and explain the who, what, where, when, why and how; the academic in me cautions against focusing on events or personalities, and to look for wider themes.

The synthesis of these potentially contradictory approaches is that this account of the contemporary history of Africa will have detailed case studies looking at the who, what and when, alongside a more considered and thematic approach to the how and the why. This book concentrates heavily on the period since the early 1970s, not just because it matches the period of my engagement with Africa first as a student and then as a journalist and an academic, but because it was a period of rapid change in post-colonial Africa. The 1970s saw the end of the last colonial empire in Africa, the Portuguese; the escalation of the struggles against white minority rule in southern Africa; the start of a global economic crisis that would shake the export-dependent economies of Africa to their narrow and vulnerable foundations; the destruction of the monarchy in Africa's oldest surviving polity, Ethiopia; and the entrenchment of authoritarian, highly personalised regimes and the apparent death of inclusive and accountable systems of government. As Stephen Ellis has identified in his work on the writing of African history,

> If one seeks to identify points of discontinuity in Africa's history since independence or, to be more precise, in the history of Africa's insertion in the world, it becomes apparent that many ruptures first became visible in the 1970s, when oil crises, currency instability and a series of related events and trends combined to create a comprehensive change in the prospects for African states and societies, and in the forms of their political life.[2]

Ellis concurs with Eric Hobsbawm in his analysis of global history that the 1970s was a very important decade of change with the end of a period of optimism of "a sort of Golden Age" and as the lustre of this age rapidly faded, "The last part of the century was a new era of decomposition, uncertainty and crisis," not least for Africa.[3]

The 1970s and 1980s were the decades of growing dictatorial and personal rule. As a journalist in Malawi, I was very well aware of the personal power of His Excellency the Life President Ngwazi Dr H. Kamuzu Banda. His word was law; no Malawian, even in the most private place, ever criticised him in my hearing. I was also able to experience, albeit from the position of an affluent expatriate, the problems of an economy that was dependent on tobacco and tea exports, was landlocked and whose transport routes to the sea were affected by South African-backed insurgency in Mozambique. There were frequent shortages of fuel, of consumer goods, even of toilet paper. Ordinary Malawians suffered from the shortages, loss of income due to falling export revenues, and increases in maize prices if harvests were low because insufficient fertiliser could be imported; these things meant not just minor inconvenience, but impoverishment and malnutrition. This in turn meant high child mortality rates and fatal or debilitating vulnerability to illnesses that I had considered uncomfortable nuisances—measles, diarrhoea, and of course, malaria.

My wider experience of African states over the years reinforced but also refined my early impressions and posed a growing number of questions. How did these leaders—Banda in Malawi, Mobutu in Zaire, Moi in Kenya, Kerekou in Benin and Bongo in Gabon, to name just a few—maintain power, and how did they wield such a strong personal influence over their states and peoples? Why have states been unable to break out of the cycle of poor terms of trade and export dependence that prevented broader and deeper economic development? How, in states with such weak institutions, could ruling elites survive while at the same time fail to control the whole of the state territory? How did ordinary Africans survive with minimal welfare and health provision?

I had no answers—and as I came to understand more about the core issues affecting African states and peoples, I was ever more aware that the simple depictions of crises, political systems and economic development provided by the media, of which I was a fully paid-up member, did not provide an accurate picture of the continent and its political, social and economic trends or provide answers when it blamed things on the incompetence, greed, selfishness or alleged tribalism of African leaders and their followers. This is no less true today, when media explanations of the violence in Kenya in 2007–8, the civil war in Sudan or the conflicts in Nigeria, Mali, the Central African Republic and South Sudan still look for simplistic, easily grasped explanations—tribal hatred, religious differences, irrational greed and violence.

Putting everything down to colonialism doesn't tell the whole story either. More in-depth studies have shown a better grasp of detail and of some of the recurring themes of post-colonial history, but they often opt for a particular structural explanation or deny structure in favour of agency as a key determinant. Some analysts have looked to personalities, the torrent of events such as conflicts[4] and theories of underdevelopment; others use theories of neo-colonialism and variant Marxisms to put structures of exploitation at the core of their explanations,[5] while still others turn to modernisation/development theory, whose strongly teleological approach located Africa in a preordained process of economic and political development from primordial to modern society.[6] Linked to these broad and contending approaches to Africa are the ideas that Africa's problems are a product of the continent's basic inability to cope with either democracy or economic development.

My experience has led me to question these either/or approaches and to examine the complex and, at times, bewildering interplay between structure and agency, between local and national or continental or global factors rather than trying to find a single theme or hypothesis that explains everything. Africans are not helpless or hopeless; they are not simply passive, powerless pawns at the mercy of structural processes. They fight to exercise their agency. But structural factors, whether Africa's subordinate and weak position in the international economic system, the artificiality of state borders and the ethnic composition of modern states, cannot be written off either, since they provide the environment in which agency is exercised.

As Marx identified in his work *The Eighteenth Brumaire of Louis Bonaparte*, "Men make their own history, but they do not make it just as they please."[7] African actors are the players in their own drama, but not the sole authors; they act out events in circumstances, locations and a wider environment over which they have little or no control.

An important point to emphasise here is that as the interplay of structure and agency has developed, there has been both continuity and change as Africa progressed from the era of pre-colonial history to colonialism and then independence. This progression does not offer clear-cut beginnings and endings, but is a continual flow that cannot be surgically separated into distinct periods with their own particular characteristics. Taking this view, this book does not treat Africa's post-colonial development as a complete end of external, colonial power over Africa. Nor do I see it as simply a continuation of that rule, a play written and directed externally with most Africans reduced to walk-on parts, bit players in a drama with a few chosen African "stars" in the heavily-directed leading roles. The institutions and cultural, social and economic structures of pre-colonial Africa were changed by colonialism, but they were not totally swept away. Pre-colonial and colonial history and institutions have had their effect on the present and will continue to do so, but not to the extent that all that has happened since the independence of states can be simply blamed on colonialism and the past.

Of course, it would also be wrong to say that colonial history is a thing of the past and can be packed away like an exhibit in a museum. Just as there was continuity in many spheres of activity between pre-colonial and colonial periods, so there have been elements of continuity from colonialism to independence right up to the present day. There is continuity and change in the physical environments Africans inhabit. Africans are subject to the power, the structures and the agency of foreign and global forces, but not to the point where they are deprived of all initiative or agency.

In this book, I try to unravel and explain how and why Africa moved from the exhilaration of independence and statehood—what former UN Secretary-General Kofi Annan describes as the "days of extraordinary hope and promise, the expectation that Africa was about to take, and that we finally had an opportunity to create for ourselves all that we had accused the colonial power of denying us"[8]—to the crisis of expectation and disillusionment, and then attempts to find new solutions. By the 1970s, the hope of creating this new world, with prosperity replacing poverty and the powerless empowered, had gone. Living standards failed to improve for the majority of people, and colonial control was being replaced not by evolving democracy and the accountability of the new governments but by variants of authoritarianism, with strong external influences on economic and political evolution. Economic independence proved to be beyond the grasp of African governments. The global economic crisis of the 1970s demonstrated how deeply African economies were integrated into the world capitalist system, and the extent to which this continued to disempower Africans and distort their states' political development.

By the 1970s, one-party systems and military governments were the norm rather than the exception. Much of southern Africa and parts of west Africa were still under Portuguese colonial rule or the rule of white minority governments. As a result, liberation struggles of varying scales were in progress in Angola, Mozambique, Guinea-Bissau, Rhodesia (now Zimbabwe), South West Africa (now Namibia) and South Africa. Civil wars had marred the early years of statehood in three of sub-Saharan Africa's biggest states—Sudan, Congo (Kinshasa) and Nigeria. Somalia had irredentist designs on Somali-inhabited regions of Ethiopia, French-ruled Djibouti and Kenya. These problems, as Annan has pointed out, are intertwined, the "coups, the mismanagement of economies, brutal regimes, the continual violation of human rights, and underdevelopment are all mutually reinforcing."[9]

The intervening decades between the 1970s and the writing of this book have been marked by conflict, the continuation of authoritarian and unaccountable rule, mounting corruption, the persistence of debilitating or fatal diseases and other threats to health, vulnerability to external intervention and to the power of the global capitalist system. But they have also seen the end of colonial occupation and white-minority rule. Some states have seen appreciable economic development and the maintenance of forms of accountability, but most have struggled economically and politically with little input from the majority of their populations. Change is constant and there are signs that it is now moving in the direction of greater popular participation, a gradual empowerment of women in what had been largely patriarchal societies, economic growth, and improvements in health provision and disease prevention.

But how deep, widespread and sustainable is this change? Is the "Africa Rising" discourse, seized on with alacrity by some African leaders and analysts, a reflection of real change and growth or is it a discourse based on optimism and a desire to represent transitory trends as lasting economic and political progress?[10] How much have Africans benefitted from the changes of the last four and a half decades? Are they more able to hold their leaders to account? Are they developing political systems that are based on their needs, political cultures and diversity of communities rather than on ill-suited Western models? Are they gaining greater control over their own economies and developing diverse and sustainable economic systems?

I have deliberately framed these as questions about dynamic and continuing processes, rather than just attempts to judge what has happened over the last four decades. This is a historical account, but one that takes history as constantly evolving, not as something that can be just stopped in its tracks and analysed.

In trying to answer the questions posed in this introduction, this book provides a narrative of events, an examination of key areas such as political change, economic structures and policies, the role of external powers and international factors while providing in-depth case studies of key events and issues. The chapters follow a broadly chronological progression but are not rigidly divided by time alone, and narratives are not truncated or split across chapters purely because they cut across decades. That would get in the way of examining long-term developments and inter-connections between events and regions. A historiographical note is included at the end of this book amplifying the concepts of the gatekeeper state, extraversion and arguments of structure versus agency.

Although the focus is chiefly on the period of African history since 1970, the opening chapter deals with pre-colonial societies, colonialism and decolonisation, demonstrating the seamless flow of history and the elements of both continuity and change in both structure and forms of the exercise of agency in that history. The second chapter covers the key themes of the early years of independence. The next four chapters deal with the period from 1970 to the present. The narrative and analysis weave together political, military, economic and social developments, local and regional factors as well as continental and international ones. The final chapter draws together the essential themes of the flow of post-colonial African history.

1

CONTINUITY AND CHANGE

FROM PRE-COLONIAL SOCIETIES THROUGH COLONIAL OCCUPATION TO INDEPENDENT STATES

The history of Africa is not one of discrete chapters or momentous ruptures. The contemporary is "only a small part of a larger whole...further evidence of the seamlessness of all history."[1] To understand it one must identify the key characteristics of precolonial African states in their diverse manifestations from loosely connected village or lineage-based communities to sophisticated kingdoms or caliphates, depicting the range of political, social and economic structures in place when the colonial powers imposed their own forms of rule which utilised or distorted existing structures. A proper awareness of the nature, consequences and African role in the slave trade is also essential, as is an appreciation of the nature and legacy of colonial rule and its role in the restructuring of key political, social and economic patterns and institutions. I will consider these points in this opening chapter, as well as the enduring impact of decolonisation and the fight for independence or majority rule in those territories where the colonisers or settlers resisted African demands. Ghana and Sudan offer useful case studies in the differing nature of the process in British, French and Portuguese territories and the way that the presence of settlers affected decolonisation in East and Central Africa.

This book is a study in the interplay of pre-colonial, colonial and post-colonial structures and the way they affected and were in turn refashioned by the exercise of agency, particularly as regards boundaries, states and institutions, elite formation and the development of extraverted economic systems.

The pre-colonial inheritance

The history of humankind begins with the evolution of the human species in Africa. Descendants of the first hominids spread across the African landmass and then peopled other continents. The early story is of human adaptation to the environment. From the struggle for survival in specific locations, distinct groups emerged as populations concentrated where food production enabled the growth of larger communities.[2] These communities developed their own structures, belief systems and languages—at least 1,500 languages have been identified in Africa. This diversity persists with the evolutionary effects of contact with the world beyond Africa over millennia through trade, imposition or adoption of foreign religions, raiding, conquest and then colonial occupation.

The structures of African communities varied hugely. There was no single, identifiable form of African societal structure. There were diverse structures, with forms evolving according to the nature of the environment and reflecting the need of peoples to have societal forms and hierarchies that accorded with the forms of subsistence most suitable to their region and climate, whether nomadic or settled, based on pastoralism, hunting or cultivation. Absolute monarchies and empires rose and fell, alongside acephalous (headless) structures in which looser forms of community lacking chiefs, kings or strong hierarchies of power developed and persisted.[3] In many areas there was no definable state, something which led early European traders and then colonisers to consider Africa a continent without history and irretrievably backward in societal and political terms—rather than accepting or attempting to understand how varying structures developed to meet varying needs. A huge spectrum of forms existed from the loosest communities without hierarchies, through confederations united by language, culture or belief right up to the hierarchical systems of the Mutapa kingdom based on the Shona people of present-day Zimbabwe, or the Ghana, Mali and Songhay empires of middle-Niger river region, the Bakongo kingdom of northern Angola-southern Congo, in Nigeria the Islamic sultanates/emirates of Sokoto, Kano or Borno, and in Southern Africa, the Zulu, Swazi, Sotho and Ndebele kingdoms.

These are but a few examples of the polities that developed and either fell before the era of colonialism or were defeated and dominated by colonial powers. The larger, more structured states had greater population densities enabled by the production of agricultural surpluses or, especially in the case of the Sahel region empires, the benefits of trade. But even the most tightly-governed societies loosened at their peripheries, and because of low population densities across the region and the physical obstacles of forests, rivers, lakes and mountain ranges, they lacked the clearly delineated boundaries between communities or states that characterised state formation in Europe. There was trade, inter-marriage and also shifting or blurred identities with language, kinship, religion and economic activity (settled agriculture vs. nomadic pastoralism, for example) all affecting how people saw and located themselves within communities and vis-à-vis neighbouring peoples. Identities overlapped and could carry different sets of meanings and values at different times or in changing circumstances and interactions between peoples were not simply governed by hard and fast identities relating to ethnicity, language or religion.[4]

Within this diversity, identities were complex. And before colonialism brought a new type of common experience and interaction beyond the local, a sense of Africa as a region or as a distinct set of peoples with common interests or shared identities did not exist. Peoples and states interacted with each other and, across the Sahara and along the Red Sea, Indian and Atlantic Ocean littorals, with non-African peoples. Trade and with it the spread of language (Arabic, in particular) and religion (Islam across the Sahara and on the east coast and, later, along the Atlantic coast, Christianity) were at the heart of interactions with peoples outside sub-Saharan Africa. Islam proved attractive to the rulers and merchants of the Sahel communities and empires, and the religion spread and evolved localised aspects across West Africa and along the Indian Ocean Coast. Early on, with the participation of African rulers, the export of people as slaves became an integral and damaging part of trade across the Sahara and on the Indian Ocean Coast.

Conflicts occurred between states or communities, but were rarely about territorial aggrandisement or the establishment of borders. Instead, they concentrated far more on resources such as cattle, gold, access to grazing or water, and on the need for labour in societies with low populations, which limited the scope for economic growth. Slaves were used to boost agricultural production or the mining and smelting of metals, and they became a tradable commodity. The Zaghawa of the Chad/Sudan region, the Tubu of Chad, the states of Kanem and Borno and the empires of the Sahel were all involved in the trade, with slaves taken from communities defeated in warfare or in raids by more powerful neighbours against weaker ones. The trade brought horses and firearms into the area of Africa bordering the Sahara and increased the military power of the trading states.[5]

It is estimated that in the14th and 15th centuries between 4,000 and 7,000 slaves were sent north across the Sahara each year, many dying on the way (as they were to on the slaves ships crossing the Atlantic from the 15th to 19th centuries).[6] Rulers, merchants and elites on the Indian Ocean coast were also involved in the slave trade, sending captives to the Arabian peninsula. The Saharan and Indian Ocean slave trade, lasted from the end of the first millennium AD until the late 19th century and saw as many as twelve million African slaves sent across the desert or seas—comparable to the number taken across the Atlantic by Portuguese, British and other slave traders from 1440 until 1867. In the main period of the slave trade, from 1400 to 1900 18.5 million Africans were sold as slaves and sent to the Americas, the Mediterranean littoral or the Arabian Peninsula, while another 18.5 million were enslaved and remained in Africa.[7] There was huge demand for slave labour in the Middle East and then in Portuguese, Spanish, French and British colonies in the Americas and an inhumane indifference on the part of those capturing, trading or using slaves to the suffering of the enslaved. Slavery became an early example of what Bayart calls the extraversion economy, in which African rulers "live chiefly off the income they derive from their position as intermediaries *vis-à-vis* the international system."[8] An early example of the gatekeeper function of African rulers developed in which they were the source of slaves, gold and ivory for export and gained power through the trade and the weapons, manufactures and wealth it brought in. The combination of pre-colonial and colonial gatekeeping and extraversion had a profound effect on the development of the economies and trading relations of independent states. The slave trade helped make Africa a subordinate and subject part of the international economic system. Through the development of dependency on exports of primary commodities and labour and reliance on imported manufactures in exchange reduced the potential for the development of diversified economies, even before the distorting effects of colonial occupation and exploitation of export commodities.[9]

Slave traders and their customers outside sub-Saharan Africa created ever more demand for this traffic in people, but relied on African rulers and raiders to supply the human raw material through warfare, raiding or tribute. Such rulers and slave traders were at the heart of the trade and used its proceeds—particularly guns, iron weapons and horses—to increase their own power regionally. There is a very strong argument that "the existence of Africans both capable and willing to capture other Africans was crucial to the emergence of the continent as a supplier of slaves."[10] The tragedy of slavery for those enslaved was paralleled by the increased wealth and power it conferred on those in Africa engaged in the trade.

The Atlantic trade developed from the Portuguese contacts with West and Central African communities along the Atlantic coast in the early 15th century. The Portuguese established plantations to grow sugar on São Tomé and purchased slaves from the Bakongo kingdom to work on the plantations. Portuguese development of its Brazilian colony and British colonial plantations on Jamaica and other Caribbean islands and the expansion of plantations on American mainland colonies led to the expansion of the trade. The Portuguese utilisation of slavery to build its colonial economy along with trade and the role of Catholic missionaries, built up the Portuguese presence on the coast of what became Guinea-Bissau, Angola and, at a slightly later period, Mozambique, as well as occupation of the Cape Verde islands and São Tomé. African states, traders and their European partners were all complicit in the merchandising of misery to meet economic demands in their American colonies. The trade, added to that of the Sahel and Indian Ocean, contributed to the under-population, slow pace of economic development and the subordinate role of Africa in the expanding world economy. It also had strong cultural and ideological effects emphasising African servitude, as perceived by Europeans and Arab peoples, but also in reverse by many Africans in terms of feelings of inferiority. Europeans justified the enslavement of Africans by referring to their alleged inferiority and backwardness and this also had a lasting effect on how Europeans viewed and treated Africans when it came to colonialism.

Colonial occupation and rule

The long-drawn-out European penetration of Africa developed from commodity trade to the slave trade and then the piecemeal establishment of trading ports or small protectorates along the coasts, and culminated in the period of colonial occupation from 1884 to the dismantling of the empires in the late 1950s and early 1960s. The occupation of the vast majority of sub-Saharan Africa after 1884 resulted in the division of sub-Saharan Africa into European colonies, with only Ethiopia and Liberia retaining formal independence. Peoples were thrown together artificially within colonially-defined territories or divided by externally-drawn borders. These borders took no account of existing states, confederations of communities or the welfare or interests of the inhabitants.

The drawing of the new colonial map of Africa at the Berlin Conference of 1884–5 was at best a haphazard affair where colonial prestige and horse-trading took precedence over everything else—including knowledge of the continent. Speaking at an Anglo-French conference in 1890, British Prime Minister Lord Salisbury admitted that, "We have been engaged in drawing lines upon maps where no white man's foot ever trod; we have been giving away mountains and rivers and lakes to each other, only hindered by the small impediment that we never knew exactly where the mountains and rivers and lakes were."[11]

The new map of Africa that emerged from Berlin demonstrated the largely unplanned nature of colonial occupation. The lines drawn by European rulers distant from and with very limited knowledge of Africa were not informed by the realities of life in African regions, communities, features or viability of territories, let alone any planned development in political or economic terms. Exact numbers are not available, but one estimate is that 10,000 communities or polities were reduced down to forty colonial territories whose final demarcation took decades, but even then, borders between colonies "were literally drawn onto the map, but left no physical trace...and indeed nothing changed after independence."[12] This negligent and arrogant construction of arbitrary boundaries created a multiplicity of small landlocked states which will always struggle economically, large multi-ethnic states whose population mix is not of the choosing of its inhabitants, and borders that by turns impede trade (cutting across old, established trade routes) and undermine state sovereignty and the hegemony or legitimacy of state institutions within national territories. The problem of inappropriate or unviable borders is not limited to Africa, as the continuing problems of borders in the South China Sea, the Ukraine and Russia, and the Balkans demonstrate, but has been particularly influential there because of the sheer numbers of communities thrown together or split by them. Beyond colonial aggrandisement, there was simply no concern for or interest in the consequences.

From the Berlin Conference to the decolonisation decade of 1956 to 1966, the newly defined territories were progressively occupied. Extractive economies based on primary agricultural produce and the mining of minerals were developed, and the major powers involved—Britain, France, Portugal, Germany, Belgium, Italy and Spain—imposed varying and generally ad hoc forms of colonial rule.

In many areas of life, colonialism only tangentially touched key pre-colonial cultural and societal structures and the institutions (formal and informal) through which people exercised agency over their lives. Those most affected were peoples directly governed or those employed in the cash crop or mining sectors. Colonialism developed new economic structures and practices, and put in place or adapted a variety of forms of government to manage the colonised. The precise nature of colonial administrations and policies differed not only between the colonising powers but also within specific empires and even territories. Most colonial powers used indirect rule where strong, hierarchical states with well-defined forms of authority, administration and legal systems already existed, and where the rulers of those states could be co-opted, bribed or coerced into becoming subordinate kings or chiefs under colonial tutelage. Those who accepted and worked within this system often had their powers enhanced and their area of control extended (as happened with the Tutsi monarchy in Rwanda). They retained authority over their subjects, often added new ones, continued to administer law, and derived income from taxes collected for the colonial government. The lives of such rulers' subjects often hardly changed; they remained subject to their own chiefs or kings and the administration of justice, land use and other key areas of day-to-day life were not significantly different.

In other areas, where there were stateless societies or very loose confederations, there was more direct rule but chiefs were also appointed to provide conduits for administration and tax collection, to implement systems of forced labour and to administer justice. While in the subjugated states there was resistance before occupation, and in some, after it (for example, Zululand during the Dinizulu and Bambatha revolts of 1883 and 1906), the more decentralised communities in colonial territories often resisted occupation and colonial rule precisely because they had looser systems of authority with elements of popular control. In the Tiv-peopled areas of what is now Plateau State in Nigeria and in eastern Nigeria, the imposition of chiefs and colonial administration was resisted "because it went against pre-colonial democratic procedure."[13]

In areas like this across colonial Africa—Tiv areas and Igboland in Nigeria, the Dogon, Bete, Kissi, Kru areas of French West Africa, and the Nuer, Luo, Maasai, Luo, Langa and Turkana of Sudan and Kenya—the colonial powers created chiefs where they did not exist or increased the powers of selected elders to be the local instruments of rule. In Portuguese colonies they were known as *regulos* and in British colonies 'warrant chiefs'. French,

Belgian and German rule was more direct, but still depended on chiefs to some extent. Along with chiefs, colonial rule introduced the concept of and the word 'tribe' to try to make sense of and label what Europeans saw as primordial forms of societal organisation that did not correspond to European experience or ideals. "Often tribes were created on the basis of territorial contiguity as villages were brought together under a single administrative authority. Chieftaincy was similarly manufactured and chiefs were imposed."[14]

Though the exact nature of this 'tribalisation' and the position of chiefs varied between the territories controlled by different powers, the process bore little relation to local agency or realities, let alone traditions. In Portuguese Guinea, for example, the imposition of a chief from one community over people from totally different communities was common, their qualification having been service in the colonial army or minor officialdom. Haphazard grouping of villages and communities into an administrative unit run by colonial officials through a proxy chief was also normal.[15] The process of creating chiefs who collected taxes, administered justice and organised labour to build roads, administrative buildings, bridges and other forms of communications or basic economic infrastructure created new opportunities for the rise of a local elite of 'big men'. They derived their power and wealth from their positions as the gatekeepers for colonialism in local communities, with the potential to become key figures in networks of power and patronage after the dismantling of colonial rule.

The other distinct area of interaction between the new rulers and their colonised subjects developed in urban areas and in the ports built to serve the export sector and facilitate imports from the metropolitan power. The administrative capitals and towns that grew up around railways, roads, ports or mines acquired very diverse populations as young men came of their own accord or were brought in as labourers, miners, dock workers, and railwaymen. Later, with the provision of mission and other forms of basic education, they came to serve as civil servants, traders, and teachers—and, in the cases of the few who gained higher educational qualifications, lawyers and doctors.

The traditional rulers had very limited hold over these new populations, which were in areas beyond their control, and the new warrant or other created chiefs had little power in the towns. The colonisers, meanwhile, had no wish to create an educated, 'detribalised' African population outside the control of traditional or new forms of chiefly authority, but necessity overrode this. Colonialism was being developed on the cheap, and it was not economically feasible to pay large numbers of European civil servants, teachers, petty traders and other professionals to work in the colonies.

The new class of educated Africans that grew up in urban areas was not inclined to submit itself to traditional authorities—and it was, in most territories, to become the core of the nationalist movements. The colonial administrations at first refused to include them alongside chiefs in bodies they established to assist with the government of the colonies, such as advisory or legislative councils, but this did not stop them developing into what the European powers had least wanted: an educated African political class which largely rejected the authority of chiefs and increasingly demanded self-government and equality.[16]

One important aspect of this new political elite was that it was generally disconnected from the mass of the population in rural areas and suspicious of or antagonistic towards chiefs and the new big men in local areas. An example of this is Ghana, where nationalists such as the moderate J.B. Danquah and the radical Kwame Nkrumah were both keen to see the educated elite replace the "collaborating" chiefs as the vehicle for an African role in colonial administration and eventually self-government and independence. Experiences were not uniform across all colonies: in Senegal and Ivory Coast, there was to be a more organic link between the political elite and the countryside.

In French and Portuguese colonies, there was another route to higher office and future political power: assimilation through the adoption of French or Portuguese language, education and culture. But this was only available to the few rather than the many, and relied on access to secondary and tertiary education and sufficient wealth to undertake it.

The French promoted their language more strongly than the British promoted English, and declared that their form of colonialism was based on the *mission civilisatrice* (civilising mission). But only small numbers of Africans were able to get education to a secondary level and engage in work that qualified them for the status of *évolués*, which gave them the same rights enjoyed by French citizens. By 1936, just 2,400 enjoyed that status out of a colonised population of over 15.5 million; approximately 100,000 Senegalese had civil rights as inhabitants of four coastal communes that had been granted full rights by the French in 1848.

In their territories, meanwhile, the Portuguese propagated the theory of Lusotropicalism, which claimed a unique absence of racism in Portuguese colonialism and set out pathways through education for Africans to gain the status of *assimilado*, or assimilated African, as distinct from the supposedly primitive *indigenas*.[17] But even though it gave greater civil rights to assimilated Africans and to mixed race *mestiços*, the Portuguese system still barred promotion for all but Portuguese settlers and colonial officials.

What the colonial enterprise did not encourage or even bring about by accident was the development of an African entrepreneurial business class. To a great extent, colonial powers tried to foster the development of an economically independent class of traders or entrepreneurs during the construction of economies, but that class was meant to serve the interests of the metropolitan power or of settlers, not to develop sustainable economic systems separate from the colonising powers. Equally, the African partners of the colonial powers had no great interest in the active encouragement of an independent business class that could challenge either chiefly power, where it was significant, or an educated, urban political elite centred on the professions and with its eyes on state power.

This meant economic activity under colonialism was largely state-directed or managed through foreign companies, whose operations helped financially support the colonial system and make it economically sustainable. Value was extracted from the colonies through the exports like ivory, palm oil, cotton, tea, coffee, sugar, sisal and tobacco, and minerals such as gold, diamonds, bauxite, uranium, cobalt and copper. In some territories, chiefs and other rural big men were able to accumulate wealth by becoming cash crop farmers, but the export sector was mostly controlled by Europeans, with a major role played by crop marketing boards established by the colonial authorities to organise cash crop production and marketing and ensure levels of production and prices that would benefit the metropolitan economies. Likewise, infrastructural developments such as roads, railways, bridges and ports and the establishment of schools and health services were closely related to the export sectors.

Full-throttle colonialism confronts African aspirations

The Second World War and the period of economic reconstruction in Europe that followed had a profound impact on the colonies in Africa, and stimulated both demands for self-government and what came to be called African nationalism.

During the war, Africans who had been drawn into the evolving imperial economic systems experienced the effects of a massive acceleration of economic activity for the benefit of the colonial powers. This exploitation was expanded and accelerated after 1945 as colonial powers tried to rebuild

UNIVERSITIES AT MEDWAY LIBRARY

their own economies after the ravages of war. The African colonies had become vital sources of raw materials, minerals, agricultural produce and cash for the depleted coffers of Britain, France, Belgium and even neutral Portugal, and economic developments in this period wrought even more substantial changes in the structures of economies than had the previous fifty years of occupation.

They also brought about political, cultural and demographic changes that had serious long-term consequences—rapid urbanisation, the creation of a wage-labour force and with it trade unionism, a growing strata of educated clerks, minor civil servants and teachers, and in some territories (such as Ivory Coast) the rise of an elite group of African farmers and traders benefitting from colonial economic growth. Through the agency of both the colonial rulers and the emerging African elites, the extractive, gatekeeping character of accelerated colonialism of the 1940s and 1950s evolved into the political and economic structures that would soon come to characterise independent African states. While colonialism had a major role in creating structures of export-centred economic development and thereby establishing Africa's subordinate position in the global economic system, the "gatekeeper state is neither an African illness nor a European imposition but a Euro-Afro-American co-production with a long history" that embodied pre-colonial influences, colonial policy and African elite choices.[18]

The wartime need for raw materials and military manpower turned what had been rather superfluous and even troublesome African appendages into major assets. The economic demands of war and the dislocation of the supply of manufactured goods from Europe led to an economic boom, with import-substitution industries and extractive industries exploding. Between 1938 and 1946, the colonies of British West Africa more than doubled their exports, notably of cocoa, cotton, groundnuts and palm oil.

Economic growth and the rapid development of small industry, mining and the processing of primary produce in turn led to higher demand for labour. Urbanisation was rapid, as many Africans were drawn to towns by the hope of work and pay, but urban development was uncontrolled, and the provision of housing, water or other services did not keep pace. The increased production of cash crops also required labour, and investment in fertilisers and mechanisation. It encouraged large-scale commercial farming and the alienation of land from traditional forms of tenure and usage. Many rural Africans became landless peasants or squatters on land taken for settlers or for large agri-businesses, often foreign-owned. The remaining smallholder agricultural sector, still encompassing the majority of rural populations across Africa, was outside the commercial/export sector and received little if any input or investment from colonial governments or, later, from independent ones, both of which concentrated what investment there was in agriculture on the export sector. Export crop production boomed and prices on global markets were high. To control output, regulate prices, ensure a good return for European commercial buyers and boost the currency reserves of the colonial powers, marketing boards were introduced or existing ones expanded. In the post-war period, colonial Africa became a cash cow and a seemingly inexhaustible source of raw materials.

Colonialism in the 1940s and 1950s established economic structures that left independent Africa "with the burden of the cash crop economy, namely the creation by the colonial states of systems of production which were organised around a handful of key commodities, and geared towards the export of those commodities rather than internal consumption and the development of an internal market."[19] The demand for cash crops was met by a combination of plantation-style agriculture owned by settlers or European (or in the case of Liberia's rubber plantations, American) companies, some larger peasant or rich farmers, who rapidly became part of the African political and economic elite, and by small peasant farmers. The richer farmers were frequently from chiefly families or sections of African society that worked closely with and benefited from colonial government. Small farmers and those in the subsistence sector were effectively marginalised, unable to influence the economic system in which they produced or the political system that governed their lives. Even more prosperous African farmers producing crops that fell under the colonial marketing boards were tied to the boards' prices. In theory, the boards would set a price and any surplus generated was available to keep prices paid to farmers stable over time and ensure continued production. But in practice, the pricing policies of the boards enabled the accumulation of a surplus that could be used for infrastructural or other development or went as profit to traders or colonial exchequers—but not to the farmers. This was to continue after independence in most states. The system discouraged entrepreneurship by African farmers or merchants and established a state-centred system that enhanced the gatekeeping role of those who controlled it, whether under colonialism or independence.

The period after the Second World War saw the colonial state expand its role in building a better road network, providing education and health services and even providing basic forms of welfare, generally funded from the surplus accumulated by export crop marketing boards. But provision was not uniform across territories; it was centred on areas of urbanisation and key economic regions, exacerbating the economic imbalance within them and increasing the marginalisation of much of rural Africa. This period of economic and colonial state expansion after the war coincided with, and fed into, a rising tide of demands for self-government from emerging political elites and the growth of anti-colonial feeling that is broadly labelled African nationalism.[20]

The gradual increase in the provision of education, whether in schools set up by the colonial administration or mission schools, produced a small but increasingly politically active class of educated Africans in urban areas and some of the larger rural towns seeking jobs in government service or the professions. The leaderships of nationalist parties or associations that developed across Africa came largely from those who had received education or studied abroad, or who had been able to benefit from the cash crop economy through social status to build economic, social and ultimately political power. Some were professionals (doctors and lawyers, in particular), others teachers, trades unionists or journalists. Trades unions expanded just before and after the war, and strikes or demonstrations by trades unionists became an important means of pressurising colonial governments and a crucial tool for those calling for self-government or independence.

Some of the leaders of nationalist movements were urban-based radicals, like Kwame Nkrumah in Ghana, or trades unionists, like Ahmed Sehou Toure in Guinea. Others were developing ideas of African socialism, like Julius Nyerere in Tanganyika; still others, like Jomo Kenyatta in Kenya or Félix Houphouët-Boigny in Ivory Coast, were more conservative and had stronger roots in rural areas and a closer affinity to chieftaincy systems. Both the radicals and the conservatives tried to harness the support of urban workers and the urban unemployed, or to represent rural grievances, but they had to do so without being organically part of a genuine mass movement. Some were quite open about this and about the role they thought that the educated elite should play. As the Nigerian nationalist Chief Obafemi Awolowo said in 1947, "Only an insignificant minority have any political awareness...It must be realised now and for all time that this articulate minority are destined to rule the country."[21]

Many of the nationalist leaders, such as Nkrumah, Kenyatta, Kaunda, Nyerere and Senghor, had studied or worked in Britain, France or the United States, where their growing desire to free their countries from colonial rule received support through their contacts with Africans from other colonised territories and with Afro-Caribbean or Afro-American diaspora leaders, who had begun to develop ideas of Pan-Africanism or black cultural liberation. Some of these ideas were practical, based on the need for joint struggle, co-operation and moves towards unity in a future independent Africa; others were less grounded in reality and more in an idealised view of pre-colonial Africa, imagining a unity that had never existed. But even the romanticised ideas "were politically enlightening and were important critiques of European colonial arrogance and is legacies. They debunk European cultural dominance discourses."[22] Afro-centric discourses were developed that were questionable in their provenance and applicability and did not necessarily lead to a realistic view of Africa's legacy or opportunities for unity.[23] Some of the leaders, such as Nkrumah and Nyerere, encountered and incorporated European socialist thinking into their approach to independence and development, though they nonetheless developed their own concepts of African socialism. Many of these Africanist and African socialist ideas were important ideological tools for developing a discourse of liberation from colonial rule and psychologically empowering Africans. They were also to play a role, as is outlined in the following chapters, in the launching of development programmes and bids for greater African unity.

One important influence on the development of demands for equality and freedom of Africans under colonial rule was the wartime experience of Africans. Over 1.3 million Africans fought in the war or served in some capacity in the British, French, Italian, Belgian and Ethiopian armies. African soldiers fought in Europe, Ethiopia, North Africa, the Middle East and Asia. They were told they were fighting for freedom and democracy against fascism and totalitarianism. Those who served had travelled to parts of the world (notably India) where nationalism was breaking down colonial rule, and saw first hand that colonialism could be challenged. This new generation would not let the colonial powers, and especially Britain, forget that the Atlantic Charter, issued by Winston Churchill and Franklin D. Roosevelt on 14 August 1941, said that a major aim of the war was to reassert the right of all peoples to choose the form of government under which they live. A Nigerian private with the Royal West Africa Frontier Force, Theo Ayoola, wrote from India in 1945 to the Nigerian nationalist Herbert Macaulay that, "We have been told what we fought for. That is 'freedom'. We want freedom and nothing but freedom."[24]

If there was a more assertive mood among African nationalists and an acceleration of economic exploitation, which created more grievances and gave rise to unions and protest movements, there was also a new international order in which colonialism looked increasingly unviable and anachronistic. The formation of the United Nations, with its expanding membership soon to include anti-colonialist India as well as Liberia, Ethiopia, Pakistan and other states outside Europe and North America, created a hospitable environment for real progress towards independence. The global balance of power, with a communist, anti-imperialist Soviet bloc set against the capitalist Western powers, led by a United States that was not going to risk lives and spend resources to preserve what American politicians saw as an anachronistic system of imperial rule, was no longer conducive to the maintenance of colonial empires.

The Cold War between East and West had contradictory effects when it came to nationalism and anti-imperialism in Africa, with the fight against communism a key determinant of Western states' African policies. At times, the Cold War helped accelerate moves towards African independence as the West tried to short-circuit Soviet backing for the anti-imperialist cause, but at others (as in the Portuguese colonies) the Cold War prolonged colonial rule, as the West tried to thwart anti-colonial movements it perceived as Soviet allies. A report written by the CIA in 1948 said that while the USA could not but support calls for self-determination, it had to ensure that in so doing it did not weaken its allies. Emphasising that this would have to become a key area for US policy, it warned that:

> The colonial independence movement, therefore, is no longer purely a domestic issue between the European colonial powers and their dependencies. It has been injected into the larger arena of world politics and has become an element in broader problems of relations between Orient and Occident...and between the Western Powers and the USSR.[25]

In 1945 there were just three independent states in sub-Saharan Africa: Ethiopia, Liberia, and white-ruled South Africa, a self-governing dominion of the British Empire in which the majority non-white population was deprived of equality and effective political, civil or economic rights. The vast majority of Africa was under colonial rule, with Britain and France controlling huge swathes of territory and Portugal, Belgium, Italy and Spain having smaller empires or single territories. Several territories had been taken from Germany after the First World War and placed under the control of Britain, France, Belgium or South Africa as mandated territories of the League of Nations, a system replaced in 1945 by the United Nations trust territory status. Britain had responsibility for Tanganyika and parts of Cameroon and Togo; France for the rest of Cameroon and Togo; Belgium for Ruanda-Urundi; Italy for Italian Somaliland; and South Africa for South West Africa.

Between 1956 and 1966, the majority of sub-Saharan African territories achieved independence, with only the Portuguese colonial empire, French Somaliland (Djibouti) and Spanish Equatorial Guinea still under European rule. In Southern Africa, Rhodesia, South West Africa (Namibia) and South Africa remained under white minority rule.

Colonialism and decolonisation have often been thought of as clear-cut beginnings and ends of eras in African history, with African nationalism seen as an essentially uniform force operating across colonial Africa that successfully pushed European colonialists into withdrawal, was ready to take over the government of territories, and had a common ideology or set of policies built on comparable aims despite the individual histories of colonised territories. But active or sustained support for nationalists campaigning for self-government or independence varied between and within the territories controlled by the colonial powers. There were major differences in the aims and objectives of the nationalist leaders—the divergent nationalisms of Ghana, Guinea, Ivory Coast and Senegal being good examples.

The diversity of territories, colonial experience and nationalist movements is so extreme that generalisation obscures far more than it reveals. A closer look at particular experiences under the different colonial systems and in the different territories controlled by them can tell us much more about the process of decolonisation.

Britain: accelerated colonial development, then rapid retreat from empire

Britain had the most diverse and extensive empire in sub-Saharan Africa, stretching from the Anglo-Egyptian condominium in Sudan to Cape Point in South Africa and from Gambia in the West to British Somaliland in the east. In some areas, colonial rule was more than a century old by the mid-1960s, but in others (such as Darfur in Sudan), physical control had been in place for barely three decades.

The systems of rule Britain imposed differed not only between regions but also within territories. So in both Uganda and Nigeria, for example, long-established kingdoms or sultanates had considerable autonomy under the system of indirect rule (through defeated or compliant traditional rulers) but the non-Buganda areas of Uganda and the south-west and south-east of Nigeria were ruled more directly by colonial administrators, having less hierarchical or acephalous forms of societal structure. In many areas, existing hierarchies of chieftaincies retained power and influence; in others, tribes and chiefs had been created by amalgamation and appointment for ease of administration. These diverse characteristics gave rise to very different responses from the colonised and a great variation in the origins and characters of anti-colonial or nationalist movements. That would in turn greatly determine the nature of politics and government in independent states—even though they all had variants of the export-dependent extroverted economic structure with the colonial authorities as gatekeepers.

Britain emerged from the war with a weakened economy and massive debts to repay. Leading members of the newly-elected Labour Party government were avowedly anti-imperialist, but as so often with parties that are radical in opposition, in power the Labour government was willing to rebuild and reform Britain at the expense of its African colonies. Cash crops and mineral production were vital to British policy, alongside a vigorous campaign to encourage settlement in Kenya and Southern Rhodesia. Eastern, Central and Southern African territories produced important crops and minerals: tea and coffee in Kenya and Uganda; tea, coffee and sisal in Tanganyika; tea, tobacco and sugar in Nyasaland (Malawi); copper in Northern Rhodesia (Zambia); and tobacco, coal and other minerals in Southern Rhodesia (Zimbabwe). In West Africa, there was little settlement but important economic resources—notably palm oil and cocoa—that could be exploited to aid Britain's economic recovery.

All the regions had developing nationalist movements based on the new urban, educated elites, though in Nigeria, Kenya, Uganda, and to a lesser extent Sierra Leone and Ghana, there were also more conservative elites linked with chiefs or surviving kingdoms and emirates. These groups were directly competing for a greater say in their own government. The paths of these regions' nationalist movements were to be diverse with a range of very different dynamics, including in some areas the complicating presence of settlers, who wanted to stay put and stay in power.

But the first British colonial territory to move from occupation to independence was one whose statehood was to prove among the most contested and costly in terms of human life and suffering on the continent: Sudan. Because of the nature of conflict in Sudan and its effects on neighbouring African states, it is worth looking at the decolonisation process there more closely.

Sudan as an independent state emerged from the complex relationship between Britain and Egypt in the closing decades of the 19th century. At the time, Britain was fighting to ensure its hegemony in Egypt in order to control the Suez Canal, a vital shipping route to India and other British possessions in East Asia. Egypt claimed sovereignty over Sudan but needed substantial British military assistance to defeat the Sudanese nationalist forces of the Mahdiya state, which had freed itself by military force from the clutches of Turkish–Egyptian Rule. The joint British-Egyptian occupation of Sudan was formalised in the 1899 condominium agreement, which established joint control. The British were militarily and economically the senior partners, and saw Sudan and the Nile as a way of linking British possessions and interests across East and North-East Africa.[26] Control of Sudan was about security and communications, though it was to become an economic asset, too, with the development of the vast Gezira cotton-growing project on the Nile providing a major source of cotton for Britain's huge textile industry.

There was serious tension in the arrangement because of Britain's political and military hegemony over Egypt and the two countries' divergent ambitions in Sudan. Egypt claimed sovereignty over Sudan, but the British governed it and tried to reduce Egyptian influence there. The situation came to a head with the growth of a northern Sudanese unification movement pushing for union with Egypt, which had become formally independent from Britain in 1922 (though still under British tutelage, and with substantial numbers of British troops and officials posted there). Protests and mutinies by soldiers in some Anglo-Sudanese military units culminated in November 1924 with the assassination of the Governor-General of Sudan, Lee Stack, in Cairo. Britain blamed Egyptian nationalists for inciting Sudanese resistance, and used its power over Egypt to force the withdrawal of all Egyptian troops—leading to further mutinies among Sudanese forces. From here on, the British became absolutely determined to prevent any future Egyptian-Sudanese union and to keep the nationalist movements in the two countries separate. They were assisted in this by many Sudanese nationalists from among the emerging Nile Valley elite, who increasingly resented Egyptian claims to Sudan.[27]

Britain's efforts to keep the territories separate resulted in the deliberate and consistent development of a northern Sudanese elite, and the encouragement of Sudanese nationalist rather than pro-unification sentiments. The British provided education to dominant groups in the Nile Valley around Khartoum and the north, with the resulting recruitment of educated Sudanese from this region to government service and into the army as NCOs and junior officers. The Arabic-speaking north was also the focus of economic development around the Nile Valley and the cotton scheme. The African south of Sudan, meanwhile, was administered separately from the north. These were two very different areas in terms of political development, culture, language and aspirations, and Britain's policy towards them was inconsistent: it "wavered between attempts to govern it as a single polity on the one hand and ruling the south as a separate entity on the other."[28] Ultimately, the culturally Arabic northern Sudanese elite was politically dominant and came to have increasing administrative and military power under British overall control, while the African south was educationally, economically and politically marginalised.

Pressure for Sudanese self-government came to a head in 1942, when a group of educated northern Sudanese called on a visiting British minister, Sir Stafford Cripps, to recognise Sudan's right to self-determination. In 1946, the British agreed that Sudan should progress to greater self-government and then independence. This angered the Egyptians, but their objections subsided when the Free Officers' Movement under General Neguib and Colonel Nasser overthrew King Farouk in July 1952. Egypt's government didn't entirely give up its ambition to unify with Sudan, but Nasser's stress on Arab and African self-determination legitimised Sudanese nationalists' demands for self-determination.

By the mid-1950s, the British had established a Sudanese Legislative Assembly, covering the north and south but dominated by the Sudanese Arab elite from the Nile Valley. Central and northern Nile Valley groups such as the Jalien, Shaggiya and Dangala dominated politics, the civil service, the professions and business during the rise of nationalism, and they have retained control of politics and the military in the north ever since.[29] The political and economic structures of northern Sudan became the dominant ones as the territory moved towards independence, and gave those who controlled them considerable power to implant ideas based on Arabised culture and Islamic belief as the ruling political ideology of independent Sudan.

In contrast, the south was undeveloped economically and politically. British policy there was one of neglect; southerners had little access to education, apart from a few mission schools, or to posts in the civil service. Many southerners joined the Sudanese Defence Force, though the majority of those made officers under the British officers were from the Nile Valley elite. Few southerners were politically active, and the south was vastly under-represented in the Sudanese Legislative Assembly and in discussions on self-government and independence. There was no great southern secessionist sentiment, but there was a growing fear of total domination by the Islamic, Arabic-speaking north—a fear shared by many other communities in Darfur, Kordofan and the Red Sea coast, who felt politically and economically marginalised in the face of Nile Valley hegemony. This has remained a divisive factor throughout Sudan's violent 59-year history.

Southern resistance to northern hegemony exploded in August 1955, when southern Sudanese troops based in Torit, Equatoria Province, mutinied after being ordered to deploy in the north. Southern soldiers rose up against their northern officers, and 366 northerners were killed in two weeks of fighting. The mutiny ended when northern army units were flown in by the British, and mutineers who were captured or surrendered were summarily executed. Those who escaped to the bush became an insurgent movement that was to develop into the Anyanya revolt of the early 1960s.

Sudan approached independence a diverse and deeply divided country. When the British handed over power on 1 January 1956, it was to a government led by the Islamic National Unionist Party, dominated by the Islamic Khatmiyya sect and led by Ismael al-Azhari. It contained two southern politicians, both of whom joined the coalition because they hoped to work towards a federation with greater autonomy for the south. They were to be disappointed, and were soon dismissed by Al-Azhari.

The new government and those that followed it, both civilian and military, remained dominated by the same small elite and pursued narrow policies that failed to deal with the demands of a very diverse state. The two main parties, the Islamic National Unionist Party and the Umma Party of Sayyid ʿAbd al-Raḥmān al-Mahdī (son of the Mahdī who fought Anglo-Egyptian dominance), were dominated by rival Islamic sects, the Khatmiyya and the Mahdist Ansar, but were both led by members of the Nile Valley elite. Together they established a Sudanese political discourse that revolved around both Islam and the dominance of the elite group over politics, the economy and the army.

Meanwhile, British West Africa was in the vanguard of the nationalist groundswell in colonial Africa at large. Before the Second World War, articulate voices had been raised in Gambia, Sierra Leone, Gold Coast (Ghana) and Nigeria demanding a greater role in the government of their territories and espousing aspirations for freedom from foreign rule. Britain responded to these calls with marginal concessions, providing seats on legislative or advisory councils for government-recognised or appointed chiefs, and later for some members of the growing educated urban elite. Where indirect rule had allowed the retention of power by traditional rulers or the delegation of it to appointed chiefs, these leaders generally continued to co-operate with the colonial administrations and were not in the front ranks of the nationalist movements.

Ghana's fast transition from colonial rule as the Gold Coast to full independence under a party and leader pledged to a radical Pan-African approach to politics gave it great prominence in the independence movement across Africa. Its first prime minister, Kwame Nkrumah, became a vocal advocate of the liberation of territories under colonial or white-settler rule and of African unity. But in 1947, as nationalism started to flex its developing muscles, the Gold Coast's embryonic nationalist movement was still dominated by a small group of educated professionals and businessmen. For the British, the colony offered opportunities for gradual Africanisation combined with economic exploitation, which meant finding collaborating elites who would, by accepting voluntarily a new form of association with Britain, help preserve the British connection.[30] The main political group, the United Gold Coast Convention (UGCC), led by a lawyer, J.B. Danquah, was a potential partner in British plans for limited reform. It wanted a gradual process of change, including the replacement of chiefs on legislative councils by educated professionals. This brought nationalists into conflict with chiefs and the Asante royal court.

Post-war economic development in Ghana emphasised the export sector, maximising earnings from cocoa, gold and bauxite. An export boom led to rapid urbanisation with the populations of Accra, Kumasi, Sekondi-Takoradi and Cape Coast rising by more than 55 per cent during and after the war. But the colony gained little economically apart from the building of roads to get produce to the coast, expanded port infrastructure and improvements in education and health necessary to provide a more skilled workforce. The UGCC leaders and indigenous businessmen wanted economic development that benefited local people, access to wider areas of trade and commerce for Africans and seats on legislative councils.

In late 1947, the UGCC asked a charismatic young man, Kwame Nkrumah, to return to Gold Coast to join the UGCC. He had been educated in Ghana, the United States and Britain and become an advocate of Pan-Africanism and black consciousness as well as imbibing European socialist and Marxist ideas—especially the anti-imperialism and organising potential of Marxism-Leninism. His writings on colonialism used Marxist language and critiques of European colonialism, but he was more "suffused with notions of African unity"[31] than with communist revolution in Africa. His Pan-Africanism had been developed in America, where he attended meetings of Marcus Garvey's United Negro Improvement Association. While studying in London, he was active in the African Students' Association and became vice-president of the West African Students' Union in the UK. He met the

Trinidadian Pan-Africanist, George Padmore, and was strongly influenced by his belief that the liberation of Africa had to lead to African unity. Nkrumah's Africanist ideas—like those of many of the first generation of nationalist leaders—developed when he was outside Africa looking back on the continent with a different perspective. Many leaders who developed within and stayed in Africa were more concerned with their own territories or locales and were less influenced by ideas of Africanness or Pan-African unity.

Nkrumah returned to Ghana in December 1947 to become UGCC general secretary. During the year there were strikes by urban workers, and anger among local cocoa farmers at government demands that they uproot plants affected by swollen-root disease. In January 1948, there was a boycott of European and Syrian/Lebanese businesses and protest marches organised by ex-servicemen, who were excluded from areas of commerce like transport by rules favouring Europeans. The shooting of a protestor by a white police officer led to rioting and a state of emergency. The British, without any evidence of their involvement, arrested Danquah, Nkrumah and four other UGCC leaders.

Upon his release, Nkrumah used the momentum generated by the riots to substantially increase UGCC membership. But his growing radicalism drove a wedge between him and the moderate UGCC founders, and in June 1949 he left to found the Convention People's Party (CPP). That October a British appointed commission recommended a new Gold Coast assembly, nearly half of whom would be chosen by chiefs, others by electoral colleges which included a role for chiefs, and only five by direct election. Nkrumah denounced it as fraudulent and demanded immediate self-government. The CPP gained the support of trades unionists and organised a campaign of civil disobedience, boycotts and protests, called Positive Action. The governor declared a state of emergency and arrested Nkrumah, along with a number of CPP and trades union leaders.

While Nkrumah was in prison, the CPP organised a successful municipal election campaign, demonstrating its substantial popular support. The government lifted the state of emergency and scheduled elections under a new constitution for February 1951. The CPP won thirty-four of thirty-eight contested seats; Nkrumah was elected to the Accra Central seat despite still being in prison. The British released him and asked him to head the first elected African government, as he led the most powerful political movement in the colony.

When it took office, the CPP was "a party in a hurry and became a government in a hurry."[32] It wanted to push for independence fast, cut the power of the chiefs over local government, bring educational and economic opportunities to ordinary people and change the priorities of development to benefit the Gold Coast rather than Britain. The British government worked with the CPP to extend self-government and then to move towards independence, but it ensured that British economic interests would be protected after decolonisation. No mining concerns were nationalised, and agricultural and trading business remained in non-Ghanaian hands. To gain independence fast, Nkrumah was prepared to accept British formulations for post-independence political structures and didn't seriously challenge the export-dominated economic structures built in the last years of colonialism. Instead, the CPP's economic policy was based on Africanisation of public services, control of export income and infrastructural development. Funds for health, education and welfare provision and wider economic development came from the surplus generated by the Cocoa Marketing Board.

This pitted the CPP against cocoa farmers, who had hoped that self-government and then independence would mean they received higher prices for their crops, but were thwarted when the CPP used the marketing board to keep prices to farmers low—despite high world prices. The board had been set up by the British to control prices for cocoa and stabilise production, but was seen by Ghanaian cocoa planters as a way for the government to retain the lion's share of export income. The CPP's trades union support did not translate into true partnership with the unions—which, with their history of anti-government activity, were seen as a threat to the CPP and the export-driven economy.[33] This created another source of future opposition to Nkrumah and his party.

As the colony moved towards independence, the cocoa farmers and chiefs developed their own party, the National Liberation Movement, which had strong support in the Asante region, where the traditional hierarchy was suspicious of the CPP, given its strong line on diminishing chiefly power. There was also growing disenchantment with the CPP in the mainly Muslim and marginalised north. But the CPP won the election in 1954, and in 1956 fought off a strong NLM challenge and the opposition of the Northern People's Party to win 72 of 104 seats in an election the British had insisted on before granting independence. Ghana became independent at midnight on 5 March 1957 under a CPP government led by Nkrumah and the CPP.

Ghana's path to independence was comparatively smooth compared with other states, including its near neighbour, Nigeria. Nigeria's inheritance at independence was a difficult one. British colonial rule had more deeply entrenched indirect rule and the power of the traditional rulers in northern

Nigeria than in almost anywhere else in Africa, with the possible exception of Buganda.[34] The Islamic emirates and the Sultanate of Sokoto had been used as the basis for indirect rule, and the power of the northern Muslim elite had been deliberately enhanced under British rule. Across this huge territory, which contained over 250 ethnic groups and 300 languages or dialects, the nature of pre-colonial societies and the colonial methods of rule differed hugely.

The British had seen the northern states as more cultured and developed and as useful tools for colonial rule, since they needed few British officials and minimal costs to run smoothly. In the eastern region, stateless societies without strong chiefs or kings had held sway and required more intrusive and more direct rule. The western region fell somewhere in between; there, Britain tried to bring together a variety of communities sharing similar languages, societal structures and customs to create the Yoruba 'tribe' out of twelve different communities.[35] These new 'ethnic' or tribal communities were created partly out of colonial administrative convenience to put in place chiefs with whom the British colonial officials could deal, but as the country moved towards self-government and then independence, many emerging leaders among these groups saw the development of western Yoruba and eastern Igbo identities as counterweights to the powerful northern potentates. Although the three dominant groups—the Hausa-Fulani in the north, the Yoruba in the west and the Igbo in the east—were made up of many different constituent groups and between them accounted for only two-thirds of Nigeria's population, they came to dominate pre- and post-independence political life, the military and the economy.

The constitutional structure adopted under British direction was built around three regions dominated respectively by each of these powerful groups, and it gave strong central power and control over export revenues and other income to whoever controlled the federal government. This set up the struggle for central and regional power that was to become and remain a central characteristic of Nigeria, and its most intractable problem. The next chapter looks in detail at the regional, political and economic problems that plagued the decolonisation of Africa's potentially most powerful state, and which ultimately led to war.

In other parts of the British colonial empire in Africa, the inheritance of the territories at independence was very different. They all had export-led and extraverted economies, and some had to cope with the same problems that faced Nigeria, bringing together a variety of different communities with differing structures of power. Uganda, for instance, encompassed both the highly-organised Buganda Kingdom and the acephalous Acholi and Langi groups, whose systems of rule and interactions had been greatly distorted by the colonial experience. Kenya and Southern Rhodesia, meanwhile, both had large settler communities whose interests had been paramount under colonial rule, and whose members had taken over the best farming land and dominated the commercial sectors of the economy. These settler communities had no intention of leaving Africa as colonial rule withered away, and the British government tried to use the settler-dominated territories as the political and economic hubs for the creation of larger federations. In East Africa, the settler problem was a major influence on the uprising by the self-proclaimed Land and Freedom Army in Kenya, but whose revolt is generally called the Mau Mau rebellion. This conflict had a decisive effect on Kenya's path to independence. Across the whole region, the opposition of African nationalist movements in Tanganyika (later renamed Tanzania after union with Zanzibar) and Uganda was enough to kill the idea of a settler-dominated federation.

In Tanganyika, the growth of a strong, well-supported grassroots movement, the Tanganyika African National Union (TANU) under Julius Nyerere, was able both to ward off federation, and attempts to establish multicultural power-sharing in which the small white and Asian populations would have been given equal political weight with the African majority. At the height of its popularity in 1960, one in five adults was a member. Because of Tanganyika's relatively low level of urbanisation and industrialisation, TANU worked hard to mobilise support in rural areas and also among women. Women played a very active role in many of the nationalist movements at this time, but were rarely prominent in the leaderships of the movement or in the governments that came to power on independence. TANU was very active in recruiting women and it established a specific women's section within the movement, but again no women rose to prominent positions in the overall movement or in government after independence.[36]

The Land and Freedom Army uprising in the Kikuyu regions of central Kenya, meanwhile, was the most violent of the nationalist campaigns fought directly against the British, and it both delayed and distorted the path to independence. It was anti-settler, but also aimed against those Kikuyu chiefs who exercised power under British tutelage. The major nationalist leader, Jomo Kenyatta, was accused of being the mastermind behind the rebellion and was imprisoned. He was only released after the rebellion had been crushed and nationalist activity allowed to resume. The defeat of Mau Mau and the radical politicians associated with it ensured that Kenyan politics was dominated by politicians unconnected with the uprising, who were willing to work with the British or Kikuyu leaders who had openly supported the colonial campaign against the rebellion.[37] Those who fought in the rebellion were effectively written out of the Kenyan nationalist story for decades. The appointed chiefs and Kikuyu elites who sided with the British and helped to brutally suppress the rebellion dominated post-independence politics, along with broadly conservative political leaders from other Kenyan communities. When Kenyatta was released he re-entered the political scene, and led Kenya to independence on 12 December 1963, first as prime minister, then president when a republic was declared a year later. He took a conservative approach with pro-capitalist economics and called on white settlers to remain.

Thanks to the alienation of both Kalenjin-speaking peoples, Maasai and Kikuyu, from land used for European settlement, land rights were a major issue in Kenya. With World Bank funding, Kenyatta launched a land acquisition programme, supposedly to allow the resettlement of landless peasants on formerly European land—but it by no means resolved the issue. Many communities, particularly the Kalenjin in the Rift Valley, felt that land taken from them under colonialism was being distributed to Kikuyu and to Kenyatta's political cronies. To this day, land is one of the most explosive issues in Kenyan politics.

In Uganda, the path to independence was more uneven. This was a linguistically and ethnically diverse territory. Britain applied a system of indirect rule in much of the country, recognising five kingdoms (Ankole, Buganda, Bunyoro, Busoga, and Toro) whose royal hierarchies were retained under British tutelage. Buganda, whose kingdom included the capital, Kampala, was the largest and most powerful of the kingdoms. Its people made up only a sixth of the Ugandan population, but they were favoured by the British in appointments to the colonial administration.[38] The colonial armed forces recruited by the British came largely from the stateless Acholi, Kakwa, Langi and Lugbara peoples of the north.[39]

As in much of the rest of Africa, nationalism became an increasingly powerful force in Uganda after 1945, fed by growing discontent over colonial policy and the pain of rising living costs, low wages and poor prices for agricultural produce. The most influential early nationalist movements developed among the Baganda and campaigned for greater self-government, but also competed for the allegiance of the kingdom's people. The movement was split along religious lines, but also in terms of the relationship with the monarchy. The Democratic Party (DP) had its base among Catholics, who felt marginalised by the dominance of Protestants in the court of the Kabaka (the king of Buganda). The Baganda Protestants, meanwhile, were represented by the Uganda National Congress (UNC), which included many non-Baganda. This fragmented, however, as non-Baganda members became wary of allowing the kingdom to dominate politics and establish hegemony over other communities.

Those who left the UNC joined the Uganda Peoples' Congress (UPC), which demanded "self-government now" but opposed the extension of Bugandan power. The UPC was led by a Northerner, Milton Obote, who used his campaign for independence to become Uganda's dominant political leader. With the decline of the UNC, political allegiances were divided between the DP and the UPC as both demanded rapid progress to independence. The rivalry within Buganda led the Kabaka, Mutesa II, and his supporters to form the monarchist Kabaka Yekka (King Alone) party. Prior to independence in 1962, the UPC became the largest non-Buganda party, while elections within Buganda to the Uganda national assembly gave the Kabaka Yekka enough seats to be included in the government in an uneasy alliance with the UPC—the two parties having little in common other than opposition to the mainly-Catholic DP.

Independence was granted in October 1962 with Obote as prime minister, and Buganda enjoyed considerable autonomy under the Ugandan constitution drawn up with British supervision. This was to be short-lived, and its demise would mark the start of an increasingly authoritarian and violent chapter in Uganda's history.

Central Africa, meanwhile, failed to fend off federation. The Central African Federation was formed in 1953 under the effective control of Rhodesian white leaders. A concerted campaign of nationalist action by movements in Nyasaland (Malawi) and Northern Rhodesia (Zambia)—led by Hastings Banda, Harry Nkumbula and Kenneth Kaunda—resulted in the end of the federation in 1963 and the independence of the two states; but majority rule in Rhodesia only came about after a long guerrilla struggle, which ended with the 1980 elections there.

In Malawi, the fight against the Federation made its leader, the ageing doctor, Hastings Banda, an icon of nationalism and independence. His success allowed him to impose his conservative and strongly pro-Western brand of nationalism on the radical young supporters who had called him back to Nyasaland to lead the fight against federation and for independence. Banda had the benefit of high personal esteem, substantial wealth, and the respect accorded elders and the highly-educated. He had been educated in the United States and Britain, but was able to build networks of support beyond the urban areas, and he used rural conservatism to help him retain power and overcome the radicalism of his erstwhile allies. This enabled him to establish himself as one of the most idiosyncratic and personally powerful rulers of the new Africa.

Meanwhile, something very different was underway on the southern tip of the continent. Three hundred years of Dutch and British settlement and British colonial occupation that started well before the Berlin Conference, created a settler-ruled independent state in South Africa. It became independent from Britain in 1910 as the Union of South Africa, a dominion of the British Empire with the same status as Australia, Canada and New Zealand. British forces had by turns crushed the Zulu kingdom in 1879 and suppressed resistance from Xhosa, Sotho and other peoples, creating a state where power was vested in the hands of an alliance of Afrikaners and English-speakers—an uneasy alliance eventually created after the defeat of the Afrikaner Republics of Transvaal and the Orange Free State in the Second South African war (the Boer War). A system of segregation developed under successive white governments, with the majority black and smaller Coloured and Indian communities in subordinate roles without equal civil, political and economic rights. As the rest of Africa experienced the rise of African nationalism after 1945, South Africa saw the triumph of Afrikaner nationalism. This saw a move further away from rather than towards political emancipation for Africans and the other non-white groups, and in 1948, South Africa's white electorate voted in the white supremacist Afrikaner National Party (NP).

The NP pursued a more rigorous segregation of races, consigning Africans to reserves except for those who were allowed to reside temporarily in urban 'white' areas through economic necessity. This was apartheid, a policy to enforce the 'separate development' of races, with economic and political power concentrated in white hands and Afrikaner nationalism as the dominant ideology.[40] The next ten years saw the consolidation of Afrikaner political power and racial separation. Laws requiring all non-whites to have passes were implemented to restrict black migration from rural areas, and the rural black population was assigned to reserves set up on a 'tribal' basis for Zulus, Xhosas, Sotho, Tswanas, Venda and other government-designated groups. The Group Areas Act was introduced to racially zone "every city, town and village in the country".[41] The black majority would have no civil or political rights outside what became known as the black homelands, and within them, white-directed homeland governments would have very limited control over their own affairs. In 1960, the population consisted of eleven million blacks, three million whites, 1.5 million coloureds, and 477,000 of Asian or Indian descent.

Unable to exercise democratic rights in any way, the main black movement in South Africa, the African National Congress (ANC), mounted protest campaigns against the pass laws and the forced removals from white areas. Formed in 1912 by educated Africans and a group of chiefs it campaigned for greater African rights and against the increasing loss of African land to white farmers. The ANC developed into a more radical organisation after the Second World War, influenced by its growing youth movement. As apartheid laws were made ever more stringent in the early 1950s, the Youth League of the ANC and the Women's League played a major role in staging protests and civil disobedience in what was known as the Defiance Campaign. These protests helped build an African nationalist movement in South Africa—and, after much soul-searching by the ANC leadership, led to co-operation with trades unions, communists, white radicals and Indian and coloured movements.[42]

ANC protests, strikes by black unions and growing international disapprobation of apartheid had little effect on the NP, except perhaps to strengthen its convictions. It entrenched its policies, shored up its power and tried to convince Western Europe, Britain and America that a white-ruled South Africa was a necessary bulwark against Soviet influence in Africa. The power of the South African economy was a huge advantage in that effort. Western countries had major investments in South Africa, which had a strong export sector dominated by gold, diamonds and other minerals and a developed commercial agricultural system that produced both a food surplus and export produce such as fruit and wine—and ultimately, the post-war West determined that South African minerals and the Cape sea route had to be kept from Soviet control.[43]

In 1960, as many African states achieved independence, the ANC and the Pan-Africanist Congress (PAC), which had split from the ANC over its alliance with Coloured, Indian and white anti-apartheid groups (especially the South African Communists Party), stepped up their demonstrations against the pass laws. This culminated in the killing of sixty-nine Africans at Sharpeville on 21 March during an anti-pass law demonstration led by the PAC. The suppression of protests over the killings led to more deaths, and the National Party government proclaimed a state of emergency, banning the ANC and the PAC and arresting 11,500 nationalist leaders and activists.

Over the next four years the main leaders of the ANC and South African Communist Party (SACP) went into exile or were detained by the police. The PAC also established an exile movement. Following a series of trials, Nelson Mandela, Walter Sisulu and other ANC and Communist Party leaders were imprisoned, while those in exile set up offices in Africa and Europe. By this time, the ANC, in close alliance and relying heavily on communist organisational skills and links with the Soviet Union, had decided that armed struggle was the only viable means of fighting apartheid.

The French experience: federation or balkanisation?

The French approach to its colonies was to treat them as part of the wider French Union. Greater African political representation would involve local government, federation-wide assemblies and the election of deputies to the French national assembly. The territories were divided into the West and Equatorial African Federations, French Somaliland (Djibouti), the islands of Madagascar, the Comoros, Reunion, Mayotte and UN trust territories in Togo and Cameroon.

In the semi-desert and savannah areas of the Sahel Francophone territories, traditional ways of life, socio-economic systems and networks of cultural religious and political power survived in various forms through the colonial period and into independence. Islam was an important social and political as well as religious force in many of the states, with a diversity of forms and the existence of strong Murid, Sufi, Ansari and other brotherhoods or local religious leaders, combining political and religious authority. They had substantial social, political and religious influence in territories as widely dispersed as Senegal, Mauritania, Mali, Niger, northern Cameroon and Chad. The lack of economic assets meant that the more arid north of territories tended to be neglected economically and marginalised politically. In Chad, the fertile food- and cotton-growing south was more developed, received more investment and better health and education services than the north. Nomadic peoples in the Sahel region, such as the Tuareg, posed problems for colonisers and then independent governments, and the difficulty of accommodating them within demarcated state borders was to become a serious cause of conflict in both Niger and Mali.

The post-war period in the Francophone countries saw similar economic development and increased utilisation of resources as in British colonies, accompanied by expansion of the colonial state and greater centralisation of administrative and state functions.[44] This also brought Africans increased representation in the French assembly and in local government. African territories gained enhanced representation, but wholly within the union. There was a strong growth in trades union activity, fed by accelerated urbanisation, infrastructural construction and economic exploitation. The general strike of 1946, which brought together educated Africans and the trades unions, and then the long French West African railway strike of 1947, demonstrated their strength and proved that they could work with the educated pro-nationalist elite to bring about changes in French policy.[45] The growth of African political activity within this system led to the rise of a number of powerful politicians—Léopold Senghor in Senegal, Félix Houphouët-Boigny in Ivory Coast, and Ahmed Sékou Touré in Guinea. These men were particularly important for the way decolonisation proceeded in France's colonies. They had very different approaches to reform: Senghor and Houphouët-Boigny wanted to work within the Union, while Touré took a more radical approach, favouring outright independence.

Senghor was a writer and theorist educated in Senegal and then in Paris, where his ideas on black cultural liberation developed as he mixed with intellectuals and activists from French-Caribbean territories and African colonies. He went on to develop the concept of *négritude* as a path to black intellectual liberation.[46] He was very much part of a reaction to the racism and alienation felt by black students in France, who rejected the idea of African inferiority, opposed ideas of assimilation and celebrated African culture and equality. Senghor's great political skill was alliance-building; he worked with rural leaders and particularly the Muslim Murid brotherhoods, which played a crucial role in Senegalese society and politics. But despite his liberating approach to culture, he was essentially a political conservative, and wanted Senegal and other colonies in West and Central Africa to remain within the French Union. He explained it in relation to his view of African family culture, saying in 1957 that:

> In Africa, when children have grown up they leave their parents' hut, and build a hut of their own by its side. Believe me, we don't want to leave the French compound, we have grown up in it and it is good to be alive in it. We simply want to build our own huts.[47]

Senghor's conservativism put him in direct opposition to Pan-Africanists, whom he infuriated by approving the deployment of Senegalese troops in the French army to fight the Algerian nationalists in their war of independence from France.

Houphouët-Boigny was from a chief's family in Yamoussoukro in Ivory Coast. He graduated as a doctor in Dakar before returning home to become a prosperous cocoa planter and organised the African Agricultural Society, which campaigned for the rights of Ivorian planters. This background and power base shored up his conservatism and nurtured his belief in the primacy of economic development, and in the importance of individual rather than state economic ownership. As an elected member of the French Assembly, he fought labour laws that enabled European planters to use forced African labour on their plantations—not just because they were exploitative, but because they put prosperous African farmers at a disadvantage by denying them access to the same labour. The *Loi Houphouët-Boigny*, which the Assembly passed in 1946, banned forced labour. The law both freed African peasants from this system and enabled African planters to compete with French settlers in the production of cash crops for export.

Houphouët-Boigny pursued his political aims through the federation and his Parti Démocratique de la Côte d'Ivoire (PDCI), part of the federation-wide political party Rassemblement Démocratique Africain (RDA). While not socialist or radical parties, the PDCI and RDA worked closely with the French Communist Party. This alliance proved problematic when the communists left the French coalition government and went in to opposition. The French government responded by trying to suppress the RDA and the PDCI, and the PDCI hit back with boycotts and mass demonstrations. The crisis was defused in 1950 when the then Minister for Overseas France, François Mitterrand, persuaded Houphouët-Boigny to break with the communists.[48]

This turned his political trajectory towards closer co-operation with the French. He began to oppose the RDA and the federation, where his conservatism was challenged by radicals like Ahmed Sékou Touré of Guinea and Modibo Keita of French Soudan (Mali). He saw greater political advantage in a purely Ivorian approach and supported the French 'balkanisation' of the African federations in 1956. This was opposed by the leaders of the other territories, chiefly by Senghor, who wanted a strong federation to aggregate pressure on France for more equal participation for Africans. But he was outflanked by Houphouët-Boigny, whose close alliance with the French government enabled him to influence the crafting of the new constitution, which dissolved the two French African federations. From that point on, negotiations on self-government were conducted between individual territories and France—greatly diluting the strength of the Francophone African territories.

The collapse of the Fourth Republic because of the Algerian War and the rise of Charles de Gaulle led to profound changes in Franco-African relations. De Gaulle wanted autonomy for the colonies, but with France protecting its economic interests and retaining control over defence and foreign affairs. He put the new arrangements before France's African subjects in a referendum on 28 September 1958, having warned that those who voted against them could go their own way if they wished, but with the complete cessation of French assistance.

The resulting vote had dramatic consequences. Eleven of France's twelve African territories voted overwhelmingly for the new constitution and continued union, but Guinea voted overwhelmingly against. On 2 October 1958, Guinea was declared an independent republic under President Sekou Touré—and the French stuck to their word, pulling out with a speed and brutality that crippled Guinea's government and economy, withdrawing all administrators, taking everything they could with them (down to light bulbs and telephones), burning government records and making French businessmen and teachers leave.

In 1960, Mali and other more pro-federation territories demanded a new arrangement: full independence, but within a union with France. Mali was granted independence on 24 June 1960, and on the other side of the continent, Madagascar became a state two days later. Ivory Coast didn't then wait for an agreement with France and declared its independence on 7 August 1960. The remaining nine French territories, along with the trust territories of Cameroon and Togo, became independent between August and the end of November. All retained close relations with France, and were part of an African franc monetary zone. Paris was able to retain extensive financial control, economic influence and a military presence in many of the states, which bolstered the power of the governments and maintained French influence in Africa.

Portugal: intransigence and armed struggle

As the pace of progress towards decolonisation gained pace across sub-Saharan Africa, it was resisted strongly by the Portuguese.

The two main Portuguese colonies, Angola and Mozambique, were situated on the borders of the settler-ruled Rhodesia, South Africa and South-West Africa (ruled by South Africa under the UN trustee system) and became part of the complex political, military and economic equation in Southern Africa; Portugal also controlled Guinea-Bissau, Cape Verde and the islands of São Tomé and Príncipe. In 1951, Portugal's African colonies were made overseas provinces. This brought them under more direct rule and emphasized Portugal's intention to maintain control and economic exploitation at all costs.

The only path to a better status for Africans or those of mixed race in the Portuguese colonies was through education and gaining the status of *assimi-*

lado; this was impossible for most Africans, who had little access to education. African political movements had existed in the colonies from the 1920s, involving both *mestiços* and *assimilados*. When the fascist New State came into being in Portugal in 1926, these were brought under tighter control than the previous governments had exerted. Open political activity was banned, and activists were arrested or eliminated by the Portuguese secrct police, the PIDE. But repression did not end the growth of small nationalist movements among more educated Africans; it just forced them underground.

Many of the Angolan, Guinean and Mozambican *assimilados* and *mestiços* studying or working in Portugal came into contact with the underground Portuguese Communist Party, which encouraged the growth of a radical, Marxist-influenced nationalism. This resulted in the formation of the clandestine Angolan Communist Party, which came together with small nationalist groups in 1956 to form the MPLA (Movimento Popular de Libertaçao de Angola)—the party had a particularly strong link with the *mestiço* and coastal Mbundu populations which had cooperated with the Portuguese, engaged at times in slaving and formed a coherent, collaborative group in the regions surrounding Luanda—these groups are still dominant within the MPLA, the government and armed forces. At the same time, exiled leaders of the Bakongo community of northern Angola formed the Union of the People of Northern Angola, calling for independence for the old Bakongo kingdom, including areas of Belgian and French Congo. At the urging of Nkrumah and other African nationalist leaders, it was renamed the Union of the People of Angola to appear more inclusive.[49]

In Mozambique, the National Democratic Union of Mozambique (UDENAMO) was established in 1960 to work for independence, and in June 1962 it formed an alliance along with several smaller political groups: the Front for the Liberation of Mozambique (Frelimo), which launched an armed struggle in September 1964. Meanwhile, in Guinea-Bissau and Cape Verde, nationalism took on its modern form with the creation of the Partido Africano da Independência da Guinê e Cabo Verde (PAIGC) by independence activist and radical theorist Amilcar Cabral in 1954. Guinea-Bissau's armed struggle began in 1963 after PAIGC members were dispatched to the Soviet Union and China for military training.

These movements were clandestine, and operated as much in Portugal and in states neighbouring the Portuguese colonies as they did in the colonies themselves. The impetus for the armed struggle across the Portuguese colonies came not only from the absolute rejection of African demands for independence, but also from the sharpening economic and social contradictions in the colonies. The New State concept relied on the colonies to contribute to Portugal's wealth and development, and to accommodate Portuguese settlers to ease unemployment at home: there were 250,000 Portuguese in Mozambique at the end of the colonial period, and 80,000 in Angola. Exports of coffee, cotton, diamonds, cashew nuts and groundnuts from the colonies paid for the cost of administration, helped develop foreign currency reserves and supported industries in Portugal. But falls in commodity prices in the early 1960s led to failures to pay coffee and cotton growers and strikes by peasant farmers—and it is not surprising that it was in the northern areas affected by this that the Angolan armed resistance first emerged.[50]

It started in 1961, when the Portuguese crushed an uprising against enforced cotton cultivation; the killing of hundreds of peasants in the crackdown helped to create the conditions for the FNLA to start guerrilla activity in 1963. The MPLA's armed struggle also started to stir in early 1961, beginning with an attack on Luanda's main prison by African slum-dwellers trying to secure the release of political detainees. Forty Angolans died in the attack, and 400 more were killed in reprisals by the security forces and settlers. MPLA activists involved in the attack fled Luanda and set up a guerrilla base in the Dembos forest north-east of the capital. Helped by its links with the Portuguese Communist Party, the MPLA developed good relations with the Soviet Union and received Soviet training, arms and financial support.

The liberation struggles in the Portuguese colonies took place in a Cold War context. The United States and other NATO countries supported the Portuguese for strategic reasons, forcing the nationalist movements to seek financial, political and military assistance from the Soviet Union, Eastern Europe, Cuba, China and radical African states. Neighbouring African states allowed them to use bases in border areas, and to bring in Soviet and Chinese weapons. That said, the USA did not ignore or totally oppose all nationalists; while wary of the MPLA and Frelimo, in particular, Washington developed relations with Roberto's UPA (later the FNLA) and the CIA subsidised his movement to enable it to offer a pro-Western alternative to the MPLA.[51]

Belgium's bungled decolonisation: sowing the seeds of conflict in Congo, Rwanda and Burundi

Infamous for its brutal and exploitative practices in Congo, Belgium did little to prepare the Congolese for any form of meaningful participation in their own government, let alone for independence, and the colonial regime allowed little scope for African political activity. Few Congolese had been recruited to the civil service, entered the professions, or been allowed to rise above non-commissioned ranks in the Force Publique, the territory's military force, and the only education available was provided by mission schools.

The colony had experienced localised revolts linked to mine strikes in mineral-rich Katanga and to mutinies by discontented troops, but no organised territory-wide nationalist activity.[52] When nationalism began to develop, it was on a fragmented regional and ethnic basis, with movements led by members of the small, mission educated bourgeois class involved in business, farming or trade—the nucleus of the elite networks that were to dominate the country under President Mobutu for nearly three decades.

Moïse Tshombe, the Katangan nationalist leader, was from a family of prosperous manioc traders. Tshombe's support base was limited to Katanga, where he formed the Confederation of Tribal Associations of Katanga (CONAKAT). A Bakongo-based organisation known as Alliance des Bakongo (ABAKO) was formed in 1950 to promote the interests of that group, and it developed a political presence in 1956 under the leadership of Joseph Kasavubu. Even when it began to call for Congolese independence, it made no attempt to become a more ethnically inclusive movement.[53]

Demands for independence were at first rebuffed, but in 1957 a process of reform was started to allow more African political participation. In 1958, a radical nationalist, Patrice Lumumba, founded the Movement National Congolais (MNC) and Antoine Gizenga and Pierre Mulele formed the Parti Solidaire Africain (PSA). These aspired to be national, inclusive movements, but a wing of the MNC led by Albert Kalonji split away to form a purely Kasai provincial movement. In 1958, Lumumba attended the All-African People's Conference in Accra, where discussions with Kwame Nkrumah and other radical African leaders convinced him that he must overcome regionalism and politics based on ethno-linguistic groups.

In January 1959, the colonial authorities tried to prohibit an ABAKO public meeting taking place, sparking riots that left at least fifty demonstrators dead at the hands of the Force Publique. Despite their hitherto co-operative relationship with Kasavubu, the Belgians arrested the ABAKO leadership. But within days, on 13 January, they suddenly announced that Congo would be granted independence. During the final months of colonial rule, the Belgians made no attempt to speed up the Africanisation of the civil service or the Force Publique. They scheduled elections for the middle of 1960, with independence to follow on 30 June. The elections produced no outright winner, though Lumumba commanded the greatest support in the new assembly; he became prime minister, with Kasavubu as president. The newly independent state was almost totally reliant on Belgian administrators in the civil service and officers in the Force Publique. They were hugely unpopular with the Congolese, but with no Congolese qualified or experienced enough to run the civil service or the army, there was no alternative. The key mining sector, meanwhile, remained in the hands of Belgian and other foreign companies.

Belgium followed a similar path in the UN trust territory of Ruanda-Urundi, which it had governed since it was taken from Germany and became a League of Nations Mandate at the end of the First World War. Belgian rule, to a great extent, was indirect and exercised through the existing caste and monarchical systems, at the top of which sat the Tutsi elite in both parts of the territory, which was to become the states of Rwanda and Burundi.

The populations of the territories were a mix of the majority Hutu group (83 per cent), the elite Tutsi (around 15 per cent) and the tiny Twa group (around 1–2 per cent). The Tutsi and Hutu spoke the same language, shared the same culture and political/social system and had inhabited the region for centuries, developing a hierarchical system ruled by the Tutsi nobility but in which Hutu could become chiefs. Historians, political scientists and anthropologists have yet to reach definite conclusions about the origins of the populations. It is unclear whether they are castes or classes of one ethno-linguistic group, or two groups which came together through migration, conquest or inter-marriage.[54] Under Belgian rule, Tutsi elite dominance was enhanced and distorted by the sacking of all Hutu chiefs and by the introduction of identity cards, which identified the ethnic origins of every individual.

In 1945, the United Nations took over supervision of the government of the mandated territories. Little attempt was made after 1945 to develop African participation in administration or prepare for independence. When tentative moves were made to increase African involvement, they were too little, too late. There was extreme wariness, and a basic lack of confidence that the Hutu could be involved in government even at the lowest levels[55]—leading inevitably to a Hutu backlash.

Tutsi supremacy fuelled a sense of injustice among Hutu elites, who set up organisations to promote the status of the Rwandan Hutu. They were assisted by changes in the attitude of the influential Catholic Church, which had previously restricted training for the priesthood to Tutsis. The

Swiss-born Bishop of Rwanda, Monsignor Perraudin, came to support the cause of Hutu equality and worked closely with one of the leading Hutu campaigners, Gregoire Kayibanda, who formed a Hutu nationalist movement known as Parmehutu. Between 1955 and 1959, the Belgians moved from grudging acceptance of Hutu aspirations to a directly supportive role. A major development of Hutu nationalism came in March 1957 with the publication of the Bahutu Manifesto. Drafted by nine Hutu intellectuals, including Kayibanda, it highlighted what it called "the social aspect of the racial problem" and demanded reforms in favour of the Hutu and to end the Tutsi monopoly of power. The ideology set out in the Manifesto accepted and developed the Belgian-inspired ethnic view, keenly adopted by sections of the Tutsi elite, that the Tutsi were a separate race which had migrated to Rwanda, conquered the Hutu and subjected them to Tutsi hegemony on the basis of an assumed ethnic superiority.[56] This would become part of the supremacist ideology of Hutu Power, and it soon started to fuel rebellion.

In the late 1950s, the pro-monarchist Tutsi elite formed the Rwandan National Union (UNAR) to defend their power and demand rapid independence. The Hutu leaders of Parmehutu stressed that they wanted an end to minority rule, with power transferred to the majority before independence. The Tutsi elite fought back, proclaiming that the Hutu could never enjoy equality with the Tutsi. When a Parmehutu activist was beaten by a group of Tutsi militants belonging to UNAR in November 1959, Parmehutu mobilised thousands of Hutu to carry out revenge attacks against the Tutsi. This was not just an attack on UNAR but on the Tutsi elite as a whole. Estimates vary, but most put the number killed at 200–300, mainly Tutsis.[57] A state of emergency was imposed, but Belgian sympathies were now with the Hutu. Between November 1959 and mid-1960, twenty-one Tutsi chiefs and 332 sub-chiefs were killed. Many more were forced to resign. Over 130,000 Tutsis fled Rwanda, mainly for Uganda and Tanzania.

In this atmosphere of fear, violence and Hutu impunity, local and national elections were held in 1960 and 1961. Kayibanda's Parmehutu won convincingly, against a background of further violence against the Tutsis. Hundreds more were killed and tens of thousands fled into exile. Independence was granted on 1 July 1962, with Kayibanda as president at the head of a Hutu supremacist government. The Tutsis had a subordinate role, with restricted access to politics, education and business.

In neighbouring Burundi, despite the growth of Hutu movements demanding equality, the transition to independence preserved the power of the Tutsi monarchy—although the power relationships in Burundi between Hutu, Tutsi and the royal caste were not as clear-cut as in Rwanda.[58] It was Burundi's monarch, Mwami Mwambutsa, who asked the Belgians for the official separation of Burundi from Rwanda as part of progress towards independence. This was not only related to a sense of Burundian nationalism, but to Burundian Tutsis' horror at the growing revolt by the Hutu in Rwanda and their violence towards the Tutsi rulers.

Parties calling for independence soon began cropping up in Burundi. The major one was the Union for National Progress (UPRONA), formally a multiracial party but in fact led by the Tutsi nobility. It won elections held in 1961, and in co-operation with the Mwami, formed a government when Burundi achieved independence in July 1961. A Tutsi political elite came to dominate politics, and it developed a supremacist bent that denied the Hutu a political role and led inexorably to decades of ethnic conflict.

Conclusion

At independence, the majority of African states inherited mixed systems, where surviving pre-colonial patterns of local and traditional authority were blended with administrative statism and centralisation of colonial rule. The resulting systems were heavily reliant on authoritarianism and the use, or threat of, force. While nationalist leaders had garnered some popular support and legitimacy through their campaigns for self-government, independence, and their discourse of African nationalism, the new elites were in most cases leaders of small groups of activists rather than parts of mass movements with organised, popular support.

In all but a few cases, notably Senegal and Ivory Coast, the new leaders had an urban bias, and bought into the retention of the export-led economic systems, and the borders and territorial structures established under colonialism. The colonial powers had been the gatekeepers of the colonial economies, controlling revenues and export income, and the new leaders of independent states simply took over this role. Though most proclaimed their intention to use those revenues for development of their economies and the raising of living standards, the systems of government bequeathed by the departing powers included few checks and balances on the misuse of state power and income.

During the decolonisation period, nationalist elites focused on ending colonial occupation and gaining state power, and little was done to develop strong civil institutions independent of government, or functioning economic sectors independent of the state. The Western-designed constitutions, as Crawford Young put it, were:

> Based on western democracy with its close relationship with civil society in various manifestations, but this was lacking, what there was of civil society was part of the nationalist elite or was viewed by it with suspicion or as something to be used to achieve independence and then controlled (like trades unions).[59]

This paved the way for the development of authoritarian systems of government controlled by the new political elites, which made control of state power and through it the economic realm their primary objectives. Marginalised communities remained marginal, and decolonisation failed to empower the majority of the populations of new states. This allowed the new leaders to tighten their grip on state power, leaving the functioning of the extraverted economy intact and fostering the development of patronage and power networks.

The new political elites were thus unaccountable to their own people—but because their roots were so shallow and their economies still so dependent on the international system, they were vulnerable to external political and economic influence.

2

THE TRIALS OF STATEHOOD

DISILLUSIONMENT, DICTATORS, COUPS AND CONFLICT

As the majority of African states achieved independence between 1956 and 1966, there was an atmosphere of euphoria and sense of expectation, encouraged by nationalists as they stirred up popular support. People hoped for better living standards, the restoration of dignity and the power to make their own decisions.

The new states inherited social, political and economic structures that were still evolving, blending pre-colonial, colonial and now post-colonial characteristics. The greatest, lasting structural changes that colonialism had brought about, and which would have the strongest influence over the history of independent Africa, were the nature of the new states established within colonially-drawn borders, and the creation of an economic system, driven by exports and heavily dependent on imports. The nationalist movements did not seriously challenge these basic structures during the decolonisation process, and did little to dismantle the statist and authoritarian administrative systems left in place.

These inherited structures and the developing patterns of elite agency in politics, society, culture and economics did not suggest harmony. African presidents and parties were in power, but the "underlying assumptions of colonialism did not disappear as Africa's last colonial governors packed their bags and mounted the aircraft steps, but became reproduced in nationalist thinking"[1]—primarily intolerance of opposition and the primacy of political and economic control exercised through the state. The new institutions of government and state were not organic outgrowths of the histories, economic, social and cultural systems of the new states but something grafted inexpertly on by the departing colonial powers and accepted by the new leaders in their eagerness for independence and political power. The agency of the new rulers of Africa was mediated through the new institutions and enforced through the coercive powers and laws the new governments retained. This marginalised much of the population, denying them all but the most symbolic participation in the running of the new states and proved inappropriate to the tasks of building new national identities and legitimacy in states that were highly diverse and vulnerable to internal and external threats to their sovereignty, security and stability.

Some of the most serious threats came from the lack of consensus over who or what constituted the new nations.

Congo: mutiny, separatism and international intervention

If Africa needed reminding of the precarious position and danger of fragmentation of the new states, it only had to look at Congo. At the independence ceremony on 30 June 1960, Prime Minister Patrice Lumumba unexpectedly took the podium and spoke of the fresh and painful wounds inflicted by Belgian colonialism. He spoke with anger of the way Africans had been treated, and proclaimed it was now at an end—but for many it wasn't.

After independence, Belgian officers remained in place in the Force Publique with unreconstructed habits of command. The force's commander, General Janssens, was openly opposed to the Africanisation of the officer corps.[2] The combination of Belgian retention of command and the expectations of immediate change on the part of Congolese was highly combustible, and on 5 July 1960, soldiers mutinied, demanding better pay and promotion. Lumumba ordered automatic promotion for each soldier and the removal of all Belgian officers, but the revolt spread throughout Congo's major towns. With no African officers, few Congolese civil servants in the administration and an unstable MNC-led coalition government, Lumumba could do little.

Belgian paratroopers occupied Leopoldville, and 10,000 Belgian soldiers were deployed across the country, seizing control. With support from the Belgian mining conglomerate Union Minière de Haut Katanga, Moise Tshombe declared the secession of Katanga from Congo; the Belgians expelled Congolese forces from the province and helped form a new

Katangese army. Albert Kalonji of the MNC, broke away from Lumumba and declared Kasai's secession. Against the wishes of President Kasavubu, Lumumba broke off diplomatic relations with Belgium and appealed to the UN to intervene.

The UN Security Council sanctioned intervention, and Secretary General Dag Hammarskjöld organised the dispatch of UN forces to Congo and provided some civilian administrators to replace Belgian officials.[3] But major differences emerged between Lumumba and the UN. He wanted the UN to expel all Belgian troops and restore control in Katanga, but this was refused. He appealed to the Americans for 3,000 troops, and again was turned down bluntly. He then asked the Soviet Union for troops and arms. After that, the Americans turned strongly against him; already suspicious of Lumumba's radicalism, they now saw the growing conflict in the stark terms of the Cold War. They wanted Lumumba out of the way and supported President Kasavubu's plan to remove him as prime minister.

The USA and Belgium backed a coup on 14 September 1960 that gave effective power to Colonel Joseph-Desiré Mobutu, the new chief of staff of the armed forces, while Kasavubu remained president. Lumumba was placed under house arrest; he escaped and tried to get to his supporters in Stanleyville, but was captured by Mobutu's forces. On 17 January 1961 they handed him over to Tshombe in Katanga, where he was tortured and killed. Mobutu worked with the Western powers to restore Congolese control in a way that did not threaten Western strategic or economic interests. The UN chief representative in Congo at the time, Rajeshwar Dayal, writes that Mobutu was heavily influenced and often more or less directed by Western diplomats and by the CIA chief in Leopoldville, Lawrence Devlin.[4]

Congo became divided into four regions controlled by different political groups with their own military forces: a Mobutu-backed government based in Leopoldville; a Lumumbist Free Republic of the Congo headed by Antoine Gizenga in Stanleyville, with control over eastern Kivu and northern Katanga; Albert Kalonji's Kasai region, backed by Belgian diamond mining interests; and Tshombe's Katanga. It wasn't until 15 January 1963 that UN forces ended Katanga's secession.[5] Conflict continued in other areas though, with government troops fighting forces loyal to Gizenga in Kivu and around Stanleyville, and the supporters of another opposition leader, Pierre Mulele, in Kwilu province east of Kinshasa.

The national government proved increasingly unable to cope, and Mobutu appointed the former Katangan secessionist leader Moise Tshombe to lead the government. He and Mobutu used the army, foreign mercenaries and

Katangese forces to crush rebel resistance,[6] but extinguishing the revolt did not lead to more effective government. President Kasavubu and Tshombe were locked in a constant struggle for power, and for access to mineral revenues and foreign aid to build their own client networks. Mobutu stepped out of the shadows on 24 November 1965, deposing the warring politicians and ending the façade of parliamentary government. Mobutu set about consolidating his power and developing what would become Africa's biggest kleptocracy.

The brutality of the Congo mutiny, the revolt, and its suppression all contributed to an image fast forming in Western eyes: a war-torn, chaotic and barbaric Africa failing to cope with independence. It also convinced many African leaders, not least Ghana's Nkrumah, that Africa needed greater unity, its own continental institutions, and the capability to intervene in African conflicts and crises.

African Unity: a fine principle, but a practical problem

Well before achieving independence, African nationalists had tried to find common cause around a wider African identity. Starting in Paris in 1919, Pan-African congresses had been organised by black American and Caribbean theorists of African unity to promote the unity of Africans and those of African descent. The fifth conference, held in Manchester in 1945, brought together future leaders including Nkrumah, Kenyatta, Banda and Awolowo.

As independence came to an increasing number of African territories, there was a desire, particularly on the part of more radical leaders like Nkrumah and Sekou Touré, to build institutions that could forge unity between states, help those still under colonial or settler rule achieve independence, and meet the political, security and economic challenges facing Africa. Some initial ideas were distinctly practical, such as aggregating Africa's voting power at the UN or dealing with the international diplomacy of the Cold War. Others, however, were more idealistic and posited ideas of a natural identity and unity of Africans across the continent—despite the fact that Africa as an entity rather than a geographical expression was invented by Europeans before being re-invented in the African diaspora; before the 20th century, very few Africans thought of themselves as Africans.[7] The attempt to forge a continental unity of interests and policy was a tall order, coming just as African states were trying to establish their own national identities and sovereignty from the contorted colonial legacy.

In April 1958, Nkrumah organised the first conference of independent African states in Accra. Eight of the continent's nine independent states attended: Ghana, Egypt, Sudan, Libya, Tunisia, Liberia, Morocco and Ethiopia. Apartheid South Africa was not welcome, and would not have attended anyway. Nkrumah said the aims were "to explore ways and means of consolidating and safeguarding our independence; to strengthen the economic and cultural ties between our countries; to decide on workable arrangements for helping fellow Africans still subject to colonial rule."[8] In the same year, he organised the All-African People's Conference, to which representatives of African nationalist movements were invited, along with diplomats from the Soviet bloc and China. This became an important forum for liberation movements to link up with the Soviet bloc, China, Egypt and radical African states willing to provide diplomatic, financial or military support for armed struggle. Follow-up conferences were held in Tunis in 1960 and Cairo in 1961. Along with the conferences, the independent states worked to build a framework for continental co-operation on issues of mutual concern.

The road to unity was not smooth. Discussions of African unity and the formation of a continental organisation were bedevilled by divisions between radicals, moderates and conservatives, and the newly independent states aligned themselves into three groups. First came the conservative Brazzaville Group, comprising Cameroon, the Central African Republic, Madagascar, Congo-Brazzaville, Ivory Coast, Dahomey, Gabon, Mauritania, Upper Volta, Niger, Senegal, and Chad, and formed in December 1960. Then there was the radical Casablanca Group—Ghana, Guinea, Libya, Mali, Morocco, the United Arab Republic and the Algerian Provisional Government—formed in January 1961. Last to convene was the Monrovia Group, bringing together Liberia, Somalia, Togo, Nigeria, Ethiopia, Sierra Leone, Libya, and Tunisia in May 1961. This was a conservative bloc, but it was not prepared to accept the domination of Francophone leaders such as Houphouët-Boigny or continued French influence and military presence in West Africa and the Sahel. Broadly speaking, the moderates and radicals supported the liberation struggle against the French in Algeria, while the conservatives backed France.

There was conflict between conservatives and radicals over the extent of African unity and its final goal, with Nkrumah seeking in-depth integration, alignment of trade and moves towards a United States of Africa.[9] He was viewed with suspicion by many states; both Cameroon's President Ahidjo and Togo's Sylvanus Olympio accused Ghana of supporting opponents of their governments. Cameroon certainly had a point, as Ghana made little secret of its support for the radical Union des Populations de Cameroon, which had fought the French and waged an armed struggle against the French-backed Ahidjo government.[10]

There were also differences over the sanctity of colonial borders. The vast majority of states were against any changes to inherited borders, but Nkrumah wanted them to wither away. Somalia too wanted changes, feeling that the inherited borders had robbed it of land and people, and laying claim to areas of Kenya, Ethiopia and Djibouti. In the first two decades of independence there were over 100 border disputes between African states, few of which have been conclusively resolved to this day—though few, other than those between Somalia and both Ethiopia and Kenya, have developed into military conflict. The Congo crisis was another cause of division. Nkrumah and the Casablanca group backed Lumumba and opposed Western involvement, while the Brazzaville group viewed Congo as a Cold War battleground and supported Kasavubu, voicing fears of Soviet interference in Africa.

Following the end of the Algerian war in 1962, the death of Lumumba and the end of the Katanga secession, the Brazzaville, Casablanca and Monrovia groups withered away. In May 1963, Africa's leaders met in Addis Ababa and adopted the charter of the Organisation of African Unity to create an institution of sovereign states. It was based on equality, non-interference in each other's affairs, the emancipation of Africa, non-alignment, and emphasised that members were "determined to safeguard and consolidate the hard-won independence as well as the sovereignty and territorial integrity of our states";[11] it enshrined the existing borders as sacred and immutable, opposing secessionist or irredentist claims. The OAU was built to champion the rights of states, and it would become a club for African leaders that foreswore open criticism of or interference in the affairs of even the most brutal or oppressive states.

At the second summit, in Cairo in July 1964, Diallo Telli of Guinea was appointed Secretary-General with Mohammed Sahnoun of Algeria as his deputy. Sahnoun says the most important early decision was to form, at President Nyerere's insistence, the OAU Liberation Committee, which set up its headquarters in Dar es Salaam."[12] The OAU aggregated African continental support for liberation, though this was often more rhetorical than practical, and the organisation was unable to prevent Malawi and Ivory Coast from openly flouting OAU policy on contacts with Rhodesia, South Africa and the Portuguese. The OAU's support for liberation was rather less crucial for liberation groups than bilateral actions such as Tanzania's and Zambia's willingness to support Frelimo in Mozambique, ZAPU and ZANU in Rhodesia and South Africa's ANC. That support allowed them to set up military camps and training bases, and to use their territory to bring in Soviet, Cuban or Chinese arms and advisers.

The OAU's principle of the sanctity of borders ran into trouble when Somalia began pressing for major border adjustments. Its claims were accompanied by support for or direct involvement in irredentist violence in northern Kenya and the Ogaden region of Ethiopia. Although the 1967 summit of the OAU in Kinshasa (formerly Leopoldville) won an agreement from Somalia that its borders with Ethiopia and Kenya would be respected, this did not stop incursions by Somali groups known as *shiftas* in northern Kenya or support for Ogadeni separatist groups in south-eastern Ethiopia.

Besides mediating disputes such as these, the OAU also tried to prevent or mediate in African conflicts and civil wars. One of the first major challenges was The Nigerian Civil War.

Nigeria: regionalism, oil and civil war

In January 1966, Nigeria experienced its first military coup. It not only overthrew the federal system, instituting years of military rule, but triggered the secession of Biafra and a civil war.

The federal structure Nigeria inherited at independence enshrined the power of the more populous but less educationally or economically developed north. Its bigger population meant that the party that controlled the north would be best placed to dominate the federal government and gain control of federal revenues. This quickly caused friction between the northern-dominated federal government and the more economically developed western and eastern regions. It became more acute as the oil industry developed in the east and began to supersede palm oil and other agricultural exports as the main source of national income.

The three regions were controlled by administrations run by mutually hostile parties, each representing one of Nigeria's three largest ethnic/cultural groups. The Northern People's Congress (NPC), built on the residual power of the northern traditional leaders in Sokoto and Kano, dominated the Northern region (Hausa-Fulani); the National Council for Nigeria and the Cameroons (NCNC) held sway in the Eastern region (Igbo); and the Action Group (AG) in the Western region (Yoruba). The AG represented Western chiefs and rich businessmen who wanted more regional autonomy within a weaker federal system. Azikiwe's NCNC was the strongest party in the east, though it also had pockets of support among Igbo and minority communities in the west and the north; it also wanted strong regional governments with greater control over their revenues. The NPC's control of the north gave it the largest number of seats in the federal assembly, but not enough to rule without allying itself with another party. The NCNC agreed to a coalition to get a share of the power and to get an edge over the AG in western areas. An NPC-NCNC coalition was formed—but there was still antipathy between the two ruling parties. There was particularly dislike between the NCNC's Nnamdi Azikiwe and the AG's Obafemi Awolowo.

Various political movements opposed the domination of these three parties, and along with representatives of ethnic and linguistic communities outside the Hausa-Fulani, Yoruba and Igbo triad, pushed for constitutional changes to dilute the power of the three dominant groups. They wanted the regions split into more states to give smaller communities political representation. These demands were publicly rejected by all three parties in their respective regional governments—but privately, they all encouraged such groups outside their home regions to weaken their opponents and undermine the political integrity of the other regions.

This divisive atmosphere intensified in the first years of independence. The NPC attempted to entrench federal power and secure a monopoly over federal revenues to fund economic and educational development in the north, citing decades of poor educational provision and economic development in the north under British rule. This was a rather self-serving justification, since many of the northern traditional leaders through whom the British governed were content to remain separate from the rest of the country and retain their own cultural identity, and that included resistance to western-style education that they feared could undercut the traditional hierarchies.

The smouldering disputes over federal powers were stoked in 1963 when the federal government moved to split the Western region in two, creating the Mid-Western region. The Western-based AG was divided at the time; Awolowo was fiercely opposed to partition, but regional premier Sam Akintola was willing, and the NPC and NCNC reached agreement with him and his supporters on partition.[13] Meanwhile, there was also growing unrest and violence in the Tiv area of the Northern region's Middle Belt, with non Hausa-Fulani groups pressing for the creation of a new region. The army had to be deployed to restore order in both the West and the Middle Belt.

Through this, the army became increasingly politicised, becoming an agent of federal political control. The structure of the army and its commanders was very regionalised and split at different ranks: the upper ranks of colonel and general were dominated by Westerners; majors and lieutenant-colonels were chiefly from the Eastern region; and captains and lieutenants were mainly Northerners, with a substantial number from the Middle Belt.[14]

By the beginning of 1966, the federal structure was disintegrating—and then, on 15 January, a group of middle-ranking army officers launched attacks that killed the NPC leaders, many of their allies and a number of Northern officers. It was called a coup, but beyond eliminating government leaders, the officers' aims were never clear. In Lagos, Federal Prime Minister Tafawa Balewa and Finance Minister Okotie Eboh were killed; in Ibadan, officers executed Sam Akintola. In Kaduna, Northern premier Ahmadu Bello was shot. No attempt was made to kill NCNC leaders. But the rebels failed to kill two key commanders, Lt-Col Yakubu "Jack" Gowon and Maj-Gen Johnson Aguyi Ironsi. Ironsi rallied loyal government troops in Lagos, and at other garrisons, and captured the rebels.

Many in the Eastern region welcomed the coup, as did the AG leader Awolowo. Northerners saw the killings as an Igbo attempt to subjugate their region—all but one of the officers leading the attacks was Igbo. To make matters worse, when the army defeated the rebels, it was an Igbo, Ironsi, who led the new military government. In May 1966, the military government abolished the regions. Ironsi declared the independence constitution and the political institutions it established unviable, and said they were the root of the country's political problems. That was an accurate summation, but the military government had no obvious answers.

To many in the north, the new system amounted to the imposition of Igbo dominance. Thousands of Igbo lived in the north and west, and having benefitted from better educational opportunities and recruitment to the civil service and institutions such as the railways, had better access to jobs than the more poorly-educated Northerners. This bred resentment among the Northerners, who were under-represented in the professions and public services. Soon after Ironsi came to power, rioting started across the north with attacks on Igbo residents, most of whom lived in specific areas known as *sabon gari* (strangers' quarters). Thousands of Igbos and other Easterners were killed.

Trainloads of Igbo fled back to their home province bearing tales of murder and Northern hatred. Ironsi toured the country trying to calm tensions, but failed. He was in Ibadan in late July when Northern troops mutinied in

Abeokuta, in the west; the revolt spread to Kaduna and Kano. Ironsi was seized by Northern troops in Ibadan, and was tortured and shot along with a number of other Eastern officers. As the Northern mutiny became a full-scale national coup, the killing of Igbos in the north continued with no attempt by the police or army to intervene.

On 29 July, a new military government was formed, this time dominated by Northerners. They chose a Northerner as head of government, but one who was also a Middle Belt Christian: Yakubu Gowon. Gowon had Northern support and the backing from Western officers, such as future military ruler and elected civilian president Olusegun Obasanjo. He lacked support, however, in the Eastern region, where military governor Lt-Col Odumegwu Ojukwu refused to accept his appointment on the grounds that Gowon was a relatively junior officer and not well-educated. The two men were on a collision course, as were the Eastern region and the rest of Nigeria, as the Eastern leadership resisted the imposition of authority by the military government. To address the crisis, a constitutional conference was held in September 1966. There was a broad consensus on a looser federal structure, though no agreement on the number of regions—but any further discussion was prevented by another wave of attacks on Igbos in the North.

Ojukwu urged Easterners in other parts of the country to return home, and ordered people from other regions out of the East. He and the other Eastern leaders seem to have decided that the region had no future in Nigeria, and that the revenues generated by the Niger Delta's offshore oil could provide enough income to make the region independent. Since the start of oil production in 1958, output had increased from 5,000 barrels a day to 415,000 in 1968—accounting for a third of Nigeria's export revenues. So, quite apart from protecting Nigeria's territorial integrity, oil revenues were not something that the military government was prepared to lose.

There was serious concern in West Africa about the consequences of Eastern secession, and the military government in Ghana and the OAU tried to mediate. But on 31 March 1967, Ojukwu issued edicts blocking the transfer of regional revenues to the federal budget (including oil income), established a separate education system, and ended the right of the Federal Supreme Court to judge Eastern cases. On 30 May 1967, Gowon announced the formation of a twelve-state Nigeria; on the same day, the east's independence was proclaimed by Ojukwu, and the state renamed the Republic of Biafra.

A civil war followed that lasted nearly three years. It was a war of blockade and of gradual occupation of Biafran territory by federal forces. The Biafran army had experienced officers, but was badly equipped and its soldiers poorly trained.[15] It was no match for the rapidly expanding Nigerian army. Biafra was subject to a UN arms embargo, but Nigeria was not; and both Britain and the Soviet Union supplied it with weapons, the latter providing modern combat aircraft and heavy artillery that Britain declined to sell.[16] Western companies had stopped paying Biafra oil revenues at the start of the war, and the Nigerian blockade starved it of resources. France gave some financial assistance and covertly supplied arms, which were flown in along with humanitarian aid deliveries. The UN, the Commonwealth and OAU attempted to mediate—but all to no avail. Biafra's defeat was inevitable. It was short of funds, food and arms; the war, blockade and diversion of food to the Biafran army led to famine among civilians. Nigerian government offensives, using an army that had grown to 250,000, ate away at Biafran territory, and the region was finally overrun by Nigerian troops in January 1970. Over one million Biafrans died during the war, a substantial portion from starvation and disease, while at least 200,000 were killed on the government side.

At the end of the war, the east was re-integrated into a Nigerian federal structure of twelve states, six in the north and six in the south. The federal government under Gowon launched a policy of reconciliation, and Igbos were taken back into the federal and regional civil services and into the armed forces. The Biafran conflict was a very bitter lesson in nation-building, but it convinced most Nigerians of the futility of secession.[17] To this day, Nigerians are searching amid corruption and civil conflict for a path to real unity, but few would now seriously promote secession as a solution to their problems.

The other legacy of the war was the domination of the military. The swollen and heavily resourced army would be hard to demobilise, and its officers came to dominate politics and much of the economy for decades. The military has continued to devour a substantial part of oil and other government revenues.

Weak states, crumbling constitutions and the rise of the 'big men'

If the Congolese and Nigerian conflicts showed the fragility of those particular nation-states, and how badly they lacked popular legitimacy within their imposed borders, events across Africa soon began to show how weak and inappropriate their political institutions and constitutions were.

In the first decade of independence, it became clear that political power and the control of economies would be increasingly vested in small groups of leaders who could use state mechanisms and revenue to entrench their power. Few checks or balances were in place to stop them using resources to build networks of clients to garner support and distribute patronage. In all but a few states, the plurality of political movements that had existed before independence, independent trades unions or other elements of civil society, either fell under the hegemony of the dominant party and leader or were suppressed. Leaders became more authoritarian, and yet institutions and the state remained weak. As Fred Cooper argues:

> Rulers in these situations were likely to fall back on the resources they could count on: institutions of state inherited from the colonial regime, revenue sources that were easily centralised, disbursement of foreign aid that is channelled through central authorities, and paramilitary and clientage systems centred on the ruler's personal connections.[18]

Just as there was to be little investment in diversified economies with thriving non-state sectors, so there was little investment in political plurality or the development of functioning, independent civil societies.

Political leaders became 'big men' in every sense. They and their client networks dominated politics and controlled state resources, including coercive force. They were gatekeepers who actively maintained and even deepened their countries' economic dependency on others; they promoted and profited from exports, the licensing of imports, the contracting of loans and aid and the resulting indebtedness.[19] And in most countries, informal networks provided a parallel means to control of state institutions for leaders to entrench their power.

The result was a drift to dictatorship. As leaders' own agency, events and the influence of the international economic and political environment transformed the new states, their inherited institutions and state structures were unable to cope with the tasks of nation-building and economic development. The absence or emasculation of crucial institutions such as independent media, civil society organisations, trades unions or viable opposition parties deprived their people of the means to limit their leaders' power. The process of decolonisation had exaggerated the power and standing of some political leaders, vesting in them powers of patronage and rent-taking, control of the media, and, crucially, monopoly over coercive force.

Of course, for a time, these leaders could rely on popular support thanks to their claims to have led their countries to independence, but that credit inevitably ran out. Kenneth Kaunda of Zambia admitted as much to me in an interview in 1991 when discussing why he agreed to end one-party rule. He conceded that his ability to maintain support or acquiescence for being the "father of the nation" had weakened as new generations grew up with no experience of colonial rule.[20] But in the years following independence, the loyalty to those who claimed credit for independence was matched by the power independence constitutions gave them to control their citizens. They could declare states of emergency at will, rule by decree, suppress dissent and limit freedom of speech, and what safeguards there were became unenforceable as institutions like the judiciary succumbed to presidential power.

Personal rule and the dominance of elite groups became prominent features of new states.[21] Those at the top of the power pyramid depended on political, economic and military networks, and had to provide sufficient benefit to key supporters and constituencies to maintain control. It was only when resources dried up or the networks weakened that regime survival was threatened. And usually, that threat came from the one institution that could claim to represent national sovereignty and which also had the power to topple governments: the military.

Across the continent, there was a crisis of expectations born out of people's hopes at independence. Nationalist leaders had used promises of a golden future to mobilise support and gain votes in pre-independence elections; instead, their citizens ended up with weak state, political and civil institutions and stagnant living standards, unemployment and unaccountable political systems. With no other means of change available, military intervention against governments became the norm in much of Africa, when the post-independence leaders could no longer exert control. But some managed to retain power and progressively accumulate more.

The career of President Hastings Kamuzu Banda and the Malawi Congress Party (MCP) is a good example of how a seemingly popular and radical nationalist movement became a highly-personalised system of rule exercised through both state and informal networks.

Banda had been called back to Malawi by the young, radical leaders of the nationalist movement to be a respectable, educated figurehead who could negotiate independence with the British—and whom the radicals thought they could control. But through his own political acumen, his personal wealth and his ability to appeal to conservative rural Malawians as well as educated urbanites, Banda dominated and outwitted his radical young lieutenants to become one of the most personally powerful rulers in Africa. Successfully portraying those who invited him back as inexperienced, hotheaded young men, he established a strong, conservative style of government, stressing the development of peasant agriculture to gain support in rural areas but also supporting large-scale, foreign-dominated farming in the export sector. He held up his own private company, Press Holdings, as an example of personal endeavour and the importance of private ownership, while also manipulating marketing boards and state companies to increase his control over key sectors of the economy and public life—a pragmatic approach that gave him considerable flexibility. He eschewed the pro-liberation nationalist ideology of his erstwhile lieutenants and of his more radical neighbours in Zambia and Tanzania, and instead developed close ties with the West—as well as with apartheid South Africa, the white government in Southern Rhodesia, and the Portuguese in Mozambique.

When I worked in Malawi for the BBC in 1981 and 1982, Banda was always referred to at public meetings or on the radio using his full title: His Excellency the Life President, Ngwazi Dr H Kamuzu Banda. He would lecture crowds under the blazing sun for two or three hours after being praised by ministers and lauded in song and dance. People were trucked in from miles around and had little choice but to obey when the enforcers of the Malawi Young Pioneers (the youth wing of the MCP) came to tell them to attend. Banda always spoke in English, with one of his ministers translating into Chichewa. This was not only because decades away from Malawi had loosened his grasp of the language; it deliberately flattered Banda as the chief of chiefs who was above the common herd.

Banda turned parliament and the MCP into his own instruments. As undisputed ruler he gave vent to his conservative ethos, introducing restrictions on men's hair length, women's dress, the press, literature and public decency. He encouraged the British tea and tobacco planters to stay, elicited foreign investment in the tobacco, tea, sugar and other industries and encouraged smallholder tobacco production in his home Central region, thereby enriching an important constituency among the peasantry.

The MCP became ubiquitous, and all adult Malawians had to pay to be members. On a number of occasions I had to persuade members of the MCP and their thuggish youth wing, the Young Pioneers, to release Malawians employed by the BBC because they had failed to pay their party membership. The Pioneers would block off the walled markets and not let people out until they produced a party card or paid for a new one on the spot. Dissent was forbidden and suspected criticism was treated harshly, including in culture and literature—the poet Jack Mapanje spent four years in prison without trial from 1987 to 1991 when Banda interpreted some of his poems as subversive.[22] This atmosphere of repression is set out brilliantly in Malawian author Legson Kayira's novel *The Detainee.*

Banda's success in crushing opposition and stamping individual authority on government was replicated in varying forms across Africa—rarely with the same conservative zeal or idiosyncratic foreign policy, but often via similar instruments of state, economic and informal power. Military or single party leaders justified ending pluralism and sweeping away or sidelining Western-style institutions on the grounds that Africa needed to concentrate on development, wealth creation and nation-building rather than supposedly divisive, European-style party politics. The need to integrate regions and communities, build identity based on the new states, and avoid political conflict arising from their cultural, ethnic and linguistic diversity were used as pretexts for authoritarianism. The emphasis new governments across Africa placed on national unity suppressed voices calling for devolution of power or federalism, both of which could all too easily be labelled as divisive and unpatriotic. And the same leaders who energetically blamed factionalism for disunity often put the most effort into fostering the interests of their client groups over others.

President Jomo Kenyatta of Kenya, for example, denounced calls for greater devolution of power to Kenya's provinces as tribalism, using the term *majimoboism*[23]—from the Swahili word for region—as a term of political abuse for those he accused of undermining national unity. But he clearly favoured the Kikuyu elite in the appointment of ministers and parastatal heads, the awarding of government contracts and import licences and the redistribution of land.

In Ghana, the opposition to Kwame Nkrumah's centralised system of rule and to his use of revenues from cocoa-producing regions to fund development nationally was evident even before independence. Once in power, his CPP administration tried to reduce the power of chiefs over local government in what were known as the 'stool lands' (after the chiefly stools, symbols of authority of the Asante kings). This meant taking control of the administration of land locally and acquiring land, as Nkrumah put it, "for development purposes".[24] Nkrumah's view of socialism, unlike that adopted by other African socialists such as Julius Nyerere, was not based on a re-imagining of pre-colonial African communalism. Nkrumah was suspicious of traditional practices and the political legacy of chieftaincy, and his socialism stressed centralisation of power and modernisation through economic development, purportedly to serve the interests of all Ghanaians rather than of elites and foreign companies. In 1959, the government adopted a five-year plan revolving around the Volta River hydroelectric power project, bauxite mining and processing, and industrialisation. The generation of electricity and the processing of bauxite were proclaimed as the basis of a new Ghanaian economy and as the end of dependence on cocoa. The plan's promise proved illusory: it took up 80 per cent of budget allocations,[25] ate up revenues and drove the country into massive debt.

In 1964, Ghana formally became a one-party state, and Nkrumah began using repressive laws to punish politicians accused of plotting against the government. Peaceful political opposition seemed to qualify as conspiracy. The state intervention in the economy and the continuing use of cocoa income to fund services and development were proclaimed as necessary to build a stronger economy and create wealth for society as a whole. This type of argument was used repeatedly by leaders across Africa to justify one-party systems, the suppression of opposition and increasing authoritarianism as the only viable means of nation-building and economic progress.

The extraction of surplus from Ghanaian exports was carried out through the cocoa marketing board, which meant cocoa farmers received barely half the income from their crops. Had the use of export earnings led to economic development and a diversified economy, history and Ghanaians might have looked more kindly on Nkrumah, but corruption, government inefficiency and falling cocoa prices instead led to economic stagnation. Nkrumah's socialist rhetoric and the development of relations with the Soviet Union and China led to American opposition, which in turn limited financial assistance from Western donors and blocked assistance from the IMF and World Bank. The Ghanaian economist Nii Moi Thompson argues cogently that there was an American policy of denying funding that would have enabled the government to ride out the fall in cocoa prices in the 1960s, while waiting for investments and development projects to bear fruit.[26]

Nkrumah's failure to deliver on the promises he made was exemplified by falling living standards. Between independence and 1965 wages fell by over 40 per cent, and cocoa farmers' income by 60 per cent.[27] The CPP was losing influence and was unable to mobilise people behind its policies, but with opposition parties banned, it no longer had to work to win elections. Nkrumah progressively alienated key sections of society, subordinating the unions and farmers' associations. The CPP itself had been weakened and reduced to an instrument of Nkrumah's vision. There was no one left to fight for Nkrumah when the army carried out its coup on 24 February 1966, while he was in China. He returned to Africa to live as an exile in Guinea.

A dramatic contrast to Nkrumah's Ghana, not least because they were neighbours and both relied heavily on cocoa exports, was Ivory Coast, which followed a radically different path under the pro-Western and determinedly capitalist government of Felix Houphouët-Boigny.

At independence, Houphouët-Boigny set about establishing a one-man system of government that entrenched personal power while giving Ivorians the impression that his government included all communities and regions. Known as *Le Vieux*, he cultivated the image of a conservative, religious and paternalistic leader. He also openly enriched himself through the development of the economy. But while other African autocrats such as Mobutu in Congo (Zaire) or Omar Bongo in Gabon secretly salted away money reaped from their peoples' harvests, the Ivorian president was quite open about his Swiss Bank accounts and about the desirability of being wealthy, exhorting Ivorians to follow his example.

Houphouët-Boigny had built the PDCI, into a strong national party, and in 1965 it was declared "a single party, for a single people, with a single leader".[28] It was one of the chief instruments of his rule, and of the carefully constructed fiction that all Ivorians were represented by the party and government. As Houphouët-Boigny increased his personal power and use of informal networks within the government, the economy and the party, the PDCI ceased to be an independent institution in its own right and became little more than a transmission belt for his policies, unable to challenge or limit his hold over politics.

The Ivorian system was designed to generate wealth through exports and small-scale industries—import substitution, textiles, brewing, food processing and the like. Order was maintained through strict government and party control, backed up by the police, the armed forces and French security guarantees. The result was a long period of growth and relative prosperity, during which Ivory Coast maintained very close economic and security co-operation with France; French troops were stationed in the country, and a wide variety of businesses were French-owned. Even as late as 1987, when I visited Abidjan, there were thousands of French technocrats working in the civil service and substantial numbers of businesses and shops were still being run by expatriates. The French population of the country increased from 12,000 at independence to 50,000 in 1980, only falling at the turn of the millennium after the country's the descent into civil war.

Under Houphouët-Boigny, Ivory Coast was a model for those who stressed the efficacy of an authoritarian system with pro-Western and capitalist policies. In the first three decades of independence there developed what Victor Le Vine has called "a distinct Ivorian political-administrative-economic elite—a state bourgeoisie of wealthy businessmen, top officials and politicians, bureaucrats, party officials...held together by networks of patronage."[29] Ultimately, though, this formula was to prove unsustainable, relying as it did on the president's political acumen, ruthlessness and ability to control a complex network of clients and patronage.

In Senegal, a different if still essentially conservative system developed based on alliances through traditional networks of political, social and religious influence in the Murid brotherhoods. President Senghor relied on his skills as an alliance builder and political thinker rather than a commanding, paternalistic autocrat. His Union Progressiste Sénégalaise—later to be transformed into the Parti Socialiste (PS)—had won all the seats in the 1959 pre-independence election. From this monopolistic position, Senghor was able to dominate both party and government, but in a more subtle and sustainable way than Houphouët-Boigny.

He maintained networks through the Murids and the party that allowed him to exert control, but which were also open to some participation and accountability. His network of support brought in a range of ethnic communities, only really leaving out the people of Casamance in the south, who were to launch a small but tenacious insurgency against successive governments. His methods encouraged a controlled form of pluralism, and he succeeded in building "a coalition of local interests, to simultaneously reinforce his power and the stability of the state."[30]

Senghor maintained stability, and his government deftly managed political conflict and headed off violence or military intervention. For example, Senghor ran into trouble when his closest political ally, Prime Minister Mamadou Dia, and younger more technocratic elements within the ruling party criticised traditional methods of growing groundnuts. Dia stressed the danger of soil exhaustion, and proposed a combination of land reform, decentralisation of control and co-operatives. If implemented, this would have disrupted the delicate balance Senghor had constructed between peasant growers, the Murids and the state marketing institutions, and he refused to endanger it. He responded by accusing Dia of plotting a coup, then sacked and imprisoned him.[31]

This was hardly the most democratic approach, but it kept the country stable, and the crucial rural/religious alliances the government relied on were left intact. The marabouts, important local religious leaders from the Murid brotherhoods who made up the majority of the largest landowners, benefited greatly from Senghor's policies; changes in land use would have undercut their clout in rural areas, disrupting the alliance system that linked the government more organically to rural areas than in most African systems.

Senghor appeared to stand above politics, presenting himself as an arbitrator and conciliator. Most Senegalese regarded him as accessible and therefore to some extent accountable, even if he was clearly in control and the fount of policy.[32]

Ujamaa: Tanzania's African socialist experiment

A very different developmental experiment was launched in Tanzania by Julius Nyerere and the TANU party. Within months of achieving independence in December 1961, what was then still called Tanganyika was set on a path Nyerere called self-reliant socialism. Basing his ideas on a vision of family-based communalism of pre-colonial society, he issued a pamphlet entitled *Ujamaa—The Basis of African Socialism.* This rejected capitalism and Marxist class-based socialism as models for Tanganyika's development and wrote of the "anti-social effects of the accumulation of personal wealth", arguing instead for a society where individuals work for each other and are looked after by society. It was based on a vision of traditional African society in which no one starved because they lacked personal wealth, a socialism in which "those who sow reap a fair share of what they sow."[33]

The farming metaphor was carefully chosen: Nyerere set out a rural-based concept of socialism founded on the idea that in African society resources were commonly held, individuals did not own land but had the right to use it, and there was no exploitation of tenants by landlords. Nyerere located his ideas in the context of an application of communalism that embodied what he wanted to achieve rather than in the context of an identifiable, functioning tradition of communalism. This was to prove to be an exaggeration of traditional communal values and an unworkable extension of the functioning of extended families to a wider community not bound by kinship.

Along with this programme for the economy, Nyerere and TANU stressed the country's identity and unity as a state, overcoming the multiplicity of ethnic identities and getting people to see themselves as Tanzanians rather than Sukuma, Maasai, Chagga, Arab, Asian or Shirazi.[34] Although ever since they were united in 1964 there have been tensions between Zanzibar and the mainland over the nature of the political system and the Zanzibari fear of domination by the mainland majority, Tanzania has avoided the regional or ethnic tension that bedevils many African states. The country has over 120 different ethnic groups, and the largest, the Sukuma, comprises only 16 per cent of the population; its politics have simply never become ethnicised, and alliance-building has been the norm—even during the period of one-party rule by TANU and its successor, the Chama cha Mapinduzi (Revolutionary Party).

The *ujamaa* policy, set out in the Arusha Declaration of 5 February 1967, established a programme of self-reliance with an economy based on rural agriculture, with nationalised banks, land and other principal means of production. The state was in control of economic activity. Nyerere stressed that this was to establish an equitable and non-exploitative economy. The plan was to expand agricultural production through communal farming to produce a surplus that could fund national economic development, raise living standards, provide services, and achieve independence from foreign control. At the centre of *ujamaa* was the concept of the mutually supportive and self-reliant extended peasant family. Nyerere believed that while colonialism had introduced capitalist relations, particularly through cash-crop production and the need for money to pay colonially-imposed taxes, it had not totally destroyed a pre-colonial family-based culture, which could be revived and turned into the ideological and spiritual driving force of development and service delivery.

What *ujamaa* meant in practice, apart from nationalisation, was the co-operativisation of agriculture and the utilisation of economies of scale by bringing peasant families together in villages—a policy known as 'villagisation'. In villages, Tanzanians could be provided with health, education, water and other services that could not be delivered to scattered peasant households. Prior to the declaration there had been voluntary villagisation in areas like Ruvuma, which had increased production and made service provision more efficient. In the 1960s, 60–70 per cent of Tanzanian agriculture was peasant subsistence farming producing food for the farmer and his extended family and with a major role in cultivation played by women.[35] Larger scale farming—both peasant farming by those able to expand and employ a few labourers and plantation-based commercial farming—produced maize for local consumption, and sisal, coffee, tea, cotton and groundnuts for export. Nyerere wanted to reduce dependence on the international capitalist system, but was not seeking to end cash-crop production or exports completely—only to change the balance of power in the economy. It was assumed that the communal work of family households would translate into co-operative work on the aggregated communal land area in new villages. This in turn would boost output, and enable the cost-effective and sustainable provision of modern machinery, fertilisers and infrastructure.

The Arusha Declaration led to the nationalisation of banks and much commercial and industrial activity. Parastatal organisations, such as the

National Milling Corporation and the National Development Credit Agency, took over the functions of Asian- and European-owned commercial organisations in the financial, marketing, and food processing sectors. These measures were popular to begin with among poor peasants, who resented the wealth and economic power of Asian businessmen in the crop purchasing, transport, retail and import sectors. But the *ujamaa* project failed to create the self-reliant communalism that the Tanzanian leadership hoped for. The top-down programme was based heavily on Nyerere's personal vision; it was unpopular with the majority of farmers, and totally opposed by prosperous farmers, international financial institutions and many aid donors. Foreign banks like Barclays, Grindlays and Standard all withdrew staff and refused to co-operate with the government after nationalisation. Tanzania still received development support from Canada, the Scandinavian countries and NGOs such as Britain's Oxfam, but this was not sufficient to provide a sound financial base for reform. There were also serious problems in the parastatal sectors (such as the sisal export sector, the East African Harbours Association and the National Development Corporation), which still relied on foreign expertise. Tanzania lacked experienced economic planners, agricultural economists, financial administrators and management personnel. When the government set up co-operative shops to replace those run by Asian or African businessmen, they were mismanaged, frequently corrupt and failed to keep local people supplied with necessary consumer goods—a huge disincentive to growing more crops.

The pace of villagisation, meanwhile, was slow. In the first three years of the campaign only 2,000 villages were established with 531,200 inhabitants—a mere 5 per cent of the population. In 1970, TANU launched large-scale operations to move people into villages led by state and party officials, and latterly, the army. Whole families were trucked to new locations, where there were often no buildings or other amenities. When peasants resisted, force and the threat of imprisonment were used. By 1973, 5,631 villages had been formed with just over two million inhabitants; Nyerere was not satisfied, and ordered that all rural Tanzanians must be living in co-operative villages by 1976.[36] The programme was abandoned before the target date was reached, but by 1976 the government estimated that nearly nine million peasants were living in villages and being provided with better education, water and health services. And even though there was little enthusiasm for communalism, the vast majority of peasants stayed in the new villages.

The villagisation process had not only failed to capture the support of the peasants—it had actually undermined agricultural output. Food production per capita fell to 99 per cent of its 1961–65 level 1972 and 92 per cent of it in 1973, only rising to 98 per cent in 1974.[37] Maize production fell from 1.8 million metric tons in 1970 to 239,000 in 1974–75. This showed that compulsory villagisation was a poor engine of growth; villages had also run up debts by using credit to buy tractors, other machinery, and fertiliser. Stagnant output meant those debts were not repaid and had to be written off, and that caused the failure of the Co-operative Bank and National Development Credit Agency. Neither the peasant farming sector nor the state had sufficient resources to continue the programme, while parastatals became repositories of debt and a drag on the economy thanks to poor management and corruption.

Even though *Ujamaa* failed to instil a spirit of communalism or provide the basis for economic self-reliance and socialism in Tanzania, it was by no means an unmitigated disaster. By 1980, largely as a result of the spread of education through the new villages, Tanzania had one of the highest literacy rates in Africa, despite being one of its poorest countries: male literacy was 85 per cent and female literacy 73 per cent. Every village had a primary school, 90 per cent of villages had shops, and over 60 per cent had access to safe water or a health centre. Better social welfare was provided, and famine and serious hunger were avoided. Tanzania had become a more equal society, narrowing the gap between high and low wage earners and between rural and urban incomes.[38] Despite the excesses of the latter phase of villagisation and the ruling party's growing bureaucratisation, political stability and basic trust in the government had been sustained.

But Tanzania was still at the mercy of the global economy. The government could not maintain the co-operative policy or resist international pressure to make punishing structural adjustments, not only because it had failed to increase productivity and because the parastatals had run up huge debts, but also because the early 1970s saw both a fall in world prices for agricultural commodities and a rise in the price of oil and manufactured imports. The mechanisation of agriculture required imports of fuel, fertilisers and capital goods that rose in price even as the exports they were used to produce sold for less.

It could be argued that a more longer-term, gradual transformation programme based on the active participation of rural people and with greater resources available might have succeeded. However, this would still have required the support of major foreign donors and financial institutions.

Nyerere saw family co-operation as the ideal end state for all peasants, but it was based on a myth. Village co-operation had only existed in a limited way at specific times and for particular purposes, like clearing land, planting and harvesting; it had never been a way of life. As Andreas Eckert says, "this function was communal in the sense of implying mutual aid and reciprocity, but not in the sense of communal ownership."[39] And while the policy tried to create a new society based on an imagined version of pre-colonial communal structures, it deprived the peasants of any agency in shaping their own economic and social relations.

Ujamaa never gained the support of the peasantry despite "a rhetoric that stressed popular participation, decentralisation, and democratisation... subsequently the government of independent Tanzania largely pursued a policy of centralisation and bureaucratic authoritarianism" which many of the peasants viewed as little different from British colonial administrative policy, marked as it was by a paternalistic, top-down approach.[40]

The military virus: coups and counter-coups

From conservative states like Ivory Coast, Senegal, Gabon and Kenya to radical or socialist ones like Ghana, Guinea, Congo-Brazzaville or Tanzania, personalised presidential and single-party systems became the rule rather than the exception in sub-Saharan Africa during the 1960s. A few states retained aspects of consent or accountability, but always in the context of paternalistic authority. But in much of Africa, the failure of plural or single-party politics to bring development, participation or to create a sense of national unity produced another phenomenon: a recurring rash of military coups and counter-coups.

Along with the insurgent, irredentist or secessionist warfare seen in Cameroon, Congo, the Horn of Africa and Sudan, the military coup became a trademark of sub-Saharan African politics. The military coup was, for several decades, the main form of regime change in sub-Saharan Africa, as civilian governments failed to bring the economic development and improvements in living standards or political participation people had been promised. Instead, leaders and parties clung to power despite their failings, like limpets to a rock in rough seas, and only the military seemed able to bring regime change. Between 1958 and April 1984, there were fifty-eight successful military coups, 65 failed coups and over 100 coups plots uncovered before they came to fruition.[41] By May 1984, twenty-one of forty-five independent states in sub-Saharan Africa were ruled by military governments, and many of the civilian governments were only there thanks to military support. The only states which had avoided the military were Kenya, Ivory Coast, Malawi, Botswana, Mauritius, Cape Verde, Djibouti, Lesotho, Mozambique, Swaziland, Zambia and Zimbabwe. Yet even amongst these states Kenya experienced and a brief and unsuccessful coup attempt by air force officers, Malawi and Ivory Coast experienced plots that didn't lead to coups, Lesotho would experience military rule after 1986, Mozambique had to endure years of South African-backed insurgency and Zambia suffered an abortive coup in 1990.

Sub-Saharan Africa's first military takeover took place in Sudan on 17 November 1958. The Nile Valley politicians that had been brought to power by independence had failed to resolve the conflict with the south, and with power held by a small group in a single region of the massive state, communities in Darfur, the Nuba Mountains, South Kordofan, Blue Nile and the Red Sea were left marginalised and alienated. The Nile Valley elite themselves were split into factions on religious and political grounds and this intra-elite conflict encouraged regular interventions by the military. The 1958 coup came about when the National Unionist Party government collapsed, and the ensuing elections failed to produce a stable government or viable coalition of parties. Perhaps encouraged by the success of the Free Officers' take-over in Egypt in 1952, General Ibrahim Abboud seized power. He adopted a more strenuous policy of Arabisation and Islamicisation of the country, including the south.[42] The army claimed to be acting as a national unifying force that could serve Sudanese interests better than the bickering politicians it had replaced.

These claims became recurring themes in the speeches of the generals, colonels, captains and NCOs who led the coups of the next four decades. This idea of the military as a reliable, unifying, national institution with a monopoly of force partially explains the prevalence of military intervention. It doesn't, however, fully explain why militaries could successfully seize power with so little opposition or public reaction, especially given the less than nationally representative nature of the leaders and rank and file of most African armies.

One explanation is that militaries had a better sense of unity than any other non-government groups. As previously independent institutions like the unions, opposition parties and non-party associations were forced into single party folds or destroyed, there was no organisation beyond the ruling elite to resist military interventions. In his seminal work on the role of the military in politics around the world, Finer captures the key factors in the political role of the military:

> Where civilian associations and parties are strong and numerous, where the procedures for the transfer or power are orderly, and where the location of supreme authority is not seriously challenged: the political ambit of the military will be circumscribed. Where the parties or trades unions are feeble and few, where the procedure for the transfer of power is irregular or even non-existent... there the military's political scope will be very wide.[43]

In Africa, coups did not take place or did not succeed where there were strong parties, well-grounded supreme authorities or alternative forms of public power and opinion. Houphouët-Boigny, Banda, Nyerere, Kenyatta, Kaunda and Senghor had built systems and networks of patronage or support that had a clearly located centre of supreme authority, often backed by a strong party or other forms of political alliance. Botswana benefited from good public accountability, legitimate forms of local and national authority, a developing civil society and a working and accepted system of plural politics and elections. But elsewhere in Africa, autocratic rulers had built their castles on sand that could be swept away with surprising ease once their popularity waned and economic failure led to discontent, and the breakdown of patronage networks or divisive policies led to an over-reliance on the armed forces as guarantors of power.

Ghana is a good example. As Nkrumah's growing autocracy weakened civil and political institutions, the growing opposition to him across a wide swathe of society and regions left him vulnerable and gave the military popular backing for the 1966 coup. The weakness of the civilian regimes installed after military interventions meant that Ghana became one of Africa's most coup-prone states, with successful coups in 1966, 1972, 1978, 1979 and 1981 and six other attempted ones.

Ghana is not the only state to have such a history of military intervention. The Central African Republic (CAR), Burundi, Equatorial Guinea, Guinea Bissau, Nigeria, Sierra Leone, Sudan and Congo-Brazzaville all suffered recurrent military coups and attempted takeovers. After the Sudanese coup of 1958, the next was in Congo-Leopoldville, when Mobutu stepped in to end the struggle between Lumumba and Kasavubu. The Togolese leader Nicholas Grunitzky was overthrown in January 1963 in a coup that put Sylvanus Olympio in office with army support; in 1967, another coup put the military directly in power in the person of General Gnassingbe Eyadema. Over the next decade there were coups in Ghana, Nigeria, Congo-Brazzaville, Dahomey (Benin), CAR, Upper Volta (Burkina Faso), Nigeria, Uganda, Burundi, Sierra Leone and Mali. In 1973, the isolated and autocratic President Kayibanda was overthrown by the army in Rwanda and replaced by President Juvenal Habyarimana, whose death in April 1994 would spark that country's genocide. In 1974, famine and misrule by a distant and negligent monarchical system led to the overthrow of the imperial dynasty in Ethiopia by radical army and air force officers.

While these military regimes were viewed with some distaste in the West and seen as a failure on the part of African politicians, who had failed to sustain the institutions their former colonisers had seen as the ideal models for political development, there was no attempt to intervene openly in favour of incumbents. The brutal strategic logic of the Cold War meant that if a government was overthrown by military men who were as or even more pro-Western than their predecessors, the West was prepared to support them. And the USSR and China were just as prepared to embrace military regimes that espoused the right doctrines, or who could be allies in the global competition for power and influence.

Civil War, Separatism and Liberation Struggles

Along with the rash of coups, there was a series of civil conflicts derived from separatist, autonomist or irredentist aims. These were often fought by communities divided by arbitrary borders and living in ill-fitting national frameworks ruled by increasingly autocratic or unrepresentative leaders. The majority of these conflicts could be classed as rural revolts, insurgencies or secessionist struggles conducted by "armed groups that are not part of national armies".[44] There were few inter-state conflicts, but many intra-state ones that involved or drew in other states or involved communities split by inherited and inappropriate borders. And as bloody and costly in human terms as the conflicts in Katanga and Biafra were, they were short-lived compared with those in Sudan, Somalia-Ethiopia, Eritrea, Chad and Burundi and with the national liberation struggles in South Africa, Rhodesia, Namibia, Angola, Guinea-Bissau and Mozambique.

When Sudan achieved independence, the seeds of insurgency in the south were already sown. The 1955 mutiny exacerbated distrust between Khartoum and southern activists. Many of the mutineers who escaped fled to the bush while northern troops carried out reprisals in the south, with reports of thousands of civilian deaths and whole villages wiped out.[45] The result was a climate of resentment and fear in the south, and growing opposition to General Abboud's Arabisation and Islamisation programmes. The military government continued to use force to try to curb dissent, and to "maintain the territorial unity of Sudan at all costs".[46]

The government assiduously tried to destroy the remnants of the mutiny, and in 1958 and 1959 the army destroyed villages in Equatoria in counter-insurgency sweeps, forcing more southerners into the bush or into neighbouring Uganda and Ethiopia.[47] Khartoum was also putting pressure on those receiving education beyond primary level to convert to Islam. In 1962, more than 600 Christian missionaries, providers of much of the education in the south, were expelled.[48] These actions led to student, trades union and church protests and increasing support for armed struggle. The surviving mutineers' leaders and those who joined them after the demonstrations and the northern attacks on villages, came together in 1963 to form the South Sudan Liberation Army (SSLA) under Emilio Tafeng and General Joseph Lagu. The movement became known as Anyanya—meaning 'snake venom' in the Madi language of southern Sudan.

Anyanya established camps in northern Congo and Uganda and launched guerrilla attacks in the south. Its forces were poorly armed and could not seriously threaten army control of major towns or defeat the counter-insurgency campaigns. There were also divisions within the rebel movement over issues such as autonomy or secession and competition for power. Political factions and competing rebel leaders exploited ethnic differences to achieve their own ambitions, and in so doing created tension between southern communities such as the Dinka and Nuer. In 1967, the rebels set up the Southern Sudanese Provisional Government, though they controlled only a few remote rural eras. There were half-hearted attempts to hold peace talks following the formation of a civilian government in Khartoum made up of the Umma Party and the Nationalist Unity Party; but they failed, and the conflict escalated after fighting near Juba prompted further Sudanese army reprisals against southern civilians.

In May 1969, the army again tired of the factional competition between the political parties and stepped in, bringing General Ja'afar Numayri to power. Meanwhile, Anyanya strengthened its military capability with aid from African states and Israel. The Israelis had developed good relations with the Ugandan government under Obote and the army commander, Idi Amin, and Uganda's support for the Sudanese rebels offered them access to Israeli training, arms and other aid. Israel was a natural ally for the rebels, since it wanted to undermine Sudan's support for the Arab states opposing it.[49] The rebels' General Lagu tried to set up a government in eastern Equatoria and became the major channel for Israeli support, which strengthened his position. Israel was also able to route some aid to the south Sudanese through Ethiopia. Britain, Egypt and the Soviet Union supported Sudan, and the USSR sent military advisers to help Khartoum's army.[50] Despite Obote's attempts to mend fences with Numayri, Israeli support for the rebels continued with the Ugandan army as the conduit. Israel backed Amin's coup in 1971, but a few years later Amin kicked the Israelis out and began developing better relations with the Arab world, receiving financial and military aid from Libya and funding from other Arab states.

All the while, Numayri followed a dual line of prosecuting the war in the south while offering an amnesty and trying to co-opt southerners who would work with him. Numayri publicly recognised the need for southern Sudanese to have a political role and more control over their own affairs. After defeating a leftist coup and crushing opposition from the Ansar sect close to the Umma Party, Numayri felt strong enough to call for talks with southern leaders. He attended a peace conference in Addis Ababa, which led to the signing of a peace deal on 27 March 1972. Khartoum enacted the Southern Provinces Regional Act to give self-governing status to the south, first made up of the three provinces of Bahr El Ghazal, Equatoria and Upper Nile, and later sub-divided to form three more provinces—Lakes, Jonglei and Eastern Equatoria. Southerners elected a regional assembly and an executive council was formed to run the administration, though with considerable oversight by Khartoum and with the continued presence of substantial Sudanese army and militia units in the south. Over 5,000 Anyanya fighters were integrated into the Sudanese army.

Sudan's neighbour to the east, Ethiopia, had its own problems with insurgency and secessionism. After Haile Selassie was restored to power during the Second World War, he sought to expand Ethiopia's borders, lobbying Britain and the United States to allow him to incorporate Eritrea (occupied by Italy under UN trusteeship) and parts of the Ogaden region of Somalia. While Italy and the Soviet Union favoured Eritrean independence, Britain, the United States and a majority of members of a UN commission decided on a federal solution, joining Eritrea to Ethiopia but allowing it a large measure of autonomy.[51] This was sanctioned by the UN on December 1950. The West supported Selassie's position largely because of Ethiopia's potential as a Cold War ally; the US's support, for instance, was conditional on Ethiopia allowing it to use the Kagnew base in Eritrea as a major surveillance, communications and air hub.

The incorporation of Eritrea into Ethiopia was opposed by half the Eritrean population. The main opposition came at first from the Muslim population, suspicious of the hegemony of the Ethiopian Orthodox Church, but resentment increased as autonomy was whittled away, with the local languages, Tigrigna and Arabic, replaced by Amharic. Increasing Ethiopian control led to demonstrations by trades unions, students and some Christian groups. The 1961 elections were an exercise in bribery, intimidation and detention of opponents by Ethiopia to ensure a puppet assembly was elected.[52]

Many Eritrean Muslims left the country seeking work and refuge in the Gulf states and Yemen, where they set up exile networks which later supported movements fighting Ethiopia. The most important was the Eritrean Liberation Movement (ELM), established in Cairo in 1958 by Muslim exiles. It formed cells in Eritrea, and, with Egyptian backing, began to prepare for armed struggle. It was superseded by the Eritrean Liberation Front (ELF), also based in Cairo but with support from Saudi Arabia and Gulf states. The first shots in the rebellion were fired in the Barka region of Ethiopia in 1961 by a group led by an Eritrean who had served in the Sudanese army.[53] The ELF sent cadres to join the group that had started the insurgency and their numbers were swollen by deserters from the police. In a pattern that was to recur across Africa, Sudan gave bases and help to the ELF to undermine the support Ethiopia and Israel were giving to Anyanya. The Eritreans were strengthened in their determination to fight when, on 14 November 1962, the federation was dissolved and Eritrea became a province of Ethiopia.[54]

The Eritrean rebellion continued to burn slowly through the 1960s and 1970s, but despite aid from Arab states, China and Cuba, the Eritreans were unable to seriously threaten Ethiopian control. The influx of radical students and Christians into the ELF increased its manpower, but also split the movement into a mainly Muslim wing and a secular or Christian and pro-socialist wing.[55] The factionalism that resulted led to Muslim leaders trying to discipline Christian and left-wing cadres. In 1968, twenty-seven Christian ELF fighters were executed for disobeying orders; in the same year, radical members of the front split and formed the People's Liberation Front. A further purge of non-Muslim cadres, in which about 300 fighters were detained or shot, increased defections both to the PLF and to the Ethiopians.[56]

In 1970, a group of Chinese and Cuban-trained fighters formed the Eritrean People's Liberation Front (EPLF), which eclipsed the ELF and PLF. The EPLF was supported by Sudan, the People's Democratic Republic of Yemen, Cuba and China. It continued to receive Arab aid, but spent most of its time fighting its rival movements rather than the Ethiopians, who had help in containing the revolt in the form of American and Israeli aid. Between 1953 and 1970,

Ethiopia was the major recipient of US military aid to sub-Saharan Africa, receiving $305 million in military assistance and arms.[57]

The contested post-war borders also created another threat to Ethiopian integrity: Somali nationalism. This took the form of indigenous revolt and irredentist claims for the return of what the Somali government and nationalists saw as traditional Somali lands in the Haud and Bale regions of the Ogaden, which had been included within Ethiopia's borders.

Under the colonial system, Somalia was divided into three parts: French-controlled Djibouti, Italian Somaliland to the south and British Somaliland to the north. But Somali nationalists maintained that the Ogaden was part of a greater Somalia, along with areas of northern Kenya. As Italian Somaliland moved towards independence in the late 1950s, Italy allowed the formation of political parties in its territory, and elections there paved the way for considerable Somali control over day-to-day administration ahead of independence in 1960. The British followed a similar policy, and on 1 July 1960, the two territories united as the Republic of Somalia. Somali nationalists believed this was the first step towards Somali unity, and were pledged to recovering the areas they claimed from Ethiopia and Kenya.

Their irredentist objectives provided a national focus for a people whose clan structure divides a linguistically and culturally homogenous population into distinct units, which form the basis for social and political organisation—a structure that has proved "a formidable obstacle to the formation of a stable, modern nation-state in Somalia."[58] Nomadism and clan are core aspects of Somali identity, but the population is not cleanly divided into nomads, settled farmers and city dwellers; instead, as Ioan Lewis writes:

> Manifestations of the nomadic lifestyle and traditions pervade almost all aspects of Somali life...Somalia's nomads are not cut off from the life or urban centres or culturally and socially separated from the majority of urban residents...From the president downwards... those living with a modern lifestyle in urban conditions have brothers and cousins living as nomads in the interior.[59]

The incorporation of French Somaliland (Djibouti) into Somalia was resisted by the French, who had no intention of relinquishing such a strategically valuable base, and fiercely opposed by a third of the inhabitants of Djibouti, who saw themselves as Afars, Arabs or Ethiopians rather than Somalis.[60] A referendum in 1967 showed a majority of the population favoured continued association with France but with greater self-government, and it was only in a vote in 1977 that the people of Djibouti opted overwhelmingly for independence, which was granted in June 1977.

If there was little Somalis could do about Djibouti, they were determined to recover the Ogaden. The delineation of the border after the war brought Ethiopian forces into the region to establish border posts and a garrison at the important pasture and watering area round Jijiga. Conflict began a year after independence, with Somali irregular forces backed by the government attacking Ethiopia's army posts, and in 1964, there was a short, sharp border war between the two countries, which ended after appeals by the OAU and mediation by Sudan. This did not end Somali nationalist aspirations, and after the overthrow of the civilian government in 1969 by General Siad Barre, claims to the Ogaden were reasserted and preparations for insurgency and regular warfare begun.

The main agitator was the Western Somali Liberation Front (WSLF), which urged Barre to do something to recover the Ogaden. Barre tried talks with the Ethiopian government and lobbied for support within the OAU, but the OAU was strongly opposed to border changes, and with Ethiopia unwilling to negotiate, Somalia took the military option. Over 3,000 fighters were recruited and trained by the WSLF with Somali help, and Barre gave the group the green light to start a guerrilla war, the aim being to seize enough of the Ogaden to enable the Somali army to establish de facto control. The WSLF seized its chance when Haile Selassie was deposed in 1974 and Ethiopian military attention switched from protecting territorial integrity, to entrenching itself in power, and in the two years following the Ethiopian revolution, the WSLF steadily increased its control of eastern areas of the Ogaden.

Somalia had built up its armed forces with considerable Soviet aid. After the coup and the development of closer relations with Moscow, the army expanded, supported by an air force with 300 MiG aircraft. To help cement relations with the Soviet Union, Barre publicly adopted what he called "scientific socialism", although it was never clear how Barre intended to apply this in Somalia's partially nomadic, clan-based society. The improved ties gave Somalia an enhanced ability to use force, while providing the Soviet Union with a strategic foothold in the Horn of Africa to match the American presence in Ethiopia.

Somalia's claims to the Kenyan Northern Frontier District (NFD), which was sparsely populated but had a significant Somali population, led to what became known as the Shifta War between 1963 and 1967—*shifta* being a Somali term for bandit adopted by the Kenyans to label the conflict as banditry rather than a nationalist struggle. The Shifta War involved both the Somalis of northern Kenya and nomadic Somalis who crossed back and forth over the border with their livestock. They fought an irregular campaign with backing of the Somali government; the Kenyan government fought back using the paramilitary General Service Unit. Somali civilians were forced to live in protected villages, and those who remained outside them were often the victims of Kenyan counter-insurgency sweeps in which all Somalis were viewed as potentially hostile. Pressure on Somalia from Western governments (with whom it was still friendly despite its Soviet links) and from other OAU members ultimately led to peace talks and a ceasefire in 1967.

Low-level Somali insurgency, which became little more than banditry with livestock raiding, armed robberies and poaching of elephants and rhinos, continued into the 1980s—to this day Somalia's problems continue to have violent effects across the Kenyan border. The 1960s left Kenya deeply suspicious of Somalis, and the destabilising effect of Somalia's collapse led Kenya to intervene militarily across the border in 2011. That intervention in turn led to an increase in attacks by Somali Islamist groups inside Kenya; notably the bloody raid on Nairobi's Westgate shopping centre in September 2013 by militants from the Islamist Al-Shabaab group. These attacks continue, examples being the bloody attack by Kenyan Somali supporters of Al Shabaab on a college in the northern Kenya town of Garissa on 2nd April 2015, in which 147 students and other civilians died.

Faltering economies: fragile structures, falling prices and failing infrastructure

Africa's economic inheritance was hardly enviable, and in the early post-colonial decades, the weaknesses of African economies and heavy dependence on exports and aid became all too evident.

Despite extensive mineral and other valuable resources, economic activity was dominated by small-scale peasant agriculture with few inputs and little mechanisation, an underdeveloped transport network in rural areas, poor provision of water and other public services, low educational levels and reliance on variable rainfall and land vulnerable to degradation. In 1960, agriculture (most of it peasant-based) accounted for 40 per cent of Sub-Saharan Africa's GDP, but 85 per cent of its labour force.[61] As populations grew, governments tried to use agricultural production to subsidise industrial development and public services, but this model became less and less viable. While the small-scale agricultural sector accounted for the livelihood of the majority of populations as well as providing the food needed to feed growing cities, it received little investment and developed little.

This was not sustainable in the long term without increasing the productivity of land and labour. Poor rural road networks, low population density and widely distributed rural communities were obstacles to growth and modernisation in the peasant sector.[62] The structure of economies was unbalanced, with the bulk of the population engaged in peasant subsistence farming but the bulk of income derived from exports of unprocessed agricultural produce or minerals. African economies and consumers were heavily dependent on imported consumer and capital goods. The more modern sectors of the economies were "limited almost exclusively to production for export, the import trade, and related collection and distribution services. These sectors did not directly engage the bulk of the population."[63] Although they brought in revenue, they did not generate enough domestic demand or resources to stimulate wider economic and especially industrial growth. Even in countries with large populations like Nigeria, industrial sectors remained small and financially unviable, requiring subsidies and running at a loss.

Africa was stuck exporting primary produce—cotton lint, cocoa, groundnuts, and latterly crude oil—and then paying high prices to import the processed versions as cotton textiles, cocoa powder or chocolate, groundnut oil, and petroleum products. A high proportion of exports earnings were then drained by remittances to the multinational companies that grew, mined, bought and marketed export produce. Where the peasant sector became involved in cash-crop production for export, the peasants had little control over the prices they received for their crops. Moreover, their earnings were eaten into by governments extracting surplus through marketing boards and by foreign multinationals harvesting profit. Much subsistence farming and local trade in agricultural produce remained outside the formal economy, and while it ensured local livelihoods and food supplies, its productivity was low and was not formally taxed or recorded.

African governments—whether Nkrumah's aspiring socialist administration or Kenya's and Ivory Coast's capitalist ones—tried to use income from taxing agricultural or mineral exports to subsidise industry, to keep urban food prices low (as wages were low and urban unrest was a more direct threat to government stability than rural grievances), and to fund public services and rent-taking by political leaders, who used power as the road to wealth accumulation and the source of funds for patronage to help maintain them in power. Some economies performed better than others during the first two decades of independence, with Malawi, Ivory Coast and Kenya encouraging peasant output and developing strong commercial farming sectors producing cash crops such as cocoa, coffee, tobacco and tea. But their success was based on just as fragile an economic foundation as the less successful economies. That much was proved when they were hit hard in the 1980s and 1990s.[64] Growth, where it was achieved, was short-term and subject to variables beyond the control of farmers, parastatals and governments.

Africa was particularly vulnerable to fluctuations in primary commodity prices and the prices of processed or manufactured goods. The early 1960s saw high primary commodity prices on world markets but as these fell in the mid and late 1960s, Cocoa and coffee prices dropped during the 1960s, rose briefly in the 1970s, trebling between 1975 and 1977, only to fall back at the end of the decade and in the 1980s. Ghana saw cocoa prices fall from a high of £460 per ton in 1954 to £222 in 1960 and then a disastrous £138 in 1965.[65] That caused a disastrous fall in export income, wiping out the surplus available for industrialisation, public service and infrastructural development and debt servicing. Ghana's external debt—resulting from loans taken out for development and to cover the trade imbalance between exports and imports—rose from £6 million in 1959 to £237 million in 1965, creating a huge annual drain on national revenues in the form of interest and capital repayments.

On top of this, terms of trade were often volatile; that obstructed long-term economic planning and led to growing indebtedness, as well as a permanent imbalance of export income and import costs: during the 1960s, African export income grew by 4 per cent annually, while imports grew by 6 per cent, hobbling the model of export-funded industrialisation and modernisation.[66] The gatekeeper role of political elites and governments meant that too little effort was put into breaking out of this cycle of boom, bust and dependence on exports, foreign loans and foreign aid—all of which were channelled through the gate controlled by governments.

This income variability was exacerbated by high levels of dependence on markets in the former colonising countries. French investment and economic influence through the franc zone financial system used by most Francophone states increased France's economy hegemony over former colonies; Senegal, for instance, sold 86 per cent of its exports to France and bought the vast majority of its imports from there. For countries reliant on mainly agricultural exports, unreliable rainfall and poor soil fertility added to export price instability. To this day, in the Sahel zone of Africa, the combination of export value fluctuations and inconsistent rainfall means that the variation of export earnings year by year can be as much as 65 per cent; in Sudan, it is 52 per cent.[67]

Comparisons are often made in the economic performance of Africa and South Asia, especially in terms of industrialisation and the development of domestic trade. By the 1980s, Africa had half the population of India, but whereas India had a strong central government and could trade with neighbouring countries, Sub-Saharan Africa was divided into forty-eight different states, all with their own markets, and with a very low-level of intra-African trade. This balkanisation impeded industrialisation and complicated trade within the continent, especially between neighbouring states that had been ruled by different colonial powers. For decades, telephone connections from Ivory Coast to Ghana or Nigeria to Benin went not directly, but via London and Paris. Most African states' domestic markets were too small to support viable industrial growth aimed at supplying local consumers or the technical innovation to make industry more productive. Small African industries could not compete with multinational companies' economies of scale, modern infrastructure and established credit and financial systems, while African commercial companies lacked capital and expertise in marketing, accounting and management, leaving them vulnerable and uncompetitive. African economies lacked developed or well-managed financial systems and networks of domestic credit, which limited development of the commercial sector. Falling export earnings in the 1960s and 1970s left most African economies increasingly dependent on foreign aid for development and budget support. As a result, aid began to account for a disproportionate level of finance available for either development or government spending: by 1994, for Africa as a whole the contribution of aid to GNP averaged 12.4 per cent, compared with 2.7 per cent for other less developed countries.

African states also suffered from poor internal and external transport systems. Infrastructural development pre and post-independence concentrated on getting exports to ports and imports to urban areas; that left rural areas poorly served, with few paved roads or rail connections. The high cost of transport for exports and imports was compounded by the disproportionate number of landlocked countries. In terms of their distance from markets, African producers are to this day unusually isolated, imposing high costs and greater problems of deterioration or damage to agricultural exports and severe trade delays.[68] This greatly restricts growth and increases economic vulnerability.

Zambia, for example, was dependent until 1975 on transport routes controlled by the Portuguese to get bulk copper exports to foreign markets, and had to use the railway network from white-ruled Rhodesia to Beira in

Mozambique or the Benguela railway to Angola's Atlantic coast. Both were expensive, and once the liberation wars had started in Mozambique and Angola, they were subject to disruption by guerrilla attacks. This prompted the Zambian and Tanzanian deal with China for the building of the Tanzania-Zambia Railway (TANZAM), for which China provided a $400 million loan. Malawi was similarly dependent on routes through Mozambique, though Banda developed good relations with the Portuguese, enabling a smoother functioning of transport.

It is hardly surprising that African countries failed to meet their growth and industrialisation targets between 1960–1975, and that Africa was the worst economic performer among the world's regions. During that period, the GDP growth target in Africa was 8 per cent, but it achieved only 4.5 per cent; agricultural growth (including food) was 1.6 per cent against a target of 4 per cent; imports rose by 10 per cent instead of 7 per cent. This was all against a background of population growth of 2.5 per cent.[69] This poor economic performance could not support development or meet the expectations generated at independence for improved living standards and welfare.

African governments also inherited a massive skills shortage in industry and few trained or experienced personnel to manage the economy. The choice of state-centric policies was unsurprising, both because most states' private sectors were so weak and because new governments with weak institutions wanted to exert as much control as possible over their economies. With the exception of a few isolated sectors in larger economies, like that of Nigeria, there was little evidence of a capitalist bourgeoisie that could become an engine of growth and a channel for investment.[70]

Instead, the emerging bourgeoisie was a dependent rather than entrepreneurial one, relying on the state and political leaders for patronage, government posts and contracts. Political leaders were primarily concerned with maintaining their political power, and using it to extract rents for regime maintenance, to fund patron-client networks or personal enrichment. Military rule (with high-spending on the armed forces), civil wars, insurgencies or separatist conflicts worsened the outlook still further, and made export commodities—like diamonds, precious metals and timber—into conflict assets for governments and insurgent or rebel movements.

3

REVOLUTION, LIBERATION WARS AND ECONOMIC CRISIS

If the period from Sudan's independence to the 1970s saw much of Africa descend from the euphoria of freedom into economic decline, political dictatorship and popular disillusionment and disaffection, the 1970s would see those ills exacerbated by two catastrophic but closely related events: the global economic crisis sparked by the Arab oil boycott, and the massive oil price rises after the 1973 Middle East war.

By the early 1970s, military rule and coups had become the political norm in much of central and West Africa. State institutions were weak and governments unstable, and their inability to fulfil the hopes of independence made worse by falling commodity prices and by the steep rise in oil prices. The economic crisis was a major driver of political evolution, as were the 1974 revolution in Ethiopia and the 1974 coup in Portugal, which led to huge changes in Africa's national, regional and continental strategic calculus and heralded an even greater intrusion of the Cold War. The independence of Angola and Mozambique had a decisive influence on the breadth and nature of the liberation struggles in Southern Africa, and through their support for liberation, both states became key targets for the developing South African strategy of regional destabilisation to protect apartheid and white rule at home and in Rhodesia and Namibia.

Borders and the make-up of states, the growing power of elite groups and their patronage/patrimonial networks, the weakness of state institutions and the hegemony of the international capitalist economy over extraverted African economies became more and more obvious.

Ethiopia: the end of empire and the bloody road to revolution

Despite being totally autocratic and feudal in its structures and practices, Emperor Haile Selassie's regime in Ethiopia had prestige as the oldest surviving independent African kingdom. The monarchy had been overthrown by the Italian invasion and occupation of October 1935, despite fierce resistance by the poorly armed imperial army. British-led troops (including units from Nigeria, Ghana, Sierra Leone, British Somaliland, British East Africa, Nyasaland and the Rhodesias) expelled the Italians with Ethiopian support in 1941 and restored Haile Selassie to the throne. After the war, he entrenched his power again with strong British and American support.

But by the early 1970s, the Ethiopian monarchy was looking increasingly out of touch with African and Ethiopian reality. Ethiopia was a highly structured and centralised statist polity that vested supreme authority in Emperor Haile Selassie, who was old, frail and remote from his subjects and day-to-day government. He ruled though a highly-personalised system of government with a prime minister and cabinet appointed by him, a supine parliament elected from among rich landowners (political parties were allowed) and the traditional nobility with power in the provinces and varying levels of influence over central government. These layers of government communicated with Selassie in personal audiences or through his closest aide, the influential Minister of the Pen.

Land was privately owned by nobles and a class of rich landowners allied to them. The vast majority of the peasantry (29 million of the 32 million strong population) were tenant farmers working land owned by others and paying anything up to 75 per cent of their annual produce as rent, or working as labour on land farmed by the owner. There was little mechanisation, and peasants had no real incentive to produce more, since most of the surplus would accrue to the landowner. Landowners had considerable economic and local political power, and shared a keen interest in maintaining this system with the hereditary nobility, which dominated provincial power through gubernatorial posts.

To stop leading noble families accruing too much power and posing a threat to his overall personal control, Haile Selassie chose his ministers and advisers from the minor nobility, educated middle class and landowners. Where he had nobles in positions of power in the provinces, he favoured those from his ancestral heartland in Shoa and Addis Ababa. This 'Shoanisation' of provincial power, combined with the highly concentrated nature of imperial power, reduced the influence of the non-Shoan regional nobility, and widened the gap between the emperor and his subjects.[1] And although Haile Selassie was not of pure Amhara lineage (he had both Amhara and Oromo ancestry),[2] he established a regime that used Amharic as the main language and stressed Amhara culture; angering non-Amhara nobles and ordinary Ethiopians, especially those of Tigray province, which had been an earlier centre of imperial power.

Under the authoritarian imperial system, peasant rebellions were frequent occurrences, as were famines affecting millions. There were risings in Tigray in 1943, Wollo and Gedeo in 1960, Bale from 1963–70, and in Gojjam in 1968; most of them over taxes on agricultural produce.[3] But these rebellions were limited to specific provinces or regions within provinces, and were directed against landowners and the nobility. The risings rarely threatened imperial control locally, let alone nationally, though the army was nonetheless deployed to suppress them.

Ethiopia depended on agriculture to provide the livelihoods and food for the majority of the population, but in the mid-1960s it accounted for only 7 per cent of national income, and only 2 per cent of the national budget was allocated to supporting farmers. Most farmers produced enough for subsistence and to pay rents in cash or kind to landowners, with any surplus sold locally. The growing urban population, the slowly increasing class of urban wage workers, and the large armed forces and police all relied on surplus peasant production for food.

In the late 1960s, aware that the government needed to increase revenues, Haile Selassie—against the wishes of landowners and the nobility—lowered the tribute levied on tenant farmers by landowners, but increased government taxes on produce. This did nothing to alleviate the grinding poverty of peasant farmers, providing them with no incentives to grow more food. When the government decided to give more support to farming in the 1970s, efforts were concentrated in the commercial sector run by prosperous landowners, both to increase food surpluses and boost export earnings through coffee production.

Coffee accounted for 50 to 65 per cent of annual export income; about 70 per cent of the country's coffee exports were purchased by the USA. Around 40 per cent of Ethiopian external trade was with the USA, which matched its trade dominance with its importance as Ethiopia's major ally. The two countries had close political and military relations. A defence agreement allowed the USA to use the Kagnew base in Eritrea, which in turn provided Ethiopia with significant military aid and arms supplies. American support for the Ethiopian army had been crucial in fending off the Somali military threat in the 1960s and deterring further incursions. US military aid to Ethiopia totalled $180 million between 1946 and 1972, and combined with US arms sales, it amounted to well over $300 million in deliveries to the armed forces. This enabled Ethiopia to build a large, well-equipped army and one of the best armed and trained air forces in Africa—a priority for Haile Selassie, who had to cope with the Somali threat, peasant insurrections, and autonomist or secessionist rebels among the Oromo (the Oromo Liberation Front) and the Eritreans.

The Eritrean war showed no sign of ending in the early 1970s, with most of the fighting between the Ethiopian army and the EPLF. The EPLF obtained most of its weapons from Ethiopian troops, especially when the Derg in Ethiopia deployed large, poorly-trained peasant militias. Prior to the Derg's alliance with the Soviet Union and Cuba, the EPLF received support from the People's Democratic Republic of Yemen and Cuba.[4] Once the Soviet Union and Cuba (though the latter remained sympathetic to the Eritrean cause) became supporters of the Derg, help for the EPLF stopped, with the exception of Chinese assistance and Sudanese backing. Both the Soviet Union and Cuba urged Mengistu to seek a negotiated solution to the Eritrean conflict.[5] Castro refused to allow Cuban troops deployed in Ethiopia to fight the EPLF.

In the early 1970s, Ethiopia experienced one of the worst of its frequent famines. Food shortages resulting from drought and from the continuing extraction of surpluses and levying of taxes, turned to famine, affecting millions. The government ignored mounting deaths from starvation, and no government aid was provided to areas suffering severe hunger. Appeals for the government to act and to request international aid, made by UNICEF and western NGOs operating in the provinces, were ignored. The government preferred to let people die rather than suffer what it saw as the embarrassment of appealing for food aid.[6] Wollo was the worst affected province. When the emperor was due to visit the region, 20,000 peasants gathered to appeal to him for help. Warned of this embarrassment, he changed his plans to avoid meeting them and had roadblocks set up to prevent hunger marchers reaching major towns and revealing the extent of hunger to the country. Around 200,000 peasants are believed to have died during the famine in 1972–73.

The government always maintained tight control of the press and, combined with restrictions on travel, this ensured that the famine remained hidden. This changed when thousands of students volunteered to assist with health and vaccination programmes in the countryside in 1972 and 1973. They saw the effects of famine for themselves, and set up an exhibition of famine photos in Addis Ababa. It was immediately closed, and six students were shot dead by police in the town of Dessie when they demonstrated against government negligence over the famine.[7] Ethiopia's students became implacable opponents of the government. What had been a student movement concerned with academic affairs became more politicised, increasingly Marxist and determined to press the case for major political and economic reforms—not least sweeping land reforms to end the system of landowning and tenancy that condemned peasants to poverty and serfdom.

Leading up to 1974, there was increasingly militant student protest. The imperial government did not take this seriously, writing it off as agitation by small, radical but weak groups. This was a major misreading of the situation. The declining economy, awareness of the famine in the countryside and the government's failure to reform Ethiopia's economic, social and political structures provoked not just student action but strikes and demonstrations among taxi drivers, teachers and the trades unions in the small wage labour sector of the economy. Despite the famine and deprivation in rural areas, the peasants and tenant farmers did not join in the gathering tide of opposition or the subsequent overthrow of the regime and there were no peasant uprisings. The government, however, could no longer hide the crisis and the level of discontent. The revolution that resulted has been described as a creeping coup, and it certainly looks as though it caught the emperor and his government unawares, despite a well-developed internal security network.

When the famine and protests combined with the steep rise in oil prices brought about by the Yom Kippur War of October 1973, the Ethiopian economy suffered. Import prices soared while export prices and volumes fell, sparking more strikes and demonstrations. The gravity of the threat to the regime was made clear when troops of the 24th brigade mutinied in Sidamo province in January 1974. The general sent by the government to negotiate was seized and only released when the emperor promised the troops that something would be done to meet their demands. A mutiny by units on the border with Kenya followed, and the same general was sent to sort it out. This time he was made to sit in the full sun for twelve hours and given only dirty water and gritty bread, to demonstrate the poor conditions suffered by ordinary soldiers. These events were not reported by the

Ethiopian media, but many soldiers were aware of them—and soon committees began to form throughout the army and air force to express grievances and co-ordinate action.

The mutinies were followed by strikes by taxi drivers, teachers and students demanding higher pay, political and land reform. On 23 February 1974, the emperor promised in a national radio and TV address that many of the demands would be met, and he increased army pay—but it was too late, and army committees began to work together to develop a common strategy. The Fourth Division, based in Addis Ababa, set up a thirty-member coordinating committee across the armed forces and police which was to become the centre of power, known as the Derg (from the Amharic for committee). While the army committees had the potential to destroy the regime and could command the allegiance of many in the ranks, junior and middle-ranking officers, the Confederation of Ethiopian Labour Unions (CELU), the teachers' union and the students were sharing the limelight and making political and economic demands identical to those of the more radical military committees.

On 27 February, Haile Selassie bowed to pressure, met representatives of the Addis Ababa-based committees and agreed to demands for the right to form political parties, land reform, the end of control of the administration by the nobility and landowners, price controls, free education and the release of political prisoners. Prime Minister Aklilou Habte-Wolde and his government resigned and were replaced by the aristocrat Endalkachew Mekonnen. While Mekonnen appeared to move in the direction of reform, he still represented the *ancien régime* and the dominance of the aristocracy and landed classes. He offered further pay increases for the armed forces but was unable to stem the rising tide of radicalism in the military.

The new government was unable to appease the unions or students either, and on 7 March a general strike began. After four days, the government met some of the union demands, but not those of teachers and students, who continued to protest. Mekonnen was shouted down when he appeared in parliament, as the normally quiescent MPs demanded answers about public corruption and what was being down to alleviate the famine. His government then promised to tackle corruption and to examine constitutional reform, but the pace of change was slow and the protests only gathered momentum. On 28 April the armed forces committees took the initiative and arrested over 200 senior figures from the armed forces high command and the previous government. To add fuel to the flames, a peasant revolt erupted in areas of Rift Valley in the south; farms were burned and landowners attacked along a 250-mile stretch of the country's most fertile farmland.[8]

Throughout April, May and June 1974 the power of the emperor and the government ebbed away as the military committees took more control, while students, teachers and the unions continued to campaign for radical socialist reforms that matched the demands of militants in the armed forces movement. On 28 June, the Derg was formally established as a body representing the armed forces and police and began to operate as an alternative government. At its first meeting, 106 delegates from military and police committees across the country elected a leadership group chaired by Lt-Gen Aman Andom, who had led Ethiopian forces in the defeat of the Somali incursion a decade earlier. Real power, though, was vested in lower-ranking officers and NCOs. The radical wing of the Derg was led by four majors, Mengistu Haile Mariam, Atnafu Abate, Sisay Habte and Fissiha Desta—and as the year wore on, they increasingly dictated the pace of change. Derg units arrested more former members of the government, including some from leading noble families and the royal family, though the young officers still pledged loyalty to Haile Selassie himself.

The officers' movement forced the abolition of the powerful and arcane post of Minister of the Pen and dissolved the Crown Council (which advised the emperor) yet Haile Selassie seemed oblivious to the progressive destruction of the whole structure of his rule.[9] But within two months, the moment of truth came. During the height of the famine, the British journalist Jonathan Dimbleby had made a documentary called *The Unknown Famine* that detailed the death, suffering in Ethiopia and the negligence of its imperial government. On 11 September an edited version was shown on Ethiopian television, with images of death by starvation crudely but effectively juxtaposed with film of the emperor feeding hunks of meat to his pets (he had many dogs and a number of lions at his palace). The film was intended to cause uproar and incite contempt and bitterness—and it worked.

While seen mainly by urban, middle-class Ethiopians, it undercut respect for the emperor and the resulting furore was used by the Derg to justify the total seizure of power. On 12 September, the Derg formed the Provisional Military Adminstrative Council (PMAC) to replace the government, with Lt-Gen Andom as chairman. Emperor Haile Selassie was taken from his palace in the back of an old Volkswagen Beetle and never seen again; he was killed in 1975 and his body buried at a secret location. The Derg proclaimed it had deposed the emperor; it dissolved parliament and the constitution, and to the dismay of the unions and student groups, banned all strikes and demonstrations.

The Derg takeover initiated nearly three years of fierce, bloody and complex political infighting, both within the Derg itself and between the Derg and political groups which emerged from the radical student movement. The Derg had taken an increasingly socialist stance, combining a basic nationalism with Marxist-Leninist ideological constructions. It adopted slogans and programmes advocated by left-wing student groups while progressively moving to destroy the student parties politically and physically. Despite its radical posture, it still embodied an Addis Ababa-centric Amhara statism, and was implacably opposed to Eritrean secession or autonomy and later to the growth of pro-autonomy movements in the provinces. The Derg's ability to exploit the programmes and policies of the student movement and then to destroy it was aided hugely by the division of the students into a multiplicity of socialist and Marxist groups—chief among which were factions which became the Ethiopian People's Revolutionary Party (EPRP) and the All Ethiopia Socialist Movement (Meison). Dissident groups existed within the military, too; these were crushed emphatically in October 1974 by units loyal to the Derg. A more far-reaching reckoning took place in November, when the Derg radicals moved against Andom and other moderate figures. Andom was killed and sixty leading figures associated with previous governments, including both former prime ministers, were executed. Although Brigadier-General Tefere Bante was the Derg's titular head, vice-chairman Mengistu was now the most powerful military and political figure.

In early 1975, the Derg programme was formalised with proclamations nationalising banks, industrial and commercial enterprises. Most importantly, given the predominance of peasants in the population, the Derg announced in March 1975 that it was abolishing private ownership of land. It banned the transfer or sale of land entirely, and said that peasants now had the right to work the land and should form peasant associations to redistribute it. A limit of 10 hectares was put on land use for each peasant family. Students and political militants were dispatched to the countryside to inculcate the new values among the peasants and to assist in the establishment of associations. The economic and political power of the landlords was broken, and there was an upsurge in peasant support for the Derg. By July 1975, four million peasants had been organised into 16,000 associations.[10]

The EPRP and Meison were critical of the Derg's approach. The EPRP condemned the state ownership of land and the way that reforms were imposed from the top down. Sure enough, the plan eventually lost the Derg the support of the peasants, who had no agency in the major structural changes in land ownership and were powerless to resist a regime prepared to use brutal force to implement its policies.

In urban areas, there was growing tension between the Derg, the EPRP and unions. Strikes were prohibited, and the military committees forged ahead with their version of socialism without any real participation by ordinary people. Urban land and property were nationalised and urban dwellers' associations set up to organise and politicise people in towns and cities. The associations would be used by the Derg in 1976 and 1977 when its conflict with the EPRP turned into a bloody urban war known as the Red Terror; during which the EPRP assassinated Derg supporters and officials, and the Derg struck back with a campaign of killings, detention, torture and summary execution of EPRP members.

As the fight against the EPRP was heating up, Mengistu was struggling to fight off other factions in the Derg. In July 1976, political infighting in the Derg leadership ended with the detention and execution of Major Sisay Habte, the head of foreign affairs. During the summer and early autumn, special army units and armed members of the urban associations carried out a thorough purge of the EPRP in Addis Ababa and other towns; a Swedish aid agency estimated that 1,000 EPRP members were killed in the first half of May alone.[11] Meison was later liquidated as a movement, and in February 1977 Mengistu's other opponents in the military were killed. Mengistu announced that "revolutionary action" had been taken against Tefere Bante and his supporters—he and six other Derg leaders had been killed in a shoot-out between the factions. Mengistu now became Derg chairman, and the all-out war against the EPRP resumed with the eventual defeat of the movement first in urban areas and then in Tigray and Gondar provinces.

In the summer of 1977 the Derg, under the highly personalised rule of Mengistu, established the Commission for the Organisation of the Party of the Workers in Ethiopia (COPWE), which took on the role of ideological vanguard. Its work would culminate in the formation of the Workers' Party of Ethiopia in September 1984, ten years to the day after the Derg seized power. Mengistu and his militant supporters had carried out a long-drawn out coup, then stolen the clothes of the EPRP and Meison to dress the revolutionary body they had built. The military-led revolution had used the student revolutionary movement to legitimise its pursuit of power, while Marxism-Leninism provided a convenient justification for a highly centralised and unaccountable state as unresponsive to the needs of the peasantry as the imperial state had been. But the revolution also sowed the seeds of its own demise by destroying those in the leftist movements capable of a more sophisticated approach to revolutionary change and driving those who survived into the countryside. While the EPRP's rural cadres were wiped out, the leftist students of Tigrayan origin who fled to the Tigray countryside established and built up the Tigrayan People's Liberation Front (TPLF) into a formidable political and military movement—one that would eventually defeat the Derg's army and overthrow Mengistu and his regime.

Conflict, the cold war and famine in the Horn of Africa

Ethiopia's transformation from a state-centred monarchy to a self-proclaimed Marxist-Leninist state ruled by the military upended the regional strategic balance. This was not just domestic regime change; it fundamentally reoriented the external relationships of both Ethiopia and Somalia. The political infighting in post-revolutionary Ethiopia encouraged Somalia to increase its support for Somali movements in the Ogaden, and to once more move into areas of that region which it claimed as part of a greater Somalia.

At the time of the 1974 revolution, the Barre government in Somalia espoused a pan-Somali ideology, and revived its claims to the Ogaden, parts of the Kenyan Northern frontier District and Djibouti. At first it did little to pursue them; while it gave sufficient support to the WSLF and Somali Abo groups to keep a small-scale insurgency rumbling on in southern Ethiopia, it concentrated on entrenching its own power and building up its own armed forces. Between 1970 and 1977, the army grew from 12,000 to 30,000 and Soviet military aid and arms sales enabled it to build up a force of 250 tanks, 300 armoured personnel carriers and 52 jet aircraft.[12] By 1977 there were about 4,000 Soviet military advisers in Somalia along with Bulgarian, East German and Cuban personnel.[13] Although the Soviet Union must have known that this force could be used to pursue Somalia's irredentist ambitions, neither Moscow nor Havana supported these aims and advised Barre against aggression towards it neighbours. But as so often in the relations between major powers and their African allies, this was no simple patron-client relationship. Somalia was pursuing its own policies rather than taking the aid and arms in return for becoming a tool of Soviet policy. And while professing socialism and trying to overcome clan rivalries that had bedevilled Somali politics (though this policy ended up being a cover for ensuring the primacy of his own Marehan sub-clan, part of the wider Darod clan), Barre also built closer links with the Arab world—Somalia joined the Arab League in 1974.

In 1975, feeling more secure in power and with an increasingly strong army, Barre took advantage of the political upheavals in Ethiopia to increase support for the WSLF and allow it to operate against Ethiopian targets from Somali territory. The insurgency escalated and Somali military assistance increased until finally, in February 1977, 1,500 Somali troops crossed into the Ogaden and fought Ethiopian units.[14] The Somali army's involvement increased, and in July 1977 a full-scale invasion was mounted. By 12 September, the key town of Jijiga had been captured and the military base at Dire Dawa was threatened.

Although the Ethiopian forces were on the back foot, a major strategic change that had taken place in the Horn of Africa meant it still had the military power and external assistance to reverse the situation. The Ethiopians were still battling the EPLF in Eritrea and had a growing insurgency problem with the TPLF in Tigray, and they needed extensive arms imports and military assistance to fight these campaigns. The army had received large quantities of American arms in 1973 and 1974 under agreements contracted with Haile Selassie, and despite growing US concern over the direction of the revolution, American arms deliveries continued after the Derg came to power, since Ethiopia remained a counter to the massive Soviet presence in Somalia. Former US Ambassador to Ethiopia Paul Henze wrote that even after protesting to the Derg over executions of members of former governments and the royal family, America still gave Ethiopia military grants and aid worth $37.5m in 1975; the following year's grants were worth $22m, and total arms sales reached $100m.[15] In turn, despite its anti-imperialist rhetoric, the Derg allowed continued US use of the Kagnew base in Eritrea. But in 1977, the Carter administration came to power in Washington, and refused to supply the arms Ethiopia wanted because of its deteriorating human rights record. That led to Kagnew's closure and the expulsion of all US military personnel from Ethiopia. And as Mengistu outflanked his opponents and adopted an ever more Marxist-Leninist posture, relations between Moscow and Addis Ababa improved.

The Brezhnev leadership in Moscow had discovered what it termed the 'revolutionary potential' of Africa in the wake of both the Ethiopian and Portuguese revolutions and the escalation of the liberation struggles in Southern Africa.[16] It didn't want to alienate Somalia, but at the behest of Cuba, the Soviets attempted to deepen their relations with both Somalia and Ethiopia at the same time. And when the Carter administration began pursuing a more human rights-oriented policy, Mengistu turned to Moscow. In February 1977, both Soviet President Podgorniy and Cuba's Fidel Castro paid visits to Addis Ababa. Moreover, that April, buoyed by hopes of socialist advances in the region, Castro tried to defuse Ethiopia-Somalia tensions, suggesting the formation of a socialist confederation between Ethiopia, Somalia and the People's Republic of Yemen. For both Mengistu and Barre, this was a non-starter. Barre had become more and more disenchanted with his Cuban and Soviet partners as they drew closer to Ethiopia. Even prior to Mengistu's victory, the USSR had agreed to supply Ethiopia with defensive weapons (anti-aircraft guns, anti-tank missiles and artillery) worth $100m. Even if it hadn't ditched Barre totally, by 1977, Moscow's commitments in the Horn had a new emphasis. Mengistu visited Moscow in May that year and was treated as a revolutionary ally.[17] A Soviet-Ethiopian arms deal estimated at $350–450 million was signed, providing forty-eight modern MiG aircraft, 200 tanks and increased quantities of anti-tank and anti-aircraft missiles.[18]

Barre was furious, and his anger was exploited first by conservative Arab states and later by Washington. Saudi Arabia offered Mogadishu aid of between $330m and $500m if it would "join the movement to eliminate Russian influence in the Red Sea."[19] After Mengistu criticised Moscow in October 1977 for its failure to act more decisively against Somali aggression, the Soviet leadership announced the cessation of all arms supplies to Somalia. Four weeks later, with Arab and US support to fall back on, Barre ditched his friendship treaty with Moscow and kicked Soviet, East European and Cuban personnel out of Somalia. He became an ally of the West in the Cold War in Africa, while the USSR, Cuba and their allies now threw their full weight behind Ethiopia, including Cuban combat troops and Soviet generals to assist the Ethiopians on the battlefield. This decision was based not just on the rupture with Somalia and the strategic advantages of an alliance with Ethiopia, but also on Mengistu's embrace of Soviet-style Marxism-Leninism.[20]

On 26 November 1977, the Soviets started a six-week airlift and sealift of military equipment and Cuban troops to Ethiopia. Between $1bn and $2bn worth of modern aircraft, tanks, combat helicopters and artillery were sent along with 12,000 Cuban soliders, 1,500 military advisers and 750 troops from Yemen.[21] The re-armed and Cuban-backed Ethiopian forces drove Somalia's army and the WSLF from the Ogaden, and defeated them by February 1978; Somalia announced its disengagement from the Ogaden on 9 March. The defeat of the Somali invasion left behind hostility and suspicion between Ethiopia and Somalia that outlasted the fall first of Barre, and then of Mengistu. The insurgencies continued in Eritrea and Tigray, and despite the huge Soviet military aid, they proved to be too well-grounded in local support to be defeated. Meanwhile, the success of the Ethiopian counter-offensive and the proof that the Soviets and Cubans were willing to commit themselves to support an ally militarily sent shivers down Western spines—but it also vastly increased the prestige of the Soviet bloc among Africa's anti-imperialist movements and states.

The Portuguese coup

As they resisted the changes across Africa, the Portuguese faced growing opposition from the peoples of their territories during the 1960s and 1970s. By 1962, liberation wars had started in Guinea-Bissau and Angola, with Mozambique following suit in 1964. This put a huge burden on Portugal, as the cost of counter-insurgency had to be balanced against export earnings. The colonies were a major part of the regime's domestic survival strategy; they had been used as a source of export revenue and repository for surplus Portuguese labour, with settlement encouraged.[22] But the cost of fighting liberation grew out of proportion to the benefits, especially when commodity prices fell in the late 1960s. This added to the growing opposition of many young people—particularly young officers and conscripts in the Portuguese colonial army.

On 25 April 1974, tanks of the Armed Services Movement (MFA) rolled into Lisbon at dawn. The movement sought to dismantle an authoritarian, fascist regime that had been in power for nearly a half-century. This started as a coup, but it drew large crowds into the streets in support, and the regime's leader, Marcello Caetano, was forced to hand power to the former general Antonio Spínola. A natural conservative, Spínola had opposed continuing the war in Guinea-Bissau, believing it could not be won, but he was not prepared to allow regime change to trigger revolution and the loss of African territories. Many young army officers and NCOs had come into contact with Marxist and other revolutionary ideas in Africa while fighting against movements that adopted these ideologies as part of the anti-colonial struggle. These radicals supported a more revolutionary approach than Spínola; they forced him out in a second coup in 1975 and installed Lieutenant-Colonel Ramalho Eanes, who worked with civilian political parties and moved Portugal towards a liberal democratic model. He also agreed to independence for the African colonies.[23] About 600,000 settlers returned to Portugal, many of them carrying out acts of sabotage, doing their best to damage the infrastructure for the incoming African governments. The liberation movements had succeeded in pushing the Portuguese out of Africa not through military victories, but by effectively undermining military and political support for both the colonial empire and the fascist state.

In Guinea-Bissau, Amílcar Cabral and a small group of educated nationalist activists had formed the Partido Africano da Independência da Guiné e Cabo Verde (African Party for the Independence of Guinea and Cape Verde, PAIGC). Initially it was a clandestine movement, but when neighbouring Guinea achieved independence under the radical, pro-socialist Sékou Touré, the PAIGC was able to operate there openly. It received training for its guerrillas in Algeria, with assistance from the Soviet Union and Cuba, and launched a guerrilla war from Guinea in 1961. The Portuguese deployed over 35,000 Portuguese troops to Guinea-Bissau, but couldn't stop the PAIGC stepping up the struggle and creating liberated zones, controlling increasing amounts of territory. The Portuguese were well armed, and were able to use US military aid and arms supplies intended for Portugal's NATO role—but they were fighting an unwinnable battle.

Under the leadership of Cabral, the PAIGC developed administration in the liberated zones based on his African socialist ideas.[24] Cabral had mixed with Marxists from the Angolan MPLA and the banned Portuguese Communist Party, and had developed an approach to revolution in Guinea-Bissau based on the principle that while there were widely shared revolutionary doctrines, revolution could not be exported and each state or movement had to develop its own revolutionary path "essentially formed by the historical reality of each people."[25] By 1968, the movement controlled over 60 per cent of the country. The liberated areas were able to feed themselves, and the PAIGC established more hospitals and schools in the liberated zones than existed in the whole of Portuguese Guinea. The movement gained strong support from the peasants, involving them in the government of freed areas through elected village committees.

A year before the Portuguese revolution, Amílcar Cabral was assassinated in Conakry by a PAIGC dissident in the pay of the Portuguese secret police. Leadership passed to Aristides Pereira, who later became the first president of the Republic of Cape Verde, and Luís Cabral, Amílcar's brother. On 24 September 1973, an elected PAIGC National Assembly met at Boe in the liberated south-eastern region and declared Guinea-Bissau's independence, which was recognised and formalised by the Portuguese in September 1974, when the new government agreed to independence for all

Portugal's African colonies. Guinea-Bissau was not to follow up the socialist ideas developed by Cabral; instead it became a coup-prone state, whose unstable and corrupt military governments turned it into a transit point for narcotics exported from Latin America to Europe.

In Mozambique, the formation of Frelimo (Front for the Liberation of Mozambique) in June 1962 led to the start of a guerrilla struggle two years later. The objective was independence, but there were different strands of ideology within the movement—a socialist wing was led by Samora Machel and Marcelino dos Santos, while the more pro-capitalist and regionalist wing was led by Lázaro Nkavandame. Frelimo's leader Eduardo Mondlane did not fall squarely into either camp,[26] but sided with Machel on the need for a united Mozambican nationalism and succeeded in making it the movement's policy.

The armed struggle had begun in 1964 after Frelimo had built up its forces in Tanzania with support from China, the Soviet bloc and Cuba. Guerrillas crossed into Mozambique and launched an attack against the Portuguese administrative post near the town of Mueda, where the Portuguese had massacred 600 peasants in June 1960, and began an insurgency centred on the two northern provinces of Cabo Delgado and Niassa. As the struggle progressed, Frelimo carved out extensive liberated zones, but there was tension between the different political wings, especially once the liberated zones were established. Nkavandame tried to develop capitalist structures within them, clashing with the socialist wing, which had the powerful support of the guerrilla army. When Mondlane was assassinated in Dar es Salaam in February 1969 (by a combination of dissidents and PIDE, as was Cabral) it was Samora Machel who became Frelimo leader. He defeated the conservative Uria Simango and Nkavandame, both of whom were expelled from the leadership bodies and accused of promoting racist (both anti-white and anti-mestiço) views and tribalist agendas.

In 1968, Frelimo launched attacks against Portuguese garrisons in the Tete province, with Zambia allowing the group to use its territory to infiltrate central Mozambique. These attacks were followed by moves into the central provinces of Manica, Sofala and Zambezia. The huge Cabora-Bassa hydroelectric dam, which supplied electricity to Mozambican towns and South Africa, was a key target. As the war developed, Frelimo allowed the guerrillas of the Zimbabwe African National Union (ZANU) to infiltrate into Rhodesia through liberated areas. As a result, Rhodesia and South Africa stepped up their military co-operation in fighting Frelimo, and Rhodesian forces carried out raids on Frelimo-controlled areas.

Poor morale among the Portuguese troops, the lack of co-operation from the peasants, access to Soviet arms and training from Cuban instructors all gave Frelimo's forces the edge. When the April 1974 coup took place in Portugal, Frelimo escalated the military struggle, and the following June, when it became clear that independence was not on offer, it broke off attempts to negotiate a ceasefire. In July, thousands of Portuguese troops mutinied and declared their support for Frelimo, and the fighting was finally brought to an end by the signing of the Lusaka Accord on 7 September 1974, which allowed for the unconditional handover of power to Frelimo. A transitional government with Joaquim Chissano as prime minister was formed in September 1974, and it led the country to independence on 25 June 1975 with Samora Machel as president.

Angola's liberation struggle was more divisive than Guinea-Bissau's or Mozambique's. At the start of the armed uprising against colonialism there were two main movements: the MPLA, which drew from the Mbundu peoples around Luanda and its hinterland and found support among the mestiço and radical sections of the white population, and Holden Roberto's FNLA (formerly the UPA). A small nationalist movement called the Front for the Liberation of the Cabinda Enclave (FLEC) developed north of the Congo river; it continues to resist rule from Luanda to this day.

The FNLA and MPLA not only had different regional and ethnic characteristics but also very different ideologies. The FNLA was a traditionalist, conservative movement based on the aspirations of the Bakongo, harking back to the powerful Bakongo kingdom. The MPLA on the other hand had a strong urban element, influenced by contacts between its leaders and Portuguese Communists and leaders from other Portuguese colonies, including Amílcar Cabral. After the Malanje peasant uprising and the Luanda prison attack of February 1961, Angola's embryonic nationalist struggle gained recognition in the Soviet Union, and the Soviet communist party newspaper *Pravda* published Soviet messages of support for the MPLA's struggle.

Regionally, the situation was complex. Both movements needed bases in countries neighbouring Angola, but only Congo-Leopoldville and Congo-Brazzaville were independent. The latter was at first under a conservative government, so the MPLA and FNLA based themselves in Leopoldville (Kinshasa). But in 1963, after Agostinho Neto became MPLA president, he and other leaders were arrested and the MPLA was forced to move to Brazzaville, where Massemba-Débat had by that time overthrown President Youlou and established a more radical regime. In Congo-Brazzaville, the

MPLA came into contact with the Cubans who had moved there after their belated attempt to support the Lumumbist forces in the Congo. The movement began to attract support from the more radical newly independent states; it used Zambian territory to infiltrate guerrillas into eastern Angola, and sent guerrillas into the Cabinda enclave from Congo-Brazzaville. It was vital for the MPLA to develop guerrilla fronts away from the Bakongo areas, as FNLA forces had ambushed MPLA fighters trying to get to the small group of fighters still in the Dembos Forest near Luanda.[27]

The FNLA was backed by the Congo-Leopoldville government and, despite its military support for the Portuguese and alliance with them through NATO, by the USA. Holden Roberto received funding and small amounts of arms from the CIA from 1962 through until 1974, when CIA increased considerably.[28] Despite declaring a government in exile (the GRAE—Governo Revolucionário de Angola no Exílio), the FNLA did not establish a major guerrilla presence in Angola. It was supported by conservative African states and China (which dropped its support for the MPLA after the Sino-Soviet split) and remained an essentially Bakongo organisation. This led to the formation of the third major Angolan movement, UNITA (União Nacional para a Independência Total de Angola) in 1966, when the charismatic Jonas Savimbi split from the FNLA on the grounds that it was a Bakongo supremacist movement. UNITA had little external support to begin with and its leader, Jonas Savimbi, concentrated on building support in his home area of Ovimbunduland in the centre and southeast of the country. Tanzania sympathised with UNITA's aim of basing itself inside Angola rather than in exile, and through Tanzania, Savimbi was able to get some Chinese support.

By the 1974 Portuguese coup, the three movements were in sharp competition, and there had been clashes between the FNLA and the MPLA, and the MPLA and UNITA. The MPLA accused both the movements of co-operating with the Portuguese to destroy MPLA military units. The scale of the guerrilla war and military threat to the Portuguese was far less than in either Guinea-Bissau or Mozambique. The FNLA's forces were concentrated in southern Zaire, and after the coup they moved into northern Angola to try to seize power. The MPLA had forces in Cabinda, Moxico and some still near Luanda (it also had the biggest urban support base), while UNITA was based in the south-east and central plateau. Attempts by the OAU and states like Tanzania to get the movements to work together failed, and despite the signing of the Alvor Accord in January 1975 and the Nakuru agreement establishing a coalition government in June 1975, it was clear that the groups would continue to fight it out for control. After the coup "they embarked on a desperate race to achieve supremacy before the scheduled date for independence"[29] in November 1975.

Key factors in the war were Angola's mineral wealth (oil in Cabinda and off-shore, and diamonds in Lunda Norte province in the north-east) and the growing involvement of external powers with interests in oil and the Cold War/Southern African political-military equation. The US, China and Zaire backed the FNLA; the Soviet Union, Cuba and Congo-Brazzaville supported the MPLA, while UNITA had some Chinese support but also assistance from South Africa. The movements were prepared to take whatever external support was available to seize power—and the FNLA and UNITA were in contact via their mutual backers to try to ensure that the MPLA was kept out.

There has been much debate over the timing of the international interventions, and their effect on the war and the following civil war between the MPLA and UNITA.[30] A month after the Lisbon coup, the Chinese sent 125 military instructors and 450 tons of weapons to FNLA camps in southern Zaire, and Washington provided funding and arms for Roberto. The CIA's John Stockwell, who worked closely with Roberto, says that the movement had 15,000 fighters, while the MPLA had around 8,000 and UNITA 3,000.[31] Moscow wanted the MPLA to adhere to the OAU plans for a national unity government, but Soviet arms deliveries in late 1974 enabled it to maintain a strong military profile. In February 1975 fighting broke out between MPLA and FNLA supporters in slum areas of Luanda, and a joint FNLA-Zairean force invaded northern Angola. By mid-year, the MPLA had taken control of the capital, but was under pressure in the north and to the south of Luanda.

By this time there was growing evidence of South African involvement in southern Angola, with troops crossing the border from occupied Namibia. South Africa wanted to ensure that the MPLA, allied as it was with the Namibian South West African People's Organisation, which was fighting for Namibian independence, did not gain control of the provinces bordering Namibia. The FNLA and UNITA were both in contact with the South Africans, and come mid-1975, South African troops were supporting UNITA in combat with MPLA units in the south. By late July, FNLA and Zairean forces were 50 km north of Luanda, and a massive airlift of Soviet weapons was underway to shore up the MPLA. The South Africans had formed a special unit, 32 Battalion, commanded by Colonel Jan Breytenbach, to fight alongside UNITA; it would be involved in supporting the movement inside Angola from August 1975 until the withdrawal of South African forces in 1988.[32]

Over the next few months the UNITA/South African force and the Zairean/FNLA one advanced towards Luanda, putting the MPLA under ever greater pressure. The MPLA asked the Soviet Union and Cuba for increased support and for Cuban troops to fight off the two forces. Cubans began to arrive in November; they fought alongside the MPLA and routed the FNLA/Zairean force, and by January 1976, the FNLA had retreated into Zaire. The MPLA/Cuban force in the south attacked the UNITA/South African units, inflicting serious casualties among the South African forces that made it domestically impossible for them to continue the fight. By February 1976, they had withdrawn most of their forces from Angola, leaving only 32 Battalion in Cuando Cubango province to help UNITA fight a guerrilla war against the MPLA.

The MPLA controlled Luanda on Independence Day on 11 November 1975 and established the government of Angola. That government received OAU recognition not because the OAU was pro-MPLA, but because the South African intervention had made it impossible for the OAU not to support a movement opposed by the apartheid regime.

Liberation and destabilisation in Southern Africa

Just as the war in Angola had profound consequences for South African-occupied Namibia, so the Frelimo struggle in Mozambique did for neighbouring Rhodesia.

African politicians had campaigned for African rights in the white-dominated settler colony of Southern Rhodesia for years. Theoretically black Rhodesians could qualify for the vote, and a few did; the settler constitution did not bar black people on the basis of colour, but tough property and educational requirements excluded the vast majority of Africans from political rights. Increasingly stringent land laws had divided land into areas for whites and areas where it was held in trust for indigenous peoples on a collective basis (tribal trust lands). African farmers who could not prove ownership of land (which was held under customary forms of ownership) were removed to the trust lands. Between 1930 and 1979, white settlers gained control of 70 per cent of agricultural land. European settlement increased rapidly after 1945, and by the end of 1958, there were 211,000 settlers, 2,590,000 Africans and 14,900 of other races (chiefly Asian traders) in Southern Rhodesia.[33]

The Southern Rhodesian government was nominally under British control, but its settler government and parliament had considerable autonomy from Britain and severely restricted African political activity at the time when Britain was granting independence to the rest of its African colonies. In the 1950s and early 1960s, the government banned a succession of African movements in Southern Rhodesia campaigning for political rights and detained their leaders. In December 1961, the latest party, the National Democratic Party, was banned for refusing to recognise Southern Rhodesia's highly discriminatory new constitution, which entrenched white political and economic power. In response, the main nationalist leader, Joshua Nkomo, and his supporters formed the Zimbabwe African People's Union (ZAPU). Nkomo was a moderate willing to compromise on nationalist demands in order to gain a small advance in rights, to the anger of more radical nationalists in the movement. But by the early 1960s, even he was facing the hard reality that the whites would not move on African rights and beginning to accept the need for armed struggle. He had visited the Soviet Union and met Chinese and Soviet representatives in Egypt, Tanzania and Guinea. ZAPU's leaders asked these states for help with weapons and military training.[34]

In 1962, the contradictions between the white political leaders and Africans sharpened with the election of a more segregationist party (the Dominion Party, which became the Rhodesian Front, RF). ZAPU opposed the more openly racist policies of the new government, but to little effect, and more radical ZAPU members accused Nkomo and the leadership of weakness. ZAPU was by this time smuggling small quantities of weapons into Southern Rhodesia and arranging to send cadres to China for military training.[35] The radicals—led by Ndabaningi Sithole, Maurice Nyagumbo, Robert Mugabe and Leopold Takawira—formed the Zimbabwe African National Union (ZANU) in 1963. This led to a period of violence between the rival nationalist movements, which paralleled preparations by both to launch guerrilla warfare against the RF government. In August 1964 both parties were banned and many of their members arrested; Nkomo, Sithole, Mugabe and Nyagumbo were among those detained. Both organisations had sent representatives abroad to set up exile offices, and from then on, nationalist activity in Rhodesia revolved around armed struggle.

Deep divisions persisted between the two movements. ZAPU was the more moderate group and had a greater proportion of Ndebele leaders; ZANU was radical, with a preponderance of Shona or Shona-related groups in leadership positions. Zambia supported ZAPU and, while it let ZANU establish offices and camps there, President Kaunda was always wary of the more militant movement. In international terms, ZAPU was more widely known, and through its links with the South African ANC, SWAPO and other groups it became part of the Soviet-supported bloc of liberation movements. ZANU, on the other hand, received support from Tanzania and China.

Both ZAPU and ZANU espoused forms of socialism, and Mugabe was to be labelled Marxist. Yet when I interviewed them two years after Zimbabwe's independence, nationalist leaders from both parties told me that while they were committed to the egalitarian and redistributive aspects of socialism and found aspects of Marxism a strong critique and useful organisational tool, they were never committed to Marxism-Leninism in the same way as the MPLA, the Ethiopian Derg or Frelimo were. They turned to the Soviet Union, Cuba and China for military and other aid because it was the only source available to them.

In the mid-1960s, both groups mounted small and generally unsuccessful guerrilla attacks, with small cadres of trained guerrillas and few weapons. They were also limited to infiltration via Zambia, and that made containment and counter-insurgency easier for the Rhodesians, who had an established army with aircraft, helicopters and armoured vehicles. A small group of ZANU members, led by Emmerson Mnangagwa (later a senior member of the Zimbabwean government and now a potential successor to Mugabe) were trained in China in 1963; they infiltrated the country and killed a Rhodesian Front politician in July 1964—the first white to die in the liberation fight.[36] In the same year, Ian Smith became leader of the Rhodesian Front, and it took an intransigent position on the granting of political rights to Africans. Britain still had theoretical sovereignty over Rhodesia, but little power on the ground. Smith wanted Britain to grant Rhodesian independence, but was not prepared to offer Africans anything like the parity in political rights that the British wanted.

Smith broke the deadlock with Britain on 11 November 1965 with the Unilateral Declaration of Independence (UDI). While Rhodesia was supported by South Africa at the time and would be for the next fifteen years, the UDI was not a development that the South African government welcomed. It would have preferred to see Rhodesia progress towards a negotiated independence rather than dragging it into a conflict not of its choosing, least of all an international crisis that would sharpen the contradictions in Southern Africa and force South Africa into ever greater conflict with the UN and the West.[37] Nevertheless, in the following years, Britain and then the UN imposed selective mandatory sanctions against Rhodesia, including an oil embargo—and South Africa and the Portuguese in Mozambique enabled Rhodesia to evade them.

The sanctions against Rhodesia hurt Zambia economically, since it relied on routes from the sea through Rhodesia, and it was forced to reroute its trade at a time when the Benguela railway through Zaire to the Angolan coast was a target for Angolan guerrillas. This was a major impetus behind Tanzania and Zambia's deal with China for the construction of the Tanzania-Zambia Railway (TANZAM), which was started in 1970 and completed in 1976. The sanctions on Rhodesia and the later closure of Zambia's border with Rhodesia in 1973 were extremely damaging to the economy, and Zambia's decision to host liberation movements made it a target for cross-border raids. But Kaunda believed that in the long-term, Zambia's true independence and economic well-being were inextricably linked with regional liberation—not least since Zambia was unique in having borders with four of the five territories then fighting for independence and majority rule.[38]

ZAPU and ZANU had a tough fight on their hands. The Rhodesian forces, backed by South African units, were well-organised and had the support of the white farming community in the rural areas where infiltration had to take place. The nationalists received training from the Soviet Union, China, East Germany, Algeria and later Ethiopia, but they were inexperienced in guerrilla warfare. At the end of the 1960s, ZANU was trying to overcome the obstacles posed by the reliance on routes through Zambia by opening talks with Frelimo, facilitated by Tanzania's Nyerere, on infiltration through liberated areas of Mozambique. Frelimo was allied with ZAPU, but ZAPU turned down an offer to use access routes through Mozambique. In 1970, the first cadres of ZANU's military wing, the Zimbabwe African National Liberation Army (ZANLA) joined Frelimo in Tete province and prepared to mount an offensive from there. The group, led by Mayor Urimbo (later ZANU's chief political commissar), established bases and routes to transport weapons from Tanzania to the border areas. ZANU was now aware that successful infiltration and the establishment of guerrilla fronts would require prior political work in rural areas of Zimbabwe.[39] That preparatory work laid the foundations for a guerrilla campaign that would begin with an attack in eastern Rhodesia in December 1972, and which would ultimately force Smith to the negotiating table and establish the political support base for ZANU's election victory in February 1980.

ZANU's strategy revolved around winning over the peasants in eastern Zimbabwe, encouraging their growing anger over the loss of land to white farmers and their desire to reclaim their land and control over their lives from a government that denied them social and political rights. There doesn't appear to have been a clearly socialist agenda for collective ownership of land; it was all about emphasising the loss of land and subordination to the white government.[40] The guerrillas also won over the spirit mediums of the Shona people in the areas they sought to mobilise. These were repositories of traditional beliefs, and by tapping into them ZANU connected this second struggle or *chimurenga* to the first against Cecil Rhodes's settlers in 1896–7. This helped ZANU win the trust of local people and the acquiescence of local chiefs. The mediums, the link with ancestors and the history of resistance, would be used by ZANU not just in the liberation struggle, but also during the 1980 election and some subsequent ones, as the group constructed a discourse of continuity between ancestors, struggle against colonialism and ZANU's programme.[41]

ZAPU, meanwhile, built up its forces in Zambia with Soviet and Cuban support, but even though by independence in 1980 it had tanks, artillery and other heavy weapons, it played a relatively small part in the fight against the Rhodesian army. Moscow refused ZANU requests for aid, seeing it as a splinter group and too close to the Chinese.

Against the background of the escalating ZANU guerrilla campaign, Rhodesia retained South African support and resisted British and American attempts to reach a negotiated settlement. But the Rhodesian army was unable to defeat ZANLA or prevent it spreading the war in eastern Zimbabwe, while South Africa put increasing pressure on Smith to negotiate and Rhodesia's economy deteriorated. This all forced first the "internal settlement" with Bishop Abel Muzorewa's United African National Council and Ndabaningi Sithole (who had been removed from the ZANU leadership while he was in prison), and then participation in the Lancaster House talks in 1979, which in turn led to elections and independence for what was now called Zimbabwe.

The liberation war in Zimbabwe had wider and lasting consequences for the region. The most immediate were in Mozambique, which provided bases and infiltration routes for ZANU, leading to raids by the Rhodesian forces on both the ZANU bases and on Mozambican infrastructure. After the Portuguese coup, Rhodesia's Central Intelligence Organisation recruited Frelimo dissidents and Mozambicans who had fought in the Portuguese army to form the Resistencia Nacional de Mozambique (Renamo). The Rhodesians also set up an anti-Frelimo radio station that broadcast into Mozambique to undermine Frelimo called Voice of Free Africa, known in Mozambique as Radio Hyena.[42] Just before Zimbabwean independence the station was moved to Phalaborwa in South Africa, where it continued to broadcast as the Voice of the Mozambique National Resistance.

Radio played a vital role in African politics at this time. High levels of illiteracy and the difficult logistics of transporting newspapers to rural areas in countries with poor road networks meant radio was a crucial medium not only for education, culture and entertainment but for news and both government and rebel propaganda. In Southern Africa in particular, political and military struggles were accompanied by radio wars. Governments controlled domestic radio in most African states, and it wasn't until the 1990s that state control over it was relaxed. The state radio stations would report the government version of news, almost always starting every broadcast with what the president had done or said that day; there was no plurality of opinion or political views, and dissent was attacked and derided. Rebels also ran radio stations from bases in neighbouring countries: the MPLA broadcast to Angola from Congo-Brazzaville prior to independence, and UNITA put out its Voice of the Resistance of the Black Cockerel from South African-occupied areas of southern Angola during the civil war.[43] Governments did not have the ability to jam radio, as both the Soviet Union and China tried to do to BBC and other Western broadcasts during the Cold War.

Radio was also an important medium for the spread of musical styles across Africa. Ghanaian high-life music became a staple in West Africa, while radio helped make the reputations of Senegalese musicians like Youssou N'Dour and Étoile de Dakar, the Cameroonian Manu Dibango and the Nigerians Fela Anikulapo Kuti, King Sunny Ade and Chief Commander Ebenezer Obey. In Central and East Africa, the Zairean music of Franco and other musicians became highly influential. The desire to keep up with music often led Africans to listen to stations other than their own government's ones. When I was travelling in northern Tanzania in October 1988, I found that local people and my driver and guide invariably tuned to Kenyan rather than their own state radio, simply because it played better music—not just African music, but also American country and western music. Music could also be a form of protest against unpopular or repressive governments: Fela Kuti repeatedly fell foul of the Nigerian military governments for his popular Afro-beat songs which fiercely attacked corruption and the military—songs like *Army Arrangement, Government Chicken-Boy* and *Colonial Mentality*.[44]

Returning to Southern Africa's political and military equation, in 1980, when Renamo moved its base to South Africa, it had fighters in Mozambique's Manica and Sofala provinces. With Zimbabwe's independence and South Africa's concern that the Frontline States could become forward bases for ANC infiltration, Renamo became South Africa's means of weakening the Frelimo government and damaging the Mozambican economy to stop it supporting the ANC. Frelimo was a staunch supporter of the ANC and allowed it to set up offices in Maputo, but didn't allow it to set up military bases or infiltration routes. Since independence, Mozambique had been receiving aid from China and the Soviet Union, but while Moscow supplied some arms and economic aid, it did not build up Mozambique's armed forces as it had Angola's, leaving Mozambique more vulnerable to Rhodesian and later South African and Renamo attacks.[45]

The new, Marxist-Leninist-oriented MPLA government in Angola was a target for South African attacks. Between March and August 1976, South Africa mounted seventeen raids against Angola. Refugee camps for Namibians and suspected SWAPO bases were targets for the South African Defence Force (SADF), and in May 1977, 612 men, women and children were killed in an SADF attack on the Kassinga refugee camp. The MPLA allowed both SWAPO and the ANC to set up military training camps in Angola, and they deployed their fighters to support the Angolan army against both UNITA and its South African backers. UNITA later gained the backing of the Reagan administration, which started supplying funds and weapons in 1985 after repealing the Clark Amendment, which banned US support for Angolan movements. Pretoria was determined to stop southern Angola being used as a base for the Namibian SWAPO liberation movement. UNITA, based in central and south-eastern Angola, claimed that the MPLA ruled solely in the interests of its Mbundu, mestiço and white members, and its leader Jonas Savimbi used ethnicity and the accusation that the MPLA was just a Soviet tool to stir up opposition to the government. UNITA and the South Africans worked to disrupt transport routes, destroy local infrastructure and cut food production; UNITA even said it was prepared to kill peasants to stop them growing food.[46]

Soviet arms supplies enabled the Angolan government to build a large, well-equipped army, supported by around 17,000 Cuban troops, and Soviet and Cuban support increased as the MPLA's political discourse moved closer to Soviet-style Marxism-Leninism. But a shortage of trained and ideologically aware personnel, combined with a growth in opportunistic behaviour and rampant corruption in the ruling party and the armed forces, meant that socialist policies amounted to little more than resolutions at party conferences, and the MPLA's elites became just as corrupt and acquisitive as many other regimes of the time. In December 1977, the MPLA renamed itself the MPLA Workers' Party and pledged itself to a programme of Marxist-Leninist revolution based on the "worker-peasant alliance."[47] This was despite the fact that very few workers or peasants were represented in the higher levels of the party, which was dominated by intellectuals, the senior officers of the armed forces and educated Angolans. The working class was a tiny part of the Angolan population, and the MPLA proved decidedly unsuccessful in mobilising much peasant support, since the top-down adoption of Marxist-Leninist policies meant little to the poor and largely uneducated peasantry. The leadership bodies of the MPLA were dominated by white Angolans, mestiços and educated black Angolans from urban and Mbundu areas. A radical group within the party, led by Nito Alves, had tried to move the movement towards a more egalitarian socialism and stressed the need for greater attention to the poor and marginalised black majority, but this faction was crushed by the MPLA and the army in May 1977, leading to a bloody purge of those suspected of disloyalty.[48] Tens of thousands are believed to have been killed and the repression established the MPLA's reputation of being willing to use maximum force against its domestic ideological as well as military opponents.

The MPLA's Marxist programme did not get in the way of close and lucrative working relationships with American and multinational oil giants in the Cabindan and offshore oilfields; in Lunda Norte, the MPLA even worked with the South African De Beers diamond company to exploit diamond resources. The spread of UNITA activity to diamond areas meant that the gems both supported the government and helped fund the guerrilla war, since De Beers representatives in southern Zaire also bought diamonds from UNITA.[49]

Despite the attacks from UNITA and South Africa, Angola continued to support SWAPO. The Namibian movement had been formed in 1960 from the regionally-based Ovambo People's Congress, and has ever since had a very strong contingent of Ovambo people, who make up just under 50 per cent of the Namibian population—though this has not meant it is an Ovambo ethnic movement. In 2015, the Damara politician Hage Geingob became president of both SWAPO and Namibia.

SWAPO was pledged to achieve independence for the territory, which was then a UN trust territory controlled by South Africa. As other trust territories achieved independence, South Africa showed no signs of giving up control and introduced apartheid policies. In 1966, the UN General Assembly voted by 114 votes to two (South Africa and Portugal) to revoke South Africa's mandate over the territory, making South Africa's occupation illegal. The International Court of Justice then ruled that South Africa was obliged to withdraw its administration from the territory—South Africa refused.[50] From 1975, SWAPO established training and garrison areas in Angola and infiltrated guerrillas into Namibia, and was no longer forced to rely on hazardous routes through UNITA-held areas or from Zambia into the Caprivi Strip.

South Africa: from Sharpeville to Soweto and the escalating struggle

After the 1960 Sharpeville massacre, South Africa's National Party (NP) government banned the ANC and the PAC and introduced draconian security laws, establishing a security and police network that gave it the power to crush the African liberation movements. Ever more stringent control of the media by the Afrikaner establishment, harassment of liberal opponents and detention without trial all enabled the government to stop African nationalists, white radicals and liberals from operating inside the country. The discourse of apartheid swamped every aspect of life, with culture, literature and the arts all affected by the efforts of the NP and Afrikaner establishment to eradicate all aspects of African nationalism from the public sphere and establish a rigid apartheid orthodoxy in public life.

Underground ANC and PAC groups remained active, but were increasingly isolated and in danger of arrest. The capture of Nelson Mandela in 1962 and then of seventeen leaders of the ANC's Umkhonto we Sizwe military wing (henceforth Umkhonto) in July 1963 destroyed the underground political and sabotage network the movement was trying to create. But Oliver Tambo, Thabo Mbeki, Joe Slovo and other key leaders of the ANC and its allies in the South African Communist Party (SACP) escaped and set up an exile organisation based in Zambia, Tanzania and London. The external wing of the ANC recruited political and military cadres and via Umkhonto launched a military campaign against the South African government, though with very limited success. The ANC and its supporters lobbied foreign governments and conducted a propaganda campaign against the apartheid system, alongside internationally-supported sports and cultural boycotts. A culture of anti-apartheid struggle developed among exiles, and musicians such as Miriam Makeba and Hugh Masakela helped popularise the struggle through their work.

The ANC received Soviet, Cuban, East German, Libyan and Ethiopian military aid and training, and established training camps and military bases in Tanzania, Zambia, and after 1975, Angola. It received financial and educational help from the Scandinavian states, diplomatic backing from the OAU, and support from foreign organisations such as the Anti-Apartheid Movement.

The ANC (and later the PAC) were forced to engage in armed struggle by the impossibility of legal, open anti-apartheid activity in South Africa. There is evidence that as early as 1955, the ANC's Walter Sisulu had raised the issue of armed struggle with Chinese Communists.[51] The ANC was at the centre of a loose alliance of African liberation movements supported by the Soviet Union and its allies, which also included SWAPO, Frelimo, ZAPU and the MPLA. The ANC relied heavily on the SACP both to develop a political and mobilisation strategy and to forge links with socialist states, and the ANC-SACP alliance introduced other African liberation movements to key Soviet decision-makers on African policy.[52] The alliance was key for both the ANC and the SACP, and ANC leaders like Mandela were co-opted in to the communist party to cement their close working relationship and mutual dependence.

The ANC's armed struggle faced huge problems. Until Mozambique's independence, the only majority-ruled African states with contiguous borders with South Africa were the small, economically dependent and vulnerable states of Botswana, Lesotho and Swaziland. While they supported the ANC, they had to avoid allowing their territories to be used for bases or infiltration because of the fear of military or economic retribution. This made getting forces into South Africa very difficult. In July 1967, a joint ZAPU-ANC force of about seventy crossed into Rhodesia from Zambia in an attempt to get to South Africa. They clashed with Rhodesian forces in the Wankie (Hwange) area; thirty-one of the guerrillas were killed, and most of the rest captured.

The failure to pose a credible military threat led to a major reappraisal of strategy at the ANC's conference at Morogoro in Tanzania in 1969. This conference saw major splits in the movement between "Africanists", who believed the ANC should remain a solely black movement, and those who believed coloureds, whites and Indians should be allowed to join. Ultimately, some of the Africanists were suspended, the ANC was opened to all races, and the movement adopted a Strategy and Tactics document that stressed the need to mobilise the black, urban youth in South Africa and the primacy of political work among the black working class. The relationship with the Communist Party—of which leading members of the ANC, including Mandela, were also members—became more overt, with communists heavily involved in drawing up the new strategy. This policy proved more viable and ultimately successful than armed struggle, particularly as NP political, economic and educational policies drove more and more black South Africans into active opposition in the late 1970s and early 1980s.

There is a debate over whether the SACP attained so much influence and power within the ANC that it (with the Soviet Union behind it) was effectively running and using the ANC for its own purposes.[53] This debate is a hangover from the Cold War days, and Western fears that an ANC government would be pro-Soviet; the dissolution of the Soviet Union before the ANC achieved power and the very non-socialist, pro-capitalist and wealth accumulation policies of the ANC's post-Mandela leadership have rendered the idea of SACP dominance irrelevant. If anything, it was the ANC that benefitted most from the relationship, since it was able to use and exploit the SACP's organisational expertise and its connections with the Soviet Union. In post-apartheid South Africa, the ANC has unquestionably been the dominant force within the alliance. One can only speculate whether things would have been different had the Berlin Wall not come down.

The ANC's new strategy based more on the working class and urban youth only began to bear fruit after the Soweto uprising of 16 June 1976, provoked by the NP's Bantu education policy. It received further impetus in the 1980s with the rise of the United Democratic Front. This was a non-racial political alliance that united opposition in urban areas and townships to P.W. Botha's policies and his tricameral parliament as they tried to bring the coloureds and Indians into the NP laager while excluding black South Africans. The ANC also forged vital connections with the developing South African trades union movement (rather than the old and out-of-touch leadership of the exiled South African Congress of Trades Unions), as well as links with the students and young people in the Black Consciousness movement of Steve Biko, Barney Pityana and others. Not unlike earlier concepts such as *négritude*, Black Consciousness aimed "to liberate black minds from the psychological shackles of white domination" and to provide an ideology of resistance that would stress black empowerment. It owed much to Africanists such as Robert Sobukwe of the PAC but also to writers on liberation like Franz Fanon.[54]

The only open black political activity that had been sanctioned inside South Africa by the NP was confined to the homelands under the Bantustan policy, which labelled all black Africans as *citisens* of government-created tribal homelands. The NP's aims were twofold: to make all black Africans in urban white areas temporary visitors whom the state could send back to the homelands at will, and whose families would be resident in the homelands; and to divert African political aspirations away from representation in central government and into the political structures of the homelands, where government-appointed chiefs beholden to the government in Pretoria would be the sanctioned political leaders. The homelands were economically unviable, with poor agricultural land, little industry, a largely migrant workforce and a disproportionately large number of the very young and very old—the unwanted blacks of the apartheid system. The territory of most of the homelands was fragmented, and even when the NP government moved to consolidate territory in 1975, they remained patchworks: KwaZulu had forty-eight separate blocks of territory, Bophuthatswana nineteen, Ciskei nineteen and Lebowa fourteen. Some homeland leaders and their subordinate chiefs co-operated enthusiastically with the government, while others were allowed at least a semblance of dissent, notably Chief Mangosuthu Buthelezi of KwaZulu. He had considerable Zulu support and had, in his youth, been close to the ANC. After the end of apartheid, Buthelezi would claim that he was always working against the system from the inside,[55] but his co-operation with the NP, opposition to the ANC and use of the government-sanctioned Inkatha movement to oppose the ANC before and after its unbanning suggest otherwise. Buthelezi did, though, reject the fictional independence that South Africa granted to Bophuthatswana (1977), Venda (1979) and Ciskei (1981).

The NP government also used the state-controlled broadcast media to deliver a message to the black majority, as well as to whites, that there was no alternative to 'separate development'. The South African Broadcasting Corporation (SABC) broadcast a diet of news and comment that furthered this discourse and ignored dissident opinion within or outside South Africa, except to criticise it. The SABC broadcast in English and Afrikaans to the white minority, and in Zulu, Xhosa, Tswana, Sotho, Venda, Ndebele and other languages to the black population. For its part, the ANC developed Radio Freedom to broadcast mobilising propaganda and its version of the news into South Africa, as well as to promote liberation and African culture.[56]

In the 1970s and early 1980s, the South African economy was the strongest economy in Africa and had a dominant position regionally, exporting food and manufactured goods even to staunch opponents like Zambia. It was also the regional transport hub. Botswana, Lesotho, Swaziland, Malawi, Zambia and Rhodesia were dependent on road and rail routes to South African ports for exports and imports, especially after South African-supported rebel movements in Angola and Mozambique cut road and rail links to Angolan and Mozambican ports. South African trade outside Africa boomed. The US became the major trading partner, but Britain, Japan and the European Community were all major traders, and foreign investment in South Africa reached $26.3bn in 1978.[57]

Although the UN arms embargo introduced in 1977 made importing modern arms more difficult, close military relations with Israel and the ability to update older weaponry enabled South Africa to keep its edge over Southern African states in military technology, while maintaining a large and well-trained army and air force. National service meant that white South African males all served time in the armed forces. There was a large reserve force of former conscripts and also local territorial defence structures, especially in rural areas thought vulnerable to guerrilla infiltration. The police were armed, and were used for domestic security and the suppression of opposition. During the 1976 Soweto riots and throughout the 1980s, the SADF was deployed in townships where the UDF and related movements were able to mobilise black opposition to the government—a tactic that dovetailed with and was encouraged by the ANC's strategy of making South Africa ungovernable.

The surface appearance of political control, economic strength and military power masked the long-term weakness of a state ruled by a small minority in the face of mounting discontent and black leaders' growing ability to stir up opposition to apartheid over issues like education. Apartheid education policies had never been accepted by the black population, who aspired to a good standard of education, not one that prepared it for menial and unskilled roles in a rich and growing economy. Black Consciousness emerged among black students in the late 1960s, and black student leaders like Steve Biko, angry at sub-standard education, broke away from the white-led National Union of South African Students to form the South African Students' Organisation (SASO) in 1969. SASO and the wider Black Consciousness movement rejected the ANC's approach of non-racial alliance and, to quote Biko, took the view that:

> Black Consciousness is an attitude of the mind and a way of life... Its essence is the realisation by the black man of the need to rally together with his brothers around the cause of their oppression—the blackness of their skin—and to operate as a group to rid themselves of the shackles that bind them to perpetual servitude.[58]

SASO rejected co-operation with white liberals, but avoided a racist approach; Biko remained friends with white sympathisers like Donald Woods.[59] Through this approach of stressing black leadership and psychological emancipation, SASO and related groups built up strong support among black university and secondary school students and started organisations in townships to run cultural, community development and health projects as well as spread Black Consciousness. Strikes broke out at a number of black universities against the system of Bantu education. The movement preached self-reliance and the rejection of victim status.

All the movements espousing Black Consciousness were banned in 1977. But they had instilled a spirit of rebellion in many young black South Africans, which led to the student protests against the Bantu education system starting on 16 June 1976. Known collectively as the Soweto uprising, this was the most serious black political action since Sharpeville. Mass demonstrations by school students were crushed with extreme violence; fifteen teenagers were killed on the first day of demonstrations in Soweto, and protests spread across the country. Township protests and attacks on Bantu Administration offices, beer halls and other targets continued until February 1977. Over 2,400 students were arrested, over 800 convicted and jailed and hundreds kept in detention for long periods without trial. The official death toll for the eight months was put at 575, but most believe that more than double that number were killed—mainly young black students.[60] The events shook South Africa and brought a hail of international criticism of the apartheid system. Many around the world saw this as nothing less than the violent oppression of a justified protest against a racist government. When Steve Biko was beaten to death in police custody on 12 September 1977, international criticism and South Africa's isolation intensified further—though it had little effect on trade or investment, or on the West's view of South Africa as a Cold War ally against Soviet involvement in Southern Africa.

Although the suppression of the demonstrations and the Black Consciousness movement gave the NP breathing space, it delivered a rude shock to those who thought that African resistance was over. Another shock was delivered in 1978 when Prime Minister B. J. Vorster was forced to resign in the wake of a scandal over the misuse of public funds to pay for clandestine propaganda campaigns to support apartheid. The Defence Minister, P. W. Botha, took over as prime minister; he later amended the constitution to create the post of executive state president at the head of a government in which the parliament and cabinet were subordinated to security structures as part of the Total Strategy. He reacted to growing international criticism and the threat of further domestic political and industrial protest with a mixture of intransigence and reforms aimed at modernising and strengthening the system rather than abolishing it.

The Black Consciousness movement survived underground, and the detention of militants brought them into contact with the jailed leaders of the ANC. Thousands of young black activists left South Africa and joined the ANC, and this new wave of recruits produced key leaders such as Tokyo Sexwale and Patrick "Terror" Lekota, who started with the Black Consciousness movement and went on to become a key ANC leader, with strong support in the Johannesburg townships.[61] Many years later, Nelson Mandela wrote that while at first there was some conflict with the new inmates, and the ideology of the younger generation was at odds with that of the ANC, the congress leadership was impressed by the spirit of protest they embodied. In his words, the leaders recognised that, "These young men were a different breed of prisoners from those we had seen before. They were brave, hostile and aggressive...In these young men we saw the angry revolutionary spirit of the times." After Lekota joined the ANC while on Robben Island, many more followed.[62] These younger activists' alignment with the ANC set the scene for the rise of the mass movement focused on the United Democratic Front (UDF) in the 1980s.

Zaire, regional conflicts and the rise of the personalised kleptocracies

The metamorphosis of Congo-Kinshasa into Zaire in 1971 was part of the troubled and deeply damaging rule of Joseph Mobutu Sese-Seko, who led the country from 1965 to 1997. He systematically plundered Zaire's resources, and developed a personalised style of rule that crushed opposition and masked the deep fragmentation of sub-Saharan Africa's largest state. Mobutu adopted the name Mobutu Sese Seko Nkuku Ngbendu Wa Za Banga, which translates as "The all-powerful warrior who, because of his endurance and inflexible will to win, goes from conquest to conquest, leaving fire in his wake". His rule was bolstered by the ideology of *Authenticité*, which encouraged and then enforced the wearing of African-style clothing and the use of African names. The country's renaming was part of this ideological justification for his rule, a very shallow attempt to harness Africanist ideas to what was a largely ideology-free and rapacious personal dictatorship. *Authenticité* was married with a growing ferocity towards opponents. In May 1966, a former prime minister and three former ministers were hanged in front of 50,000 spectators on charges of complicity in a coup planned by senior army officers. Mobutu justified this action with a pronouncement that epitomised his style: "One had to strike through a spectacular example, and create the conditions of regime discipline. When a chief takes a decision, he decides—period."[63]

Mobutu was an important Cold War ally of the West in a region rich in strategic minerals but beset by war and regional revolts, and Western states tolerated his plunder of the country's resources, appalling human rights record and interference in the affairs of neighbouring states to keep him on their side. The level of support was demonstrated in 1977 and 1978 when French, Belgian and Moroccan troops were airlifted, with US logistical aid, into Shaba to suppress two attempts by former Katangese gendarmes to seize the province. The military incursions by the Katangese had the blessing of the pro-Soviet MPLA government in Angola, and Mobutu's Western patrons clearly saw them as a Soviet proxy threat. The protection of mineral resources, Western investments and the propping up of a pro-Western regime were of primary importance, and they are the only explanation for the support given to a corrupt and brutal regime headed by a leader who became known as the Great Plunderer.[64] Prior to his overthrow in 1997, the US State Department estimated that President Mobutu's personal fortune, derived from the long-term theft of Zairean mineral revenues and loans contracted by his government, amounted to $5bn.[65]

Mobutu's domestic political strategy involved appointing and replacing ministers on a regular basis, rotating members of his government to prevent them from building up independent support bases, constituencies or informal networks that could threaten his dominance. His treatment even of close political allies could be brutal and inconsistent. The veteran politician Jean Nguza Karl-i-Bond, for example, was fired as foreign minister in 1977, sentenced to death, imprisoned and tortured. Mobutu commuted his sentence to life imprisonment, released him after a year, and then made him prime minister. After another falling-out with Mobutu, Nguza fled the country in 1981 but returned in 1985 to serve as Zaire's ambassador to the US and later as foreign minister again. This game of political musical chairs was enabled by Mobutu's support from the army, control of export earnings and incoming loans and assistance from the American, French and Israeli intelligence communities. The army was as venal as its commander-in-chief and had a fearsome reputation for brutality, rape and looting when deployed against rebels.

Mobutu's was the ultimate African gatekeeper regime, using state companies like the mining giant Gécamines to enlarge the leader's personal fortune and provide the patronage to buy off those clients he did not control totally through terror. The carrot and stick were employed in combination to ensure loyalty and subordination. Networks of clients, particularly in the military, maintained control across the vast country, but did not work to develop a viable institutional framework for government or management of the economy. Mobutu's rule depended on coercive power applied by his subordinates, who used their authority and control of military force to establish their own patron-client networks in the regions they governed.

The stability of this edifice was threatened in the mid-1970s by a drastic fall in world copper prices, which halved Zaire's export income. During the preceding boom years export earnings had been plundered; massive loans were contracted, then disappeared without any obvious benefit to the country. Zaire was unable to repay interest or capital to creditors. To save their ally from a financial crisis that could have threatened his regime just as the Angolan civil war was developing into a major Cold War concern, Western nations rescheduled the country's $3bn debt. Zaire defaulted again in 1977, during the first Shaba crisis, and yet more money was poured into the bottomless pit of Mobutu's treasury. Mobutu used his strategic position and Zaire's mineral wealth to go to Washington and "shake the money tree".[66] Only after the Cold War was over did Western governments and the IMF take a chainsaw to that tree and begin to cut away the branches that supported Mobutu.

Mobutu was far from the only leader of his time who failed to distinguish between state and personal wealth. In the Central African Republic (CAR), Jean-Bedel Bokassa was indulging in even greater delusions of grandeur than Mobutu, declaring himself emperor and renaming the country the Central African Empire. The French paid for his enthronement in 1977, but when their patience with his despotism ran out, they organised an overthrow and gave it militarily support. The CAR was underdeveloped even by colonial standards, with few educated or skilled people at independence, but it had diamonds, gold and uranium deposits. It remained close to and very dependent on France, with most government contracts and extensive technical and economic aid deals going to France and French companies, and with French troops stationed in the country. The presence of French troops enabled Paris to repeatedly intervene to overthrow or bolster chosen partners. Decades of coups and minor rebellions characterised political life, and to this day, the CAR remains one of the most unstable and poorly governed states in a central African region beset by division and conflict.

In March 2013, regime change occurred when a movement known as Seleka, which united rebel groups from the mainly Muslim and marginalised east of the country, used support from Chadian forces to oust the government of Francois Bozize, which had itself originated as a rebel movement by dissident officers against an unpopular government. This led to a prolonged period of instability and growing communal violence between Muslim and Christian groups. A small African Union intervention force proved powerless to stop the violence, forcing France and the UN to step in. In late 2013 and early 2014, there was horrific sectarian violence following the growth of a movement called Anti-Balaka, which was set up in Bangui and other areas seized by Seleka. Its members claimed that Seleka was a Muslim organisation and was targeting Christians. The upshot was serious violence in Bangui and other towns, as Anti-Balaka and vigilante groups attacked and killed Muslim civilians and Seleka struck back at Christians. In January 2014, amid growing violence between these groups, a group of neighbouring states led by Chad forced Seleka from power and established an internationally-backed interim government under Catherine Samba-Panza, the CAR's first woman leader. By the time of writing in mid-2015, CAR remains unstable and beset by outbreaks of violence.

In Uganda, Idi Amin was another military ruler who became a violent and seemingly irrational tyrant. He did so during a decade in which Africa was increasingly depicted in the Western media as a basket case continent ruled by brutal dictators hellbent on personal power and the accumulation of wealth at the expense of their peoples. It was not an accurate image of the whole continent, but it became a stereotype that still persists and informs much media coverage of Africa. Of course, the forces at work were far more diverse and complex than just the power and rapacity of a few powerful political or military leaders. When Amin seized power in 1971, he was welcomed by many in Uganda because of the increasing unpopularity of Milton Obote. Amin released political prisoners and established a government dominated by technocrats rather than politicians. His power base was the army, in which his own small and politically weak Kakwa community was strongly represented. Soon after taking power, Amin sought to purge Langi and Acholi groups from the military because of their close association with Obote's support base in the north. This became an ethnic purge; troops loyal to Amin killed Langi and Acholi officers, soldiers and prominent civilians.

Violence escalated in 1972 when Ugandan exiles in Tanzania (where Obote had taken refuge) launched an attempt to overthrow Amin's government. Amin responded with a wave of purges and killings of those suspected of supporting the incursion. In August 1972, with the economy faltering and resources to fund patronage dwindling, Amin ordered the expulsion of Uganda's Asians and the seizure of their property. The Asians had played major roles in the commercial sector of the economy and in the professions. Many of the expelled Asians had British citizenship and duly fled to Britain, whose relations with Uganda were soured by their expulsion. Israeli military advisers and instructors were expelled in 1972 after Amin began to look increasingly to Libya and the Arab world. It is said that when he went abroad for official visits, Libyan troops were flown in and assumed control of security.[67]

Amin's unpopularity increased as the economy declined and as more and more communities were accused of disloyalty. He became ever more dependent on his own Kakwa troops and soldiers of Nubian descent from the West Nile area, including Sudanese Nubians. His area of effective control shrank, and military commanders around the country became virtual warlords in their own areas. Despite Amin's growing unpopularity and shrinking support base, his ability to deploy fear and force was so great that it took a Tanzanian response to bring him down.

In late 1978, mutinies by Ugandan garrisons near the Tanzanian border were crushed, and the mutineers fled into Kagera. Ugandan troops invaded to kill them. Amin claimed that his action was in response to a combined Tanzanian-Cuban invasion of Uganda. This was pure invention; Cuba had no troops in Tanzania. The Ugandan incursion continued, with its air force bombing the town of Bukoba. On 1 November 1978, Amin announced that he had annexed the region.

President Nyerere denounced Amin as a savage, and promised to hit back hard. Libya still had forces in Uganda and Gaddafi tried to mediate, but Amin refused to withdraw from Tanzania. On 11 November, Tanzanian forces began a counter-attack and drove the Ugandans back. In January 1979, Ugandan exiles and over 40,000 Tanzanian troops invaded Uganda; the Ugandan army's resistance was weak, and by the end of February the anti-Amin forces were nearing Kampala, at which point Gaddafi flew in arms and troops to support Amin. When the Tanzanians and their Ugandan allies advanced towards the capital, Libya threatened to declare war on Tanzania. Nyerere refused to call a halt and said, "We will not change our stand on Amin. Amin is a murderer, a liar and a savage...By threatening to send troops to Uganda, Colonel Qadhafi has declared war against Ugandans who have the right to remove any dictatorship."[68] Amin fled on 11 April 1979, and an interim government was put in power by the Ugandan exiles and the Tanzanians.

In 1980, elections were held and won by Obote's UPC. Opposition parties accused him of rigging the result, but he was nonetheless inaugurated as president and proceeded to rule with as much use of force as he had during his first term in office. Obote's support was concentrated among the Langi and Acholi in the north, and he soon faced a revolt by opponents from within the anti-Amin alliance representing Ugandans from the south and west of the country. A guerrilla war and savage counter-insurgency campaign ensued, centred on the area near Kampala known as the Luwero Triangle. The fight against Obote was led by the National Resistance Army (NRA) of Yoweri Museveni, who had trained with Frelimo in Mozambique and been part of the Ugandan exile force that overthrew Amin.

There followed four years of war in which nearly 500,000 people died; most of them were civilians killed by Obote's northern Ugandan troops, and Acholi forces in the Ugandan army were accused of widespread atrocities. The NRA had developed strong support in central and southern Uganda and was backed by radical African states, including Libya. By July 1985, Obote was increasingly politically isolated. Before the NRA could seize power, army commander Tito Okello led a coup to depose him. He was soon defeated and overthrown by the NRA, his support base having been weakened by conflict between Acholi and Langi army units. In January 1986, the NRA took Kampala and Museveni was sworn in as president, a post he still holds.

By the 1980s, military rule was becoming the norm in much of Africa. Soldiers who seized power pledging to end corruption and the factional or regionally/ethnically-based policies of their civilian predecessors rarely proved willing to give up the reins of power or to be any more accountable than the civilians they overthrew. Many—Mobutu, Bokassa, Amin, Macias Nguema in Equatorial Guinea, and Rwanda's Juvenal Habyarimana—retained power until they were overthrown or killed by other factions within the armed forces. The remaining civilian rulers—Ahidjo and then his successor Paul Biya in Cameroon, Kenyatta and then Moi in Kenya, Banda in Malawi, Kaunda in Zambia and even the more accountable Senghor and Diouf in Senegal—also clung to power and established *de jure* or *de facto* one party states in which popular participation was prevented, or at best limited.

Africans who were not part of the ruling elites could only exercise their agency in informal ways beyond the control of governments, or through networks that enabled economic subsistence outside the cash crop economy and the depredations of its gatekeepers. Informal networks were also used by political leaders through clients, patronage and appeals to identity on the basis of language or ethnicity[69]—this necessitated the distribution of state or national resources in the form of patronage. Examples include the way Kenyan politicians generated support with appeals to ethnicity and the development of overtly tribalist politics, and the way they informalised political violence, as seen in 2007–2008. Equally, Robert Mugabe has long used informal networks of power, alongside the army and security forces, to support his regime and intimidate his opponents. But the use of traditional/informal types of public discussion—the *baraza* in Tanzania, the *kgotla* in Botswana—did enable ordinary citizens to hold political leaders to account in limited ways outside formal political institutions, and these should not be forgotten.

It must be stressed that in the autocratic or one-party systems of this era, personalised rule and control of the instruments of coercion and military force did not imply that states and formal structures were strong. Quite the reverse: they were often weak and had shallow roots in their nations and societies, frequently a result of the inappropriate or illegitimate nature of inherited or developed institutions, and the gulf between formal political structures and the actual behaviour of both rulers and ruled. The weakness of state institutions enabled autocracy and corruption, rather than preventing or limiting it.

Economic crisis: oil prices and commodity dependence take their toll

One area where the weakness of formal state structures and institutions became more apparent in the 1970s was economic management. The economic structures of the colonial period had scarcely changed in the first decade or so after independence; and Sub-Saharan Africa's economies were still export-led, with weak, struggling industrial and commercial sectors and undeveloped agriculture. The main change was that the gatekeepers for export revenues and import tariffs, skimming off foreign aid and misusing loans, were now the leaders of the new states rather than colonial authorities. They used this extraversion tactic to maintain political power and accumulate wealth—but power became something dependent on external as well as internal factors, maintaining the subordinate position of African states in the global economy.

The dominant approach to post-colonial economics was export sector development, with industrialisation through import substitution. Systems developed in which national, regional and local gatekeepers extracted rents from import tariffs, export revenue, incoming loans and aid.[70] This ate up surpluses and foreign loan or investment capital that could have been used to modernise agriculture, build infrastructure or alleviate poverty. European and North American multinational companies had major roles in the export sector; Western donors and states and international financial institutions retained strong influence over African states' macro-economic and financial strategies. Rent-seeking and vulnerability to foreign control left state institutions powerless to control economies; financial monitoring was weak and inefficient, with great dependence on foreign expertise, the World Bank and the IMF. An over-reliance on aid and foreign personnel weakened states' control over economies and attracted a deluge of economic advice—much of it inappropriate to African needs.

Attempts at industrialisation used export revenues, loans and aid to diversify economies away from their dependence on primary produce exports and manufactured imports. This in itself was not an unreasonable strategy, or rather would not have been had global and national economic conditions provided a conducive environment, and had the expertise been there to implement it in a planned and resourced manner. All too often, markets were too small for successful or cost-effective import substitution, and the trade networks needed to develop African markets for African-processed or manufactured goods were not there. Industries became uneconomic, costly and dependent on subsidies and protection—these costs were only exacerbated by the drain of corruption.

Governments contracted loans on the basis of high export earnings in the 1960s to fund projects that devoured funding and produced no revenue to pay the debt interest or capital, including over-ambitious projects such as Ghana's Volta Dam, Zaire's Inga hydro-electric scheme and Maluku steel mill, Nigeria's Ajaokuta steelworks and the Trans-Gabon railway. The latter, for instance, consumed $4bn of oil revenues and loans in the 1970s and 1980s and was never commercially successful.[71] States became increasingly dependent on aid to support budgets: in the first eight years after its independence Ghana received $90m in aid, while Africa as a whole was given aid or loans worth $950m.[72]

Loans built up indebtedness, while rent-seeking behaviour combined with loss-making industries and projects to reduce the capital available to pay interest on debts, to fund the provision of public services (notably health, education and transport infrastructure) and invest in agricultural development. Yet these development policies implemented by African governments, even though inefficiently or corruptly managed, were in line with the accepted global mantra of development through industrialisation and import substitution.[73]

Although states like Tanzania and post-revolutionary Ethiopia attempted to communalise or collectivise agriculture, farming methods scarcely changed and peasant agriculture was not made more productive, still lacking inputs and government support. Subsistence agriculture mixed with small-scale cash crop production dominated, and there was little investment in irrigation, fertilisers or improved rural transport. Between 1960 and 1985, alone among regions of the world, Africa experienced a decline in food production; agriculture, the source of livelihood for 70 per cent of Africans, performed badly.[74] Loans, aid and export earnings were not used efficiently to build economic foundations for the development of indigenous capitalism, and nor were there the funds or skilled economic planners needed to successfully implement alternative socialist strategies.

A capitalist, entrepreneurial bourgeoisie, the driving force of capitalism in Europe, North America and East Asia, was largely absent, with economic power concentrated in the hands of those who ran the state. Government jobs, contracts and tenders and other forms of top-down patronage were the sources of wealth accumulation, not entrepreneurship or the development of a strong, wealth-creating private business sector. In the state-centred and socialist-oriented states, there was not enough expertise to manage resources, and not enough was done to win peasants' support for land reform or communalisation. African socialist experiments such as Tanzania's failed, as did later Marxist-inspired attempts at state socialism in Ethiopia, Angola, Benin and a number of other states. The lop-sided development pattern in most of Africa shored up export dependence, aid dependence and the power of global markets and companies at the expense of the future of African economies. This system suited powerful donor nations who wanted to maintain their global economic dominance and the political power of the modern-day gatekeepers, who were left free to extract whatever they wanted. The gatekeepers' motivations were selfish, and while there may have been an element of reality in their governments' arguments that the need for development had to take priority over democracy, and that strong governments had to be in place to direct development, these justifications for autocracy and a lack of accountability were self-serving and deeply damaging in the long run.

The result, as Robert Bates put it, was that, "African states extracted resources and used them to underpin high levels of consumption by political elites. Rather than power being concentrated in the hands of those who accumulated and invested, power in Africa was instead concentrated in the hands of those who spent and consumed."[75] African peoples experienced low political participation, political and economic marginalisation, and falling living standards. The problems were compounded by optimistic beliefs that growth in the size of African economies or gross domestic product could be equated with development, while a lack of progress or often even a decline in agriculture was ignored. The Nigerian economy, for instance, grew by 6.9 per cent between 1960–70 and by 7.5 per cent between 1970–9, boosted by oil production and prices—but Nigerian agriculture declined by 0.4 per cent and 0.3 per cent respectively. Ivory Coast and Kenya, held up as beacons of successful capitalist-style development, also registered much higher growth in GDP than in their key agricultural sectors.[76]

For most of the 1960s and early 1970s, the growth of industry through government emphasis on the sector, the use of loans and aid to support industrialisation and the favourable prices of export commodities gave the appearance of development. Between 1965 and 1973, industry in Africa expanded by 14.6 per cent annually, more than double the continent's GDP growth, but much of this industrialisation was in mining and extraction industries related to exports. Most states had markets that were too small and underdeveloped to sustain cost-effective manufacturing, while poor transport, water supply and power generation systems combined with a shortage of skilled labour and of competent managers and accountants to militate against the successful development of manufacturing.

While export earnings were high during commodity price booms, the contracting of loans and the growth in debt did not seem catastrophic. When harvests were bad or global prices fell, the revenues to repay capital or interest dried up and debts grew. Outside the oil sector, there was not enough inward investment to fund industrial or agricultural development. Across Africa, investment per capita dropped from $80 in 1970 to $73 in 1997.[77] This only exacerbated dependence on aid or loans and encouraged indebtedness. The investment problem was worsened by a very low domestic savings base, and by capital flight. Those wealthy Africans who obtained rents from the system frequently deposited or invested their wealth abroad, rather than using it to develop the commercial sector of economies. By 1990, it was estimated that 37 per cent of Africa's domestic wealth had been sent abroad.[78]

It was against this background of economic inertia and mounting debt that the world was hit by the OPEC/Arab oil boycott of late 1973, following the October 1973 Arab-Israeli war, and the subsequent quadrupling of oil prices that led to a global recession. The World Bank calculated that oil import costs for most states rose from 4.4 per cent of export earnings in 1970 to 23.2 per cent in 1980. Economic growth stalled in the developed economies of Europe, North America and Japan, reducing demand for agricultural produce, minerals and metals for industry. The African commodity boom was over. Prices for commodities fell dramatically, as did the volumes imported by the industrial economies. At the same time, the petro-dollars deposited by the oil-producing states in Western banks funded a flood of lending to African states feeling the oil price pinch. This hugely increased their indebtedness.

In the decade after the oil crisis, African economic output declined by 20 per cent. In Zambia; which was badly hit by the nosedive in copper prices, the rise in oil import prices and the knock-on effects of sanctions against Rhodesia, gross national product fell by a staggering 36 per cent between 1976 and 1986. The crisis destroyed many of the illusions about industrialisation and import substitution, as these were dependent on imported capital goods, oil and other processed products—the prices of which stayed high. The only beneficiaries were oil producers like Nigeria, Congo-Brazzaville and Gabon.

Agriculture was hit hard, too. Despite a temporary increase in prices of coffee and cocoa between 1976 and 1978, commodity prices for agricultural exports stayed low and the lack of investment in the sector hit production hard. Ghana's cocoa output, for instance, fell by half between 1965 and 1979. Across Africa, food production failed to keep pace with population growth, and nearly two-thirds of sub-Saharan African states showed a decline in food production between 1970 and 1980. Drought exacerbated food shortages and led to catastrophic famines in Ethiopia, Sudan and the Sahel. Many states moved from being self-sufficient or even food exporters to being net importers. Imported food was often too expensive for poor workers, the unemployed or the under-employed in urban areas. To avert political unrest, imported food had to be subsidised by the state, putting an even greater strain on stretched government resources.

Overall, the picture for African economies as the 1970s drew to a close was poor, with little sustained development and continued reliance on a few vulnerable export commodities, corruption and mismanagement, widespread food insecurity, an increasing reliance on costly imports, unequal and damaging terms of trade between primary exports and manufactured, processed or refined imports, and a massive and growing problem of indebtedness. The scene was set for the drastic surgery demanded of and imposed on Africa by international financial institutions and donor countries: structural adjustment.

4

STRUCTURAL ADJUSTMENT, FAMINE, ENVIRONMENTAL DEGRADATION AND AIDS

While the global image of Africa during the 1980s and into the early 1990s may have been one of crisis, suffering and a perfect storm of economic decline, famine, war, corruption and environmental degradation, the picture on the ground was far more mixed. There is not one story of Africa during this period, and it was not a period of unrelenting doom and gloom. Many events of the 1980s and early 1990s were catastrophic for Africa, but there were also signs of positive and constructive approaches to political, economic and environmental development.

A core influence on events was the period's major economic development: the implementation of Western-driven structural adjustment programmes, which had lasting economic and political effects across sub-Saharan Africa. Amid all the other major events, themes and developments, this one was continental, with only a handful of states escaping its cold, hard clutches. Almost as pervasive, though with uneven effects across Africa, was the threat of deforestation and desertification tied inextricably to destructive climatic events in many regions, especially the Sahel and Sudanic zones. Africa also experienced the onslaught of HIV/AIDS, with its debilitating human, social and economic consequences.

Yet even in the face of these tragedies, Africa was not in a state of irreversible decline or a mere basket case continent. In the midst of the dire challenges to life, development and progress, one can detect the resilience and inventiveness of people, and the crucial role of informal, non-state approaches to potentially devastating challenges as well as to government policies.

Structural adjustment: the hegemony of global markets and institutions

International financial institutions and Western donor governments chose structural adjustment as their favoured instrument in thc facc of the economic crisis and failures of development that became most apparent in Africa in the wake of the oil crisis of the mid-1970s and the resulting global recession. After a decade of the imposition of structural adjustment in Africa, one leading academic wrote that "the I.M.F. has imposed 'conditionalities' in sub-Saharan Africa as integral elements of Structural Adjustment Programmes (SAPs) that affect not only the lives of all the inhabitants, but also the nature and landscapes of the nations concerned—their very geographical composition."[1]

The economic crisis as it affected Africa was the result of complex, interlinked forces. The most important were falling export earnings and rising import prices, capital flight, the growing burden of debt, failures of economic management, the debilitating effects of rent-seeking and the misuse of revenues, growing dependence on aid and grants, stagnant agricultural production, the costly failure of industrialisation, rising populations, damaging swings in climatic patterns and environmental degradation, poor transport and communications infrastructure, and conflict.

The need for change was overwhelming. Reforms in economic management, use of resources and control of revenue were long overdue. Economies were still too dependent on a limited range of vulnerable exports, and there had been little meaningful industrialisation or diversification. Those managing the economies were aware of this fact. Even the most rapacious economic gatekeepers wanted economic development, if only to increase their wealth and powers of patronage; so did aid donors, trading partners, creditors and international financial institutions. The latter were playing an ever-greater global role, under US tutelage, in dictating policies for economic management and charting strategies for growth and wealth production for states that were part of the global capitalist economic system. Africa might have been internationally marginalised in many ways, but it was integrated into international financial and trade systems—and subordinate to them. Even those states that opted for socialism and closer relations with the Soviet Union, like Ethiopia, Angola, Guinea-Bissau and Mozambique, were still part of the international economic system by virtue of their reliance on exports. Soviet and East European assistance was of limited economic value, did little to stave off or reduce indebtedness, and displayed an ignorance of African needs and conditions, matching the worst efforts of Western donors and NGOs, who also thought they knew best.[2] The global economic crisis affected all sub-Saharan African states, though not equally or with identical results.

The oil-producing states benefitted from oil price rises and gave the appearance of boom economies, but the majority of states were in crisis, their economies weakened by falling commodity prices and rising import prices. The basic statistics spoke volumes: African economic growth, which averaged 2.1 per cent per annum between 1960 and 1990, was outstripped by population growth of 2.8 per cent per annum, while the economies of comparable countries in Asia grew by an average of 5.8 per cent. Even 'model' pro-Western states such as Ivory Coast and Kenya, which achieved reasonable growth rates and attracted more inward investment than many of their neighbours, were beginning to falter. Donor nations were less and less willing to give aid that they perceived as being wasted through incompetence or corruption. After the petro-dollar boom of the mid-1970s, banks were disinclined to lend more to states so deeply in debt that rescheduling or defaulting on existing loans were their only options. The world's major financial institutions—the World Bank and the IMF—realised that radical change was necessary, and this view was reinforced by political changes in major Western nations.

Between 1979 and 1981, Britain, Canada, the US and West Germany, four of the key donor and trading partners for Africa, had conservative governments elected to power. They were wedded to reducing the economic role of the state, privatisation, deregulating currency markets and liberalising trade—all means of encouraging global economic growth that would benefit their economies.[3] They were representative of what became a new capitalist economic orthodoxy, reasserting the central role of the market as the engine of growth, and their policies would not only be applied in their own countries but aggressively encouraged through trade and aid policies, and, most importantly for Africa, through the IMF and the World Bank.

Although some conditionality had been applied to IMF and World Bank assistance to Zambia in 1976 and had been part of other programmes after that, the first clear application of structural adjustment came in 1979 as part of a programme agreed by the IMF and Senegal. Senegal had developed a widening balance of payments deficit as its agricultural production stagnated, reducing exports at a time when oil prices were increasing. The country's small industrial sector was dependent on subsidies and government revenues were stretched past breaking point, with debt at $1.47 billion and export earnings from groundnuts, fish and phosphates falling. The servicing of the debt was unmanageable and the budget in deficit. The World Bank provided an initial loan to lessen the effects of the financial crisis. This was followed by a three year loan facility with the IMF that was contingent on the implementation of a stringent SAP, including what became the standard set of conditions: reductions in public spending and the economic role of the state, privatisation of state companies, freeing of exchange rates, and the deregulation of trade to encourage imports.[4] The IMF set these conditions even though it blamed the Senegalese crisis not on poor government policies or corruption but on years of drought, which had reduced cash crop and food production.[5]

Senegal's problems were part of a wider African economic crisis, and the financial institutions' responded by establishing almost identical SAPs that applied the same solutions to problems that had a variety of causes, many of which were not overtly addressed by the economic narratives the institutions used when putting together programmes. For example, if Senegal's economic crisis was caused by drought, why an SAP rather than funding for food security and drought alleviation? In the years to come, similar questions would be asked across Africa and by many African and Western analysts and NGOs.

Between 1979 and 1989, thirty-seven African countries signed up to 241 structural adjustment or related schemes with the IMF or World Bank. Of those, eleven countries received ten or more loans. Only Botswana, Angola and Djibouti did not apply for SAP facilities between 1980 and 1991. During this period and into the 1990s, the Fund and the Bank were the dominant influences over African economic policy.[6] In the whole period of decline, crisis and adjustment, to quote K. Y. Amoako, former Executive Secretary of the UN Economic Commission for Africa, "A major irony is that theories and models of economic performance and problems in Africa have all come from the outside. No other region of the world has been so dominated by external ideas and models."[7] The new ruling approach to African economies took it as read that the root causes of poor economic performance, poor growth and growing indebtedness were the failure of policy, the setting of unrealistic exchange rates, the protection of industry, restrictions on imports, and the dominant role of the state in the economy.

The Western view of the causes and cures of Africa's economic crisis was set out in the Berg Report for the World Bank, published in 1981. The report blamed structural factors for economic stagnation, something with which few could argue. It identified structural problems both external (terms of trade, climatic effects, role of international financial system, conflict in Africa) and internal (price controls, exchange controls, state role in economy, import restrictions), but the World Bank and the IMF chose to ignore the external factors and concentrate SAPs on domestic policy.[8] This was perhaps because tackling external structures such as terms of trade and international financial networks would mean restructuring the foundations of the international capitalist economy and reducing the profits made by Western multinationals and financial institutions from their roles in Africa.

SAPs concentrated on what their framing institutions saw as obstacles put in place by governments that inhibited the working of the market and of private enterprise. Rather than tackling states' reliance on primary produce exports with widely fluctuating prices and their resulting economic vulnerability, the SAPs promoted greater dependence on exports while encouraging states to remove price controls, scrap domestic food subsidies, liberalise exchange controls to subject currency values to the market, and remove import restrictions that protected domestic industries. It was believed that freeing currencies would make exports more competitive and provide better prices for producers, encourage domestic food production by raising prices, cut spending by reducing subsidies, and encourage enterprise in local industries by introducing competition. The assumptions on which these beliefs were based were flawed, and African economies were too weak to compete in the markets they were forced into.

While in the short term states such as Ghana experienced economic growth,[9] the overall outcome of the SAPs was not good. By the early 1990s, a decade of SAP across the majority of African states had increased indebtedness, kick-started capital flight to service debts, massively increased unemployment and poverty, boosted the incidence of malnutrition, undermined health and education services, degraded infrastructure, and driven down the adjusted states' balance of payments. Export earnings—as vulnerable as ever to fluctuations beyond the control of now even weaker African states—could not meet the combined costs of debt servicing and imports, which had both spiralled thanks to devalued currencies and higher oil prices. The increase in the burden of debt only added to other consequences of SAPs such as unemployment and environmental degradation.[10] Privatisation did not lead to a rebirth of private commercial activity, nor did it stop those in power using their position to gather rents from economic activity and incoming capital. The lack of a strong, independent private sector and the existence of patron/client networks among political and business elites meant that when states divested themselves of assets, the process was neither efficient nor free of corruption. SAPs did not take place in an environment of economic rectitude, but in one where powerful politicians still wielded substantial influence and where kickbacks were commonplace, the valuation of privatised assets haphazard, and the revenue from the sale of assets minimal or pocketed by politicians. Tendering for contracts by the private sector simply became a new form of patronage.[11]

The removal of food subsidies and price controls, meanwhile, was supposed to encourage agricultural production and reduce government spending, but the actual effect was to raise the prices of imported fuel, food, medicines, agricultural inputs and capital goods for industry. Agricultural production scarcely increased as any price incentive to grow more for sale was offset by land infertility, the lack of fertilisers and other inputs, and the diversion of produce into informal local networks rather than formal trade and pricing systems. Government services were cut back, unemployment rose and living standards fell. Few benefited apart from those businessmen granted import licences and access to foreign exchange; ordinary people suffered. Across African economies, costs of production and trade rose rather than fell because the high value of oil drove a universal increase in the cost of transport.[12] Export crop prices rose, but this had no effect on the volume of export crops purchased, which was dependent on external markets and global demand. The same was true of other export commodities. In Zambia, the devaluation of the kwacha had no effect on copper or cobalt exports, since demand was internationally determined, there was no black market or cross border-smuggling of copper, and devaluation merely raised the foreign exchange costs for the mining industry and worsened Zambia's terms of trade. Increasing food prices, caused by cutting of subsidies, were unsustainable because of falling employment and incomes in urban areas. Poor prices for copper, falling volumes of exports and dependence on loans meant that by 1990, Zambian debt servicing had reached 150 per cent of export income.[13]

One of the most serious effects of the SAPs was a catastrophic increase in indebtedness. At the start of the adjustment period in 1980, African external debts totalled $84bn, but after twelve years of adjustment had increased to $150bn, while debt servicing was consuming 20 per cent of export revenues.[14] Ghana, held up by the IMF and the World Bank as a success story, experienced a devastating rise in its debt as adjustment loans and other financing mushroomed while income fell. In 1989, cocoa prices dropped by 29 per cent, and this brought an end to the brief period of economic growth for which the SAP architects had tried to take credit. Ghana's debt service/export income ratio more than doubled, with servicing taking 53 per cent of earnings by 1987, alongside a massive increase in urban unemployment, a fall in the real value of wages and little of the promised increase in foreign aid and investment.[15] This story was common across the continent.

Despite the growing evidence that the SAP exercises had damaged infrastructure, reduced the ability of already weak institutions to manage economic policy, lowered living standards and increased poverty, the international financial institutions and their powerful backers continued the programmes well into the 1990s. The only change was an increased emphasis on the new mantra of 'good governance'. There had been no adjustment in the major structures affecting African economic development, notably global terms of trade and the dependence of most African economies on a very limited and vulnerable range of primary agricultural and mineral exports. There had also been little economic diversification. Instead, African states had largely lost what little control they had had over their economies. As Julius Nyerere asked in 1980, "When did the IMF become an International Ministry of Finance? When did nations agree to surrender to it their power of decision-making?"[16]

The answer is of course that in the face of economic crisis and mounting indebtedness, African leaders felt they had little choice but to bow to the IMF's will. The resulting prescriptions left Africa dependent on primary or semi-processed exports, while subject more than ever to the vagaries of the world market. In 1965, the proportion of African exports taken up by primary commodities was 92 per cent; the figure in 1991 was identical, while East Asia had reduced this figure from 89 to 28 per cent over the same period, and South Asia from 63 to 28 per cent.[17] And dependence on Western financial aid, rescheduling of debt and contracting of new loans actually served to reinforce the power of the gatekeepers, while deepening dependence.

Drought, famine and conflict: Ethiopia, Sudan and Chad

> "Dawn, and as the sun breaks through the piercing chill of night on the plain outside Korem it lights up a biblical famine, now, in the Twentieth Century."
>
> Michael Buerk, BBC News, 23 October 1984

For much of the world, the abiding image of 1980s Africa is the TV footage that alerted outsiders to the extent of the Ethiopian drought and famine of 1983–1985. It had a huge effect globally, and launched a fundraising and relief effort that elicited unprecedented sums and brought famine to the fore as an international concern. It also helped create a lasting frame for the representation of Africa that shed light on a tragic and oft-repeated cause of death and suffering, but which also distorted the way people saw the continent as a whole. The other upshot was an explosion in the size and influence of Western non-governmental organisations (NGOs) in Africa in the fields of economic development, health and disaster relief.

The vulnerability of African agriculture and food security to prolonged periods without rain was nothing new but the early and mid-1980s saw droughts that rivalled the worst periods of the previous decade, during which hundreds of thousands died of starvation or malnutrition-related diseases across the Sahel, Sudan and Ethiopia. Drought destroyed or drastically reduced harvests, wiped out livestock and depleted scarce water resources, leading to soil degradation and reduced the ability of the land to recover.

The Sahel, Sudanic and Ethiopian regions and areas of eastern and southern Africa have long been prone to drought and will be for the foreseeable future. Individual countries, regional and international organisations have tried to learn from the catastrophic droughts of the 1970s and 1980s to develop early warning systems and improve food security to prevent droughts causing persistent malnutrition and famine. These systems are based on "a range of environmental and socio-economic data such as rainfall levels, the condition of pasture, migration of people and livestock, level of crop storage and animal sales." These methods are an improvement, but are only useful if governments are willing to maintain monitoring and act to get food to those affected before shortages become famine.

Famines are more or less a thing of the past in Asia but not Africa. The 2011 Somali famine killed an estimated 260,000 people, half of them under the age of five. The aid community believes that tens of thousands of people died needlessly because the international community was slow to respond to early signs of approaching hunger in late 2010 and early 2011. The death rate was exacerbated by militants from the Somali al-Shabaab movement, which prevented aid organisations and Western NGOs delivering food aid. This brings us to a key point about famine, one that is vital to understanding why it recurs with horrifying regularity in Africa when elsewhere in the world it is prevented, even at times of severe drought or natural disaster: famine is man-made.

The Nobel laureate Amartya Sen has identified key factors that lead to famine and the conditions for prevention. Sen's critics have questioned his criteria, but his arguments about famine and entitlement, and the relationship between famine, democracy and a free press are nonetheless useful. They go beyond the effects of climate, environment and natural disaster and incorporate all-important forms of human agency: government negligence, the progressive marginalisation of peoples, conflict, and poor or deliberately exclusionary economic and food security policies. And of course, the policies and prescriptions of international financial institutions, aid donors and even NGOs can also play roles in creating the conditions for famine or failing to avert them.

Sen writes that, "Starvation is the characteristic of some people not having enough food to eat. It is not the characteristic of there being not enough food to eat. While the latter can be a cause of the former, it is but one of many possible causes." He goes on to point out that, "While famines involve fairly widespread acute starvation, there is no reason to think that it will affect all groups in the famine-affected nation. Indeed, it is by no means clear that there has ever occurred a famine in which all groups in a country have suffered from starvation." In normal times, an African peasant or pastoralist (the most affected groups during famines) can command entitlement to food through growing it, working as a wage or payment-in-kind labourer to earn it, selling livestock or other produce to buy it, or combinations of the three.

Drought may affect all of those entitlements, not just by reducing food availability in a particular area but by increasing food prices and depriving people of produce they sell to buy food. The failure of governments to provide food aid, food for work, welfare payments or other schemes for those who have lost their entitlement can turn local or regional food shortages into famine. The distribution policies of governments can mean the marginalised lose their entitlement to food, and during conflicts, deprivation of food, destruction of harvests, food stocks and livestock can all be used as weapons to combat rebels or insurgencies; so too can forced resettlement, in which food is used as an incentive to move, or the lack of it as a disincentive to stay.

Accordingly, the catastrophic famine in Ethiopia in the early to mid-1980s cannot be understood without taking into account that a conflict in which food was used as a weapon, a government prepared to conceal famine, and NGOs that were negligent or duped by a government they wanted to co-operate with at almost any cost. Ethiopia is vulnerable to drought, and for centuries droughts have led to famines when harvests have failed and livestock died, but nothing has been done to alleviate the hunger. The Selassie government's failure to deal with persistent and widespread hunger led to a famine that was instrumental in starting the creeping revolution that overthrew him. The worst affected were poor and marginalised pastoralists and peasant/tenant farmers, expendable as far as the monarchy was concerned. The new revolutionary government in Ethiopia pledged to institute land reform and prevent famine recurring. The land reforms freed peasants from indebtedness to landlords and abolished rents, but the government established the Agricultural Marketing Corporation to buy food from peasant farmers at low prices to feed the urban population, the growing army and peasant militias fighting rebels. Those low prices removed incentives for peasants to grow more than required for subsistence. As so often happened in Africa, events in rural areas had sparked major changes in government, but the rural poor had little or no role in enacting those changes. The result was further impoverishment, and the only options Ethiopia's peasants had were to withdraw from the system through lower production, deny food surpluses to government, or withhold food from sale altogether. A range of Derg policies had disastrous effects on the food system: quotas, restrictions on rural markets, movement restrictions in rural eras, a ban on migrant labour, and use of food as a weapon against the insurgencies in Eritrea and Tigray.

The famine that received world attention in October 1984 began in 1983 and lasted into 1985. Estimates of the number who died vary, with the UN figure of a million for the whole period contested by De Waal, who puts the figure for the main area hit, northern Ethiopia, at 400,000, including those who died from causes other than starvation but as a result of the diseases that accompanied the famine. Ethiopia's Relief and Rehabilitation Commission (RRC) said in 1983 that the number of people at risk of starvation was 3.9 million, up on the previous year but still below the critical levels of several years before. The RRC was established after the revolution to prevent famine, but had become enmeshed in the Derg's collectivisation and resettlement campaigns. Western NGOs working in Ethiopia largely failed to register the famine, partly because they were excluded from many of the conflict zones in the north but also because they were trying to move from relief to longer-term development. In February and March 1983, the first signs of famine were obvious, but the RRC was unable to persuade the Derg that it was a priority.

The most serious problems became apparent in Tigray, and in May 1984, the RRC announced that there was a catastrophic drought there. Food was short, harvests were down, and food stocks had been seized or destroyed as part of the counter-insurgency strategy against TPLF guerrillas. Grain prices in Tigray had almost doubled between 1982 and mid-1984. The combination of shortages and high prices led to starvation for many poor peasants. The cause was not drought alone, but this served as a convenient cover for the RRC and the Derg, which was remarkably successful in keeping its military activities out of the famine narrative emanating from NGOs and the international media. Michael Buerk's famous report for the BBC from the feeding centre at Korem was a masterpiece of disaster reporting that was re-broadcast by more than 450 TV stations around the world; it helped spark a major relief effort, elicited hundreds of millions of dollars in public donations, and forced the Ethiopian government to admit the famine was happening. But the reporting itself and the media coverage and NGO campaigns that followed gave a far from accurate account of the famine and its causes, ignoring the deliberate withholding of food aid and the destruction of markets, crops and livestock to prevent them from falling into TPLF hands. The famine was depicted as a result of drought and poor harvests in an area affected by environmental degradation and overpopulation. This served the Derg's purpose of diverting attention from the war, while highlighting the arid and infertile nature of the region and implicitly making the case for people to be resettled away from there for their own long-term good. The government exploited feeding stations and camps run by the aid agencies for those fleeing hunger, which became "magnets with which to draw unsuspecting people who were then whisked off to resettlement camps hundreds of kilometres from their homes."

Little was spent on famine relief by the government, which was spending an estimated 46 per cent of GNP on the armed forces and fighting the Eritrean, Tigrayan and Oromo insurgencies. It is clear that the counter-insurgency campaign in Tigray was the chief cause of the famine. The army and government militias used scorched earth tactics against the TPLF and its supporters, and forcibly requisitioned food to feed the army and militia. Government military offensives in 1983, 1984 and 1985 displaced hundreds of thousands of rural people and worsened the effects of drought and food scarcity. Once the international relief effort was underway, the Derg turned the whole operation to its advantage. It was able to manipulate the UN Emergency Office for Ethiopia (UNEOE) in Addis Ababa to ensure that drought was blamed and the war hidden, and the UNEOE played down reports of forced resettlement. The organisation's head, Kurt Jansson, would later admit that a substantial portion of the aid sent to Tigray by the international community never reached those in need and was used to feed the forces fighting the TPLF; only 5.6 per cent of the food aid delivered reached Tigrayans, even though they made up between 20 and 33 per cent of those affected. The Relief Society of Tigray (Rest) was the conduit for international aid supplied either to Tigrayan refugee camps in Sudan or to TPLF-controlled areas, and there is evidence that substantial amounts of food aid and hard currency sent to buy food were diverted to buy weapons for the TPLF.

The famine weakened TPLF control of parts of Tigray, but by the late 1980s, a series of better harvests and the failure of the Derg's military campaign to eradicate the insurgents laid the groundwork for a new TPLF offensive, one that was assisted by a major military defeat for the Ethiopian army at Afabet in Eritrea in March 1988. Unable to defeat the EPLF in Eritrea or the TPLF in Tigray and steadily losing territory to both, the Derg was further weakened by the reduction and then cessation of Soviet military support as Gorbachev realigned Soviet foreign policy and the Soviet Union disintegrated. By February 1990, the Ethiopians controlled just a few towns and major roads in Tigray and had lost the key Eritrean port of Massawa. Pressure was growing on all sides, and soon after Massawa's fall, Mengistu gave in to political pressure and announced that the Workers' Party of Ethiopia—formally established in the midst of the worst period of the 1984 famine—would be replaced by a multi-party system. This did not stave off defeat, and between early 1990 and 21 May 1991, when Mengistu fled to Zimbabwe, the TPLF was able to ally itself with other anti-Mengistu groups, including Oromo insurgents, to form the Ethiopian People's Revolutionary Democratic Front (EPRDF), which took power from the Derg after Mengistu's escape.

On 24 May, EPLF forces took Asmara. The new Ethiopian government and the EPLF negotiated a referendum in Eritrea that returned a result of 99.79 per cent in favour of independence, and Eritrea became independent on 24 May 1993. This ended over thirty years of war between Ethiopia and the Eritrean movements, and was the first time that the OAU-supported sanctity of colonial borders had been overridden, but it didn't end the conflict between Eritrea and Ethiopia. The EPLF and TPLF had been uneasy allies against the Derg—an uneasiness that periodically turned into outright hostility—and once in control of independent states, they developed an animosity that descended into inter-state war and a nagging border dispute.

In neighbouring Sudan, conflict and drought also went hand in hand to cause massive humanitarian suffering. The Nile Valley elite had a tenacious hold on power both in political parties and the high command of the armed forces, and the fragile peace agreed at Addis Ababa in 1972 had brought a semblance of peace in southern Sudan, and limited self-government in the south dampened down southern resentment of Khartoum's control of the national government and the economy. But as time progressed and the arrangement brought no obvious economic benefits to the south, disenchantment grew, and was exacerbated by periodic droughts that starved millions. The Khartoum government maintained a policy of almost total neglect of drought and food shortages outside the central Nile area. Eastern, southern and western Sudan were left vulnerable and "in an extreme state of underdevelopment," and the marginalisation of those areas would be a major cause of conflicts in Darfur, Blue Nile, the Nuba Mountains and other parts of South Kordofan, even after the negotiated secession of the South in 2011. Where development did take place in some of these regions it was on large holdings owned by the Nile Valley elite, funded by the World Bank and Arab states. Far from bringing any benefit to local communities, it pushed pastoralists and peasant farmers off the best land and limited their access to water. This had particularly debilitating effects on the Baggara of Darfur, the Kordofan and the Nuba, and variously prompted revolt or left them vulnerable to government attempts to use them as informal militias against Khartoum's insurgent enemies—for which they were paid in both cash and weapons. In this volatile environment, it was only a matter of time before Sudan would see a renewed conflict on a massive scale. The spark that ignited that conflict was ultimately supplied by Khartoum.

Initially supported and armed by the Soviet Union, President Numayri moved from the Soviet to the Western side in the Cold War as a result of his support for President Sadat in Egypt (who had broken with the Soviet Union) and his growing hostility towards the Derg in Ethiopia. Numayri backed the EPLF and the TPLF and allowed them to use Sudanese territory, and his animosity towards Ethiopia and the USSR increased after a series of coup attempts involving the Sudanese Communist Party and radical army officers. Numayri formed the Sudanese Socialist Union (SSU) to give political weight to what was essentially a military government; he also developed closer relations with the Muslim Brotherhood and its leader, Hasan al-Turabi. The SSU and the government emphasized Arabic culture and Islam, but were nonetheless seen by the US as a bulwark against Soviet expansion, and Sudan became the largest recipient of US aid in sub-Saharan Africa. This did little to develop the economy, and the aid just disappeared into the "vortex of corruption" around Numayri. That corruption, the huge cost of the armed forces, drought and underdevelopment in much of the country, drained the economy and brought hardship even to Khartoum itself. This weakened support for Numayri even within the traditional support base of Sudanese governments. His response was to launch projects in the south aimed at helping northern-owned commercial agriculture, and to bolster his support from the Muslim Brotherhood and other Islamist groups, he turned to sharia law.

In 1983, Numayri instituted sharia as the basis for all law in Sudan, including in the non-Muslim south. He also redrew the provincial borders to move the oil fields that the US multinational Chevron was developing in the south into Kordofan province from Upper Nile, and thereby out of the autonomous south. In 1981, he had already announced plans to re-divide the south into more provinces, taking advantage of tension within the southern political leadership between powerful Dinka politicians and those from the Shilluk and Nuer communities. The final straw for the southern leaders was the decision on 5 June 1983 to dissolve the southern Regional Assembly and create the three weaker regions of Equatoria, Upper Nile and Bahr al-Ghazal, where Arabic would be the official language and the provincial governors would be appointed by Khartoum. This broke the letter and the spirit of the Addis Ababa accords, and for many former Anyanya fighters it was unacceptable.

They had already begun to re-establish contacts with those in what was called Anyanya II, a movement of Nuer dissidents who had stayed outside the agreement and were variously in camps in Ethiopia or in small groups in Upper Nile, Jonglei and Bahr al-Ghazal. They had gradually increased military attacks in these areas, and had put out feelers to army and police officers serving in Sudanese units in the south. One officer, Colonel John Garang, helped smuggle arms to some of the groups. A highly educated officer, Garang had a strong following among Dinka troops in the Sudanese army.

When Numayri scrapped the deal with the south, he provoked a mutiny in a southern battalion in Bor, which was supported by Garang. After an unsuccessful attempt by northern units to retake the base at Bor, most of the battalion and Garang took to the bush or to camps in Ethiopia, where remnants of Anyanya II were based. In July 1983, the Sudan People's Liberation Army (SPLA) and its political wing, the Sudan People's Liberation Movement (SPLM) were founded by Garang in Ethiopia, amalgamating the defectors and Anyanya II. The new movement was more organised than its predecessors, under a single command and had backing from Ethiopia and through it the Soviet Union. Garang's charismatic leadership had both advantages and disadvantages; he was able to galvanise the movement, but was accused of being autocratic and of favouring the Dinka by rebel commanders such as Riek Machar of the Nuer and some Shilluk leaders. These divisions allowed Khartoum to play divide and rule among the southerners, prolong the war and further split the south—but without fatally undermining the SPLA.

The SPLA's recruits were sent to Ethiopia for training and then back to their home areas as guerrillas and recruiters, which proved a good way to build up local support. Khartoum deployed its army in massive, indiscriminate and destructive counter-insurgency sweeps, and as the cost of counter-insurgency mounted, used militias recruited from dissident groups in the south or impoverished Arab pastoralist communities like the Baggara.

The actions of the army and the militias worsened the effects of a drought that had started in 1981 in northern Kordofan and parts of Darfur, but which had spread to the south by 1983–4. In many areas, food production was down to a quarter of the normal level, and the combination of circumstances made it into Sudan's worst famine for 70 years. Numayri's government, just like Haile Selassie's and later Mengistu's, was totally negligent, failing to send food aid to Darfur, Kordofan or the south. It was willing to use starvation as a weapon against those who supported the SPLA, while the government's allies among the grain traders and northern Banks, like the Faisal Islamic Bank, used the shortages to make huge profits from vastly inflated food prices. Numayri refused to admit there was a famine, and by 1985 an estimated 250,000 Sudanese had died. The shortages had not been felt in the Nile Valley, though starving peasants from Darfur, Kordofan and the south had migrated to areas around Khartoum in the hope of finding work or food. This made the famine obvious to most Sudanese and to Numayri's allies in Washington. Under pressure from the US, Numayri acknowledged the famine in January 1985 and asked for aid. But by then, sections of the army and the SSU had turned against him because of his gross mismanagement.

When he was in Washington on 6 April 1985, the army deposed him in a coup believed to have had the support of Washington and the Mubarak government in Egypt. The new government allowed the re-emergence of parties and trades unions, which had been suppressed by Numayri, but it did little to combat famine; food was provided by NGOs, and as in Ethiopia after 1985, they became the main providers and distributors of famine relief and medical assistance in many poor and marginalised areas.

The coup paved the way for elections in April 1986, which brought Sadiq al-Mahdi back to power at the head of a series of unstable coalitions.

Although the interim government called on Garang to come to Khartoum and said it would reinstate the Addis Ababa accords, there was no progress towards peace and the war continued. Despite the expansion of the army and the increased use of Baggara and later Nuer militias (after Machar defected from the SPLA rejecting Garang's personalised style of leadership and apparent favouring of the Dinka), they were unable to stop the steady advance of the SPLA and its consolidation of liberated areas in Jonglei province and along the border with Ethiopia. The Sudanese army was increasingly trapped in garrison towns, and militia became the government's main tool for raids on SPLA territory to kill, seize livestock and destroy crops. Those captured by the militias in their raids became virtual slaves, forced to work unpaid.

Various attempts were made to find a political solution during al-Mahdi's time in office, including meetings between al-Mahdi and Garang in Addis Ababa, but the Khartoum political parties (including the Umma party and the opposition National Islamic Front, NIF) were committed to making Sudan an Islamic state and opposed autonomy for the south. The result was the continuation of the war and the development of insurgencies in the Nuba Mountains, South Kordofan and later Darfur. The search for peace was complicated by the shifting nature of the alliances between the Umma party, the Democratic Unionist party and the NIF. The political turmoil came to a head on 1 July 1989, when Colonel Omar al-Bashir, with the support of Turabi's NIF, overthrew Sadiq al-Mahdi. Although Turabi was briefly detained after the coup, it became apparent that he was the ideological driving force behind the Bashir government's more militantly Islamic approach. This made a peace deal less viable.

In August 1991, Nuer and Shilluk SPLA units led by Machar and Lam Akol tried to displace Garang, accusing him of dictatorship and of putting too many Dinka in leadership positions. The coup failed but led to fighting between the SPLA and Machar's Nuer factions, who had support from Khartoum, and accusations of massacres of Dinka civilians by Machar's supporters. By 1995 the SPLA was on the offensive again, and the Sudanese government faced co-operation between the SPLA and Sudanese opposition and insurgent groups working together within the umbrella group, the National Democratic Alliance (NDA). Nigeria's President Babangida and states in the Intergovernmental Authority on Drought and Development (IGADD—it later dropped "Drought" and became IGAD) tried to mediate but failed to make real progress. That said, their attempts to bring the SPLA, NDA and Khartoum together made it clear that in the wake of

Eritrean independence from Ethiopia, there was an acceptance in the region that, despite Garang's attachment to Sudanese unity, a lasting solution to the conflict might have to come through self-determination for South Sudan. This idea gradually took hold and led to the prolonged negotiations that concluded with the Machakos Protocol of July 2002 and the Comprehensive Peace Agreement, which ended the war between the SPLA and the Sudanese government, paving the way for South Sudan's independence on 9 July 2011.

Neighbouring Chad also experienced decades of war, resulting again from the sorts of structural and demographic problems facing many African states and the actions of emerging political leaders and movements. The population was three million at independence in 1960, but consisted of 200 different ethnic groups who spoke 110 languages. The south of Chad is fertile and populated by a mix of African communities; the most numerous are the mostly Christian Sara. They constitute a third of the country's population and grow most of the cotton, rice, groundnuts, corn, millet and sorghum that make up the export and food crops upon which Chad depends. In the pre-colonial era they were subject to heavy slave raiding by groups from the central Sahel area of Baguirmi, the Fulani people to the north-west and the Oueddai sultanate to the east. Under French colonial rule, they were the main source of recruits for the colonial army and colonial civil service, and were favoured over the more scattered and nomadic Muslim northern communities. This history left lasting suspicion between the settled Christian agricultural communities in the south and the Arabic-speaking and closely linked Maba and Tubu communities in the centre, north and east of Chad.

Notwithstanding these ethnic, religious and cultural differences, there wasn't a simple north-versus-south, Christian-versus-Muslim or agriculturalist-versus-pastoralist divide. Chad's political, economic and social cleavages were far more complex, and the conflicts which developed were not simply southerners against northerners but involved serious divisions among Arabic-speaking, Muslim Chadian groups as well as splits between southern politicians. Shifting alliances were affected not only by domestic relationships but by French ambitions in Africa, the indissoluble links between Chadian and Sudanese communities, and cross-border conflicts and disputes involving Libya. Prior to French colonisation of northern Chad and Italian occupation of Libya, the Libyan Sanussi dynasty exercised considerable power over the north of Chad, and Libya claimed ownership of the Aouzou strip along the border.

At independence, the southern Chadians were economically stronger, better educated and dominated the army and civil service. They had also developed more organised political parties. The arid, thinly populated Bourkou-Ennedi-Tibesti (BET) region to the north of the capital, Fort Lamy (later renamed N'Djamena), was not well represented politically and was under French military control for five years after independence. The French remained with the agreement of the first Chadian government because of the fear of a backlash against the dominance of southern and Fort Lamy-based politicians in the new state.

The first government was formed by François Tombalbaye, leader of the Parti du Peuple Tchadien (PPT), which had the support of many Sara and also among Arabic-speakers in the capital. Tombalbaye followed an increasingly authoritarian path and began to eliminate opponents within his own party and ban other parties. In January 1962 the PPT was declared Chad's sole legal party. A reduction in Muslim representation in the government and the arrest of senior Muslim politicians led to rioting between Muslims and Christians; over 100 people were killed, and more leading Muslims leaders were arrested. This was followed by the start of a violent revolt against Tombalbaye in November 1965 in the predominantly Muslim Batha region, just south of the BET.

In June 1966, the Front de Libération Nationale (Frolinat) was founded by Muslim Chadian groups at Nyala, the capital of South Darfur. Frolinat wanted to bring down the southern-dominated government, and was able to use Sudanese territory as a conduit for arms and a base for incursions. Libya's backing reflected its support for the Tebu people, many of whom had fled Chad in late 1966 after Tombalbaye had stripped their leader of his traditional judicial role and refused to appoint his son, Goukouni Oueddei, to a major judicial position in the BET. Goukouni was to become Libya's main ally in Chad, and a leader of one his country's strongest factions.

The history of Chad's conflicts over the next 45 years is complex. Interwoven as they were with those in Sudan and the Central African Republic and involving as they did Libya and Gaddafi's Sahel and West African-recruited Islamic Legion, Chad's struggles are testament to the intricacy of the factors that still fuel conflict and division across the Sahel and Sudan region today. The conflict in the CAR in 2013, for instance, was exacerbated by the involvement of Chadian forces supporting Muslim groups in the Seleka rebel coalition—and the relationship between those movements cannot be divorced from decades of complex and shifting relationships between Chadian governments, Chadian rebel forces, and movements and governments in neighbouring states.

The war in Chad itself was governed by constantly changing military/political coalitions, with the initial Frolinat alliance of Muslim groups fracturing into factions led by powerful regional leaders with backing from their own communities and neighbouring states. The involvement of France in support of first Tombalbaye then Hissein Habre, and Libyan backing for a range of factions from the north of the country and its ambition to annexe the Aouzou Strip, both internationalised the conflict. Gaddafi would follow a consistent policy of interference and intervention in Chad, but he was inconsistent in his support for his allies, frequently changing sides for short-term gain. Beyond Libya and France, the movement of Chadian forces back and forth across the Sudanese border into Darfur and also into eastern CAR brought those countries into the regional mix and involved them in the Chad conflict—and Chadians in theirs.

Between 1975 and the early 1980s, leaders like Habre and Goukouni were part of a succession of alliances, variously with the government in N'Djamena or with rebel groups backed or opposed by Libya. Nigeria and the OAU repeatedly sought to mediate a lasting ceasefire and find the basis for governments of national unity; these attempts all foundered in the face of mutual suspicion among the warring factions and the interference of both Libya and France. Both countries committed troops to fight alongside their Chadian allies in the 1980s, and French airpower helped Habre seize and maintain power in the face of Libyan-backing for Goukouni. Despite a French-Libyan agreement to withdraw in September 1984, the Libyans kept their forces in northern Chad, blocking a military or political solution. Fighting continued for the next three years, but the Goukouni-Libyan alliance was gradually weakened as several factions revolted against Libyan hegemony over the north, attacking Gaddafi's Islamic Legion and Libyan army units in Chad.

Eventually Habre's forces, armed by France and the US, launched a series of offensives that inflicted crushing defeats on the Libyans and their Chadian allies. On 8 August 1987 Habre's army occupied Aouzou, and on 4 September they carried out a raid into Libya, destroying a major base at Ma'tan al-Sarah, killing 1,713 Libyan troops and destroying large numbers of tanks and aircraft. I was in Accra and Ougadougou soon after this attack, and the pro-Libyan Ghanaian Foreign Minister and Burkinabe ministers and officials told me that most Africans were proud that the forces of an African government had inflicted such a defeat on a foreign army from a country that had been involved in the slave trade across the Sahara. This was despite the fact that at the time, both Ghana and Burkina

Faso were closely allied with Libya and received financial and military aid from Gaddafi.

Habre remained in power until 1990, when his repressive and autocratic style of government led a former ally, Idriss Deby, to overthrow him. Deby was supported in his coup by Sudan, where he had the support of communities in Darfur closely related to his own culturally and linguistically. He established a government that remains in power today, despite continuing insurgency and the periodic interference of foreign forces, and under him Chad has become a major political and military force in the region, by turns influencing the conflicts in Darfur and the CAR through its support for warring factions. At the time of writing, Chadian forces were playing a major role supporting the Nigerian army in its fight against Boko Haram insurgents. Chad's involvement led to a series of suicide bomb attacks by Boko Haram in N'Djamena in the summer of 2015.

Drought, desertification and environmental degradation in the Sahel

Drought and deforestation affect much of sub-Saharan Africa outside the wetter rainforest regions and their neighbouring well-watered grasslands. They are two of the major causes of food insecurity that combine with human agency to cause famine or malnutrition. In the Sahel and other arid areas, they lead to desertification, serious soil erosion and deepen the problems of rural poverty. Low levels of agricultural inputs, such as fertilisers, poor or intermittent water supplies for irrigation and over-grazing by livestock mean that the Sahel environment and agricultural land is extremely vulnerable to the effects of climate.[18] In the long-term these combine with over-intensive use of marginal land to accelerate desertification. As a result, agricultural development has been disappointing across Africa with only slow and uneven growth in crop yields—and the worst affected region is the Sahel.

The Sahel suffered a long drought from 1968 to 1973, and farmers in the region were then only able to increase the output of the staple drought-resistant sorghum and millet crops by about one per cent a year until the next drought in the early 1980s. This low growth in crop production went alongside a population increase of 2.5 per cent annually. A 1982 United Nations study of the developing world's capacity to feed itself found that half the Sahel countries would not be able to produce enough food to feed their populations in the foreseeable future. The most arid area of the region, directly bordering the Sahara desert, is thinly populated by nomadic or semi-nomadic pastoralists at a density of only two people per square kilometre, but the carrying capacity of the land is only 0.3. To the south, where slightly higher rainfall and more fertile soils support pastoralists and arable farmers, the population density is twenty people per square kilometre, and the carrying capacity fifteen.[19] With the population still growing, food insecurity is worsening over time, and this has been exacerbated by the allocation of the best agricultural land to the growing of cash crops, especially cotton and peanuts. For governments trapped between commodity dependence, world market prices they cannot control and rising debts, the only way to increase export earnings is by the allocation of more and more land to cash crops and the use of more intensive farming methods. Combined with a paucity of agricultural extension services and affordable fertilisers, this greatly erodes land fertility, while fuel shortages mean wood is cut at a greater rate than can be sustained by new growth or planting.

Declining soil fertility and deforestation lead to further soil erosion, worsened during periods of prolonged drought. Pressure on land prevents farmers from being able to allow cultivable areas to lie fallow, and the limited areas for grazing are constantly overgrazed. The SAP programmes of the 1980s also sped up the process of environmental damage by demanding the expanded cultivation of export crops. That meant more and more land in West Africa was used for the production of crops such as cotton and groundnuts, to the long-term detriment of food security. Even in Ghana, in the more fertile region south of the Sahel, the SAP-inspired push to increase cocoa exports led to deforestation and long-term ecological damage.[20] Over the last two decades, regular droughts and falling harvests in Niger have led to severe food shortages and chronic malnutrition. The World Food Programme (WFP) estimates that "2.5 million people in Niger are chronically food-insecure and unable to meet their basic food requirements even during years of average agricultural production."[21]

In 1973, aware of growing threats to the global environment from a range of issues, the UN set up the UN Environmental Programme (UNEP), based in Nairobi. Its studies of Africa concentrated on issues such as desertification and water resources, and demonstrated that between 1959–84, the population in the Sahel doubled and farmers extended cultivation into marginal areas while livestock populations grew substantially, resulting in overgrazing and deforestation. Efforts have since been made to develop drought-resistant crops and improve agro-forestry, so that cultivation goes hand in hand with forest restoration; better soil and water conservation techniques are also being developed. But for the majority of poor farmers and pastoralists in the Sahel these techniques are out of reach, both for economic reasons and because of governments' unwillingness or inability to offer sufficient support for small-scale agriculture as they continue to concentrate on export crop production. The result is that, as a UNEP study found in 2006:

> The intertwined processes of land degradation and desertification, which have prevailed in the Sahel over the last few decades are nothing more than the embodiment of a degenerative process that started several decades back. The drought years of the 1970s, 1980s and 1990s were...the culmination of this environmental crisis...the Sahel remains an environmentally sensitive region and climate change is likely to exacerbate the vulnerability of its ecological and socio-economic system.[22]

The droughts and consequent food scarcity of 2011–12 demonstrated the Sahel's failure to make major advances in food security, and in 2012, the UN's Food and Agriculture Organisation (FAO) reported that, "A combination of drought, chronic poverty, high food prices, displacement and conflict has led to dramatic declines in food production across the Sahel," concluding that more than seventeen million people were directly at risk that year."[23] Poverty, government mismanagement and environmental degradation are as closely entwined as ever, and also contributed to the conflicts that developed in the Sahel in the first decade and a half of the 21st century.

Coup, coup and coup again: the search for political stability in Ghana and Nigeria

The overthrow of Ghanaian President Kwame Nkrumah in 1966 by General Joseph Ankrah's National Liberation Council (NLC) was hardly the first coup in Africa, but it was a key moment nonetheless, as one of the leading voices for independence and pan-Africanism was removed from the scene. Led by senior army and police officers,[24] the coup against Nkrumah was in large part a reaction to the proliferation of corruption and abuse under his government.[25] In contrast to Nkrumah, Ghana's new government adopted a strongly pro-Western, anti-Soviet foreign policy, which was welcomed in London and Washington. This continued when Ankrah was himself deposed after an internal army split in 1969, the new regime arranging the election of a conservative civilian government led by Kofi Busia.

Busia had strong support in Asante areas, and had been a Legislative Council member for the Asante Confederacy in 1952. Along with the backing of an important traditional constituency, he also enjoyed the support of the prosperous educated elites and the cocoa farmers Nkrumah had alienated. Busia continued the pro-Western external policies, but he proved as incapable of ruling Ghana and managing the economy as Nkrumah's CPP had been in its failing years, doing little to change state control of wages and prices. When there was a temporary boom in cocoa prices, Busia permitted a liberalisation of imports that led to a flood of goods and a depletion of the foreign exchange reserves earned by improved commodity prices. His attempts to impose austerity and devalue the cedi were opposed by the Trades Union Congress and the Union of Ghanaian Students, which were promptly banned. When he tried to impose austerity measures on the army, it overthrew him and set up the National Redemption Council (NRC) under Colonel Ignatius Acheampong.

Under Acheampong's NRC government, economic policy went into a tailspin. Exchange rates were reversed to vastly overvalue the cedi, while large parts of the timber, mining and embryonic oil industry were acquired by the government and mismanaged. Corruption "reached unbelievable heights as government decisions on fundamental issues such as import permits were made largely on the basis of personal connections."[26] The NRC did try to give greater weight to agriculture in the economy, but high exchange rates meant lower prices for cocoa farmers, while global oil price rises and corrupt import policies led to even greater trade imbalances and indebtedness.

The cycle of coups was an indication of the weakness of Ghana's state and political institutions. What was evident throughout this period and later the long years of rule by Jerry Rawlings—whether under the overtly military Provisional National Defence Council or in the guise of a civilian government formed by his National Democratic Congress (NDC)—was that most Ghanaians accepted economic incompetence, corruption and a lack of political accountability almost as a fact of life. This enabled governments and military leaders to proceed in the knowledge of a "Ghanaian desire to avoid conflict and that they will stand for almost any government action."[27] The same point has been made in relation to evidence of rigging in successive elections for civilian governments in the 21st century, where Ghanaians accepted clearly fraudulent results just as they had acquiesced in the failings of the past. Through this relative passivity, they have avoided the politically-generated violence and incitement of ethnic conflict by ambitious politicians or military leaders that has blighted other states.[28]

Ghana's extended game of military/civilian musical chairs did not lead to innovative economic policy. The only innovators were traders with import licences and cocoa farmers of means, who circumvented the government-mismanaged economy by creating the *kalabule* black market system and creating networks for smuggling cocoa to Ivory Coast, where they could get much higher prices for the crop. The black market system worsened the overall problems of corruption and weak state power, but it at least made goods available to Ghanaians at a price and provided farmers with an incentive to keep planting cocoa. It was an example of how those unable to exercise agency over their own produce and economic well-being through formal or government-controlled structures often did so through informal networks instead. When I was in Ghana in November 1987, bribery and corruption were the order of the day and I had to bribe an airline official with dollars to get the boarding pass to leave the country. Even under the more stringent rule of the PNDC, the informal economic sector flourished and was vital for the survival of many people, especially in urban areas.

The Acheampong government lasted six years until it was overthrown in another coup by General Fred Akuffo, who legalised political parties and prepared Ghana for civilian elections. As this process developed, Ghanaians for once protested against the corruption of the military and the rich business classes. The demonstrations in Accra encouraged a group of radical junior officers and NCOs to stage a coup on 15 May 1979; it failed, and the leader, Jerry Rawlings, was imprisoned. On 4 June he was freed when another coup took place, and he became head of the ruling Armed Forces Revolutionary Council (AFRC). He moved fast and ruthlessly to publicly punish former heads of state and senior officers, trying to destroy the aura of impunity that surrounded them. In a break from the tradition of bloodless coups, the AFRC executed Acheampong, Akuffo and six other senior army officers and established tribunals to try officials and businessmen accused of hoarding and price-fixing. Rawlings argued that executions were necessary to stop popular anger from developing into destructive violence. It also removed from the scene potential opponents who could disrupt his attempts at change.

The AFRC allowed the elections to go ahead, and a coalition of parties led by Hilla Limann won. But because the AFRC held the ring for the elections, Limann had a massive credibility problem; people saw the shadow of Rawlings and the military looming over his two-year rule. Limann inherited an economic mess, and could do little to extricate Ghana from it. Industry was operating at a quarter of capacity, and cocoa farmers were either not planting to replace depleted crops or were smuggling their produce to Ivory Coast. Debt was rising to levels that put a huge repayment burden on government finances, and inflation was running at well over 100 per cent. Aid donors and financial institutions were wary of working with Ghana: World Bank figures show that by 1981, Ghana was receiving $13.3 a head in official development aid, compared with the average of $26.3 for sub-Saharan Africa. Per capita incomes had fallen from 640 cedis in 1971 to 460 in 1981.[29]

The Limann government's inability to act decisively brought on the inevitable coup. On 31 December 1981, Rawlings seized power and broadcast over Accra radio that the people of Ghana had little point to their lives and a revolution was needed. The broadcast was long on rhetoric and short on detail of how the new military government would cure the ailing economy. Over the next ten years, against a background of radical pronouncements, socialist-style political organisation and the development of close links with Cuba and Libya, Ghana ironically became the star pupil of the IMF and World Bank by implementing structural adjustment programmes.

At first, the Rawlings government's economic policy was hardly different from that of its predecessors, though it had a strong emphasis on fighting corruption, especially in the granting and use of import licences. Politically, the ruling Provisional National Defence Council (PNDC) worked to establish organisations of citizens and workers to mobilise the population in a way not really attempted since the early days of Nkrumah's radicalism. Workers' Defence Committees (WDCs) were established in workplaces to organise the support of workers and—though it wasn't an explicit objective—to undermine the power of the trades unions, which were a potential source of opposition.[30] The People's Defence Committees (PDCs) were organised on a local basis to generate support for the radical political policies of the regime. As usual, the rural areas were largely ignored, and the regime remained military-based and urban-biased.

This early period saw political in-fighting within the PNDC, from which the Marxist Chris Atim and his supporters were eventually purged for opposing the decision to negotiate with the IMF and World Bank over an adjustment programme.[31] There were several coup attempts during 1982 and 1983 by factions within the armed forces, but Rawlings and the PNDC had developed sufficient stability to weather the storm of attempted coups and even to cope with the forced return of over one million Ghanaian workers expelled from Nigeria in early 1983, when the Nigerian economy went into decline. Having defeated their radical critics, Rawlings and the PNDC introduced a budget in December 1983 that included sweeping reforms to liberalise the economy and meet the demands of the financial institutions for changes to exchange rates, trade and more besides in return for an SAP facility and financing. The new approach included price incentives, assistance with the supply of fertiliser and pesticides, and encouraging farmers to plant more cocoa—many plants had been destroyed in the preceding years by drought or bush fires and had not been replaced.[32] Rawlings lasted so long in power, and remains a force in Ghanaian politics, because he worked hard to build support networks and did not rely solely on the army and the use of force, though this of course was employed when expedient.

The incentives worked: cocoa production rose, smuggling declined and export revenues increased. There was also an increase in food production. A rise in cocoa prices gave the impression that SAP had turned the economy round, but there had been no major structural changes and debts increased to $3.087 million, with debt servicing rising to 48.9 per cent of export earnings. This came at a high social cost, with growing poverty and poor welfare, health and education provision as public spending was slashed, and yet there was little public protest or union opposition. The new WDCs in urban workplaces, while not totally negating the role of trades unions, did enable the PNDC to channel worker militancy and avert strikes. The PDCs and WDCs were later replaced by the Committees for the Defence of the Revolution (CDR), which were clearly tasked with mobilisation but also with control and surveillance. The PNDC developed alternative institutions to the old parties or traditional sources of authority, with the PDCs, WDCs and CDRs playing overtly political and economic roles. They didn't provide freedom to organise, criticise or exercise agency outside PNDC control, but in the long term, they formed a political base which Rawlings could exploit when domestic and external pressure forced political liberalisation and a return to civilian rule.

Nigeria suffered an even more prolonged period of military take-overs, attempts at civilian rule and reversions to what the musician Fela Kuti called the Army Arrangement. The end of the civil war in 1970 had stirred a desire for reconciliation, unity and reconstruction, and victory in the war had bolstered the prestige of the military leader, Yakubu Gowon. But this positive atmosphere did not last, even as the Nigerian treasury benefited hugely in the 1970s and early 1980s from a massive increase in oil revenue. The urgent priority after the war was constitutional restructuring and the development of political institutions to prevent further conflict. Accordingly Gowon set the target date of 1976 for a handover to civilian rule under a new constitution, but he appeared to have no clear plan for new institutions that could cope with regional, religious and ethnic diversity. There was clearly a desire to retain some form of federal structure, but even as smaller communities tried to make themselves heard, the three-way battle between the north, east and west continued—despite the country being divided into twelve states in 1967 to split the three big post-independence blocks.

During the war, Gowon had appointed military governors and state commissioners in each of the twelve states of the federation to ensure control while the federal military government concentrated on the war. The governors and commissioners had gained their positions with the support of the military, and used them to amass huge wealth and build client networks in their states.[33] The oil boom and the distribution of the bulk of the revenues through the federal and state governments offered those in public posts a lucrative source of patronage, which in turn bolstered these regional client networks. The military and senior officers in government posts were major beneficiaries of the new wealth, and the state governors became significant obstacles to Gowon's uncertain moves towards reform.[34]

The armed forces had grown from 10,000 in 1967 to 250,000 in 1970, and there was no serious attempt to cut numbers at the end of the war, when stability and the reincorporation of former Biafran officers and soldiers were paramount concerns. The share of government spending on defence grew from 9.4 per cent in 1967 to 45.9 per cent in 1975; 85 per cent of that was spent on salaries. The army was the largest institution and major employer in Nigeria, the most powerful player in the political process and the strongest institution in a weak political system. When the constitution was drawn up to replace military with civilian rule in 1979, it made the seizure of power by the military illegal. Nobody, however, addressed the issue of who could enforce this provision when the military was the only functioning coercive power in a system with a weak executive, political institutions and judicial system. This was to be the leitmotif of Nigerian politics until the new millennium. The country spent decades with weak institutions unable to reduce the power of the military, which in many ways still decides which civilian politicians and former generals compete for office and who benefits from access to oil revenues and government contracts. It was no surprise that former military ruler, General Muhammadu Buhari, was elected as president in 2015 to replace the ineffectual and increasingly unpopular Goodluck Jonathan.

But if Gowon ultimately failed in his domestic polices and left Nigeria with the unsolved problem of corruption and the residual power of the military, he did have one major achievement: his leading role in the formation of the Economic Community of West African States (ECOWAS).

Regionally, Nigeria was the biggest economic and military power, and competed for influence with the Francophone states (especially Senegal and Ivory Coast) and France. Nigeria was keen to integrate its economy more closely with the region to fulfil its potential to be the manufacturing hub of West Africa. The approach it took was functionalist; Gowon wanted to start with trade, transport and communications co-operation rather than political or foreign policy integration.[35] West Africa was replete with organisations that had secretariats, officers, periodic meetings but no obvious effect—from the large Francophone economic community of West African States to the three-member Mano River Union. Nigeria proposed the ECOWAS idea after the Biafran War and was supported by a number of states, particularly Togo. Others, led by Ivory Coast, were wary; the French government, too, was opposed to the community, and tried to use its influence in Abidjan to put obstacles in its way. But Nigeria's openness (later reversed by President Shagari when it suited Nigeria to do so) to the free movement of labour between states won over the doubters, as they could see the obvious advantage of receiving remittances from migrant workers employed in Nigeria's booming economy.

The ECOWAS treaty was signed in Lagos in May 1975 by fifteen states: Benin, Gambia, Ghana, Guinea, Guinea-Bissau, Ivory Coast, Liberia, Mali, Mauritania, Niger, Nigeria, Senegal, Sierra Leone, Togo and Upper Volta (later Burkina Faso). Two years later, Cape Verde joined. ECOWAS has survived for thirty-nine years, and has developed a political and peacemaking role, as shown during its intervention in the form of ECOMOG (the community's military monitoring force) in Liberia and Sierra Leone and its role in the aftermath of the Mali coup and conflict in 2012–3. It has been less successful as an economic union and an engine to promote regional trade; the hoped-for customs union has not materialised, and the growth in trade between member states has been slow.

Domestically, Gowon failed. He was unable to overcome the competition and suspicion between the three major regions. A census held in 1973 demonstrated the problem, finding that the northern states now comprised 64 per cent of the population, up from 53 per cent ten years before, while the percentage for the western states was down. The Yoruba political leadership in the west cried foul at these findings, leading to a dispute that prevented the official acceptance of the result. The formula for dividing up oil revenues was just as controversial. The oil producing states wanted the major share, not unreasonably since it derived from their territory and given they paid the price in terms of relocation of people, acquisition of land for terminals and pipelines, and massive pollution in the Delta. The states of the west and north, meanwhile, wanted export earnings to accrue federally and to share them. Gowon came up with a formula in which 20 per cent of on-shore oil earnings and rents from the oil companies would go to the Delta states, with the rest distributed by the federal government; off-shore earnings went to the federal authorities. This formula didn't satisfy anyone. Along with the consequences of pollution and lack of local employment in the oil industry, grievances over revenue led to conflict in the Delta between local people, the oil companies and the federal government, and between local communities such as the Ogoni and Ijaw.

Between 1965 and 1973, oil earnings increased federal revenues more than fivefold. In 1972, half of all revenue was from oil; it was 87 per cent by 1987.[36] High oil prices enabled the Nigerian economy to grow 7.5 per cent annually throughout the 1970s, but this didn't lead to development or the raising of the living standards of the millions living in poverty. Imports surged and local consumer-related manufacturing grew, but agriculture contracted, with food and export crop production falling. A class of rich entrepreneurs grew up through access to foreign exchange, import deals and contracts to supply goods or services to the massive public and oil sectors. The members of this business class were closely linked to and even members of the military and the political elite in the states and Lagos. Domestic production was concentrated in areas that served the hunger for consumer goods—textiles, brewing, soft drinks, soaps and other detergents, and construction materials (with the important exception of cement). There was little in-depth development of manufacturing, industry or the private commercial sector.

While export earnings were booming, so were import costs, and there was little financial control. In 1973/74, the government and the armed forces ordered twenty million tons of cement, but Nigerian ports only had the capacity to cope with two million tons of imported goods in total. As a result, by late 1974, ports were blocked and Nigeria's shipping lanes were backed up for months. The government was paying $500,000 a day in demurrage charges for freight sitting at sea on ships.[37] At the time, there were serious food shortages resulting from poor rains and a lack of planting. It had become more profitable for merchants to import food than to buy it from Nigerian farmers and transport it within the country. The port problem slowed vital food imports. The use of oil revenues to pay for imports masked a growing crisis in the economy and a damaging imbalance between the oil sector and what one could call the human economy of Nigeria.[38]

The level of corruption was extreme, and Gowon's weak attempts to combat it were resisted at every stage by vested interests in the army, federal and state administrations. Gowon launched a policy of indigenisation aimed at ensuring Nigerian control of economic activity, including control of the iron and steel sector, majority shares in local subsidiaries of oil companies, the formation of the Nigerian National Oil Corporation (NNOC) and a 40 per cent share for Nigerians in commercial banks. This became yet another form of patronage for the government to dole out, giving posts in state companies or government contracts to political allies and former officers with no economic rationale. The normally elitist Chief Obafemi Awolowo said in October 1973 that, "A situation such as we now have, under which the good things of life are assured to a small minority of Nigerians and almost totally denied to the vast majority of our countrymen is pregnant with unpredictable dangers for all of us, if allowed to continue for much longer."[39]

Not all sections of the military were willing to tolerate the oil-driven race to economic anarchy, and on 29 July 1975, when General Gowon was at the OAU summit in Uganda, a northern general, Murtala Muhammed, staged a coup, pledging to clean up corruption and prepare the way for civilian rule. Within months, 10,000 public employees, police and army personnel had been sacked for abuse of office or incompetence. The new Supreme Military Council (SMC) government launched a mass demobilisation to reduce the size of the military by 100,000 and started divesting state resources, encouraging a greater private sector role in the economy. The twelve state governors who had resisted change under the previous regime were summarily dismissed and had their assets seized. In a bid to decentralise power, the military government announced that the twelve existing states would be sub-divided into nineteen, another attempt to break up the three regional power blocks and open up political participation at state level for smaller communities.[40] The SMC set up a Constitution Drafting Commission, with a target date of 1979 for the handover to civilian rule.

The process was nearly derailed in 1976 when a senior army officer attempted another coup and Muhammed was assassinated. But troops loyal to the SMC restored it to power under Muhammed's deputy, General Olusegun Obasanjo. Obasanjo continued the drive against corruption. His government also enacted land decrees that vested control of substantial areas of land and mineral rights in the central government, rather than in local bodies or people. Intended to make better use of land, it led to more state involvement in the economy and alienated land from the people in areas such as the Delta, exacerbating the Delta peoples' growing anger at the loss of control over their resources and their further marginalisation. Regardless, Obasanjo forged ahead with constitutional reform. In 1977 he oversaw elections to a constituent assembly meant to finalise the new constitution, which would create a federal structure of nineteen states, governed with a strong measure of central power exercised by an executive president and an independent judiciary. Parties competing nationally had to have offices in every state and had to register with the military government. This gave the military the power to ensure that parties pledging to hold the military to account for its years in power were not registered.[41]

One idea that came up during the constitutional process, and whose importance would only grow despite being left out of the constitution, was increased power for Islamic sharia courts in the north and the formation of a federal court of appeal for sharia cases. Northern politicians and religious leaders wanted more power for the sharia courts, but this was opposed by Middle Belt and southern Christians, who feared growing northern and Muslim dominance. A compromise was reached, but the issue encouraged the development of radical Muslim groups in the north, who worked to recruit poor, frustrated northerners who had benefited little from Nigeria's wealth. These twin issues—sharia law and Islamic movements combining fundamentalist religion with confrontational politics appealing to the marginalised—would come back to haunt Nigeria time and again. In the late 1970s and early 1980s, the northern cities of Maiduguri, Kano and Kaduna came under attack from the extreme Muslim Maitatsine sect. This violence was followed by Muslim-Christian clashes in the north, linked to the institution of sharia law in mainly Muslim states.[42] The movements that formed were crushed but the inheritance they left helped provide the fuel for the inferno of Boko Haram insurgency, again feeding off poverty, poor education, marginalization and resentment of the poor and non Hausa-Fulani peoples in the north east.

Elections were held in five stages from local government to the presidency between July and late August 1979. The main parties fighting them were the National Party of Nigeria (NPN) led by Shehu Shagari (a former NPC politician with easterner Alex Ekwueme as his running mate), the Unity Party of Nigeria (UPN) of Obafemi Awolowo, the Nigerian People's Party (NPP) of Nnamdi Azikiwe, the Greater Nigerian People's Party (GNPP) of Alhaji Waiziri Ibrahim, and the People's Redemption Party (PRP) of Aminu Kano. These were familiar names for the most part, dating from the previous round of civilian politics but now organised into national parties, in which dominant groups—such as Shagari's supporters from the old NPC—sought allies in other regions. The NPN won the election narrowly, with Ekwueme able to garner sufficient eastern support to give Shagari the necessary spread across states to be declared the winner. But with only 168 of 449 National Assembly seats, the NPN lacked a majority in either the senate or the house of assembly at federal level, and only controlled seven out of nineteen states. This was not a strong position from which to cope with the economic and serious political problems facing Nigeria. The elections did nothing to create a sense of national unity when the new government came to political power, and emphasised rather than diminished the country's deep regional, religious and ethnic differences. The distribution of public offices and corrupt disbursement of national revenue through informal networks was used to paper over some of the cracks. The mainly eastern/Igbo NPP went into alliance at the federal level with Shagari, more or less excluding the western states from federal power. Awolowo decided not to join the alliance, leaving the main western party in total opposition; the state governments controlled by his party refused to formally recognise the Shagari government.[43]

The federal government and state administrations proved inept and corrupt. There was gross mismanagement, graft and an accelerated flight of capital that totalled $15bn in the four years between Shagari's installation and the 1983 coup. Nigeria's foreign debts climbed to $18bn and when oil prices fell in 1982, GDP dropped by 8.5 per cent.[44] The oil slump of 1982 continued into 1983, and the Shagari government's attempt to deal with the loss of earnings through import and foreign exchange controls were poorly implemented. The government tried to allay growing poverty, unemployment and popular anger by expelling over two million West African migrants in early 1983; the expulsions were condemned by the governments of Ghana, Cameroon, Benin, Chad and Niger, and ECOWAS decried them as a violation of the community's free movement provisions. As the elections of August and September 1983 approached, Awolowo and Azikiwe refused to co-operate to oppose Shagari, who used his position in government to rig the elections,[45] ensuring a very unlikely and disputed victory.

On 31 December 1983, a Supreme Military Council led by Major-General Muhammadu Buhari seized power. It ritually denounced corruption and mismanagement, pledging to clean up government and economic management and warning there would be no rapid return to civilian rule. Politicians were arrested, or, like former Transport Minister Umaru Dikko, fled abroad. The military government later kidnapped him from Britain and tried to fly him back to Nigeria trussed up in a packing crate; he was discovered and released by the British authorities. It was a huge embarrassment for Nigeria, and only drew attention to corruption and the illegality of its government's actions. There were serious attempts to cut the government's inflated wage bill and tighter control of imports and exports, introducing the death penalty for smugglers of key commodities like petrol. This was used liberally, and public executions by firing squad were carried out on a popular Lagos beach. Street traders in Lagos sold simple wooden carvings depicting the executions, which had proved popular with poor Nigerians sick of corruption. Buhari's popularity explains his adoption as a candidate and his victory in presidential elections in 2015.

Debts continued to rise, and Nigeria was unable to come to an agreement with the IMF for financial aid in return for adjustment. Nigeria's foreign exchange crisis, resulting from debt and the flight of capital, led to barter trade with oil exchanged for imports. Political agency was increasingly exercised through the military, with loans and aid used for corruption and oil money distributed to clients and used to buy off potential opponents. Nigeria was a gatekeeper state writ large; as Richard Dowden put it,

> Everyone is for sale...In a state totally dependent on oil like Nigeria, the ruler derives his power from outsiders; the companies that extract oil and Western countries that buy it. Power oozes down from the ruler reducing the population to dependency...successive military rulers drew the oil revenue to themselves and with it, power.[46]

Nigeria suffered massive capital flight; between independence and 2008 it totalled $296.2 billion. In 2005, the Nigerian Finance Minister, Ngozi Okonjo-Iweala, revealed that "Nigeria owes $34 billion, much of it in penalties and compound interest imposed on debts that were not paid by the military dictatorships of the 1980s and early 1990s...We make annual debt repayments of more than $1.7 billion, three times our education budget and nine times our health budget."[47] Corruptly distributed or stolen money was invested or banked outside Nigeria, while debt repayments and interest bled the exchequer dry, preventing infrastructure development and service delivery. This continued under the military regimes that succeeded Buhari's period in power.

Major-General Ibrahim Babangida seized power in August 1985, accusing Buhari of failing to rescue the economy, of excessive concentration of power and of excluding powerful groups within the military from decision-making. The almost total exclusion of civilian politicians and the populace at large did not seem to be an issue. Babangida gained popularity by releasing human rights activists and journalists detained under Buhari's repressive decrees, but soon the corruption of the new administration became notorious, and journalists uncovering graft became targets for attack. One, Dele Giwa of the popular news magazine *Newswatch*, was killed by a parcel bomb while investigating stories that Babangida's wife Maryam was involved in drug smuggling.[48] Babangida was not just a thug, however, and he earned the nickname 'the Maradona of Nigerian Politics' because of his seeming ability to inflict economic and other pain on Nigerians while dodging responsibility for their suffering.[49] He tried his hand at political engineering in a way that previous military regimes had largely avoided. To try to get round the problem of regionally based parties and shifting, patronage-dependent alliances, he tried to establish parties of the left and right with economic, social and political policy at the heart of their identities, rather than regional or ethnic interests. But they proved to be nothing more than state creations funded by the military government and with their programmes written for them.[50] They could not establish roots or compete with vested military and regional networks and interests.

The path to planned elections in June 1993 was not smooth, with riots in the south in 1989 after the sacking of a leading southern officer and an attempted coup on 22 April 1990. But the transition proceeded with strong competition to head the left-leaning Social Democratic Party (SDP) and the right-leaning National Republic Convention (NRC). Moshood Abiola—a Muslim Yoruba businessman who had been a member of both Azikiwe's NCNC and Shagari's NPN—won the nomination for the leadership of the SDP. A northern businessman, Bashir Tofa, won the NRC nomination. In what has been viewed as one of Nigeria's fairer elections, perhaps because of the less obvious regional split and the lack of wheeling and dealing between regionally based parties,[51] Abiola won by a large margin. Abiola had been close to Babangida, but observers believe that Babangida never expected a party led by a southerner to win.[52] He backed away from handing over power to Abiola and cancelled the whole process before results were officially announced. Rioting by Abiola's supporters was violently suppressed, and Babangida was forced to step down by the military. For a brief period there was a civilian caretaker government, but in November 1993 it was replaced by a military government led by General Sani Abacha.

Abacha had none of Babangida's charm or political skills, and turned out to be every bit as corrupt and twice as ruthless. Angered by Abiola's protestation that he was the elected president and by the formation of a National Democratic Coalition to demand the formation of an elected civilian government under him, Abacha imprisoned Abiola. Despite appeals from across Africa, the Commonwealth and the UN, Abiola remained in prison until his death on 7 July 1998. Abacha's five years of rule were marked by brutality, the imprisonment of human rights campaigners and journalists, and the suppression of opposition. In March 1995, former military leader Obasanjo and deputy leader General Yar'Adua were arrested along with dozens of officers, accused of plotting a coup, and sentenced to death; it took the intervention of Nelson Mandela and Archbishop Desmond Tutu to get the sentences commuted. But extensive international appeals and the threat of suspension from the Commonwealth failed to stop Abacha imprisoning and then executing the Ogoni rights activist Ken Saro-Wiwa in November 1995.

Saro-Wiwa was a well-known writer and the leader of the Movement for the Survival of the Ogoni People (MOSOP), which launched a concerted but largely non-violent campaign against the pollution of the Niger Delta by oil companies. He was fiercely critical of successive governments for failing to prevent environment damage, ignoring the development of the Delta and diverting oil wealth away from the region. MOSOP demanded changes in the regulation of foreign oil companies, greater political rights, and reparations for the damage caused to Delta communities by the oil industry. The failure to take the Delta peoples' grievances seriously led to the development of movements among the Ogoni and Ijaw communities, such as the Ijaw Youth Council and the Movement for the Emancipation of the Niger Delta (MEND). Attempts to crush these movements led to greater violence and the formation of militia groups, especially after the Nigerian military killed over a thousand Ijaw civilians in raids on villages near oil installations in Delta State in January 1999. Groups such as the Niger Delta People's Volunteer Force (NDPVF) and the Niger Delta Vigilante (NDV), both primarily made up of Ijaw, carried out attacks on oil targets and the Nigerian military in the Delta. They were also involved in the theft of oil from storage facilities and pipelines, known as bunkering, which caused massive losses of oil earnings and many deaths in oil fires. The insurgent activity was accompanied by widespread banditry, and it became impossible to tell real insurgents from bandits.

This conflict has continued under the civilian governments that followed. When Abacha died in office he was succeeded by General Abdulsalami Abubakar, who oversaw the transition to civilian government. Elections were held, and former military ruler Olusegun Obsanjo was voted into power in May 1999. Obasanjo won a second term in office in 2003 and then handed over to the next elected president, Umaru Musa Yar'Adua, in May 2007. There seemed to be an acceptance in political circles that there should be alternating southern and northern presidents. This form of elected but regionally sensitive succession, was interrupted by Yar'Adua's death in office on 5 May 2010, and the inauguration of his southern vice-president, Chief Goodluck Jonathan. Jonathan's succession was one of the reasons for the growth of Islamic militancy among the deprived and marginalised peoples of north-eastern Nigeria, with Northerners complaining they had been cheated of their turn to rule.

The attraction of militant Islamist groups was also a result of Nigerian governments' failure to address poverty in the less developed north. The inability to find solutions to the alienation of poor northerners or win the battle for hearts and minds in the region has been responsible for years of violence and insurgency, often with an anti-southern and anti-Christian edge, carried out by north-eastern based Islamist groups like Boko Haram. They all appeal to the poor and powerless outside the Sokoto, Kano and Kaduna Muslim military, religious and political elite of the north that the earlier Maitatsine movement did.

Boko Haram launched its insurgency in 2009, and by 2014 thousands of civilians (both Muslim and Christian) had been killed by its attacks. The group's commonly used name can be translated as 'Western Education is forbidden', and encapsulates a total opposition to anything but a very narrowly interpreted form of education and lifestyle based on Salafist Islamic principles. The full name of the movement—Jamā'atu Ahli is-Sunnah lid-Da'wati wal-Jihād—is translated as 'People Committed to the Propagation of the Prophet's Teachings and Jihad'. The group wants to see Nigeria become an Islamic state along the lines of its particular interpretation of the religion, an interpretation not accepted by many Muslims in Nigeria and in direct opposition to the traditional practice of Islam in the north, which revolves around a centuries-old religious and political hierarchy based on the northern Nigerian sultans and emirs of Sokoto and Kano.

The Jonathan government's efforts to deal with Boko Haram were not successful. The movement has a loose structure of units spread across north-eastern Nigeria, is well-armed and able to evade capture. A massive government offensive by the military's Joint Task Force alienated the people of many areas of the north and destroyed whole villages, with huge loss of life but without seriously reducing the incidence of attacks—which in Boko Haram's case include mass killings of students and attacks on churches and mosques. The kidnapping of nearly 300 schoolgirls from

Chibok in Borno State by Boko Haram in April 2014 brought Boko Haram to international prominence and led to mass demonstrations in Nigeria over the government's failure to find the girls or deal with the causes of insurgency. Jonathan's failure to be seen to be working to rescue the girls led to growing unpopularity. As Boko Haram gained in strength and began to occupy towns and large areas of Borno, Yobe and Adamawa states, its leader Abubakar Shekau, whose profile was raised by the regular release of his videos in which he set out his aims, announced the formation of a caliphate in Boko Haram-controlled areas. The failures of the Nigeria army to cope with the insurgency and its humiliating defeats in a number of engagements were largely a result of corruption and poor leadership in the Nigerian military. Frequently army units lacked weapons, ammunition and armoured vehicles, as corruption in the allocation of the huge defence budget had enriched senior officers, defence officials and their political allies while depriving army units of the equipment with which to fight the well-armed insurgents.

This worsening military situation forced Jonathan to seek aid from neighbouring Cameroon, Chad and Niger. Boko Haram insurgents were both using border areas of these states as refuges but also carrying out attacks there. The cementing of a military cooperation pact in February 2015 led to the use of Chadian and Cameroonian troops in border areas and inside Nigeria to retake territory and limit the scope of Boko Haram attacks—though not to rescue the kidnapped girls or decisively defeat Boko Haram. The insurgency forced the government to delay the 2015 elections from February to the end of March. President Jonathan's failure to exert leadership and seeming lack of interest in the fate of abducted women and children was undoubtedly a factor in his defeat by Muhammadu Buhari. Buhari came to office pledged to defeat Boko Haram and in July 2015 sacked all the armed forces chiefs and the National Security Adviser. By the time he took office, Boko Haram had lost ground to the combined armies but was still able to mount suicide bomb attacks across the north-east and in Plateau State. They also carried out bombings in Chad in retaliation for the Chadian role in supporting the Nigerian army.

Southern Africa: destabilisation and township revolt

The upsurge in domestic opposition to apartheid in the early mid-1980s put greater domestic pressure than ever before on the apartheid system. The opposition united many black, Indian, Coloured and radical white anti-apartheid activists in the United Democratic Front, and through trade union movements that came together in the Congress of Trades Unions (Cosatu). The changed regional/strategic position after the independence of Zimbabwe in 1980, and the persistence of pro-socialist governments in Angola and Mozambique meant that external pressure on South Africa was maintained.

The National Party government's reaction was to implement what it called its 'total strategy' to resist what it said was the total onslaught against the apartheid system. This strategy's underpinnings have been described as "a paranoid, Manichean view of a world in which the West was threatened by a total strategy led by an aggressive communism."[53] This world view was held with varying levels of sincerity and credulousness by the NP's members, but was adopted partly to appeal to the Cold War sentiments of Western leaders and thereby to stave off the threat of economic sanctions or support from Western governments for the ANC or PAC.

The proponents of the strategy, Prime Minister and then State President P.W. Botha, and his Defence Minister Magnus Malan, wanted to combine limited domestic political reforms in South Africa and the encouragement of a small and anti-ANC black middle class with an aggressive propaganda campaign against SWAPO, the ANC, Cuba and the Soviet bloc both inside and outside South Africa, and an interventionist regional strategy to protect white control in Namibia and South Africa. The homelands policy would be pursued vigorously to try to divert black political aspirations and maintain the fiction that blacks were actually citizens of homelands, not South Africans. Alongside this would be attempts to give very limited political roles to Indians and Coloureds as part of a divide-and-rule policy.

South Africa wanted to work with the West strategically. It tried to get American support or at least acquiescence for its use of force against the ANC and the states that supported it, and for destabilisation to keep its neighbours weak and vulnerable. It continued to promote the idea of a constellation of states in Southern Africa based around South Africa, Namibia, the homelands and friendly states like Malawi and Swaziland.[54] When regional resistance proved this was unviable as a long-term policy, South Africa was prepared to use military force to undermine governments that supported the ANC, PAC and SWAPO. Angola and Mozambique were the main targets, but Zimbabwe was hit as well and pressure put on Malawi and Zambia in the form of threats to their transport links to the outside world—there were also sporadic attacks against specific ANC targets in Lesotho and Botswana. One objective of this strategy was to undermine regional transport and communications, which would weaken economies and make them more dependent on South Africa. In Angola, South Africa continued to support UNITA and deployed special forces in the south. Not only was UNITA a strong ally with potential to challenge the MPLA militarily, but the zones it controlled with South African backing in the south and south-east of the country formed a buffer zone to help protect the Namibian border. With support from the SADF, and later with American funding and arms supplies, UNITA was able to establish substantial areas of control and larger areas of operation in south, east and central Angola.[55]

Angola was also a prime target because it both embraced Marxist-Leninist ideology and allowed SWAPO and the ANC to establish military camps and training facilities there with assistance from the Soviet Union, East Germany and Cuba. That allowed South Africa to ward off Western criticism of its military tactics by citing the Soviet/Cuban threat. Attacks by the SADF in the late 1970s escalated into a major invasion of southern Angola in 1980, which captured the important town of Mavinga, 250km north of the Namibian border.[56] South African forces destroyed major towns and economic infrastructure in the south and displaced 130,000 people. Between 1981 and 1984, the South African army and air force attacked key economic installations in Angola, including the iron mines at Kassinga, the Lobito oil terminal, a Luanda oil refinery, and an oil pipeline in Cabinda; they captured towns as far north as Cangamba, 450km from the border. In late 1983 and early 1984, a major South African offensive to capture Lubango and Kassinga only ended when the Soviet Union privately warned South Africa against escalation of the conflict. In the mid-1980s, Soviet diplomats based in Ivory Coast and Tanzania told me that Moscow had warned it would supply arms to support a combat role for Cuban troops in Angola against the South Africans.[57] The USSR increased arms deliveries and training for the Angolan army and air force, and Cuban advisers played a bigger role in Angolan operational units—though according to a well-placed Soviet source, they stopped short of a major commitment of Cuban troops in the south.[58]

Angola launched a major offensive against UNITA in late 1983, in which SWAPO and ANC forces fought alongside the Angolan army. The threat of a major escalation brought diplomatic pressure from the US, which was worried by the possibility of a Cuban counter-offensive in the south. With support from President Kaunda of Zambia, US Assistant Secretary of State for African Affairs Chester Crocker tried to scale down the military confrontation. Crocker wanted to get both the South Africans and the Cubans to withdraw, and he later wrote that he was not prepared to have US policy in the region "stalled while South Africa stoked regional wars and the 'military track' became an end in itself."[59] This pressure, and South Africa's realisation that Angola was prepared to use the Cubans in the south, led to a disengagement agreement in Lusaka in February 1984, under which the SADF pulled back to near the Namibian border. But it never withdrew entirely, and retained a military presence in areas of Cuando Cubango and Cunene.[60]

South Africa's raids on oil and other installations and the effective defensive shield it provided enabled UNITA to operate freely in the south, east and parts of central Angola, with a liberated area based at Jamba in Cuando Cubango province. UNITA received a major boost when the US congress repealed the Clark Amendment, which banned US support for the group, and from 1986 Washington provided UNITA with financial and military aid. The weapons supplied by the Americans were sent to UNITA via South Africa, but there was also evidence that President Mobutu was allowing the Kamina air base in southern Zaire to supply UNITA forces in eastern Angola. But the American supplies weren't sufficient for UNITA to withstand the well-equipped and better-trained Angolan forces, and in September 1985, the Angolan army recaptured Mavinga. To prevent a major defeat for UNITA and Savimbi, the South Africans returned in force, using aircraft, helicopters and troops from 32 Battalion to destroy the advancing Angolan column near Mavinga.[61]

By early 1987, Soviet deliveries of advanced air defence equipment and MiG-23 aircraft began to turn the tide in southern Angola. The commander of the South African air force, General van Heerden, admitted that the Angolans now had the capacity to provide air support for their ground forces across southern Angola and into Namibia. The Americans continued their aid to UNITA, but stepped up the search for a negotiated solution. Washington's priority was to get the Cubans out and reduce Soviet influence in the region. Angola began to talk to Washington about these aims, something which reportedly angered Castro.[62] But at the end of July 1987 he and President dos Santos signed a communiqué proposing a phased re-deployment and then withdrawal of Cuban forces linked to progress on Namibian independence, which the Americans and South Africa saw as a step towards a deal.[63]

Militarily, the South Africans felt that despite the improvement in Angolan air strength, the Angolan defeat near Mavinga had weakened its army enough to stop it carrying out further major offensives against UNITA. But in August 1987, Angola launched a new offensive near Mavinga.

The South Africans initially pushed the Angolans back, inflicting heavy losses on them at the Lomba river and forcing them back to the strategic town of Cuito Cuanavale. The SADF and UNITA laid siege to the town, and large numbers of UNITA guerrillas died in attacks on its defences. Although much of the town was destroyed, the Angolans held out; the Angolan air force shot down between a dozen and twenty South African aircraft, and about 230 SADF troops were killed. This level of losses was unexpected, and was politically unsustainable for the SADF.

At this point, Dos Santos asked the Cubans for help, and Castro sent a Cuban division in Angola to the south. In early 1988, Dos Santos threatened to use the Cuban division against the South African forces around Cuito Cuanavale. By May 1988, there were 12,000 Cuban combat troops in southern Angola supporting Angolan and SWAPO forces.[64] When a South African attack ended with a tank unit trapped in a minefield with the loss of several irreplaceable tanks, the South Africans and UNITA were forced to pull back. With the rainy season looming and Angolan and Cuban troops to the north and south of the SADF units, Pretoria risked a deeply damaging loss. It couldn't afford further loss of life and equipment, or the regional and domestic effect of a major defeat. This realisation coincided with a change in Soviet policy, with Gorbachev keen to reduce commitments and involvements in Africa. This convergence allowed a series of meetings to start in London in May 1988, bringing together the Angolans, Cubans, Americans, Soviets and South Africans. The result was an agreement on a South African and Cuban withdrawal.

The negotiations also led to movement on Namibian independence, and the passing of a series of resolutions by the UN Security Council that set in motion the withdrawal of South African forces, the unbanning of SWAPO, and elections held under the auspices of the UN Transitional Assistance Group (UNTAG). By the end of June 1989, President de Klerk of South had formally declared the dismantling of apartheid in Namibia and an amnesty for returning SWAPO members. In elections in November 1989, SWAPO won 57.3 per cent in a UN-supervised election, and on 21 March 1990, Namibia became independent under a SWAPO government led by President Sam Nujoma. SWAPO remains the governing party, with victories in a series of elections, but with regular changes of president, rather than the Mugabe style of retaining power in the hands of one man.

Mozambique also suffered from South Africa's regional destabilisation campaign, with Pretoria using the Mozambique National Resistance Movement, Renamo,[65] as its weapon against the Frelimo government. The entire

Renamo operation had moved to South Africa just before Zimbabwe's independence in 1980. The South Africans provided it with weapons, funds, bases near the Mozambican border and boosted the reach of the Voice of Free Africa station, which they ran for the movement. Renamo's move to South Africa coincided with serious defeats; its rebels were driven out of their Gorongosa stronghold and Manica province in 1980. South African aid kept Renamo fighting, with helicopters and naval units delivering arms to rebel forces scattered across central Mozambique. This was combined with the direct involvement of South African special forces in sabotage, which damaged Mozambican economic infrastructure and cut road, rail and oil pipeline links from Zimbabwe to Mozambique's ports.

The first successful attack was in November 1980, when the Mutare-Beira pipeline was cut, acting as a warning to the Mugabe government that its support for Frelimo, the ANC and SWAPO could end in tears. But the Renamo attacks also damaged the economy of Pretoria's ally, Malawi, which was dependent on oil and other supplies freighted in from Beira and Nacala. When I was working in Malawi in 1981 and 1982, there were frequent petrol shortages as Renamo or the South Africans disrupted rail and road links. Although South Africa retained close links with Banda's government, the wily Malawian leader was aware that the tide was gradually changing, and he joined the Southern African Development Co-ordination Conference (SADCC) when it was formed in 1980 to promote regional integration and to "mitigate the effects of economic dependence" on South Africa.[66] Diplomats and Malawian politicians told me at the time that attacks on routes to Malawi coinciding with the November 1981 SADCC summit were a warning that Pretoria would not allow its friends to get too close to the frontline states.[67] But Malawi continued to try to cut it both ways; it was an active member of the SADCC, but also allowed South Africa to use Malawian territory to supply Renamo and offered Renamo fighters sanctuary. This came to a head in September 1986, when Mozambique's President Machel and Zimbabwe's Robert Mugabe personally threatened Banda face-to-face that they would take military action to blockade his borders if he didn't end his support for Renamo.[68]

A month later, as Machel was returning by air from a summit in Zambia where Southern African leaders put pressure on President Mobutu to end his support for UNITA, his plane hit a mountain in South Africa, near the Mozambican border, and all on board were killed. South African military forces and the Foreign Minister, Pik Botha, were at the scene remarkably fast to grab documents from the wreckage. They claimed it was an accident, but SADCC leaders believed the plane had been guided into the mountainside by a South African radio beacon; I was in Dar es Salaam at the time of Machel's death, and a Tanzanian Minister, Ben Mkapa, told me that his government had evidence that the plane had been brought down by the South Africans. South Africa's Truth and Reconciliation Commission later uncovered evidence that this account was correct.[69]

The most far-reaching effect on Mozambique was the destruction of economic infrastructure, local government and agricultural output. The combination of destabilisation, insurgency, droughts and floods caused a major humanitarian crisis in 1984, and aid agencies such as Oxfam and Save the Children mounted major relief operations. Renamo had residual support in areas where Frelimo was weak and the effects of the civil war weakened Frelimo even further, while not necessarily strengthening overall support for Renamo.[70]

By 1990, civil war and South Africa's military and economic destabilisation had reduced Mozambique to total dependence on aid and financial support from the IMF and World Bank. It became one of the most indebted countries in the world on a per capita basis.[71] The combination of pressures forced the country to join the World Bank and IMF and accept structural adjustment, to end most of its socialist policies, and to reach a peace agreement with Renamo. South African support had made Renamo into a true political movement, one that had to be politically accommodated when Mozambique sought peace. The peace deal gave Renamo the legal status of a party in a new multiparty system, and offered amnesty for the crimes it had committed. The end of the war enabled reconstruction to start in Mozambique, but Renamo remains a thorn in the side of the government and despite its repeated defeats in national and local elections, it remains a threat, with the retention of military forces and periodic threats to go back to the bush by its embittered leader, Afonso Dhlakama.

The destabilisation campaign was part of South Africa's doomed attempt to protect apartheid, but it also worked to serve the broad Western attempt to force states to accept Western trade, financial and economic policies or models and give up alternative routes to development.[72]

Zimbabwe was also a target for South Africa's destabilisation campaign. The ZANU election victory in 1980 was a shock for the South Africans; along with the British, the Americans and states like Zambia, the NP had expected Joshua Nkomo's ZAPU to win and lead a government willing more inclined to compromise with South Africa. Mugabe had a radical reputation, although he was not on the best of terms with the ANC, which was allied with ZAPU. Zimbabwe made clear its support for liberation, but said it would not allow the ANC to set up camps in Zimbabwe. Mugabe's government had a lot for fear from a hostile South Africa; trade had developed under the Smith government, and as a result of sanctions, was heavily dependent on South Africa, particularly on South African ports. Zimbabwe was also militarily vulnerable to South Africa due to an extensive shared border, and ZANU was aware that members of militias loyal to Bishop Muzorewa and Ndabaningi Sithole (who had co-operated with Smith in the failed internal settlement) had fled to South Africa, as had military personnel from the Rhodesian army's controversial Selous Scouts, Grey's Scouts and Special Air Service units. In August 1981, a South African hit squad made up of former Selous Scout members assassinated the ANC representative in Zimbabwe, and the following month there was an attack on the Zimbabwean army's Inkomo barracks in which $36 million worth of military equipment was destroyed. Mugabe held South Africa responsible, and accused it of bombing ZANU party headquarters in December 1981.[73] In July 1982, ten combat aircraft from the Zimbabwean air force were blown up on the ground at the Thornhill air base, including new Hawk jets supplied by the British government.

Pretoria was then given a golden opportunity to intervene in Zimbabwe with the growing conflict between ZANU and ZAPU. The two parties had co-operated unwillingly under frontline states' pressure in the Patriotic Front alliance, and Mugabe had appointed Nkomo and other ZAPU leaders to his first cabinet. But in March 1982, large arms caches were found on ZAPU-owned properties across the country. Nkomo was accused of hiding arms for use in the event of conflict with ZANU. ZAPU leaders Nkomo, Josiah Chinamano and Joseph Msika were sacked from the government, and former commanders of ZIPRA (ZAPU's military wing), Lookout Masuku and Dumiso Dabengwa, were arrested.[74] ZAPU properties were confiscated and financial assets frozen. This directly hit former ZIPRA combatants and ZAPU members working for ZAPU-owned companies and farms; it also added to ZIPRA's grievances over being the junior partner in the formation of the new Zimbabwean army.

In early 1982, a ZIPRA backlash began with attacks against ZANU officials and government targets in Matabeleland. ZIPRA cadres returned to the bush, taking their weapons with them. As the violence increased, so did the ferocity of the ZANU government's response; it accused ZAPU of plotting to overthrow the elected government and working with South Africa, although to this day there is no direct evidence that Nkomo or ZIPRA/

ZAPU leaders collaborated with the South Africans. As the violence escalated, attacks were carried out by South African-trained and directed units, which were made up of former auxiliary forces loyal to Bishop Muzorewa and which became known as Super-ZAPU. There were three groups active in carrying out attacks on government targets in the south-west: ZIPRA, Super-ZAPU, and assorted ex-guerrillas or others who had seized weapons and were little more than bandits.[75] The conflict lasted for four years and was marked by the brutal actions of army and police units, particularly the predominantly ZANU-staffed and North Korean-trained Fifth Brigade.

The government military campaign hit the region very hard, and coincided with a drought. The Fifth Brigade was indiscriminate in its violence against civilians and suspected dissidents. Estimates of the numbers killed have varied dramatically, with reports by the Catholic Commission for Justice and Peace—the most reliable source until the Zimbabwean government allows access to government documents—saying that between 1982 and 1987, over 20,000 civilians were killed by the army, police and other security forces.[76] The security forces destroyed homesteads and even entire villages; it detained civilians en masse, and subjected them to torture, including rape and mass beatings.[77]

Dissident activity was brought to an end with the 1987 Unity Accord, which integrated ZAPU into a broader ZANU-PF coalition. This ended the political violence but emasculated political opposition, and seemed to vindicate the use of violence to crush opposition,[78] a lesson Mugabe did not forget. But South African destabilisation continued: on 19 May 1986, the SADF and air force launched a two-pronged attack on Harare and Lusaka against ANC targets in both capitals.

The South Africans also attacked ANC offices in Botswana and Lesotho. In December 1982, the SADF attacked ANC offices and homes of members in Maseru, killing thirty South African exiles and twelve Basotho civilians. The pressure was escalated during the 1980s with South African financial and military support for the opposition Lesotho Liberation Army of Ntsu Mokhehle, which sought to overthrow the government of Chief Leabua Jonathan. This included SADF help for sabotage operations, such as the destruction of oil storage tanks in Maseru in February 1983. Botswana, the most democratic state in sub-Saharan Africa, did not have a dissident movement to support, but South Africa conducted military raids across its border on a number of occasions, notably on Gaborone in June 1985; that raid killed twelve and destroyed the ANC offices.

While some Southern African countries turned to the Soviet Union, China, Cuba or North Korea for arms and training to resist South Africa, the broader regional response was the formation of the SADCC. This was an effort to foster regional economic co-operation and free the economies of member states from their dependence on and vulnerability to South Africa. Botswana's President Seretse Khama said this was not only a response to South African attacks and economic pressure, but part of a bigger effort: that, "Only in co-ordinated action can small independent states of Southern Africa achieve the economic strength and power necessary to resist those who are tempted to exploit us and to perpetuate our economic fragmentation and dependence."[79] While there were serious attempts to co-ordinate policy in transport and communications, the SADCC was chiefly a symbol of resistance to South African power. Little was done to integrate economies and break down trade barriers. That said, the SADCC did establish the foundations of today's Southern African Development Community (SADC), which is trying to make good on post-apartheid South Africa's economic strength and potential while protecting the interests of economically weaker states. It too has had limited success, partly because of competition between Zimbabwe and South Africa for leadership and Mugabe's resentment of the arrival of Mandela, Mbeki and a powerful, democratic South Africa. Like other African regional and economic organisations, the SADC has had limited effect on the overall structures of international economic relations or regional trade.

Domestically, P. W. Botha's total strategy led to cosmetic reforms to apartheid structures and removed some petty aspects of separate development while retaining the core of white political and economic domination.[80] Botha tried to split opposition to apartheid by bringing Coloureds and Indians into the white laager. Changes included lifting the ban on mixed marriages and abolishing influx control in the hopes of developing regulated urbanisation—which was meant to help create a black middle class—and the establishment of elected councils in black townships. But ultimately, white control was not negotiable, and minor reforms were only ever going to have a marginal effect. The councils and homeland governments would be the limit of black political participation, and the piecemeal reforms only served to heighten the contradictions in the system.

Trades unions reform, for example, opened the way not just for more successful pay bargaining, but also for black workers to organise and to play an important political role in emerging mass organisations. The reform process, limited though it was, proved too much for hardline conservatives in the NP. The leading conservative voice within the party, Andries Treurnicht, led a revolt within the Transvaal National Party, but was outmanoeuvred by Botha and F. W. de Klerk. Treurnicht then led an exodus of intransigent supporters of apartheid and formed the Conservative Party. A plethora of other groups began to spring up on the far right of white politics, including the paramilitary Afrikaner-Weerstandsbeweging (AWB) of Eugene Terre'Blanche, fiercely opposed to any concessions to the black majority or to international pressure for change.

Through his role as defence minister, Botha had close ties to the military command, to military intelligence and other security organisations. Under his leadership, the security apparatus was to become the dominant group within government. Botha made the State Security Council the apex of the national security management system; it dominated the remaining years of NP rule, to the extent that it eclipsed the cabinet and parliament.[81] On the political front, Botha implemented plans for a tricameral parliament that would give representation to Coloureds and Indians, though retaining white control, with the whites having a built-in majority.[82] The office of executive state president was created; elected by an electoral college of fifty white MPs, twenty-five Coloureds and thirteen Indians, the state president would have far-reaching powers and control over the administration of black affairs.

These plans were greeted with outrage by the black majority and by most Coloured and Indian organisations. The planned reforms and the continued exclusion of the black majority from political participation outside the homelands or tame local councils sparked township revolts, and in August 1983 it led to the formation of the United Democratic Front (UDF). An alliance of 565 civic, community, church, union, student, women's and youth groups, the UDF started its political life with protests and mass demonstrations against the tricameral parliament and township councils. While whites had voted in a referendum to accept the new constitution, when black township elections were held only 19 per cent of people voted in Durban, 15 per cent in the Vaal Triangle, 11 per cent in Port Elizabeth, and 5 per cent in Soweto.[83] Elections for the new parliament were held amidst countrywide demonstrations by the UDF and violent repressive responses by the security forces; only 16 per cent of Coloureds and Indians voted. Through its protests the UDF gained a high profile as a non-racial mass movement.

While it was not founded on the initiative of the ANC, many of the UDF's leading members, including Archie Gumede, Oscar Mpetha and Albertina Sisulu, were very close to or former leading members of the ANC, and the group's patrons were the ANC's Nelson Mandela, Walter Sisulu and Govan

Mbeki. Many of its leaders were drawn from the ranks of those who had supported the Black Consciousness Movement of Steve Biko, but who now supported the ANC. Although officially unaligned—since openly siding with the banned ANC would have got it banned too—the UDF and its allied trades union movement Cosatu rapidly became, to quote activist and later ANC MP Andrew Feinstein, "a thinly-disguised, mass-based internal wing of the ANC that developed a remarkably open and non-racial culture."[84] The UDF contained a wide variety of groups and differing ideologies—pro-ANC, Africanist and Black Consciousness as well as various shades of socialism and Marxism. Its general secretary, Popo Molefe, had been part of the black consciousness-styled Azanian People's Organisation. Molefe was detained without trial for three years and then sentenced to jail after a trial at which sixteen UDF leaders were accused of treason (in a re-run of the 1950s trial used to try to break the ANC). Like many UDF leaders, Molefe later became an ANC member, and was premier of North-West Province until 2004.

The UDF's success in mobilising against the NP's meagre reforms led to a wave of repression and violence. Demonstrations in townships in Johannesburg and the Vaal triangle were brutally suppressed and violence followed protests against the new black councils' attempts to put up rents. At least 175 people were killed in township violence in 1984; most died at the hands of the police, but some were black councillors who supported the government. ANC guerrilla attacks inside South Africa increased in the early 1980s, starting with the spectacular blaze after an attack on the Sasolburg oil plant in 1980. But the ANC's actions were less important than the combined UDF mass actions and Cosatu strikes. The year saw rent, bus, school and other boycotts, demonstrating the ability of black protestors and boycotters to make the townships largely ungovernable—something called for repeatedly by ANC leaders from exile and by the ANC's Radio Freedom, which was heard and discussed widely among UDF activists.[85]

In 1985, 879 people were killed in political violence, and there were 390 strikes involving 240,000 workers.[86] In the townships most black councillors resigned, leaving UDF-linked local organisations in effective control. In areas like the informal Crossroads settlement outside Cape Town, the government's security and internal intelligence groups—such as the notorious Civil Co-operation Bureau (CCB)—funded, armed and helped conservative or even criminal groups to attack UDF supporters.[87]

Cosatu, meanwhile, became a mass-based and powerful body that worked closely with the UDF. It included powerful unions like the National Union of Mineworkers (NUM), and between 1980 and 1987, strikes increased five-fold. In 1987, an NUM strike closed down a third of gold and coal mines for three weeks, ending in a negotiated settlement that established the reputation of the NUM head Cyril Ramaphosa, who would go on to be chief ANC negotiator with the NP and then South Africa's deputy president. The growing power, militancy and political role of the unions was crucial; UDF/Cosatu actions, South Africa's economic problems and foreign financial pressure would all ultimately combine to force the NP to dismantle apartheid and unban the ANC.[88] By the end of the process Cosatu was highly politicised, and it later became part of the ANC-SACP alliance.

The government declared a state of emergency in thirty-six districts across the country in July 1985, giving the police and army wide powers to use violence and to detain people without trial, while banning the media from reporting most of the events. This did not stop the violence; the total death toll in 1985 and 1986 exceeded 2,000 and tens of thousands were detained, including more than half the regional leaders of the UDF. Several hundred of those killed were black policemen, councillors or suspected informers, but the majority were protestors killed in police, army or vigilante violence. The violence spread to include resistance to the repression attempted by homeland leaders, notably in KwaNdebele and Bophuthatswana. Large-scale killings by the security forces attracted international condemnation and made it hard for South Africa's allies in London and Washington to hold the line against the rising pressure for sanctions. There was also growing violence in Natal, KwaZulu and the townships around Johannesburg between UDF supporters and those of KwaZulu Chief Minister Mangosuthu Buthelezi's Inkatha movement. By 1987, the security forces had deployed 8,000 troops to support the police; vigilante groups in the townships and groups such as the CCB were involved in the kidnapping, torture and assassination of UDF activists and suspected ANC members. Alongside growing economic problems, with mounting industrial unrest, high inflation and increasing indebtedness, the extent of the protests and violence seriously threatened South Africa's stability.

The final element that tipped the balance for change was international pressure for sanctions and disinvestment. This was brought to a head on 15 August 1985 by a speech Foreign Minister Pik Botha had promised would be a turning point. Western political and business leaders hoped that amid the violence, the Botha government would move to enact serious reforms that would bring the black majority onside—but in his speech, President Botha made it clear he would make no further concessions to black demands. This disappointed leaders like Ronald Reagan and Margaret Thatcher, who had been hoping for reforms that would give them room to keep resisting calls for international action.[89]

A crucial international response to South Africa's crisis was Chase Manhattan Bank's calling in of South African loans. South Africa owed $13 billion, due to be repaid by December 1985; other banks followed Chase, causing a massive outflow of capital. Disinvestment by US state or local administrations saw $4.5 billion in investments withdrawn, while sanctions were imposed by Canada, Australia, New Zealand, the Scandinavian countries and then the USA, where Reagan's veto was overridden by a congress influenced by a massive public opinion swing against South Africa. Despite the Conservative government's opposition to sanctions, British companies began to shed their South African investments. In private, even Reagan and Thatcher were beginning to put pressure on South Africa, while appearing publicly sympathetic.[90] In the late 1980s, leading South African businessmen such as Gavin Relly of the mining giant Anglo-American and non-NP politicians met ANC leaders in Zambia, Senegal and London. Alongside this were constant global calls for the release of Nelson Mandela. By the end of 1988, recognising the key role he would inevitably play in the future, the South African government moved Mandela to a cottage in the grounds of Victor Verster Prison near Cape Town, where he was able to receive visitors and gradually engage in the political process, meeting Botha in July 1989.

The NP was besieged in its laager by the combination of domestic resistance, economic decline, industrial unrest, global financial and diplomatic pressure and by the force of regional strategic issues—not the least being the debacle at Cuito Cuanavale and the moves towards Namibian independence. And when President Botha suffered a stroke in August 1989 and was replaced as president by F. W. de Klerk, the writing was on the wall for apartheid.

Walter Sisulu was released from prison in October 1989, and it became clear that Mandela wouldn't be far behind.[91] De Klerk met Mandela in prison, and was more willing than his predecessor to take radical steps to end apartheid. On 2 February 1990, he announced to parliament that the ANC, SACP and PAC were unbanned, and that Mandela would be released. After twenty-seven years in prison, Mandela walked to freedom on 11 February.

The scene was set for the long negotiations, accompanied by much verbal and physical violence, which led to the total dismantling of apartheid and the elections that brought Mandela and the ANC to power.

HIV and AIDS: a threat to life and development

Although HIV/AIDS is thought to have originated in Central Africa in the 1930s, the first recorded major outbreak was in Kinshasa in the 1970s, and it only began to reach epidemic proportions in Africa in the early to mid-1980s.[92] Transmitted sexually, from mother to child in pregnancy or through contaminated blood transfusions or needles, the virus destroys the immune system, leaving the sufferer vulnerable to a range of infections; tuberculosis is endemic in Africa, and is the major cause of death for those who have contracted HIV.

Speaking in London on 13 March 2000, a decade and a half after HIV/AIDS had been recognised as a deadly disease that could kill millions and drastically undermine social cohesion and economies alike, the Ghanaian-born UN Secretary-General Kofi Annan said that, "AIDS is a major crisis for the continent, governments have got to do something. We must end the conspiracy of silence, the shame over this issue." Announcing the launching of a UN study of AIDS in Africa, he conceded that this would meet with resistance from some African leaders; identifying what was one of the key political problems in combating AIDS, he said that while some leaders had begun to speak about it, most were still reluctant to confront it. "If I say that we must get people to use condoms, I find I'm said to be encouraging people to be promiscuous—this won't do." Annan pointed out that where the crisis was addressed—as it was by Ugandan President Yoweri Museveni, who called for the use of condoms and changes in sexual habits—previously catastrophic rates of infection were reduced.[93]

At the turn of the millennium, twenty-three million of the world's thirty-six million people infected by HIV/AIDS lived in sub-Saharan Africa. Annan lamented that in Ivory Coast one teacher died because of AIDS every school day, and that in Botswana a child born in 2000 had a life expectancy of 41, as opposed to 70 before HIV/AIDS. Quoting UN figures, he added that in Zimbabwe, government projections showed that within a few years HIV and AIDS could consume 60 per cent of the health budget, and that AIDS permeated the military and police to such an extent that neither group could be used as blood donors. But in countries like South Africa, Malawi and Zambia, where infection rates were extremely high, the subject was still taboo.

A decade after Annan spoke, thirty-four million people worldwide were living with AIDS, of whom 68 per cent or 23.12 million were in Africa. 1.9 million people per year were being infected, and over one million were still dying annually from the disease's effects—the majority of them in Southern Africa. It was the most common cause of death and illness in Africa.[94]

Yet despite major epidemics in Ethiopia, Nigeria, South Africa, Zambia and Zimbabwe, and catastrophically high infection rates in Uganda, Kenya, Botswana and Swaziland, the last ten years have seen a gradual decline in infection and improvements in health care and anti-AIDS campaigns, with the overall incidence in sub-Saharan Africa declining by 25 per cent between 2005 and 2009.[95] The sexual transmission of the disease has enhanced the stigma attached to it, and has inhibited public discussion and government action, while the attitude of the churches, especially the Catholic Church, towards the use of condoms and the discussion of safe sex has greatly obstructed efforts to halt the spread. Only major government efforts, such as Uganda's, have been able to mount campaigns, distribute condoms and address the crisis head-on to start slowing the disease's spread and help its sufferers.

In Southern Africa, one of the worst affected regions from the 1990s onwards, some governments were slow to react or were staunchly opposed to the accepted approaches to prevention and drug treatment. In South Africa, where Nelson Mandela and his wife Graca Machel broke the silence on the disease, AIDS sufferers were often stigmatised, and until his political demise in September 2008, Thabo Mbeki and his government stood out against supplying antiretroviral drugs to sufferers.

Mbeki came out with bizarre ideas about the infection, its causes and what to do about it. In 1999, six million South Africans (15% of the population) were reported as HIV positive, yet Mbeki still opposed the mainstream position on HIV/AIDS, asserting that HIV does not necessarily cause AIDS and that antiretroviral treatments were toxic. Mbeki's health minister, Dr Manto Tshabalala-Msimang, was known as Dr Beetroot because of her insistence that beetroot, garlic and other vegetables or herbs would cure or prevent AIDS; she resisted the allocation of resources to the necessary information campaigns, drug provision and health programmes. When she was removed from office in September 2008 by Mbeki's successor, Kgalema Motlanthe, her replacement was AIDS campaigner Barbara Hogan, who revolutionised AIDS policy in South Africa with the support of the ANC and AIDS campaigning groups. In 2008, HIV/AIDS researchers at Harvard estimated that Mbeki's policy had led to the deaths of 300,000 people who could have been saved with more viable science-based policies.[96]

Outside South Africa, Botswana and Swaziland have been particularly hard hit, perhaps due to histories of labour migration, small populations and social mores. When I interviewed Botswana's then Vice-President

Festus Mogae in Gaborone in 1993, HIV/AIDS was a problem; in June 2001, President Mogae told the UN General Assembly that without assistance and concerted action, "We are threatened with extinction. People are dying in chillingly high numbers. It is a crisis of the first magnitude."[97] But the Botswana government, aid organisations, the World Health Organisation and major companies all worked to fight the epidemic, which threatened serious demographic, social and economic decline. Campaigns about safe sex or abstinence, the supply of free condoms and the provision of antiretroviral drugs all helped stem the spread and combat high death rates. By 2009, while a quarter of the population over the age of fifteen were HIV positive (300,000 out of 1.2 million in a total population of two million) the campaigns were beginning to have an effect. Life expectancy had risen from the low of under forty in the first five years of the new century to 53 in 2011.[98]

Swaziland was even worse affected than Botswana. Health monitoring programmes showed that by 1996, the incidence of HIV among pregnant women was 26.3 per cent, and the national rate of infection was the worst in Africa. By 2005, the Swazi government estimated that within a decade it could lose 32 per cent of its adult workforce to HIV/AIDS;[99] 75 per cent of the country's orphaned children had lost their parents to the disease. The mounting crisis caused King Mswati III to declare AIDS a national disaster in 1999 and establish the Crisis Management and Technical Committee (CMTC), which developed a national plan to fight HIV/AIDS. Programmes were started to try to change sexual behaviour and to ameliorate the disease's effects, though the need for significant resources was not always translated into policy in a country where the King, his numerous wives (at the time of writing they numbered thirteen) and his retinue eat up a huge proportion of government income while poverty alleviation remains a low priority. Swaziland's progress in dealing with AIDS has accordingly been slow: statistics for the number of pregnant women infected show the 1996 level rising to a massive 42.6 per cent in 2004, and only falling a little to 41 per cent in 2010.[100]

When UNAIDS Executive Director Michel Sidibé visited the country in 2010, he emphasised the need for Swaziland to improve its HIV prevention efforts and said that estimates suggested three in every 100 people in Swaziland would be infected with HIV every year if prevention was not improved. Swaziland is, though, one of just five sub-Saharan African countries to achieve the target of getting more than 80 per cent of eligible people on antiretroviral treatment, with access to the drugs among pregnant women at 95 per cent. As the AVERT organisation has pointed out, there is a need for more work to prevent the spread of infection among women, since two out of every three newly-infected people are women and "one in three women experience sexual violence before the age of eighteen showing how vulnerable young girls are in the country. The common practice of polygamy also puts women at greater risk of becoming infected with HIV as this practice often involves multiple sexual partners."[101]

If progress has been made in some countries, HIV/AIDS is still a major humanitarian, social and economic crisis for Sub-Saharan Africa—and the chief reason, as with other diseases like malaria, diarrhoea and TB, is poverty. HIV leaves people vulnerable to other pathogens, and Africa's deepening poverty has created fertile ground for the spread of infectious diseases, with low living standards, poor access to clean water, sanitation and basic health or welfare services ensuring that infectious diseases are still rife and are a deadly threat to those who are HIV positive. Almost half of all Africans lack access to safe water and adequate sanitation. The lack of resources to maintain or develop health services, with greatly reduced health spending in the wake of the IMF and World Bank's structural adjustments and privatisation programmes, has meant that most African states don't have the capacity to substantially reduce the impact of HIV/AIDS—a problem compounded by the threat posed by malaria and other endemic diseases.[102]

Of course, HIV/AIDS should not lead us to ignore the threat to health and economic development from other health issues and diseases, notably the poor provision of potable water across Africa and the massive problem of fighting malaria. Malaria kills a child every minute in Africa, and the continent loses an estimated US$12 billion annually in economic output because of the effects of malaria and the costs of combating it. Over one million Africans die from malaria each year, and the continent accounts for 85 per cent of the world's malaria cases. WHO figures suggest that over recent decades malaria has caused more deaths in Africa than HIV/AIDS and tuberculosis combined.[103] The only glimmer of light is that the WHO reports that countries such as Cape Verde, Eritrea, Namibia, Botswana, Swaziland, South Africa, Sao Tomé and Príncipe, Rwanda and Tanzania have all made some progress in combating the disease through mosquito eradication programmes, the supply of insecticide-treated mosquito nets and education about prevention.[104]

In 2014 and 2015, the Ebola virus emerged as a major threat to life in areas of West Africa. An outbreak starting in Guinea spread to neighbouring areas of Sierra Leone and Liberia. The poor state of the health services in these countries—a result of years of civil war and the effects of SAP-inspired cuts in public spending—meant the countries were poorly prepared for the disease, which spread rapidly through contact with bodily fluids of the victims, often during preparation of bodies for burial. Between March 2014 and July 2015, at least 11,193 people were reported by the WHO as having died from the disease in six countries—Liberia, Guinea, Sierra Leone, Nigeria, the USA and Mali—though the organization believes more may have died unrecorded. Nigeria, with more developed health services, rapidly contained the outbreak, but the first three countries suffered the most and continue to fight pockets of the disease. The Western media discourse presented the outbreaks as a result of the states being backward and corrupt, playing up the role of Western agencies while to a great extent ignoring the sacrifice of Guinean, Liberian, and Sierra Leonean health workers. It led to a Ebola scare in the USA and Europe, as small numbers of aid workers returned with the disease, some of them dying. Yet again, Africa as a whole was represented as affected, with scare-mongering media reports depicting it as a continent ravaged by ebola. Only a few accounts detailed the problems of poverty, poor sanitation and water supply and the effects of war and SAP as responsible for the spread of the disease and the difficulty in fighting it.[105] Little coverage was given to Nigeria's success in eradicating Ebola or similar positive stories from previous outbreaks in Uganda.

5

THE RAINBOW NATION, RWANDA'S GENOCIDE, AND THE GOOD GOVERNANCE BALANCE SHEET

As African states wrestled with the challenges and pains of structural adjustment, the international environment changed dramatically with the end of the Cold War and the demise of the Soviet Union. The ensuing realignment in the structure of global power had major consequences for the changes that were beginning to take place in Africa, particularly the upsurge in popular, chiefly urban, demands for greater political participation and accountability.

From the last days of the 1980s and into the new millennium, news from Africa was dominated by South Africa's progress to democracy, the disintegration of the state in Somalia, the horror of the Rwandan genocide and its legacy for the whole Great Lakes Region, and the complex web of wars and insurgency in West Africa. The combination of events proved Africa's potential for democratic development. But it also revealed the continuing structural weakness of African states and their institutions, their economic and political vulnerability to external influence, and the struggles African peoples faced as they tried to exercise their agency in the face of resistant authoritarian elites.

Good Governance: the new mantra for Africa

Growing popular impatience with incompetence and corruption, combined with the maturing of the first generations born since independence, meant that the late 1980s and early 1990s saw an upsurge in demonstrations, strikes and demands for democracy and accountability in many states. These protests were closely linked with the growing economic pressures on populations, exacerbated by structural adjustment, economic decline and the failure of governments to deliver acceptable living standards. They also coincided with or closely followed the dismantling of authoritarian, statist systems in Eastern Europe and the Soviet Union.

Inevitably, the African democracy movement was attributed to copycat motives or to external actors; African autocrats such as Gabon's Omar Bongo were keen to jump to this conclusion, and to divert attention from their people's dissatisfaction with them. Bongo described the end of the Cold War as "a wind from the East that is shaking the coconut trees,"[1] and Western decision-makers and commentators often took a similar view. Former US Assistant Secretary of State Chester Crocker wrote that the West's Cold War victory in the Third World set the stage for the dramatic turn away from one-party autocracy and "towards democracy and political reconciliation", and that African dictators had lost their freedom of manoeuvre.[2] He could have added more candidly that Western governments no longer had any need to support corrupt autocrats like Mobutu, Doe, Banda and Bongo. The West pulled the financial and military plugs. But not straight away, and not always in ways that helped establish more democratic and viable systems.

As demands for democracy spread across Africa, Western governments became obsessed with pressuring states to hold multi-party elections rather than helping them create their own systems of accountability and representative government. Western governments which now demanded good governance as a condition for financial aid gave too little attention to building non-political civil society organs: free media, neutral civil services, independent judiciaries and other institutions that would end impunity and encourage accountability. Instead, elections and other Western-set criteria became part of the 'good governance' agenda, which was added to the SAPs still being forced on struggling economies.

The end of the Cold War and the use of conditionality for aid and loans did not cause the surge in demands for democracy, although they did weaken regimes whose poor accountability, political misrule, economic incompetence and corruption had undermined their legitimacy, while increasing the grievances of ordinary people. The big mistake of Western policy and of many of Africa's new opposition parties was to concentrate on party politics, plurality of choice at elections and the elections themselves—rather than on the broader challenges of building democratic civil societies.

The end of the Cold War also reduced the bargaining power of those leaders who received Soviet bloc support, and governments in Ethiopia, Angola and other Marxist-leaning states lost both an ally and source of arms. Strongly pro-Western governments found they could no longer play the Soviet threat card to resist conditionality or Western pressure for change. Even those who were non-aligned suddenly had less room for manoeuvre, as the end of the Cold War meant Africa was even more marginal internationally and more vulnerable to Western pressure, having lost its strategic value. Until China came on the scene as a major no-strings economic player in Africa at the end of the 1990s, there were no alternative sources of aid or economic models available.[3] But it must be emphasised that, as Bayart put it, "external dynamics played an essentially secondary role in the collapse of authoritarian regimes—however much a tenacious myth suggests otherwise."[4] The challenge to authoritarianism in many states preceded the fall of the Berlin Wall and the disintegration of the communist states.

The good governance and democratisation process was superficial, and it became simply another tool used by Western governments to try to exercise control. The cutting of public spending and weakening of public institutions through SAPs had damaged service delivery and the capabilities of states, but without fatally weakening political elites and their patronage/client networks. An example of this is years of Western sanctions have, signally failed to weaken Robert Mugabe's hold on power in Zimbabwe, but have helped impoverish the population.

Many leaders were able to adapt their systems of rule to the new realities and to manipulate multi-party systems just as adroitly as they had the independence constitutions and military or one-party systems. There were changes and there have been huge advances in many countries in political participation, including development of freer media and freedom to organise, but the African political world was not totally turned upside down in 1990. Adept leaders were able to hang on using the advantages of state power or informal instruments of violence for political ends—whether the security forces, police, party militias and even criminal gangs on hire to the highest bidder (as happened with the use of the criminal Mungiki sect and Kalenjin street gangs in Kenya in 2007–8). In many states, elections have proved to be "one-time only vehicles through which governing elites consolidate their domestic hegemony, snuffing out the *institution* of free elections and short-circuiting other elements of constitutional democracy."[5] Equally, they were periodic episodes, frequently leading to the recalibration of informal networks and patron-client relations and providing opportunities to air grievances—episodes often roundly exploited by political actors, with only a limited exercise of popular choice.

The mere existence of opposition parties was not in itself an indication of a society in which freedom of association, speech and action were entrenched and in which groups that were apolitical and independent of parties could exist and operate to articulate opinion and, along with functioning opposition parties, ensure accountability outside election periods. Colonialism had severely restricted the activities of what one could term open civil society; colonised populations' freedom of speech was heavily curtailed, and formal organisations were channelled into ethnic or tribal networks. Decolonisation had generally seen unions, women's groups and youth groups destroyed or absorbed into ruling parties. When multi-party politics re-emerged, the new parties tended to be built around politically active individuals who had left or been excluded from ruling groups. That meant politics was based on personalities and/or sectional interests rather than policy, issues or ideological differences, and it remained very urban in character. The democratisation movement did little to end the marginalisation of rural people; attention was only paid to them when politicians needed to mobilise the vote at election time or drum up opposition to new parties (as President Moi did in Kenya's Rift Valley in the early 1990s). In extreme situations this led to unrest, as national or regional/local incumbents sought to exclude challengers, through force or through promises of patronage or the incitement of suspicion or hatred of 'otherness'. This is what happened in Kenya in 2002 and 2007 and in Rwanda, in the lead up to the 1994 genocide.[6]

Yet it would be wrong to suggest there was no change. In the first two years of the 1990s, eleven African heads of state were removed from power as protests escalated—though only four were removed through elections (Kerekou in Benin and Kaunda in Zambia being the most prominent leaders voted out). By 1992, eighteen heads of state had lost power, and many of those who remained had had to change their tune; even Félix Houphouët-Boigny of Ivory Coast bowed to domestic pressure and to President Mitterrand's demands that Francophone countries become more democratic or risk cuts in aid.

In the late 1980s, opposition to Houphouët-Boigny's authoritarian rule and to the austerity imposed by his government led to strikes by teachers, public servants and students. By early 1990, the momentum for change in Ivory Coast was so strong that when Mitterrand weighed in, it became too much to resist. Ever the astute political operator, Houphouët-Boigny refused to hold a national political conference, which had been the vehicle for change in many Francophone countries, and instead organised multi-party elections for the end of the year. This gave his ruling PDCI party a decisive advantage as his opponents, led by Laurent Gbagbo, a former history professor Houphouët-Boigny had jailed in the 1970s, had to start the task of building and financing a party from scratch. Gbagbo gathered considerable support, but he lacked the state resources that his opponent could harness and had little access to the media, which was controlled by the ruling party. He received 18.7 per cent of the vote, against 81.7 for Houphouët-Boigny. This pattern was repeated in countries such as Togo, Gabon and Cameroon, where Presidents Eyadema, Bongo and Biya (who had replaced Ahmadou Ahidjo when he stood down in 1982) were able to use state power, media control and coercion by party thugs and the security forces to ensure that the attempt at democracy, even with a multiplicity of parties and periodic elections, was conducted within an overall structure that ensured the locus of power remained unchanged.

Donors and international financial institutions had naïvely expected that privatisation and the divestment of state resources would encourage plurality and end the monopoly of patronage and resources enjoyed by ruling parties and presidents. But divestment usually saw state resources sold off to allies of the political elite within a privatised patronage network. The granting of government contracts, therefore, became a way to simultaneously reward allies, maintain patron-client relations and deny economic resources to opponents. The state patronage system was simply replicated, and in its new form it could still enable the retention of political power and gatekeeping networks. Where there was a change of president and ruling party, countries really did little more than shuffle the pack of established political actors, with new parties and their leaders drawn from political elites who saw multi-party politics as a route to power at the expense of their former patrons. Elections or protests could become a means for people to get on the gravy train rather than derail it—as Kenyans say, politicians, their clients and communities saw opportunities to ensure that "it's our turn to eat."[7]

The democratisation movement has not been what campaigners hoped for in the early 1990s, but it started a process that continues to this day, with the development of more freedom to criticise and campaign against governments and the space for greater media freedom. Journalists, editors and their papers, radio or TV stations and websites remain subject to harassment, intimidation, bribery and arbitrary use of repressive laws. Nonetheless the press, broadcast and online media have expanded, and a majority of countries now have a plurality of media and a growing climate of criticism.

In Zambia, for example, the growth of the free media began with journalists like Fred M'Membe and the establishment of the *Post* newspaper in 1991—before the multi-party elections that voted Kenneth Kaunda out of power.[8] Since the early 1990s, many states have developed vibrant newspaper, media and online services that have become very critical of governments. In Nigeria, newspapers like *Punch*, *Daily Trust*, *Vanguard* and the *Premium Times* have reported both criticism of and demonstrations against the government and military over corruption, the scandals in the oil sector, and the failure to provide security for schools and civilians against Boko Haram attacks. These are just some examples of how the African media has begun to operate in a more effective way.[9] The plethora of newspapers, websites and commercial radio or TV stations that have developed may often be sensationalist, partial and closely linked with political elites (often owned by them through proxies) but the media environment is freer, discussion and criticism more open and political debate is taking place publicly.

The course of the democratisation surge that began in the late 1980s varied from state to state, but it often started—in Benin, Ivory Coast, Madagascar, Mali, Niger and Zambia, for example—with strikes and student protests. As demonstrations developed in one country they spread to neighbours; discontented urban groups with greater access to news realised that they could wring concessions from governments through protest, and that conditionality and good governance provisions for aid could assist their campaigns. This knock-on effect was particularly evident in Francophone Africa after Benin's President Kerekou was voted out of office. A number of states followed the Beninois example of holding a national conference to rewrite the rules of the political game, including Congo, Gabon, Madagascar, Mali, Niger, Togo and Zaire; they led to elections or other forms of regime change in Congo, Madagascar, Mali and Niger,[10] while Gabon and Togo's ruling presidents managed to use them to retain power and to call elections before the opposition could organise itself.

Another good example of change in one state prompting demands in others came in Zambia, Tanzania and Zimbabwe. Tanzania was a one-party state under the rule of the Chama cha Mapinduzi (CCM) and Julius Nyerere's successor, Ali Hassan Mwinyi. Zimbabwe had a multi-party system, but one in which state and military power had been used to crush the opposition and there were moves towards a *de facto* if not *de jure* one-party state. When, President Kaunda signalled the end of one-party rule in Zambia at the end of 1990 and opposition parties began to form, this encouraged activists who were agitating to develop or protect plurality in Tanzania and Zimbabwe.[11] The two states' governments went in opposite directions: Tanzania ended its system of one-party rule and allowed opposition parties and competitive elections. By contrast, Zimbabwe used all forms of state and informal power to intimidate both opponents and the electorate, while rigging elections to ensure that Mugabe and ZANU-PF stayed in power (see next chapter).

In Zambia, which did not have a history of harsh repression of dissenters, the Kaunda government had been unable to tame the strong confederation of trades unions, the ZCTU, which was based on the mineworkers of the Copperbelt. With opposition to structural adjustment mounting, an alliance of young activists, trades unionists, and politicians expelled from or marginalised by the ruling party forced Kaunda to concede to the principle of multi-party politics. He allowed parties to form and held elections, perhaps hoping that his standing and the institutional power of his ruling UNIP party would see him through. But the new Movement for Multiparty Democracy (MMD) chose ZCTU head Frederick Chiluba as its candidate, and had the support of sections of the business community who were disenchanted with the government's economic incompetence. It also appealed to younger Zambians. By the early 1990s, a significant proportion of population of sub-Saharan Africa had been born since independence and known nothing but independence, and for them, single-party or single-ruler government could not be justified on the basis that the rulers had won independence; they wanted higher living standards and the chance to question or even remove their governments if they did not perform.

Kaunda himself listened to his electorate, and when Chiluba and the MDD defeated him in the October 1991 elections, he stepped down with some grace. Sadly, Chiluba, about whom there had been accusations of fraud when he was head of the ZCTU and which circulated at the time of his election as MMD leader,[12] proved to be more personally corrupt than Kaunda. He was no better than his predecessor at preventing corruption among his ministers and officials, and was little inclined to accept that electoral politics meant he needed to be accountable, that the opposition had a right to criticise him, or that his own party would contain varying shades of opinion. Chiluba passed legislation to strip Kaunda of his right to stand in future elections on the grounds that his parents were Malawian.

He won re-election in 1996, and in 2001 he tried to amend the constitution so he could run for a third term—not just to retain power, but because by being in office he could avoid corruption charges. But his own party had had enough and refused to back him; his successor as MMD leader, Levy Mwanawasa, won the 2001 elections and instituted corruption charges against him—though the trial fell apart. In a civil case brought against him in Britain, Chiluba was found guilty of stealing $46m. The British judge said Chiluba had shamelessly defrauded his people and flaunted his wealth amid the poverty of his nation.[13] Up to the present, Zambian politics have been lively, marked by fierce verbal conflicts within and between parties and the continuation of corruption as part of the currency of politics and economic life. But there is real and regular competition for power and the basis for further progress—the system has been able to cope with the death in office of Mwanawasa and then Michael Sata (who defeated Rupiah Banda, the incumbent, in 2011).

The demand for an end to one-man and one-party rule spread to Malawi, which soon saw growing opposition from groups with a measure of independence, such as the Catholic church, along with protests by students and workers. Banda's close relationship with the West and his conservative economic policies had failed to bring development or reduce dependence on tobacco, tea and sugar, and that poor record combined with the changes taking place in the region to give domestic protest more force. In addition, the end of the Cold War meant that could no longer rely on South African aid or automatic Western backing based on geopolitical calculations. With the defeat of Kaunda in Zambia and the introduction of plural politics in Tanzania, Banda was more isolated than ever. He had ruthlessly crushed domestic dissent, and had created a climate of fear in which people dared not speak out or even privately question his actions, but he began to lose control as the economy faltered and crucial donors demanded changes in governance—especially the breaking up of agricultural parastatals and Banda's Press Holdings, the basis of his complex web of patronage.

In March 1992, amid the suppression of growing opposition, a Pastoral Letter issued by Malawi's Catholic bishops denouncing the oppressive policies of Banda and the Malawi Congress Party was read out in churches across the land. A deeply religious country, Malawi reeled from the church's open attack on Banda, and it sparked a wave of protests in favour of a multi-party system. Banda resisted, but the suspension of $174m in budget support by international donors forced him to hold a referendum on the issue. Held on 14 June 1993, the vote resulted in a strong majority in favour of political reform, despite extensive harassment of campaigners by the MCP's youth wing and the police. There were large majorities in favour of reform in the marginalised northern region and the commercial centres in the south; Banda had more support in his home area in the central region, which had benefited most from his rule.[14] He was ultimately voted out of office in May 1994 in Malawi's first multi-party vote since independence—Bakili Muluzi, a former minister and MCP leader who had fallen foul of Banda, became president.

Malawi's road to developing an accountable and workable democratic system has been a rocky one ever since, with Muluzi trying to change the constitution to stay in office and his successor, Bingu wa Mutharika, becoming increasingly corrupt and autocratic—resorting to lethal force to crush student demonstrations in 2011. Unable to change the constitution as Muluzi did, Mutharika was thought to be preparing the way for his brother to become president, partly to avoid a successor pursuing corruption charges against him, but he died unexpectedly in April 2012.

This resulted in a brief attempt by his brother and a group of cabinet ministers to override the constitution to prevent the vice-president, Joyce Banda, from succeeding him. But support for the constitution from the police and the army and a wave of press and social media criticism of what amounted to a constitutional coup stopped the plotters in their tracks. There wasn't time for popular protest, but the educated elite used Twitter, Facebook and other social media to generate opposition to a coup, with the army and police supporting Joyce Banda. Following the rapid development of this online and social media campaign, I could see and record the way the head of steam generated among Malawi's politically literate class helped convince the army, police and judiciary to stick to the constitution rather than disregard it.[15] Joyce Banda was sworn in as Malawi's first, and Africa's second, woman president on 7 April 2012, an example not only of growing support for constitutionality and the impact of an increasingly free media, but also of the expanding role of women in African politics. Nonetheless, her two years in power—she lost deeply flawed elections to Mutharika's brother, Peter, in May 2014—were marked by a series of corruption scandals. Some related to long-standing forms of graft, but the 'Cashgate' scandal, when ministers and senior public officials were caught with huge quantities of embezzled currency in their houses, showed that Banda had failed to get to grips with the problem of integrity in political and public office.

In Kenya, President Daniel arap Moi had succeeded to the presidency after the death of Jomo Kenyatta in 1978, and had taken over Kenyatta's network of patronage and political clients—though without depriving the Kenyatta family of the fortune they had amassed since independence. Moi became head of the ruling party, KANU, and over the following years he built his own networks based on the Kalenjin communities of the Rift Valley, the Masaai and other smaller ethnic communities, gradually pushing out the Kikuyu grandees like Charles Njonjo, who had been a mainstay of Kenyatta's period in power.[16] Other leading Kikuyu politicians were bought off or disgraced. The Luo of Oginga Odinga (and later his son Raila) remained marginalised. Moi used his client network and the coercive powers of the state to retain power and to ensure that when he began to move towards plural politics—under heavy domestic pressure and American and British threats to withhold aid—he did so in a way that enabled him to keep tight hold of the reins of power and wealth accumulation while building ever stronger patronage networks in the Rift Valley.

The movement for political liberalisation in Kenya was led by a mixture of former ministers and KANU leaders who had fallen from favour under Moi, alongside nascent civil society groups from the legal profession, human rights activists and sections of the church. Moi tried to deny them the chance to propagate their views with arrests, harassment and a ban on meetings and by trying to prevent the broadcasting of their views—but the sheer breadth of opposition,[17] supplemented by Western pressure, forced Moi to agree to the legalisation of political parties and the holding of elections in 1992. He moved fast to hold the elections before the fragmented opposition had time to organise. But Moi had been less inclusive than Kenyatta and many communities felt excluded, providing a focus for opposition.

As Moi liberalised Kenyan politics, he began a very clear strategy of informalising political power and coercive force, a means both of retaining a power base in the Rift Valley and protecting the wealth of his client network should he lose power nationally. This informalisation was "characterised by the looting of the Kenyan state, and by transforming some of Kenya's gangs into ethnic militias."[18] The result was a groundswell of overtly ethnic politics encouraged by ambitious elites for whom community grievances over land, development or access to education could be politically exploited through emotive appeals to fear and ethnicity. It needs to be stressed that these ethnic rivalries were developed and manipulated by political leaders. They were not, as the media often presents them, primordial, primitive ethnic or tribal antagonisms. There was no concerted or consistent history of hatred or violence between different groups in Kenya; divisions were caused by poverty, marginalisation and the frustration of those outside the patron-client networks rather than by abiding ethnic enmity.[19]

The financing and arming of local militias made violence a theme of Kenya's elections, and there were major incidents in 1992, 1997, 2002 and 2007. Moi used armed Kalenjin militias to break up opponents' meetings, drive "outsiders" such as the Kikuyu and Kisii from areas of the Rift Valley (land then being seized by Moi's local clients). His Kalenjin supporters were accused of carrying out ethnic cleansing in the Rift Valley in the 1990s, a period which saw over 2,000 deaths and 500,000 displaced in land conflicts.[20]

Rwanda and the Congo: civil war, genocide and descent into regional war in the Great Lakes

The genocide in Rwanda had its origins in the way that the complex and centuries-old political and economic relationships between the state's Tutsi and Hutu populations had been distorted, first by colonisation and then by the Hutu revolution that preceded independence. After independence, the Hutu supremacist Kayibanda government's rule benefited relatively few Rwandans, even among the majority Hutu community. Kayibanda's ideology was based on the Hutu supremacy set out in the 1957 Bahutu Manifesto: his government concentrated power and distributed patronage among those from his own regional power base in southern Rwanda, and excluded northern Hutu. Under Kayibanda, Tutsi were excluded from politics and deprived of access to education. They were labelled as outsiders who had subjugated the Hutu majority by force, and who must now be permanently excluded from power.[21] Hutu fear of the Tutsi was entrenched though the use of racist ideology, and given impetus in 1963 when Tutsi guerrillas based in Uganda and eastern Congo mounted raids into northern Rwanda.

Tutsis forced into exile had established insurgent groups; they received some support from neighbouring states such as Uganda or Burundi, or operated in border areas of Zaire where the government had little or no control. In December 1963, a Tutsi insurgent raid on the Bugesera region of Rwanda resulted in a government-encouraged pogrom, and in the weeks that followed, "Rwanda lived through an unprecedented orgy of violence of murder targeted against Tutsi"; the final death toll was estimated at between 10,000 and 14,000.[22] Tens of thousands more Tutsis fled Rwanda, many of them joining the guerrillas in Uganda. The government labelled the insurgents *inyenzi*, the Kinyarwanda word for cockroaches, and that term was used to make fear and dehumanisation of the Tutsi a part of everyday political discourse.

This ethnic scapegoating did not protect Kayibanda from the discontent caused by economic decline, which arose from Rwanda's dependence on fluctuating revenues from coffee and tin. On 5 July 1973, he was overthrown in a coup led by the army chief, Juvenal Habyarimana. The coup enshrined the dominance of Hutu groups from the previously marginalised communities in the north and north-west.[23] While Habyarimana was a northerner, he was not from the strongly-anti-Tutsi clans of the north-west. By October 1990, when the Tutsi-led Rwandan Patriotic Front (RPF) invaded northern Rwanda from Uganda, Hutu from the north and north-west held a near monopoly of senior positions within the government, the army and the economy.[24] After taking power, Habyarimana had moved to soften the racially-based ideology of Hutu; this didn't mean the Tutsi gained equality, but they were now viewed as a Rwandan ethnic group rather than as racially different outsiders. This was intended to reduce tensions and outbreaks of violence by ending concerted persecution. The Tutsi were still excluded from higher positions in local and central government, the civil service and the army they had better access to education and more freedom to engage in commerce.

Habyarimana created his own political party, the Revolutionary Movement for National Development (MRND), to replace Kayibanda's Parmehutu and entrench his regime as the sole power in Rwandan politics. Administrative reforms established systems designed to ensure maximum political control down to village level. This system was an adaptation of the pre-colonial hierarchical political culture, and its potential to mobilise ordinary Rwandans on a mass scale would be central to the organisation and implementation of the 1994 genocide.[25]

The identity card system for all Rwandans was made more rigorous, with both ethnic origin and place of residence included on the cards. But the government failed to halt Rwanda's economic decline, with the country still at the mercy of adverse weather and falling coffee and tin prices. Overcrowding and land shortages became extreme, and the expanding population had no surplus land to increase export crop or food production. The resulting fall in export income sapped the regime's resources for the patronage it relied on to maintain political control and ensure a minimum level of client loyalty, and competition for new means of accumulating wealth and political influence was intense.

The main conflict was between government and party leaders gathered around the president's wife Agathe and her clan members, and Hutu elites outside this network. The network was known as *le clan de Madame* or the *Akazu* (Kinyarwandan for Little House). It had extensive influence over the president, and since they were drawn from the north-western clans, who had been the last Hutu in Rwanda to be brought under Tutsi control during the period of Belgian rule, its members had a fierce hatred and suspicion of the Tutsi. The *Akazu*'s powerful political, military and business leaders wanted harsher policies towards the Tutsi than Habyarimana.

Just as most other African states did, Rwanda experienced a surge in demands for democracy in the early 1990s as students, educated people from the professions and businessmen demanded greater accountability from the government. Many came from Hutu communities in central and southern Rwanda that had been marginalised under northern Hutu dominance. Aid donors, including the French and Belgians, put pressure on Habyarimana to democratise, and in September 1990 he bowed to the pressure and established a commission to examine political reforms—but its work was delayed when northern Rwanda was invaded by the Tutsi-dominated Rwandan Patriotic Front (RPF) and its army, the RPA.[26]

The RPF's hallmark was its military leadership and experience. Its main leaders, Fred Rwigyema, Paul Kagame and Adam Wasswa, were exiles who had fought for and gained senior positions in Ugandan leader Yoweri Museveni's NRA in the 1980s; Rwigyema became the NRA's chief of staff and then Uganda's deputy minister of defence. Once Museveni had taken power, the prominence of large numbers of Rwandan Tutsi exiles in the army and government became a political embarrassment for him and the NRA, and in November 1989, Rwigyema and other leading Tutis lost their posts. This spurred them on to use the RPF to force change in Rwanda.

Their initial aim was to bring about the return of Rwandan exiles with guarantees of their safety. To achieve this and their bigger goal of equality for Tutsis within Rwanda, they could call on the military experience of the large numbers of Tutsis who had fought for the NRA. The RPF claimed to represent all Rwandans, but it was Tutsi-led and made up largely of Tutsi exiles and their descendants. The 2,500-strong RPA force that invaded Rwanda on 1 October 1990 had a strong officer and NCO corps of 150, all with combat experience in Uganda. It was well-armed, most of its weapons having been taken from the Ugandan army—most likely with the NRA's knowledge.

The RPF posed a serious threat to Habyarimana, and its invaders exploited the element of surprise, advancing 60km into Rwanda. But when

Fred Rwigyema and two senior officers died in fighting (or, as some accounts have it, in a factional internal struggle),[27] the RPF was pushed back towards the Ugandan border and Paul Kagame took command, opting for a strategy of guerrilla warfare. The Habyarimana government reacted with a military offensive, along with internal repression and propaganda against Tutsi and pro-democracy activists. Within days of the invasion, the government arrested over 13,000 suspected opponents, most of them Tutsi, and adopted a harsher attitude towards the Tutsi minority. The *Akazu* group, Hutu businessmen and senior army officers all feared for the future of their power and wealth, and they started building an alliance that would become the genocidal Hutu Power movement.

While Habyarimana's first concern was to stay in power, Hutu Power wanted above all to exclude the Tutsi from any share in government or the economy. Encouraged by the government and supremacist propaganda, ordinary Hutu were mobilised to oppose the RPF, which Foreign Minister Casimir Bizimungu described as a terrorist organisation hellbent on "leading the nation's dynamic forces back to feudal drudgery and enslavement."[28] Everything about the conflict was framed by government sources as being about Tutsi hegemony and Hutu subjugation. The RPF was supposedly attempting to bring Rwanda back under Tutsi dominance and to reinstate the exploitation of the Hutu. In the Gisenyi prefecture, local leaders told Hutu that "their communal work duty for the month would consist of fighting their Tutsi neighbours," and initiated a massacre: "The Hutu went to work with singing and drumming, and the slaughter lasted three days; some 350 Tutsi were killed."[29] The government even staged a fake RPF attack in Kigali in October to increase fear and elicit military support from France, Belgium and Zaire. France had sent 150 troops to Kigali immediately after the RPF invasion to protect French nationals and the airport; this force was increased to 600 following the Kigali 'attack'.

The president tried to use the RPF invasion to unite Hutu and prevent the rise of political groups that could threaten his hold on power. But Hutu supremacists feared that Habyarimana had gone soft on the Tutsi and on moderate Hutu politicians, and would sell out Hutu hegemony to retain power for himself. While the government used Radio Rwanda and government newspapers to get across their message, the Hutu Power group had founded a violently anti-Tutsi newspaper, *Kangura*, and in mid-1993 had set up the virulently pro-Hutu Radio-Télévision Libre des Mille Collines (RTLM), which broadcast a stream of Hutu extremism and incitement against the Tutsis.

As the war with the RPF escalated, the political environment in Rwanda changed. Moves towards ending one-party rule and legalising opposition parties continued under domestic and foreign donor pressure, and by the middle of 1991, Habyarimana had been pushed into allowing the registration of opposition parties. A plethora of parties emerged: the main ones were the Republican Democratic Movement (MDR—Parmehutu reborn), the Liberal Party (PL), the Social Democratic Party (PSD) and the Christian Democrat Party (PDC). Alongside this political activity, the Hutu Power movement was growing. In March 1992 the Coalition for the Defence of the Republic (CDR) was formed, representing militant Hutu increasingly worried that Habyarimana was giving in to the opposition parties and foreign pressure; it would vehemently oppose the peace process with the RPF.

With a tightly regimented population who had either lived through the final days of Tutsi dominance or been brought up in a climate of Hutu supremacy and demonisation of the Tutsi, it was not hard for Hutu supremacists to use the war to raise the spectre of a Tutsi resurgence and the prospect that the Hutu could be enslaved. Alongside this propaganda, the Hutu were being organised into local defence groups and militias. In 1990 the government launched a civil defence programme that established local patrols organised by commune or prefecture officials and armed with traditional weapons such as machetes. Hutu Power politicians within the MRND and the more militant CDR also established, trained and armed militias with the assistance of army and police commanders. The largest militia was the Interahamwe, which had developed from the MRND youth wing and provided employment for large numbers of jobless, poorly educated rural and urban youths.

In March 1992, Habyarimana gave in to pressure and signed an agreement with opposition parties to form a coalition government. The new government had little real power and could not challenge the president's control of the administrative machinery, the security forces or militias, but the changes it signalled nonetheless scared Hutu supremacists. The new education minister, Agathe Uwilingiyimana (of the MDR), ended the quota system that limited Tutsi access to education, and the new government wanted to negotiate with the RPF. Habyarimana let the talks proceed, and a ceasefire was agreed on 6 July 1992. Negotiations on the constitutional future and integration of military forces began in the Tanzanian town of Arusha, but Habyarimana obstructed progress and the talks dragged on. The ceasefire did not last; the RPF accused the government of killing innocent civilians, and it launched a new offensive in February 1993, in which it advanced to within striking distance of Kigali.

Negotiations continued amid the renewed fighting, and the Arusha Accords were signed in Tanzania on 4 August 1993, establishing a new ceasefire and the process for forming a broad-based government including ministers from both the RPF and the five parties in the existing coalition. The implementation of the accords was to be overseen by a 2,500-strong UN force, the UN Assistance Mission to Rwanda (UNAMIR) led by Major-General Romeo Dallaire of the Canadian army. The ceasefire and the accords were not welcomed by many MRND members or Hutu Power, and the army was fearful of integration with the RPF. The first UNAMIR troops arrived in Kigali in November and a 600-strong RPF battalion was stationed in Kigali, but there was no progress on setting up the broad-based government laid out in the accords. At the same time, UN commander Dallaire was getting information from his informers within the Interahamwe that it was training young men across the country, and that lists of the Tutsis living in every commune were being drawn up so that when the time came they could be rounded up and exterminated.

In the last week before the start of the genocide, the Hutu Power radio station RTLM and other Hutu Power media warned of a coming bloodbath in Rwanda and accused the RPF of intending to break the ceasefire.[30] On 2 April 1994, RTLM broadcast clear threats against the new prime minister, Agathe Uwilingiyimana, calling her a traitor and saying she had had betrayed the Hutu people. The station also broadcast a warning to Habyarimana that the nation would not tolerate a leader without popular support, and that there would be no escape for him.

Habyarimana flew to Tanzania for a meeting with regional leaders, including President Cyprien Ntaryamira of Burundi; they put pressure on him to fully implement the Arusha accords. He then left Dar es Salaam in his presidential jet, accompanied by Ntaryamira. As it came in to land in Kigali on the evening of 6 April, the aircraft was shot down. The identity of whoever fired the missile is unlikely ever to be proved conclusively, but the most recent and believable version is that it was shot down by a ground-to-air missile fired from within the Presidential Guard camp, suggesting that Hutu militants in the armed forces were responsible. This was the result of an inquiry by a French judicial and forensic team, and it supports the view that Hutu Power killed Habyarimana, blamed his death on the RPF and then used it as justification for their pre-planned campaign of extermination against the Tutsi and Hutu moderates.[31]

The speed of the reaction to the president's death, with targeted attacks immediately launched against political leaders and the beginning of the general assault on the Tutsi, certainly indicated extremely careful planning. Interahamwe roadblocks were in place within forty-five minutes of the plane going down; editing that night's BBC World Service *Newshour* programme from London, I'd barely read the first reports of the president's death when news came through of roadblocks being set up and of shooting in Kigali. Within hours of the death, RTLM accused the RPF and the Belgians of killing the president and called for vengeance.[32] Hutu militias and the Presidential Guard forces were already at work in Kigali, killing prominent Tutsi on prepared lists. Within twenty-four hours, Prime Minister Uwilingiyimana was killed along with her ten-man Belgian UNAMIR protection force and several moderate ministers. The UNAMIR commander, Romeo Dallaire, says that within a few hours of the death of the president he was getting reports that the Presidential Guard, gendarmerie and Interahamwe were going from house to house in Kigali with lists of names of those to be killed. UNAMIR forces were kept out of Kigali city centre on the night of 6 and 7 April by roadblocks manned by heavily armed troops and militiamen.[33]

The genocide was implemented on a massive and organised scale, with Hutu civilians joining the army and the militias in hunting down and killing Tutsi and suspect Hutu, and between 6 April and mid-July 1994, between 500,000 and 800,000 were killed. The slaughter was going on alongside a new phase of the war with the RPF, which the Hutu army ultimately lost. A few days after the start of the mass killings, the RPF launched a new offensive and steadily pushed back the Rwandan army, taking Kigali on 4 July. On the following day Pasteur Bizimungu (a Hutu and former MRND member who had joined the RPF) was sworn in as president, with Kagame as vice-president; sixteen out of twenty-two cabinet ministers were Hutu. RPF control of the whole of Rwandan territory was only prevented by the presence of French troops in much of the south-west of the country. They were there ostensibly as part of a mission to provide a safe haven from the war and genocide, but many still suspected them of providing a refuge for fleeing Hutu leaders responsible for the genocide but allied to France.[34] France withdrew its troops in August 1994, bringing the whole of Rwanda under RPF control.

The establishment of control by the RPF and the mass exodus of Hutu had lasting consequences for the whole Great Lakes region. The *Génocidaires* retreated to Zaire, driving nearly two million Hutu into exile. One witness has described how the retreating Hutu militants were among the wealthiest refugees in African history: they had systematically looted Rwanda before their flight, leaving little. They took huge amounts of cash in Rwandan francs, foreign currency, all the buses from the Rwandan national transport company, the country's fuel reserves, much of the year's coffee crop, tanks, armoured vehicles, huge stocks of weapons and ammunition, and six military helicopters.[35] Among those who fled into Zaire were the bulk of Rwanda's regular army and thousands of Hutu militiamen. The areas around Goma, Bukavu and Uvira in Zaire became almost exclusively Hutu provinces, with organised armed forces, militias and around 1.2 million Hutu civilians camped there.

This was extremely destabilising. The complex ethnic make-up of the Great Lakes region is not in itself a cause or "central determinant"[36] of conflict there, but the dislocation of communities by colonial borders, the movement of economic migrants and refugees and the porous borders, and the lure of valuable mineral resources all make it vulnerable to self-serving political leaders and to foreign interference. This generated conflict and sharpened ethnic differences—and the arrival of over a million Rwandan Hutu and the extension of the Rwandan conflict across the border had an explosive impact.

The international community, which had at first refused to accept that a genocide was being perpetrated, suddenly saw the human tide flowing into eastern Zaire as a humanitarian disaster of major proportions—while continuing to pay little attention to what had been left behind in Rwanda. The result was a massive and dangerously ill-advised aid effort. In a miscast act of repentance for ignoring the genocide and its victims, the UN and USA launched a huge operation to airlift tents, water, food and other vital supplies to the refugees. The USA sent over $400 million and 4,000 military personnel to eastern Zaire, but nothing to the survivors in Rwanda, where over two million people had been displaced and hundreds of thousands killed. As the NGO effort went ahead full speed, with clinics and feeding stations set up to serve the dozens of refugee camps set up in Zaire, "the old, extremist Rwanda that had settled undisturbed in Goma was being reborn as a state within a state. The Hutu leaders created *préfectures* in the camps, which they subdivided into *communes* and *secteurs*" with the old-style hierarchical leadership imposed on the camp under the leaders of the genocide.[37] The Interahamwe was in charge.

The UN and NGO authorities were aware that a Hutu Power administration was operating in the camps. Appeals to UN member states to provide a UN military force to police the camps, disarm the army and disband the militias went unheeded. The Hutu leadership set up its own camp, known as Lac Vert, and arranged for young recruits from the refugees to be given military training on a daily basis in preparation for an offensive and guerrilla war against the RPF government.[38] Those who opposed the restoration of Hutu extremist leadership or tried to return to Rwanda were dealt with summarily, and murder became the chief cause of death in the camps. When the Hutu forces started launching attacks into Rwanda, the new Rwandan government warned it would take action, and it pressed Zaire and the UNHCR to start repatriating refugees and control the Hutu forces. But President Mobutu was in no hurry to send back the Rwandans, since they brought in valuable international aid and sympathy for Zaire at a time when the end of the Cold War and Mobutu's well-earned reputation for corruption had badly eroded his former American and European alliances. Mobutu also used the Hutu military groups to counter local politicians in Kivu, an area he deemed insufficiently loyal or dependable.[39]

By 1994, Zaire was bankrupt, with external debts of $8bn and a debt service requirement far beyond the government's ability to pay. Mobutu had always maintained his rule through the use of both patronage and violence, but his powers of patronage waned as finances dried up. Ordinary Zaireans had long given up expecting anything from the state—water, power, health, education—and relied on informal local networks to survive.[40] Official US development aid was terminated in June 1991, with Congressman Stephen Solarz denouncing Mobutu as having "established a kleptocracy to end all kleptocracies" and "set a standard by which all future international thieves will be measured."[41]

Domestic and international pressure had forced Mobutu to end the one-party system in 1990. There was a rush to form parties, and many current or former Mobutu allies formed their own. Most had regional or sectional biases, and few were truly national in character. They were mostly "simple cliques of ambitious individuals, with no popular base"[42] with the possible exceptions of Nguza Karl I Bond's Uferi party, based in Katanga and openly in favour of Katangan chauvinism, and Etienne Tshisekedi's Union for Democracy and Social Progress (UDPS) in Kasai. They joined with other groups to form the Sacred Union, which put pressure on Mobutu to hold a national political conference. But the competing personalities with their divergent regional/linguistic/ethnic support bases did not make for a united opposition or a political system designed to improve accountability. All the major political leaders were former Mobutu ministers, and Mobutu was able to use the divisions among them to thwart his new opposition. Ahead of the national political conference, Mobutu appointed Tshisekedi as prime minister. He accepted the post, prompting demonstrations against him for selling out; he could not work with Mobutu, who sacked him after a few weeks.

But Mobutu's power over his provincial networks of patronage was declining. Kasai and Shaba were now loyal to Tshisekedi and Nguza, while North and South Kivu were slipping from his grasp—increasing his need to use the Rwandan Hutu forces to bolster his power. His fall came not as a result of overwhelming pressure from people and politicians, but because of his divisive role in regional conflicts. Mobutu's backing for the Rwandan Hutu, their control over large areas of eastern Zaire and insurgency in border areas of Rwanda backfired, and Uganda and Rwanda began supporting an anti-Mobutu alliance in eastern Zaire, led by veteran Mobutu opponent Laurent Kabila.

The eastern region of Kivu had been a refuge for anti-Mobutu forces since the wars of the early 1960s, with Lumumbist and other rebel groups surviving in remote border areas of North and South Kivu. Kabila's small group had survived by smuggling gold and ivory to Tanzania, where Kabila himself spent most of his time. As Mobutu's power declined, Kabila's ambitions revived and he allied himself with other groups in the east, including the Alliance Democratique des Peuples, which was dominated by Zairean Tutsi known as Banyamulenge. The Banyamulenge had migrated into the region from Rwanda in the 19th century (as had some Hutu) to escape growing overpopulation and land shortages; they lived alongside other Congolese ethnic groups. In the 1960s they became Mobutu's allies, and were rewarded with provincial government jobs and business opportunities. Other local Congolese communities resented the advantages they gained from allying themselves with Mobutu, and there were massacres of Banyamulenge in the mid-1960s. Thirty years later, by which time Banyamulenge politicians linked with Mobutu were in disgrace, conflict spread across the whole region and there were further attacks on Banyamulenge, some carried out by the Rwandan Hutu, who were now Mobutu's allies—and this prompted the Banyamulenge to join forces with Kabila.

In October 1996, spearheaded by Rwandan troops and the Banyamulenge, Kabila's new alliance (known as the Alliance of Democratic Forces for the Liberation of Congo, the ADFL) moved into South Kivu and the Rwandan border area.[43] As Kabila's forces moved towards Bukavu, the Zairean governor demanded that all Banyamulenge left the province, and the local radio station broadcast a stream of incitement against them.[44] Soon afterwards, the Rwandan army crossed the border in force and attacked the Hutu camps around Goma. They forced the refugees to flee, and burned the camps to the ground. Vice-President Kagame rejected criticism of the attack and blamed the NGOs who ran the camps for enabling the rebuilding of a Hutu force.[45] The Rwandans and ADFL occupied Goma and launched an attack on the Mugunga refugee camp, to which most of the Hutu had fled after the initial raid. The Hutu militant forces fled after putting up a desultory resistance, while hundreds of thousands of civilian refugees crossed back into Rwanda. Many of the refugees who tried to remain in Zaire were killed by the Rwandan army and its local allies. Nearly 200,000 Hutu, a mix of militants, their families and civilian refugees, moved further into Zaire and even today remain a serious cause of regional destabilisation and an almost permanent excuse for Rwandan interference in Congolese affairs; they are known as the Democratic Forces for the Liberation of Rwanda, or FDLR.

Backed by Rwanda, Uganda, Angola and Zimbabwe, all of whose governments wanted to see the end of Mobutu, Kabila's ADFL continued to push Mobutu's army westwards after the capture of the two Kivu provinces. This was a brutal war even by 20th Century standards, with as many as 200,000 people—some soldiers and militiamen, but mostly civilians—killed during the advance by Kabila's alliance.

Mobutu's end was not long delayed, but when it came it started a new round of regional alliance-making and breaking, and the development of a complex series of conflicts. Kabila turned against his Banyamulenge allies and came into conflict with Rwanda and Uganda. Angola and Zimbabwe supported Kabila and used the conflict to get access to valuable minerals such as coltan (used in mobile phones), gold and diamonds. The Hutu FDLR still threatened border areas, and allied itself with whoever would fight with it against Tutsi groups. There were internal power struggles within Kabila's new Congolese army and conflicts over land and livestock between Congolese communities such as the Hema and Lendu, many of which were made into vicious local wars by external interference, insecurity and the deprivation brough on local peoples by the Great Lakes conflict. This was a conflict in which sheer greed, the dislocations caused by colonialism, the imperatives of national and local actors, and communities' struggles for survival were all thrown together—a potent cocktail of structural, individual and external factors.[46]

Once installed as President, Kabila renamed Zaire the Democratic Republic of the Congo (DRC) and set about using state power to strengthen his own position and eliminate rivals. When he was assassinated in January 2001, sections of the army, with Angolan and Zimbabwean support, ensured the succession of his son Joseph. The new President Kabila had to cope with the continuing war in the east, the presence of large numbers of foreign troops on DRC territory, and all forces' plundering of valuable export commodities. With South African mediation, he negotiated a peace agreement in April 2002 that involved the withdrawal of Rwandan and Ugandan troops and of the units from those countries supporting the DRC. It did not bring peace.

With no period of respite, a plethora of armed militias and splinter groups from mutinies in the DRC army, and local armed groups—such as the M23 movement in the Goma area—have continued to compete for control of territory,[47] people and valuable mineral resources. A UN force, MONUSCO, is based in the region, and in 2013 it was given the mandate to use military force where necessary to disarm or neutralise rebel groups. Some success was achieved by the UN rapid reaction force deployed in eastern DRC, and it ended the M23 revolt and is now involved in combating Ugandan rebels groups in the north-east.

As insurgencies have swept across the eastern DRC, they have enabled groups such as the Ugandan Lord's Resistance Army to move between the DRC, CAR and South Sudan, and created links to conflicts in South Sudan, Darfur and the CAR.

This conflict has many causes. There are those who take the view, now increasingly contested,[48] that greed and economic advantage are the primary drivers of civil wars and localised conflicts and are more powerful than grievance.[49] In the DRC, access to gold, diamonds, coltan, timber, ivory and other commodities was often seen simply as something to sustain combat and militia forces; and not least as a means for the Rwandan, Angolan, Ugandan and Zimbabwean armies to profit from their pursuit of regional and security interests. But greed was not the main motivation for rebels groups or for intervening powers: resource theft and economic advantage were just complementary factors in a multi-layered series of inter-linked conflicts. The key motivating factors were the political ambitions of the DRC's leaders and factions, its inadequate state structure, its competing and uneasily coexisting communities, Rwanda's desire to destroy the Hutu FDLR and establish a buffer along its border, and the Hutu FDLR's desire to oust the RPF in Rwanda and attack its allies in the border areas. Local militias, such as the Mai Mai, often become swept up in the wider conflict simply by acting in defence of their own communities and taking whatever resources they needed to survive and buy weapons.

Before leaving the Great Lakes, it must be said that the task of peace and nation-building there is not hopeless. In Burundi, a peace process backed by the OAU involving mediation by Nelson Mandela and Thabo Mbeki, with strong UN backing, helped end a terrible conflict in the early 2000s. The timely deployment of a 700-strong South African stabilisation force gave protection to the Burundian politicians engaged in peace talks to end the fighting. The talks resulted in elections in 2005, which brought a former Hutu rebel leader to power and led to a ceasefire agreement with the rebel movements who had refused to take part in the elections. With continuing UN, African Union and NGO involvement and funding, power-sharing institutions have been constructed, and they have worked sufficiently well for the 2005 and 2010 elections to be held without significant violence. The Hutu and Tutsi communities are represented in Burundi's National Assembly and Senate, and parity has been established within the armed forces to end decades of Tutsi dominance and use of the armed forces to achieve hegemony. A deal based on power-sharing has so far had a positive effect in bringing peace and security.[50] This success, though, is now in danger through the political ambitions of President Nkurunziza and his fiercely contested election to a third term in office. This sparked demonstrations and violence in Bujumbura and other towns by his opponents, an attempted military coup and the delaying of presidential elections. East African states became involved in trying to find a political solution, with the bizarre development of President Yoweri Museveni (still clinging to power after nearly thirty years in office) trying to mediate between Nkurunziza and his opponents.

Somalia: civil war, disintegration, secession and the power of local networks

In the twenty-four years since the overthrow of Siad Barre, Somalia has been portrayed in the global media and among Western policymakers as the ultimate failed state: a humanitarian disaster area dominated by clan-based militias out to control and plunder resources and aid; a state with no state structure; a breeding ground for anti-Western Islamist groups; and a base for maritime piracy. There have been invasions by neighbours, disastrous interventions by the UN and the USA, and a concerted and comparatively successful intervention by an African Union force with international backing. There have been international conferences, regional conferences, transitional governments, and unrecognised statehood for Somaliland. But most of all, there has been little real understanding of the dynamics of the Somali situation and of the structures and factors at work.[51]

Somalia is a clan-based society, with strong religious and cultural influences that set it apart from most of its near neighbours. The depth of these clan, religious, local and regional networks mean that viewing Somalia as a failed state in purely Western, Westphalian/Weberian terms is shallow and misleading—a hindrance rather than a help. Barre's military government claimed to be working to diminish the dominant role of clan rivalries, engaged in a divide-and-rule strategy that for more than twenty years prevented serious challenges to its power, while enabling Barre to advance the interests of the Marehan sub-clan and Darod clan at the government's heart.[52] Barre's regime was first bolstered by massive Soviet military aid and then with the help of an estimated $800m in military and other aid from the USA and $1bn from Italy. Somalia did not achieve its irredentist aims of recovering the 'lost' territories of Djibouti, the Somali-speaking areas of Ethiopia, or parts of northern Kenya. But it did use this substantial assistance to build a huge army and air force that kept the military in power and diverted Somalis' attention away from clan competition and lack of government accountability.

When the Cold War ended, so did the West's rationale for backing Barre. At the same time, the fruits of decades of conflict ripened: Ethiopian support helped the Somali National Movement (SNM) and the Somali Salvation Democratic Front (SSDF) to establish themselves in northern Somalia. At first they were more of an irritant than a threat to Barre's government, though the SNM was able to feed on the grievances of northerners (especially the Isaq clan) who felt marginalised by a system dominated by the Marehan and Darod. In 1987, the SNM launched a series of offensives around the northern capital, Hargeisa, and the strategic port of Berbera. Barre counter-attacked, killing thousands of SNM fighters and an estimated 50,000 civilians and more or less destroying Hargeisa—ensuring the enduring enmity of the Isaq. In the north-eastern area known as Puntland, the SSDF garnered support among the Majeerteen sub-clan of the Darod and established itself as an alternative to Barre. In central and southern Somalia, the politically marginalised Hawiye clan formed the United Somali Congress (USC), which took advantage of growing regional opposition to the government and its waning international support to launch its own insurgency.

In August 1990, the SNM, USC and smaller groups representing other clans formed a united front. Barre tried to fend off the growing armed opposition by announcing the legalisation of political parties and plans for multi-party elections, but it was far too late, and armed groups began to challenge the power of the army in Mogadishu. By the end of the year, the Hawiye and the USC had taken control of much of the capital, and in

January 1991 Barre fled, leaving behind a fragmented and heavily armed country with little trust in the concept of central government and a plethora of clan-based militias.

The rival militias and movements fought each other, splitting on clan or sub-clan lines. In a naked demonstration of the gatekeeping aspect of political and military control, they fought fiercely for control of Mogadishu's airport and harbour and the port of Kismayo. In the capital, USC fighters launched a witch-hunt against the Darod, even those from movements that had been allied to the opposition. The USC then split into factions led by provisional President Ali Mahdi Mohamed of the Abgal sub-clan and Mohamed Farah Aideed of the Habr Gedir, who also declared himself president. Mogadishu became a battleground, with civilians caught in the middle of faction fights.[53] Control of territory and resources was constantly shifting, and alliances were made and broken for short-term advantage. One of the most acute observers of Somalia's recent history admits, "The unpredictable and fast-moving situation was bewildering for everybody, both inside and outside Somalia."[54] Somalia's international image became dominated by reports of violence and pictures of militias tearing around Mogadishu in four-by-fours mounted with heavy weapons.

This failed state image was reinforced by ill-conceived foreign interventions by the UN, the USA, and later Ethiopia. Far from improving the humanitarian situation or bringing the clans, militias and warlords to the negotiating table, the interventions sharpened the conflict, drew international attention to what seemed like insoluble and inexplicable violence, and hindered Somalis' attempts to find solutions. The UN intervention of 1992–3, Operation Restore Hope, had a lot to do with President George H. W. Bush's view of the US's role in the new world order he wanted to dominate after the Cold War. But it was also a reaction to images of starving Somali children, the plunder of aid by militiamen and the deaths of civilians in militia clashes. The UN and US did not restore hope, and only marginally and temporarily improved the delivery of humanitarian aid. The operation harmed Somalia in the long term; it was not informed by clear aims, but was, "Culturally ignorant and oblivious to the hostility of Somalia's clans to central authority," while "a naïve international community blundered as it tried to restructure local power configurations."[55]

The USA sent 28,000 troops to Somalia during Restore Hope, and then supplied a quarter of the soldiers for the UNOSOM II force starting in March 1993. UNOSOM II had a mandate to seek out, disarm and demobilise the militias rather than just ensure the safe passage of humanitarian aid, but

American operations in Somalia became tragically farcical. They twice attacked UN buildings after false tip-offs about the whereabouts of Mohamed Farah Aideed; they then launched another attack in which they failed to get Aideed but killed hundreds of Somali citizens, most of them women and children, with machine gun and rocket fire, losing eighteen soldiers in the process. The bodies of the Americans killed were dragged through the streets of Mogadishu. The episode was recreated in the hugely inaccurate film *Black Hawk Down*, which for many outside Africa was their only experience of Somalia beyond scattered news reports. The Americans pulled out within a month, and the entire UN operation was doomed to failure. The international community then largely left Somalia to its own devices.

On the ground, Somalis began to find solutions on a local or community level, through trade, money movements and traditional, religious and clan-based forms of justice. From the latter grew a movement that showed signs of restoring security, offering more hope than the series of transitional governments formed at conferences held in neighbouring states, which had no power and were unable to even return to the country. This new movement was the Union of Islamic Courts (UIC).

The UIC arose out of clan-based sharia courts, which provided widely accepted forms of authority. The courts began to coalesce in a loose organisation in central and southern Somalia, particularly in Mogadishu, and gained the support of a population weary of clan conflict and lawlessness. They were part of a pre-colonial Islamic structure of social control that had survived colonial rule, Barre's military rule and the clan conflict of the early nineties. The UIC had a particularly strong link with the Ayr sub-clan of the Hawiye; it also had access to weapons, and by early 2006 it had established itself as the major power in Mogadishu. The union was supported by religious groups, by businessmen who wanted an end to the economic chaos of militia depredations, and by ordinary people who wanted security above all. It was initially non-political, but in September 2006 it was included in the Transitional National Government (TNG) created at a conference in Djibouti.

In the wake of the 9/11 attacks, the US's "War on Terror" began to intrude into Somali politics, and UIC members who had been involved with Islamist movements were included on US lists of wanted terrorists.[56] There were some links between Somali Islamist activists and international groups like al-Qaeda, but no evidence of common purpose; the UIC was concerned with domestic rather than international issues. Washington viewed the UIC exclusively through the prism of the War on Terror and backed an alliance of warlords, funding their fight against the UIC, and encouraging Ethiopian hostility towards Somali Islamist groups. But the courts had sufficient support to defeat the warlords. Roadblocks began to be dismantled around the capital, rubbish was cleared up, and the port and airport were reopened and cleared of clan militias. Alongside these positive developments, they also implemented harsh sharia punishments and strict restrictions on women and cultural activities.

The courts were able to create a level of security that had never been achieved in the post-Barre era, and to establish some legitimacy among the population.[57] But as they grew in power, they were joined by Islamist fighters who had received military training in Afghanistan. These militants soon gained control of many of the UIC's militias, which became known as Jamaa'a al-Shabaab. These militants alienated moderate supporters of the courts, exaggerated the influence of the Ayr sub-clan and then declared jihad against Meles Zenawi's government in Ethiopia. At this time, Zenawi had troops inside Somalia to secure territory for the Transitional Federal Government (TFG), which had been formed at extended talks in Kenya to replace the defunct TNG and to which the UIC was opposed. On Christmas Day 2006, Ethiopian aircraft attacked Mogadishu's port and airport; the Americans provided military aid and intelligence for an Ethiopian invasion, having concluded that the UIC was under the control of al-Qaeda (something for which there was no conclusive evidence). The TFG supported the invasion seeing it as a means of defeating its main domestic opponent. The UIC was driven out of Mogadishu, and Ethiopian troops seized territory formerly under its control on behalf of the TFG.

The courts movement fragmented, but the more militant elements came together to form Al-Shabaab, a shortened version of Harakat al-Shahaab al-Mujahidin (Youth Movement). This movement was now more overtly jihadist, and made no secret of its contact with al-Qaeda. There was some residual support for the legacy of the UIC among Somalis, especially as the two years of Ethiopian occupation of Somali territory ensured that the TFG lacked legitimacy. That meant Al-Shabaab could don the garb of Somali nationalism along with some of the kudos of the Islamic Courts—but the group still could not secure the willing acceptance that had been accorded the UIC.

In the north, the SNM was more united than the movements of southern and central Somalia, and when Barre's government collapsed it was able to control most of the territory now known as Somaliland. In May 1991, the SNM declared Somaliland an independent state—one that has yet to be recognised internationally or by the African Union. Essentially encompassing the former British colony of Somaliland, the region "was probably the most comprehensively destroyed part of Somali territory" by the time Barre was forced out. However, it managed to cultivate its own identity and gradually rebuild itself, creating a working and increasingly democratic system of government with no interference or social/political engineering from outside.[58] With considerable popular support, the SNM was even able to bring the various militias in the territory under control, as was the regional government in Puntland, which was effectively autonomous but did not declare independence.

In 1993, two years after Somaliland declared independence, a conference was held at Boroma bringing the SNM together with traditional and other politically or socially active groups from the region. They tried to find a political solution that combined traditional politics with more modern structures to create a hybrid and totally Somali political system, one decided upon by the mix of groups at the conference—not imposed by departing colonialists or foisted on competing groups by outside powers or donors. The conference drew up new political structures and appointed Mohamed Ibrahim Egal, a prime minister of Somalia in the pre-Barre era, as Somaliland's president. He was the first to preside over a system that combines an elected parliament with a senate made up of a council of elders or *guurti*, with the traditional leaders taking particular responsibility for the resolution of conflict. This is an inventive model, incorporating both old and new structures; it was accepted locally rather than fitting a donor or IMF good governance checklist, and was very much a grassroots-up solution, rather than one imposed by the SNM.[59] It reflects rather than ignores or works against Somalia's clan make-up, and uses respect for traditional elders in a constructive way.[60]

International and African non-recognition may have been a political blessing in disguise for Somaliland, even though it has created problems economically. Yet even the economic problems of isolation have led to searches for local and, interestingly, Somali diaspora solutions. To a great extent, this has helped rebuild a shattered society and construct an economy from the bottom up with little international funding or aid from NGOs. The foreign NGOs working in Somalia as a whole competed with local groups; they failed to contribute to capacity-building in Somaliland, and were viewed with some suspicion by indigenous NGOs. Somaliland has instead relied very heavily on the return of skilled people from the diaspora, remittances from Somalis living abroad, and on networks of foreign and Somaliland-based businessmen who can raise funds privately for local projects that meet identifiable needs—bridges, irrigation, small-scale farming ventures. The Dahabshiil money transfer company has worked to connect the diaspora with Somaliland and also greater Somalia. It is now used not just by Somali individuals and businesses as a way of transferring money quickly and safely, but also by NGOs to pay local staff and fund projects. As the head of Dahabshiil said in July 2013,

> Remittances from the diaspora provide essential support to 40% of the Somali territories. We have nearly 300 branches in the territories and thousands of agents servicing people in towns and rural areas. For them, money sent from relatives overseas is an economic lifeline. It is mainly spent on food, medicines and school fees.[61]

While the Somaliland government still wants international recognition and the funding it would bring, there is also the danger that it could see resources wasted on the "trappings of statehood"[62] and be dragged into the donor- and international institution-dominated approach to development that has caused so many problems in Africa by ignoring local needs, expertise and solutions. As it is, Somaliland has capitalised on its strengths and continued to develop its livestock-based agriculture, the backbone of its economy both domestically and in terms of exports, which have continued despite political isolation with sheep, camel and cattle exported to Gulf Arab countries such as Saudi Arabia and the UAE.

If Somaliland has made careful, gradual process towards solving its problems, Somalia at large is still wracked by conflict—some internal, but much of it exacerbated by external forces. Al-Shabaab fought the Ethiopian army in Mogadishu in 2007 and 2008 in a bloody and very brutal war, which included the targeted assassination of TFG officials and businessmen who worked with the transitional authorities. The Ethiopian response was extreme, with counter-insurgency sweeps that killed hundreds of civilians while alienating most of the Somali population. Al-Shabaab, meanwhile, continued to receive funds from abroad; its agenda was still centred on events in Somalia, though its rhetoric matched that of other Salafist groups around the world, who saw its fight against the Ethiopians and the TFG as part of a war against US involvement in Somalia and the Horn of Africa.[63] There's little doubt that the Ethiopian intervention was responsible for "transforming the group from a small, relatively unimportant part of a more moderate Islamic movement into the most powerful and radical armed faction in the country."[64]

After 2008, Al-Shabaab gradually occupied more and more territory as the Ethiopians pulled back, but the movement's aims and leadership became more opaque as it spread and gained strength. Rather like the Islamic Courts, it was an amalgam of Islamist factions and clan-based groups trying to utilise Islam. There were serious rifts between the groups over clan allegiances and the influx of foreign fighters, which Al-Shabaab's now more overt links with Jihadis abroad encouraged. In some areas it occupied, the group was much like the UIC and implemented a tough but broadly accepted version of sharia law that some welcomed as at least offering security; in other areas, where it was less welcome, it adopted what were little more than terror tactics.[65] These tactics have been used against the African Union mission, known as AMISOM, whose troops were sent into Somalia to replace the Ethiopians and support the transitional government.

On 20 February 2007, the UN Security Council authorised the AU to deploy a peacekeeping mission to support a national reconciliation conference, in which more than 3,000 people from across Somalia and from the diaspora participated during July and August 2007. The resulting AMISOM force, led by Ugandan and Burundian troops, entered Mogadishu in March 2007 in support of the transitional government. Originally given a six month mandate, AMISOM has been operating under renewed authority from the AU with EU, UN and US support, ever since it was created, and it was there to provide security when Sheikh Sharif Sheikh Ahmed, a former UIC leader, was elected head of the transitional government in 2009. AMISOM has had some success, forcing Al-Shabaab out of Mogadishu and reducing the areas it controls, but it has been unable to decisively defeat Al-Shabaab or to stop bombings in the capital. While security has improved somewhat, attacks continue in the capital.

AMISOM's offensive was assisted by the Kenyan army's invasion of Jubaland in the south in October 2011, and by the painstakingly slow Kenyan push to capture the port city of Kismayo. The Kenyans wanted an Al-Shabaab-free zone along their northern border, and hoped to end the flood of refugees into camps on its territory and gain influence in a region of Somalia vital to their own border security. The Kenyan force remains in Jubaland and operates as part of the AMISOM force, though Hassan Sheikh Mohamud's Somali government has accused Kenya of siding with certain southern Somali factions and thereby weakening the transitional government. Kenya, meanwhile, has suffered domestically as a result of its involvement in Somalia, suffering periodic bombings and a growth in Islamic militancy and violence in Mombasa—along with the 2013 Westgate Mall attack in Nairobi and the 2015 Garissa University massacre. The large Somali population of Kenya has been persecuted and viewed with suspicion ever since the *shifta* war of the 1960s and because of the large informal smuggling economy that involves many Somali businessmen and transport operators—smuggling ivory poached in Kenya, charcoal and sugar across the porous border. The smugglers had links with Al-Shabaab, which benefitted financially from the smuggling. The development of a Kenyan wing of Al-Shabaab is now a serious security threat in many areas of north-eastern Kenya and the government has failed so far to combat it either politically or militarily.

In September 2013, the fragile government of Somalia was forced to accept that Jubaland was slipping from its control and gaining a degree of autonomy, and the government in Mogadishu signed a deal in Addis Ababa recognising Jubaland as another partially independent entity.[66] The deal was rubber-stamped by the UN, EU and the AU, whose chairperson, Nkosazana Dlamini-Zuma, welcomed the decision as an indication of Somalia's ability to overcome its regional divisions.[67] But the autonomy or semi-independence of Jubaland damages both the transitional government's claim to control beyond Mogadishu and the nation's legitimacy, with Somaliland effectively independent and Puntland enjoying its own self-proclaimed autonomy. The port of Kismayo is of huge importance to Somalian trade and to the economy of the whole of southern Somalia, and will only become more vital if oil exploration off the coast of southern Somalia yields results. Oil deposits have been found along the coast near the long-disputed Kenya-Somalia border, and if a tug-of-war over off-shore oil begins, a weakened Somalia and a Jubaland owing its existence to Kenya would clearly be to Kenya's advantage.

International concerns over Somalia have also focused on piracy, with Somali armed groups attacking and hijacking merchant ships, tankers and yachts in the Indian Ocean and holding crews and boats to ransom. Navies from NATO countries, Russia, China and Australia have been deployed to combat it, and merchant ships often have guards recruited from what are euphemistically called private security companies but are basically mercenaries, especially from South Africa and the successors to the Executive Outcomes mercenary group. An economy developed around piracy in impoverished coastal areas where fishing had been destroyed by international fleets plundering fish stocks, and where war had damaged rural economies. By early 2014, the international efforts combined with anti-piracy measures in Puntland had dramatically reduced the number of pirate attacks from Somali territory.

The end of apartheid gives birth to the rainbow nation—but where's the gold at the end?

In the 1990s, South Africa was seen as the great hope for Africa, and Nelson Mandela the personification of that hope. Portrayed as an icon of the struggle against apartheid by the ANC and anti-apartheid campaigners around the world, his release in February 1990 heralded a new era for South Africa and Southern Africa at large. His speech on the day he was released from prison struck notes of humility, his steadfastness about his goal tempered with reconciliation:

> I stand here before you not as a prophet but as a humble servant of you, the people. Your tireless and heroic sacrifices have made it possible for me to be here today ... Negotiations cannot take place above the heads or behind the backs of our people. It is our belief that the future of our country can only be determined by a body which is elected on a non-racial basis...There must be an end to white monopoly on political power and a fundamental restructuring of our political and economic systems... I have cherished the ideal of a democratic and free society in which all persons will live together in harmony with equal opportunities.[68]

After Mandela's release, the ANC, NP, IFP and other parties began a complex process of negotiations against a background of violence in the townships and escalating conflict between the ANC and Mangosuthu Buthelezi's IFP. There is considerable evidence that Buthelezi supporters were covertly funded, armed and encouraged by elements within the security/intelligence network established to defend white rule. The Civil Cooperation Bureau (CCB), set up by the apartheid security services to combat opposition to apartheid using violence, assassination and kidnapping, played its role in provoking township violence, and was the "third force" the ANC accused the NP of using to attack and undermine it during the 1994 elections.[69] F. W. de Klerk always denied any NP role in inciting violence, and blamed it on the ANC. There is evidence that IFP cadres were trained by South African special forces, armed with weapons left over from the SADF's support for Renamo in Mozambique and encouraged by elements within SA Military Intelligence to try to eliminate ANC supporters in Kwa-Zulu and the Vaal townships.[70]

The ANC and the National Party pledged themselves early on to peaceful negotiations and ending the climate of violence; the ANC suspended the armed struggle, but did not end it. In interviews I conducted at the time, ANC insiders like Ronnie Kasrils and Tokyo Sexwale told me Mandela was dubious about the suspension but was talked into it by Joe Slovo, the Umkhonto chief of staff and general secretary of the SACP. Slovo was a voice of compromise and caution during the negotiations, and helped chart the reformist course the ANC ultimately took.

The formal multi-party talks involving the ANC, NP, IFP, Democratic Party and fifteen other parties got underway at the Convention for a Democratic South Africa (CODESA). The opening session on 21 December 1991 took many by surprise with a bitter and very personal row between de Klerk and Mandela, yet the talks continued, and the participants signed a declaration of intent. Five working groups were established to deal with the constitution, setting up an interim government, the future of the homelands, the timeline for implementing changes, and the new electoral system.

The three main parties came to the talks with very different ideas of what they wanted to achieve. The ANC wanted majority rule on the basis of a totally non-racial franchise and to redistribute wealth; the IFP wanted much the same, but with a strong element of regional power, aware that it could not compete nationally with the ANC but could win in KwaZulu-Natal. The NP, meanwhile, wanted a system that recognised the equality of all, but with a constitution that would entrench property rights and give minority groups (notably the NP's white constituency) a guaranteed share in decision-making.[71] The gaps seemed unbridgeable, and it is hardly surprising that it wasn't until 1994 that elections were held under an interim constitution.

The combined effects of township protest and violence, the increasing power of black trades unions, the declining economy, international banks calling in loans, and the withdrawal from Angola and Namibia had forced the NP to unban the ANC and start the dismantling of apartheid. Nonetheless, de Klerk's party used all possible means to try to salvage what it could for the whites, particularly when it came to control and ownership of economic resources. On paper, the ANC was in a stronger position, but it was struggling to bring together the disparate elements of its membership and support base: the exiles, the Robben Islanders who had been in prison for years, the internal mass movement led by the UDF/Cosatu, the Communist Party and Umkhonto cadres. All these groups wanted representation in the leadership, the ability to influence policy and a slice of the post-apartheid pie. The ANC had not overthrown apartheid by force, and the sheer breadth of its alliance meant its position was not as powerful as Mandela's standing, its appeal to the majority of black South Africans and its eventual victory would make it appear. The ANC was especially vulnerable when it came to economic policy, which had not been a priority in the struggle; suddenly it had to deal not only with the NP but also with the

Anglo-South African business elite, international investors and international financial institutions, whose goodwill would be vital for a post-apartheid South Africa.

Violence was a recurrent problem during the CODESA process and at times threatened to bring it to a bitter end. Far from ending violence, the release of Mandela and the unbanning of the ANC was followed by an escalation. In 1989, 1,403 people were killed in political violence but this rose to 3,699 and 2,760 in the next two years. The most serious fighting was between ANC and Inkatha supporters in the townships around Johannesburg and the Vaal Reef region, while rural areas of KwaZulu-Natal saw fierce and bloody fighting between local leaders trying to ensure control for their chosen parties. The Reef War started in July 1990 when Inkatha supporters killed more than thirty ANC followers in Sebokeng; in September 1990, 26 black workers were killed on a Johannesburg commuter train, which the ANC blamed on the 'third force'. The role of the NP security forces and military intelligence was revealed in 1994 when the Goldstone Commission, appointed by de Klerk to investigate the violence, exposed the NP's operations to undermine the ANC. An internal SADF report also confirmed that military intelligence was involved in the Sebokeng train massacre, the assassinations of ANC supporters, and supplying weapons to political and vigilante groups fighting the ANC.[72] The revelations forced de Klerk to remove his defence minister, General Magnus Malan, and Minister of Law and Order Adriaan Vlok from their security posts, though not from the cabinet.

As the violence spiralled, the CODESA talks began to falter. They had been suspended in May 1992, and Buthelezi had staged a walk-out. There was deadlock over the key issue of the parliamentary majority necessary for voting on the new constitution. Then came the Boipatong massacre of June 1992, in which forty-eight ANC supporters were killed by IFP militants from a nearby workers' hostel. There was strong suspicion that the security forcers had assisted in the massacre.[73] The ANC responded by abandoning direct negotiations, and Mandela declared that "I can no longer explain to our people why we continue to talk to a regime that is murdering our people and conducting war against us."[74]

The ANC launched a campaign of demonstrations, marches, civil disobedience and strikes organised by its ally, COSATU. A general strike at the beginning of August 1992 saw millions of workers stay at home. The cycle of violence, strikes and the breakdown of negotiations was having a huge impact not just on domestic politics, but on the economy. This forced the ANC and the NP back to the negotiating table. After a deal that involved the policing and disarming of migrant workers in township hostels, the talks restarted, but this time without Buthelezi. He joined a group of parties opposed to the ANC and NP's dominance of the negotiations—a coalition that included the far-right Conservative Party. But the NP still had the support of a majority of the white population, and in a whites-only referendum on whether to continue the reform process, held on 17 March 1992, more than two thirds voted 'yes'. By April 1993 enough common ground had been found for the resumption of multi-party talks. This process was nearly destroyed by the assassination on 10 April of the SACP, ANC and Umkhonto leader Chris Hani, a murder organised by the extreme right-wing Conservative Party member Clive Derby-Lewis.[75]

The ANC's control in the townships meant it was able to prevent massive retaliatory violence, but it nonetheless used the anger generated by Hani's murder to extract concessions from the NP, above all to hold an election in April 1994 creating a deadline for the negotiations.[76] The talks then focused on setting up a process to create a government of national unity after the elections. The NP wanted a permanent unity government to ensure a white role and calling for a two-thirds majority for all cabinet decisions, but it had to retreat from these demands; it was ultimately agreed that the unity government would last five years, and that any party winning more than twenty seats would be represented in the cabinet. The IFP initially planned to boycott the elections and declare its own KwaZulu-Natal constitution, but eventually took part after some powers were reserved for the provinces. An interim constitution was drawn up, and became law in December 1993.

While township violence had declined by the time of the 1994 elections, they were held in an atmosphere not only of enormous expectation and excitement, but also of tension and fear. A total of 3,794 people had died in political violence in 1993, and in the months preceding the election there had been an upsurge in violence by the extreme white AWB militia, along with bombings blamed on other white supremacist groups. Bophuthatswana's chief minister, Lucas Mangope, decided to resist incorporation back into South Africa, and when a series of demonstrations and strikes by ANC supporters threatened his hold on power, he called on the newly-formed right-wing Freedom Front of former SADF chief General Constand Viljoen to come to his aid. Viljoen sent 1,500 lightly-armed volunteers, who were joined by a group of armed AWB members; they started shooting at people on the streets of Mmabatho. The Bophuthatswana defence force mutinied, attacking the AWB units and killing three AWB men in front of TV cameras. The Freedom Front and AWB withdrew their forces, and this spelled the end of the AWB's reputation as anything but a lunatic fringe element.

The elections took place over the three planned days at the end of April 1994 with little violence and few serious hitches. The count then took far longer than expected, leading to endless speculation about rigging and extra or missing ballot boxes—but in the end it was all deemed fair, and most South Africans believed that verdict was the right one. The ANC won 62.6 per cent of the vote, with the National Party receiving 20.3 per cent and Inkatha 10.5 per cent. That deprived the ANC of the two-thirds majority needed to control the constitution-making process, but it was nonetheless the dominant party; it won all but two of the provincial votes, with the IFP taking KwaZulu-Natal and the NP the Western Cape. A new unity government was formed with Mandela as president and Thabo Mbeki and de Klerk as deputy presidents. Buthelezi became minister of home affairs.

As president, Mandela will be remembered for his policy of reconciliation and for forming a government that appeared to bring the races together—the creation of what Archbishop Tutu called the 'rainbow nation'. Under Mandela, South Africa gained serious clout in regional and international affairs, and every world leader wanted to be seen with Mandela. Domestically, he reached out to white South Africans and famously donned a Springbok rugby shirt when South Africa won the rugby world cup in South Africa in 1995. This was an important symbolic gesture, adding to white South Africans' delight that the years of painful exclusion from international sport were over. Suddenly South Africa could play international test cricket and rugby again. This may seem trivial, but it was hugely important to white South Africans and the rugby-mad Afrikaners.[77] But the rainbow image obscured some of the raw realities of post-apartheid South Africa, most of which took a few years to emerge, as even the poorest black South Africans were willing to give the new government time to fulfil their expectations not just for political rights, but for economic improvements.

Early on in the Mandela presidency, it became clear the government of national unity was not really going to function. While IFP ministers, including Buthelezi, remained in the government until after the 2004 elections, de Klerk withdrew from the cabinet in June 1996 and went into opposition; the NP entered a terminal decline, and eventually dissolved in 2005. The multi-party nature of South African politics has been maintained in the three national elections since 1994, with the ANC predictably winning more than 60 per cent of votes in each one. It remains politically dominant nationally and provincially, except in the Western Cape, where the Democratic Alliance forms the government.

Mandela retired in 1999 and Thabo Mbeki replaced him as president, with the Zulu ANC leader Jacob Zuma as his deputy. Both were part of the old guard, and many of the UDF or COSATU-linked leaders—like the ANC's constitutional negotiator and former National Union of Mineworkers leader, Cyril Ramaphosa, and UDF stalwart and one-time Free State premier, Patrick Lekota—were pushed out of the ANC leadership and into business or opposition, having been seen as potential threats to Mbeki's autocratic style of government. Mbeki had run the government day-to-day under Mandela, and both then and as president he oversaw the entrenchment of ANC political power, the appointment of ANC members to senior civil service and provincial administration posts, and the implementation of a neo-liberal, free trade, export-centred economic policy. His policy of opposing the conventional wisdom on AIDS and refusing to distribute antiretroviral drugs was fiercely opposed and derided in South Africa and abroad.

In terms of black advancement, Mbeki relied on appointing ANC members to public service posts and the introduction of the Black Economic Empowerment (BEE) programme. This was heralded as a broad-based policy that would work to redress the economic imbalance between black and white. In practice, "it has benefited only a small group of African elites, some of whom have become fabulously rich,"[78] including Cyril Ramaphosa and Tokyo Sexwale. Ultimately, the Mbeki era was marked by growing disenchantment for poor black South Africans and by a major increase in corruption. And at the centre of the accusations of ANC corruption was Jacob Zuma.

Zuma has long been the subject of a huge array of corruption allegations, including those relating to multi-billion dollar arms deals and now to the building of his huge family complex at Nkandla, utilising public funds in a way that remains at the centre of political controversy in South Africa.[79] The allegations seemed to be of no interest to Mbeki until he began to see Zuma, a populist critic of his economic policies, as a major threat to his leadership. In 2005, Zuma was removed from the post of deputy president; within a few months, the mass of corruption accusations against him had multiplied, and to make matters worse, he was also put on trial for rape. During the trial Zuma pleaded his innocence, and there were daily demonstrations by ANC Youth League members outside the court in support of him. Leading many of the demonstrations was Youth League leader Julius Malema, who would become one of Zuma's main supporters in the following years as the ANC was rent by increasingly acrimonious factionalism.

Eventually cleared of the rape charge and successfully fending off prosecution for corruption, Zuma was not prepared to give in to Mbeki. At the ANC's December 2007 conference in Polokwane, Zuma used his support network in the party, the youth league and the intelligence services to engineer Mbeki's downfall and secure his own election as ANC president. Mbeki's position was untenable, and he resigned as South Africa's president in September 2008. He was replaced by Kgalema Motlanthe until the 2009 elections, when Zuma was voted in.

Once in office, Zuma's populism and campaigning on behalf of poor black South Africans, which he'd used as a stick to beat Mbeki, turned out to be little more than rhetoric. His government did little to dismantle the conservative economic policies of the Mbeki period or to embark on redistributive policies that would raise the poor majority's living standards or deliver vital welfare, health and other services. Along with growing corruption, this failure of service delivery became a main theme of Zuma's first term in office. The ANC was unchallengeable in national elections, but enmeshed in a web of formal and informal political and economic networks that began to seriously damage its integrity. It was still formally allied with the SACP and COSATU, but it remained the dominant partner. The SACP may have had cabinet posts and members in senior ANC positions, but it was impotent as a political force; COSATU, meanwhile, was key in mobilising voters during elections, but had little influence over economic policy. COSATU's leaders, were increasingly critical of economic policies that did little to raise wages, alleviate poverty or tackle rampant corruption; General Secretary Zwelinzima Vavi became one of Zuma's chief critics within the alliance, and is still battling to retain his position within COSATU against factions led by Zuma supporters. At the time of writing a COSATU special congress is taking place pitting Zuma allies against Vavi and unions such as the National Union of Metalworkers of South Africa (NUMSA), which is threatening to form an anti-ANC political party. COSATU's days as a national union body may be numbered.

There was growing industrial unrest across South Africa, culminating in the Marikana platinum mine strike in August 2012. The violence there ultimately claimed at least forty-four lives when police fired on striking miners. The mine strike was a crystallisation of many aspects of modern South Africa: the strikers had left the NUM, a member of COSATU, and joined an alternative union; the police acted at Marikana as they had during the apartheid era, shooting down striking and demonstrating miners; and one of the directors of the company running the mine was a former NUM head and ANC leader, and later the party's deputy president—Cyril Ramaphosa.

How did the ANC reach this low point? In 1994 it seemed to hold all the aces in the political pack, and to have national and international backing for the task of building a new South Africa. Its programme, derived from the Freedom Charter, committed it to redistribution, nationalisation of key parts of the economy and the economic empowerment of the black majority. But as some of its leaders have since admitted, it did not play its cards well, particularly not in behind-the-scenes negotiations with the white English-speaking business elite, which controlled the commanding heights of the economy through the mining conglomerates, the banking, financial and manufacturing sectors.[80] If the constitutional talks leading to the 1994 elections were important for the political empowerment of the black majority, the economic talks behind closed doors ensured the continuing dominance of the white business elite.

A leading SACP member and former ANC government minister, Ronnie Kasrils, put it this way:

> What I call our Faustian moment came when we took an IMF loan on the eve of our first democratic election. That loan, with strings attached that precluded a radical economic agenda, was considered a necessary evil, as were concessions to keep negotiations on track and take delivery of the promised land for our people...Big business strategies—hatched in 1991 at the mining mogul Harry Oppenheimer's [former chairman of Anglo-American and De Beers] Johannesburg residence—were crystallizing in secret late-night discussions... Present were South Africa's mineral and energy leaders, the bosses of US and British companies with a presence in South Africa—and young ANC economists schooled in western economics...All means to eradicate poverty...were lost in the process. Nationalisation of the mines and heights of the economy as envisaged by the Freedom charter was abandoned.[81]

This view is shared by some leading analysts of South Africa's continuing poverty and vast economic inequality. One has described how in the early 1990s, the ANC lacked a coherent economic policy, and that its agreement on the 1993 IMF loan tied it to economics not based on redistribution and socialism, but on "a neo-liberal, export-oriented economic policy" that prevented a seriously redistributive approach and turned South Africa into a capitalist enclave, enabling "the corporate sector to take core ANC leaders in tow on economic policy."[82] This led to conservative economic policies that liberalised trade (to the detriment of South African manufacturing), emphasised exports, incorporated the ANC elite into the capitalist class that owned and ran the South African economy, and diluted the ANC's commitment to vigorously pursue policies based on social action.

Consequently, South Africa's black political elite has prospered, while the black majority has become ever poorer and marginalised. The incomes of the top 20 per cent of African households increased by over 60 per cent over the last thirty years, while the incomes of the bottom 40 per cent fell by the same amount. The ANC has become an almost unassailable political elite, and the enrichment of the ANC-linked black political and business class has fostered an attitude of "arrogance and indifference" towards the poor black majority. As Desmond Tutu said, the white South African gravy train was not halted and its wealth never redistributed; instead, the train, "Stopped only long enough for the black elite to climb on."[83] Much as in other African states, a leadership class's pursuit of political dominance and the trappings of power has trumped any attempt to seriously restructure the state's social and economic foundations.

Despite Zuma's 2014 re-election, growing factionalism and disenchantment could yet undermine majority support for the ANC unless a post-Zuma leadership emerges to clean up the movement's act. Despite the growing factionalism and evidence of incompetence and corruption in the ANC under Zuma, it still manages to hold on to just over 62 per cent of the national vote—though with the moderate Democratic Alliance gaining 22 per cent, and Julius Malema's populist Economic Freedom Fighters, appealing to disenchanted black youth, taking 6.3 per cent. One of the tactics which helped Zuma and the ANC hold on to a substantial vote was the playing of the 'Mandela card'—his death in December 2013 and the ceremonies to celebrate his life were milked, as was his contribution to changing South Africa. But a year on from that victory, the ANC remains a troubled and tarnished party, even though it is yet to be seriously threatened in its hold on power.

West Africa: Ghana heads for plurality, but Ivory Coast, Liberia and Sierra Leone for civil war

Ghana is not Sub-Saharan Africa's richest or most politically powerful state, but has often been a benchmark for political and economic development across the continent. It was the state that first 'sought the political kingdom' (in Nkrumah's famous phrase), was a dynamic force behind the OAU's formation, and was later held up as the poster boy of structural adjustment. It also became a model in the search for plurality and accountability. Under the radical Rawlings regime, Ghana's leaders groped for a system of governance based on local committees and without political parties, trying to meet growing demands for a return to civilian rule and greater participation—without loosening Rawlings's grip on power. Pressure for political change was magnified by the effects of structural adjustment; although a programme had been introduced to alleviate the social costs of adjustment, unemployment suddenly hit many thousands of Ghanaian civil servants, employees of the cocoa board and workers in industries that declined or downsized as adjustments began to bite. Unemployment remained high as hoped-for foreign investment failed to materialise after the PNDC applied its adjustment policies. Urban workers, professionals and students were hit hard. These were groups that the PNDC hoped would support its radical politics, but instead they began to join opposition parties after political reforms took place.[84]

Rawlings and the PNDC said they wanted to develop a democratic system in tune with Ghanaian customs, tradition and culture. Justice Annan, the chairman of the PNDC-appointed National Commission on Democracy, said, "We must measure the performance of the modern political system since independence against our traditional system and see whether the modern period could not have been improved by an interrelationship with the traditional system."[85] But this made little sense, since Ghana's social and political culture was anything but uniform, instead made up of 100 ethnic and linguistic-cultural communities. And as Col Assassie, the co-ordinator of the Committees for the Defence of the Revolution, told me in Accra in 1987, the PNDC had no intention of restoring power to chiefs. It wanted a system of politics and participation that incorporated elements of tradition that would foster grassroots systems of popular involvement and accountability of institutions—but ordained from the top, not nurtured from the roots or by conservative, traditional leaders.

The reform process started with proposals for local government structures from a PNDC appointed commission, which had consulted Ghanaians through the network of Committees for the Defence of the Revolution. The commission's proposals emphasised local democracy and grassroots participation through district assembles far more than previous systems had. Elections were held in 1988–89; two thirds of assembly members were elected, while the remainder were chosen by the government from recognised civil society groups, with traditional chiefs and elders being consulted on these appointments.[86] The candidates for the local assemblies were not affiliated to parties, though many benefited from being part of the established committee network or of nascent opposition groups.

The success of the local elections and increasing pressure from disgruntled urban political activists pushed Rawlings into announcing a return to multi-party politics in 1991, with elections for the presidency and parliament. A draft constitution was put to a referendum in April 1992, and was approved with 92 per cent of voters in favour. The new system had an executive president voted for by the electorate and a single chamber parliament of 200 MPs; they would be elected on a first-past-the-post, single constituency basis. Ghana's political system rapidly came back to life; political 'clubs' were established prior to the formal legalisation of parties, which meant that by the time parties were legal, groups basing their programmes on known political lineages could quickly form parties in time for the November 1992 elections. The PNDC converted its local structures and the committees into the National Democratic Congress (NDC), led by Rawlings; the old J. B. Danquah-Kofu Busia conservatives became the New Patriotic Party (NPP) under Adu Boahen. Despite the unpopularity of the SAP's implementation, Rawlings was able to use his charisma, the committee network and the advantages of incumbency to win 58.3 per cent of the vote for the presidency, with Boahen some way behind. In what has become a tradition in Ghanaian elections, the NPP accused Rawlings of rigging the vote, against the strong opinion of a Commonwealth election monitoring team, which said that the vote had been free, fair and devoid of serious harassment.

To this day, one of the main problems of the Ghanaian electoral system is that voter registration is poorly or corruptly managed, and voter lists are bloated beyond belief. In some areas there are hundreds of thousands of "ghost" voters, people who have died but remain on voting lists for years and whose votes can be used corruptly. People seem to be able to register in a plurality of districts without being found out. This always gives fertile ground for the losers in an election to cry foul, as happened in 2012, when the incumbent NDC president, John Dramani Mahama, defeated his main challenger, Nana Akufo-Addo of the NPP. Commonwealth and EU observers said the elections were fair, but the NPP launched a court challenge over the issue of out-of-date or inflated voters' lists and voting returns that did not seem to add up. The courts rejected the challenge.

But despite all the disorganisation and malpractice, the plural system has worked. Ghana's system of government is broadly accepted, with energetic debate and regular peaceful transfers of power at elections, Rawlings's NDC losing to the NPP in 2000 but returning to office in 2008. Plural politics seems to have finally put down roots in Ghana, helped by a vigorous newspaper, web and broadcast media and an improving economy boosted by the discovery of oil. Although corruption, which successive NDC and NPP governments failed to deal with successfully, remains a serious problem in government, public service and in the awarding of tenders/contracts. The main risk to further political and economic development is a decline into unaccountability and the revival of patronage as the driving force of politics.[87]

If Ghana has been a relative success story, its long-time rival and neighbour Ivory Coast moved in the opposite direction. Like Rawlings, Félix Houphouët-Boigny was able to win the first election after the restoration of multi-party politics. He did so by calling very fast elections and using state, party and informal networks of power and patronage to make sure the opposition had little chance to organise beyond its core supporters. Houphouët-Boigny's system "relied on distributing rewards for continued political support...Patronage funded from economic growth, could be a substitute for political participation. Legitimacy would come from material provision...State resources were offered to local communities who supported the president."[88] But despite the electoral success, Houphouët-Boigny was having increasing trouble finding the resources to pay supporters and buy off potential opponents. The economic boom was over, and France less generous and more demanding in return for its aid. This seriously threatened the PDCI's local support networks.[89]

Before this could seriously threaten his hold on power Houphouët-Boigny died, in December 1993, resulting in a power struggle between Henri Konan Bedié, who inherited the support of the PDCI/military elite, and the prime minister, Alassane Ouattara. Ouattara was a skilled economic manager, having been a senior official at the IMF, and was appointed by Houphouët-Boigny to stave off economic crisis and curry favour with the IMF and the World Bank. Ouattara did not have the political networks to defeat Bedié, who duly became PDCI head and president. Bedié was no fool, but he lacked Houphouët-Boigny's prestige and political skills, and given the legalisation of opposition parties and the lack of resources to maintain a broad, national patronage network, he could not be sure of retaining power in elections due in 1995. His response, which would have long-lasting divisive consequences, was to pass an electoral code that banned those with a foreign parent or who had not been resident in Ivory Coast for the preceding five years from standing. That excluded Ouattara, who was Ivorian but of Burkinabé origin and had worked abroad at the IMF and the Banque Centrale des États de l'Afrique de l'Ouest for several years before becoming prime minister. He was prevented from running, and the PDCI-controlled media started publishing or broadcasting material that was anti-immigrant and specifically anti-Burkinabé (there were an estimated two million Burkinabé immigrants or people of Burkinabé parentage in Ivory Coast out of a population of over fourteen million).

Having barred Ouattara from standing, Bedié was assured of victory when Ouattara's Rassemblement des Républicains (RDR) and Gbagbo's Front Populaire Ivorien (FPI) boycotted the election. These events, the government's anti-Burkinabé xenophobia and the continuing economic crisis meant the first four years of Bedié's rule were marred by political unrest, violent demonstrations, strikes and growing ethnic tensions. Relations with Burkina Faso had been close and co-operative under Houphouët-Boigny (whose goddaughter/ward, Chantal Terrasson, married Burkinabé president Blaise Compaoré), but became strained under Bedié, prompting Burkinabé meddling in the political violence that soon developed.

Faced with falling world cocoa and coffee prices, Bedié was unable to restore economic confidence and growth. By the start of the campaign for the 2000 presidential election, there was still plenty of support for Ouattara, while Laurent Gbagbo retained the backing of his supporters in the southwest. Regional and ethnic differences were increasingly exploited for advantage by political leaders. Before the elections could take place, the Ivorian army overthrew Bedié and installed a former army chief, General Robert Gueï, as head of a military government. This suited none of the politicians or their supporters, and there were violent demonstrations in Abidjan and other towns. In July 2000 there was a mutiny and rioting by troops in Abidjan over unpaid wages, and an attempt to assassinate Gueï. The discontent only mounted when the new Supreme Court, appointed by Gueï, disqualified many candidates from the major parties by enforcing the electoral rule that all candidates had to have two Ivorian parents and to have never been a national of another country. This barred Ouattara and several other RDR candidates from running. The RDR called for a boycott, resulting in a low turnout in the race between Gueï and Laurent Gbagbo. When the early results put Gbagbo in the lead, Gueï and his supporters in the army stopped the count and the reporting of results, declaring the general the winner.

The attempt to deny Gbagbo backfired. His supporters, backed by the police, took to the streets of Abidjan. Protesters attacked the guards protecting the presidential palace, and were joined by disgruntled soldiers. Gueï fled, and Gbagbo was declared president. The RDR demanded new elections, but the police and army units backing Gbagbo joined his party's youth gangs in attacks on Ouattara's supporters. Hundreds died in street fighting, which continued until Ouattara called for peace and agreed to recognise the Gbagbo presidency in return for negotiations. The two leaders reached a temporary accommodation and local elections were held successfully in March 2001, with all political parties participating and the electoral bar on Ouattara and other descendants of immigrants removed. The RDR won a majority of locally contested seats, with the PDCI coming second and the FPI third. In August 2002, after further talks and urging from France and other donors, many of whom saw Ouattara as a better economic manager, Gbagbo formed a government of national unity that included ministers from the RDR.

But the newfound stability didn't last, and on 19 September 2002, 700 soldiers threatened with demobilisation took to the streets in what became a full-blown army insurrection, during which Gueï and his wife were murdered by a pro-government death squad.[90] A movement calling itself the Mouvement Patriotique de Côte d'Ivoire (MPCI) launched a revolt against the government. The MPCI, which later said it was the political wing of the Forces Nouvelles de Côte d'Ivoire armed movement, was led by a northerner called Guillaume Soro, who was fiercely opposed to the *Ivorité* ('Ivorienness') ploy Gueï and Gbagbo had used to disenfranchise northerners and those of Burkinabé descent. Burkina Faso may have helped the MPCI launch its campaign, and the Ivorian government accused foreign forces of assisting the rebellion and the mutiny. Those accusations heightened the xenophobia directed at northerners and immigrants, and the result was a pogrom by Ivorian security forces and civilians against the country's large community of immigrant workers, especially those from Burkina Faso.

Gbagbo was not the only one who suspected other states of backing the rebel movement. In the wake of the Liberian and Sierra Leone wars (see below) and the roles in them of rebels and mercenaries funded by Burkina Faso and Libya, ECOWAS leaders were alarmed at the situation and demanded action. Nigeria and Senegal were particularly keen to end the fighting and ensure it did not encourage Libyan interference. When Ivory Coast's ambassador to the UN said the country was rearming its forces to combat what he claimed were rebels mainly drawn from Burkina Faso, Sierra Leone, and Liberia,[91] Senegal appealed to France to take a more active role and help the Ivorian government; French troops did ultimately assist the Ivorian army, though without engaging in combat. The combination of French intervention, direct military support from Nigeria and Angola, and pressure on Burkina Faso from ECOWAS leaders brought the fighting to an end. Ivory Coast found itself in a military stalemate, with a ceasefire line dividing the country and French troops in place to deter further rebel attacks. The MPCI controlled the northern 60 per cent of the country, while two smaller rebels groups backed by Liberia's Charles Taylor had seized small areas on the western border. The division was a measure of the frustration among peoples marginalised and impoverished in the previous decade of political factionalism and economic decline[92]—and one of the effects of the factionalism and the disintegration of centralised control was the proliferation of armed groups.

French and ECOWAS pressure and the military stalemate forced Gbagbo and the rebels to negotiate a peace accord in Paris in January 2003, and a formal ceasefire the following May. Over the next four years there were repeated outbreaks of fighting and massacres, blamed on attempts by armed groups to cleanse their territories of political opponents or potentially hostile ethnic communities. Nevertheless, in March 2007, the Gbabgo government and the MPCI/Forces Nouvelles under Soro signed a power-sharing agreement installing Soro as prime minister, and Gbagbo declared that the war was over. But despite the presence of UN peacekeepers, there were still repeated outbreaks of violence.

Economically the conflict had been disastrous, with a decline in cocoa and coffee exports and a massive increase in cross-border crop smuggling. The national economy was in tatters, and debt had soared. But in April 2009, recognising the political progress that had been made and the restoration of central control, the IMF and creditors agreed to write off $3bn of the country's total debt of $12.8bn. By mid-2010, there was sufficient calm to schedule elections and they were held at the end of October.

When Alassane Ouattara was declared the winner of the second round of the presidential election, Gbagbo refused to accept the result, and his party and supporters in the army launched a violent attempt to retain power. Forces supporting Ouattara resisted, and there was heavy fighting in Abidjan. Most regional support and international opinion was in favour of Ouattara; the UN (which still had peacekeepers in the country), the African Union, ECOWAS, France and the US recognised Ouattara as the rightful winner. Fighting in Abidjan worsened, but French forces—with UN approval—seized the airport and then helped capture Gbagbo, which brought his attempt to retain power to an end. Ouattara was inaugurated as president in May 2012, and Gbagbo was handed over to the International Criminal Court to face charges of crimes against humanity.

The civil war in Ivory Coast resulted from a breakdown of central authority, as long-standing patron-client networks fragmented in a succession struggle sharpened by economic crisis. This destroyed the veneer of unity and order created by Houphouët-Boigny's authoritarian and patrimonial system. The violence and bitterness of the conflict stemmed from the way old local and regional networks had been turned into divided political constituencies loyal to competing leaders who were prepared to incite ethnic hatred for political gain, while the interference of Burkina Faso and the links between Ivorian and Liberian rebels only made the situation worse. While ECOWAS and the AU attempted to mediate and other African states became militarily involved, it was only the intervention of France and the UN that halted the war and snuffed out Gbagbo's armed resistance after he lost the election.

For decades, Liberia was an elite-run, US-backed state. Its government was made up of American-Liberians, with a few clients among the majority Liberian indigenous population. The American-Liberians were descended from freed slaves who were settled on the Liberian coast in the mid-19th century, who became a political and economic oligarchy controlling government and external trade, through the rule of the group's True Whig Party. The country's mineral and rubber became assets for US businesses, which ran plantations and mines—the Firestone tyre company being a major landowner. This was an extreme example of a gatekeeper state, with the small population of descendants of freed slaves dominating politics, domestic business and foreign trade. The elite kept itself aloof from the people of the interior. Peasants were recruited into the army, and only in the last years of the True Whig Party's rule in the 1970s were attempts made to extend patronage networks to other groups.[93] These included Mandingo traders (a Muslim trading community which was present in towns throughout Liberia but viewed by many Liberians as foreigners and envied for its wealth) and government-recognised chiefs among other indigenous communities.

As late as 1975, the Liberian constitution included the statement that the love of liberty had "brought us here" and that part of this destiny was to enable the "enlightenment of the benighted continent". But the elitist system kept non-American-Liberians out of power and denied them access to wealth or education: in 1960 there was a literacy rate of barely 10 per cent outside the elite.[94] Generous investment terms had attracted American, German and other European investments in rubber, timber and iron ore, but much of the export-oriented commerce was limited to concession areas where foreign companies had financial and other privileges. As David Harris wrote,

> People at the bottom of the scale could only look at the huge disparities between the inside and the outside of the concession areas. Those who might have benefited in acquiring skills and a better standard of living from positions in the companies or from their own entrepreneurship were kept out by predominantly

> American and European expatriate workers, and actively discouraged from business by a government fearful of other nodes of economic and political power."[95]

The diverse nature of Liberia's ethnic communities, who speak many languages or dialects (even among related peoples, such as the Krahn subgroups) and have different societal structures and traditions, meant that political opposition to American-Liberian dominance was slow to develop. The Krahn, for example, had no tradition of centralised power or chieftaincy, which instead was foisted on them by the American-Liberian government to make administration simpler.[96] A common feature across many of the groups was the prevalence of secret societies based on age groups within communities. Known as Poro among the Mende-speaking communities, these were networks among cultural, ethnic and age groups both for spiritual belief/observance and as a means to organise in times of violence or threat. Seniority in the Poro meant local political clout; they were important informal centres of power within communities, and could be used to generate support for politicians or militia leaders who won their allegiance. Samuel Doe and Charles Taylor would both use them in their pursuit of power.[97]

By the end of the 1970s, the patrimonial system in Liberia was creaking at the seams, especially as falling raw material prices and increased oil prices sapped the True Whig Party's powers of patronage. Aware of the inherent weakness of a system run by a small, transplanted elite with few organic links to the majority of the population, President William Tolbert began to try to extend his informal networks to include both the indigenous peoples of the interior and also young people who had flocked to Monrovia and other urban areas.

Unemployed urban youths were recruited into the army but were ill-suited to army discipline, while indigenous soldiers were still not promoted above the rank of NCO. The urban recruits upset the army's balance of regional/ethnic recruitment and power, destabilising the very institution the ruling elite relied on to retain power. In April 1979, a steep rise in rice prices led to riots in urban areas; they were so serious that Tolbert couldn't rely on his own army, and he called in Guinean troops to keep order. The elitist and unpopular ruling group could not hope to deal with widespread grievances and the problems of the narrowly structured political system, and within a year Tolbert had been overthrown in a coup led by NCOs from the Krahn, Gio and Mano communities.

The first military government represented most of Liberia's ethnic groups except for American-Liberians. The head of the military government was

Master Sergeant Samuel Doe of the Krahn group, while the new head of the army, Thomas Quiwonkpa, was a Gio from Nimba County. Doe and his allies were bloody and brutal in their elimination of the ruling elite; Tolbert was killed during the coup, and ten days after seizing power a hastily convened military tribunal convicted thirteen leading members of the ousted government of corruption. They were publicly executed on the beach in Monrovia.[98] In a rash and ultimately self-defeating move, Doe ignored his promise to President Houphouët-Boigny to spare Tolbert's son Adolphus, who was married to Houphouët-Boigny's goddaughter Désirée Delafosse.[99] The Ivorian leader became implacably opposed to Doe, as did Ivory Coast's Francophone allies—notably the Burkinabés under Compaoré.

At first, many rural and urban people looked to the military to improve their living standards, access to education and government posts. Conflicts within the regime gradually narrowed down its support base until it was dependent on the Krahn—and even some Krahn groups began to oppose Doe after he sacked and executed the vice-president, Thomas Weh Syen, and three other members of the ruling People's Redemption Council (PRC). Doe soon found he had to rely on American-Liberian public servants after all, as his army support base lacked educated personnel who could run the government. One American-Liberian brought in was Charles Taylor, who was married to a relative of the new army commander, Thomas Quiwonkpa. Taylor became part of the cabinet, where he enjoyed huge influence over economic affairs.

In search of external support, Doe aligned himself more closely to the US and reluctantly acquiesced to its demands to end military rule. He prepared to transform the PRC into a civilian government. When Quiwonkpa was told that he was to be removed as head of the army and given a senior civilian post, he fled the country along with other Gio leaders. Taylor escaped to the US, from where Doe tried to extradite him on charges of corruption. He then travelled to Libya, where he gained the support of Colonel Gaddafi against the strongly pro-American Doe. Doe now allowed the formation of political parties, and held an election in 1985. By this time US aid had increased from US$20m to $90m, and Doe received $500m over the first five years of his rule. During the elections, Doe used control of the state and the army to harass opponents, deny them freedom of speech and ban those he accused of importing foreign ideologies, like the radical Liberian People's Party of Amos Sawyer.[100] After a massively rigged vote, Doe declared himself the winner in the face of considerable evidence that Jackson Doe, of the Liberia Action Party, had really won. Despite obvious fraud and intimidation, the US welcomed Doe's win—the US Assistant Secretary of State for African Affairs, Chester Crocker, endorsed what he called the "noteworthy positive aspects" of the process, presumably meaning a victory for Washington's client.[101] The Americans seemed willing to accept the jailing or forcing into exile of educated, capable politicians like Ellen Johnson-Sirleaf; they put pressure on Doe to prevent her serving ten years' hard labour, but she still had to flee the country.[102]

In 1983, supporters of Quiwonkpa invaded Nimba County from Ivory Coast and attacked the iron ore mines, killing a number of government officials. Prior to the incursion, there had been some tension between the Krahn and Gio and Mano leaders within the PRC leadership, but little violence. The attack was used by political leaders to stoke a Krahn-Gio ethnic rivalry that ultimately took on horrific proportions. Quiwonkpa's attempted uprising a month after the 1985 elections prompted a brutal counter-insurgency and anti- Gio and Mano campaign by the army in Nimba. Quiwonkpa was captured, tortured and killed, and members of Doe's army openly hacked pieces off the body and ate them. This was not specifically an act of cannibalism, but a ritual act; Liberia's traditional society still held strong spiritual beliefs about sacrifice and the use of magic as a protection against enemies.[103] Doe now ensured that economic networks in Nimba were in the hands of Mandingo traders rather than Gio or Mano, further increasing the grievances of local people.

The political and ethnic enmities Doe stirred up rebounded on him, the Krahn and the Mandingo in December 1989, when Charles Taylor led an invasion of Nimba County from Ivory Coast. While in exile, Taylor had formed the National Patriotic Front of Liberia (NPFL) from former Quiwonkpa supporters and from Gio and Mano who fled the Doe terror. With substantial support from Ivory Coast, Burkina Faso and Libya, Taylor assembled a force of Liberians, Burkinabé mercenaries and assorted West African dissidents who had come under Gaddafi's wing. Burkina Faso had become a key supporter since Adolphus Tolbert's widow, Désirée, had become part of the entourage around Blaise Compaoré. Compaoré had Libyan backing, and brought this to bear in an alliance with Ivory Coast to support Taylor against Doe.

The 1989 NPFL invasion was a small one to start with, fought by only about 100 fighters, but Taylor was able to project his image as a potential liberator to amplify its impact. He was well aware of the importance of radio as a medium of communication and propaganda; the reach and size of the West African audience for the BBC African Service, and particularly its *Focus on Africa* programme made it highly influential. Taylor regularly phoned the station to give interviews and to try and put across his often-exaggerated military claims and his views on the future of Liberia.[104] The Nimba invasion was successful as the Liberian population were receptive to anyone trying to overthrow the hated Doe. When the army couldn't defeat the insurgents it resorted to vicious reprisals against the Gio and Mano, raping, plundering and killing its way across Nimba. The NPFL gathered more fighters from Liberia, but also used increasing numbers of Burkinabés and other Libyan-trained West Africans; it is estimated that as many as 700 Burkinabe were involved in the NPFL offensive.[105] Doe started rounding up and killing Gio and Mano in Monrovia; prominent members of the community were kidnapped and killed, and their headless bodies left on the streets.[106]

By mid-1990, the NPFL controlled nearly 95 per cent of Liberia, but was unable to capture Monrovia from Liberian army units loyal to Doe. On 1 July 1990 the NPFL launched an attack on Monrovia and cut all road links to the city, disrupting power and water supplies. The Doe loyalists reacted by attacking a group of two thousand Gio and Mano refugees sheltering in a Monrovia church. At least 600 unarmed civilians, mainly women and children, were killed. The NPFL and its offshoot, Prince Johnson's Independent National Patriotic Front of Liberia (INPFL), were just as brutal; there were massacres of Krahn and Mandingo at the port of Buchanan and in Lofa County, with between 500 and 1,000 civilians killed in the two atrocities.[107]

Nigeria and other ECOWAS states (though not with the support of Burkina Faso or Ivory Coast) tried to negotiate an end to the fighting. Nigeria and Sierra Leone were particularly keen to stop what they saw as a Francophone and Libyan attempt to destabilise the regional balance of power. A summit of leaders decided to send a military force, ECOMOG, to stop the fighting to allow for the formation of a unity government. But when it arrived at the end of August 1990, the force had no clear mandate about the use of force and was woefully ill-equipped. Doe had taken refuge in the presidential mansion with sufficient forces to resist an attack. On 10 September he visited the ECOMOG headquarters, where Prince Johnson's rebels seized him and killed most of his bodyguards as the West African peacekeepers failed to intervene. Doe was wounded and taken to Johnson's headquarters, where his torture and killing were videoed. His mutilated body was then exhibited in Monrovia, dumped in a wheelbarrow.

The presence of ECOMOG and the hostility of Johnson stopped Taylor taking control of Monrovia, despite Doe's death. ECOWAS called for a conference of all Liberian parties to establish an interim government, but Taylor rejected the invitation and was not part of the ECOWAS-backed interim government that was set up, headed by Amos Sawyer. Taylor expected that he could take Monrovia, and openly threatened ECOMOG with retribution for any NPFL fighters they killed.

By the time Houphouët-Boigny tried his hand at mediation, Taylor's anger at Sierra Leone's backing for ECOMOG and for a new armed movement, the United Liberian Movement for Democracy (ULIMO, an alliance of Krahn and Mandingo formed in Sierra Leone) had led him to arm and host the Sierra Leone Revolutionary United Front (RUF). The Ivorians hosted a series of meetings that produced an accord in March 1993 establishing in principle that all armed factions would disarm and move towards elections. Taylor accepted the deal and then reneged on it, as his forces fought an on-off battle against ULIMO. In Sierra Leone, ULIMO forces supported the Sierra Leonean army against an RUF invasion from Liberia. The Nigerian, Sierra Leonean and Guinean ECOMOG forces sided with one ULIMO faction and helped it try to push the NPFL from areas bordering Sierra Leone and Guinea.

At stake was access to diamonds and timber in areas on both sides of the Sierra Leone-Liberia border. In both the Liberian and Sierra Leonean wars, access to valuable primary commodities sustained rebel movements. Short-term greed was not a primary motive in these conflicts; at best it was a secondary by-product. The basic political goals of protecting communities or seizing power on their behalf were more important.[108]

Thanks to Nigeria and ECOWAS's mediation efforts and with a decline in violence, Liberia held elections in July 1997—and with three-quarters of the vote, Taylor was the clear and largely undisputed winner. This clear mandate installed a man anything but committed to democracy or reconciliation, and Taylor continued to use violence as a means of governing. Corruption only worsened as Taylor became a very personal gatekeeper, having personal access to and control over income from the export sector and concession areas where foreign companies ran plantations. Taylor and the National Patriotic Party (NPP, the party that replaced the NPFL before the elections) did well out of their period in power and also accumulated wealth by becoming the conduit through which the RUF smuggled diamonds out of Sierra Leone; Liberian diamond exports jumped to $450m at the end of the 1990s, far in excess of the country's own mining capacity.[109]

Taylor's meddling in other countries and their conflicts inevitably rebounded on him. The eventual defeat and disintegration of the RUF and the failed sponsorship of a rebel group trying to overthrow President Lansana Conté of Guinea weakened Taylor's regional influence. The Guineans responded by backing yet another Liberian rebel group, Liberians United for Reconciliation and Democracy (LURD).

With help from Sierra Leonean militiamen, LURD first helped Conté defeat the Guinean rebels and then pushed into Liberia with strong Krahn and Mandingo support. Liberia's power to resist was weakened by an international arms embargo and trade sanctions by Western governments. LURD advanced on Monrovia, proving just as brutal as those it was trying to overthrow, and the capital was inundated with armies of bizarrely dressed fighters and child soldiers. The recruitment of children and arming of civilians, combined with beliefs among Poro and other societies that encouraged strange forms of dress or the wearing of masks, meant that Liberian armed groups presented terrifying images to ordinary civilians—and, via a sensation-hungry media, to the world. The most perceptive account of the role of Poro societies and ritualistic spiritual beliefs on the conflict is by Max Bankole Jarrett, a Liberian journalist with the BBC African Service:

> The behaviour and costumes of many fighters must, however, be seen as a bastardisation of Poro practices and symbolism. Their actions (cannibalism, mutilation of pregnant women and so forth) are influenced by the Poro code of symbols but they do not represent actual Poro practices...men [the fighters] have left most of the traditional ways behind, but they have chosen to interpret essential symbols from the traditional secret society in order to gain spiritual power in a modern war...Ritual violence is used to instil terror...many fighters have simply used the armoury available in their traditional cosmology to succeed on the battlefield.[110]

In August 2003, another ECOWAS military force was dispatched to Monrovia and Taylor went into exile in Nigeria, despite an indictment from the Special Court for Sierra Leone for his arrest on charges of crimes against humanity. US forces were also sent to keep order in the Liberian capital. Despite rioting in Monrovia in 2004, a relatively smooth transition to elections ensued, and in November 2005, Ellen Johnson-Sirleaf was elected president. The elections were seen as the most honest in Liberia's history, and the new president was the first woman to be elected head of state in Africa. The path towards reconciliation and the replacement of conflict with civilian politics was not smooth, with fighting in Lofa County between Christian and Muslim Liberians, but Johnson-Sirleaf established greater trust in her government domestically and internationally. Moreover in 2010, the IMF and World Bank agreed plans to relieve Liberia of the heavy debt burden built up over years of plunder and conflict. The next year Johnson-Sirleaf was joint winner of the Nobel Peace Prize, and she won re-election that November, though her opponents cried foul and boycotted the second round of elections.

Charles Taylor's retirement in Nigeria lasted only until 2006, when that country's President Obasanjo complied with a request from Johnson-Sirleaf to send him to trial. He was flown first to Liberia and then Sierra Leone before being transferred to the Special Court for Sierra Leone in the Hague. On 26 April 2012 he became the only former head of state since Nuremberg to be convicted for war crimes or crimes against humanity for his role in Sierra Leone's armed civil war and his plundering of the country's resources. He has not stood trial for his actions in Liberia, where a Truth and Reconciliation Commission investigated the crimes committed during the country's wars to no great effect. Taylor lost his appeal against his fifty-year sentence in 2013, and is now serving it in the UK.

The Liberian episode was part of a wider regional conflict that demonstrated both how porous West Africa's borders were and yet how easily they could become a focus for conflicts involving communities split across two or more states. But Liberia's war was not at its core an ethnic one; as Stephen Ellis has written, the explosion of armed movements:

> Did not have its origins in any generalised ethnic hatreds, but in the factionalism of ambitious politicians seeking to carve themselves a following. Once small groups of combatants, identifying themselves by ethnic labels, had begun to fight, and their activities had been reported in the media or by word of mouth, it easily led to more generalised suspicion of one group towards another. All of Liberia's current ethnic feuds started at the top and spread downwards.[111]

Settlers' domination and marginalisation of indigenous Liberians only began to end with the Doe coup. What followed was nearly three decades in which violence became the currency of power as the inadequate institutions and structures of Liberia's politics, society and economy power failed to accommodate change.

Sierra Leone's conflict had many similarities with Liberia's, and was inextricably bound up with it, but there were also important differences between the two, and they should not be conflated. Nonetheless, it can be argued that without the Liberian civil war, the RUF would never have received the Liberian and Burkinabé support necessary to make its Sierra Leonean offensive more than an isolated insurgency. Sierra Leone was fertile ground for the seeds of revolt, but none materialised until the government of General

Joseph Momoh backed ECOMOG and helped ULIMO launch its attacks into Liberia, provoking Taylor to strike back. Sierra Leone had social and cultural similarities with Liberia—both had Mende-speaking communities and an urban, educated elite descended from freed slaves. The Creole aristocracy that developed in the Sierra Leonean capital, Freetown, opposed the joining of the city with the 'up-country' protectorate administered separately by the British. The union of the two zones in advance of decolonisation in 1961 seemed to have created a certain unity between the Temne speakers of the north and the Mende in the south as a counterbalance to the educated, economically privileged urban Creoles.[112] But this unity began to fray when parties began to be formed to fight elections in the late 1950s.

A powerful southern movement formed around Milton Margai and the Sierra Leone People's Party (SLPP), which had strong support from Mende chiefs; it could benefit from traditional power structures in the south, but did not become a national mass party.[113] Siaka Stevens' All People's Congress (APC), meanwhile, dominated the north. The SLPP was able to generate enough support beyond the south to make Margai prime minister in 1958, and he led Sierra Leone to independence in 1961.

The north considered itself comparatively disadvantaged in comparison with Freetown and the south, which had alluvial diamond deposits and as a result inherited a better colonial-era system of transport and trade. The SLPP assiduously promoted southern, Mende interests, and chiefs benefited hugely from diamond revenues and government patronage. But by the 1967 elections, Stevens' APC had gained ground among the youth in the north and other undeveloped areas thanks to its reformist, populist platform and criticism of the power of Mende chiefs. Stevens won, with a clear electoral split between the APC-dominated north and the SLPP's southern stronghold. But the army, led by a Mende officer corps, stepped in and seized power to prevent northern political control—but it was handed back to Stevens as the new prime minister after northern soldiers and NCOs turned on their officers and secured his return from a brief exile.[114]

Stevens was a populist, but he ruled through a remodelled patronage network little different from Margai's. He replaced Mende officers with northerners, stripping the army leadership of southerners and bringing the influential role of Mende chiefs to an end.[115] His patronage was based on a small but far from stable elite connected with the diamond trade, and he used imported rice, Sierra Leone's staple food, as a means of buying support from the army, the business sector and important regional leaders in the north. The diamond trade slipped more and more out of the formal economy and into informal networks with Stevens at their centre. Recorded diamond exports fell from two million carats in 1970 to 595,000 in 1980, then 48,000 in 1988; the real earnings remained substantial, but went unrecorded. To avoid dependence on southerners in the diamond areas, dealing licences were given to Lebanese and Afro-Lebanese traders, who had no political constituency or ambitions and so did not pose any threat, and who also enabled Stevens to establish business relations with the Middle East, bringing in funds that had been unavailable to his predecessor.[116]

The army was the other key to Stevens' grip on the country, but despite promoting northern officers, he never entirely trusted it, and there was an attempted coup in 1971. It involved Corporal Foday Sankoh and several other low ranking soldiers, who were later to emerge in the leadership of the RUF. Stevens declared Sierra Leone a republic in 1971 and became its executive president. He relied more and more on informal economic networks, and established his own security system separate from an increasingly marginalised army; named the Special Security Division (SSD) and recruited from among APC militants, it was violent and acted with impunity against the president's opponents. It became known as Siaka Stevens's Dogs.[117] Stevens used it to intimidate opponents and ensure victory in the elections of 1973 and 1977, after which he declared the country a one-party state. The system changed little after 1985, when Stevens handed power to one of the few army officers he trusted, Maj-Gen Joseph Momoh.

Momoh took over just as the IMF and World Bank pressed the government to reform the management of the economy. Little was achieved. When the state did divest itself of loss-making or costly enterprises they were distributed among Momoh's tight-knit circle, which became known as the Binkolo mafia, after his home town. As in other African states, the IMF adjustment requirements hit the urban and rural poor the hardest via drastic reductions in food subsidies, while rising petrol prices affected domestic trade.[118] The whole political and economic system served only a small elite, with rural people, the urban poor and those outside Momoh's northern-dominated clique impoverished and marginalised. A recipe for conflict and revolt.

It was against this domestic background that Sierra Leone became a staging post and supplier of troops for the ECOMOG operation in Liberia—and therefore a target for the RUF. The RUF was formed by exiled Sierra Leoneans, and proclaimed a populist, anti-corruption, anti-elite platform that appealed to those excluded by the post-independence governments; it is not clear to what extent Taylor used the RUF as a tool, and to what extent it was his creation. Its fighters included former Sierra Leonean soldiers, Sierra Leoneans who had fought for the NPFL, and an assortment of West African political militants and mercenaries recruited through the Burkinabé and Libyan backers who helped Taylor fund the RUF.

On 23 March 1991, the RUF made its first incursion across the border, with around 100 RUF insurgents entering eastern Sierra Leone from Liberia. Their attacks were brutal, and the non-Sierra Leonean fighters were later blamed by the RUF for early atrocities and looting. The RUF's attacks on villages and civilians did not give much credence to the movement's purported radical programme of ending corruption and restoring democracy.[119] The poorly armed, poorly trained and poorly-led Sierra Leone Army (SLA) was unprepared for the incursion, and the RUF soon seized most of Kailahun region. Only the arrival of Guinean troops enabled the SLA to stop the RUF moving on the key eastern towns of Bo and Kenema. But now the movement controlled the diamond areas in Kailahun, it had a means of supporting its rebellion and repaying its backer, Taylor.

It would be simple to chalk the war up to sheer greed, but the RUF was more than that: both a tool the Liberians could use to destabilise Taylor's enemies and a movement that, for all its rapacity, did manage to appeal to some of those marginalised by a greedy and incompetent government. But over time, the RUF failed to demonstrate that it had a political programme beyond stock diatribes against corruption and promises of change. Many people still might have been swayed had the RUF implemented democratic rule in areas it controlled and moved away from the extreme brutality that characterised its rebellion from the start.[120]

The RUF invasion was seen in Freetown and across West Africa (especially in Guinea, Senegal and Nigeria) as an extension of Liberia's war and evidence of more interference in the region by Burkina Faso and Libya.[121] The Liberian angle of the conflict was only highlighted by the Sierra Leone government's use of ULIMO insurgents to fight the RUF and to seize areas inside the Liberian border to try and cut its supply lines. Guinean and Nigerian troops from ECOMOG were deployed in Sierra Leone and border areas of Liberia to fight the RUF.[122] As the insurgency continued, it emerged that the RUF was relying on forced recruitment, the use of child soldiers and brutal retribution against those who failed to support it. It became notorious for the amputation of hands or arms as a punishment for people in areas it overran. The BBC's West Africa correspondent at the time, David Bamford, wrote that whereas the RUF started with high-minded ideals about ending corruption and creating democracy, it "quickly degenerated into a movement dominated by young and impoverished men seeking opportunities to loot the countryside and enrich themselves" and with a leadership prepared to deploy forcibly recruited child and teenage soldiers to control territory through the use of terror.[123]

In April 1992, the RUF was both given an opportunity and at the same time faced a new threat. A coup in Sierra Leone led by young army officers removed Momoh and established the National Provisional Ruling Council (NPRC), led by Captain Valentine Strasser. This was not a planned coup, but rather a mutiny by junior officers over poor pay and the lack of support for the army fighting the RUF. The NPRC suspended the constitution and banned political parties, which had been legalised by Momoh in 1991 under domestic and international pressure. The new military rulers not only appealed to the young, but included southerners in the government after a long period of northern domination. The NPRC said it would bring a quick end to the war, and the RUF claimed at the time that it offered to negotiate an end to the fighting,[124]—but Strasser made no move to seize this opportunity, and the NPRC concentrated on entrenching its hold on power in Freetown. All it offered the RUF was an amnesty in return for unconditional surrender, and no serious attempt was made to start talks. The RUF survived a brief offensive launched by Strasser and then advanced into the Kono area, taking more of the diamond fields. By 1994, it controlled territory that included bauxite and titanium mines, eating into the government's export income.

By 1995, the RUF was within reach of Freetown. Strasser's NPRC was on the back foot and turned to mercenaries to train the SLA and local militias. The South African Executive Outcomes mercenary group became involved in command, logistics and combat roles.[125] Part of the deal with Executive Outcomes, as would later be the case with the British Sandline mercenary group, was that it would gain diamond concessions. The mercenaries and SLA were able to clear the RUF from the vicinity of Freetown and to recapture the Kono diamond fields. Local militias known as *kamajors*, recruited from among hunters in Mende areas of eastern Sierra Leone, also helped push back the RUF and keep control of the areas recaptured. These militias were a localised initiative supported by the NPRC and subsequent governments, but they were not disciplined and were hated by the SLA. Another phenomenon developed at this time: the 'sobel', a soldier by day and a rebel by night. Poorly paid, badly trained and unmotivated, soldiers would join the rebels at night while serving as SLA soldiers during the day, only adding to the confusion over who was fighting for whom and why.

The NPRC's fortunes progressively declined. Strasser tried to cling on to power, announcing that he would stand in elections to return the country to civilian rule. This was too much for his fellow officers, and in January 1996 he was overthrown by his deputy, General Maada Bio, who ensured the elections went ahead without Strasser's candidacy. By then, at ECOWAS's insistence, peace talks had started in Abidjan between the NPRC and the RUF. The elections were Sierra Leone's most peaceful and fair up until then,[126] and were won by the SLPP. Ahmad Tejan Kabbah became president, and negotiated a peace deal with Sankoh's rebels involving an amnesty for RUF fighters—effectively giving impunity to those involved in atrocities. The final agreement provided for the withdrawal of Executive Outcomes, but not ECOMOG forces. There were provisions for an international peacekeeping force, but no central or local government posts for the RUF; a new army was to be formed incorporating the RUF and the SLA.

Kabbah was doomed from the start. He lacked the support of the army, which opposed his plans for unification of forces and was strongly opposed to the use of the *kamajors* as part of the security apparatus. Promised international aid was slow to arrive, and the RUF showed it had little intention of sticking to the Abidjan agreement. The planned demobilisation, disarmament and reintegration programme, supposed to be paid for by donors, received only a fraction of the $232m promised. In the vacuum that resulted, restive elements in the army and the rebels started to find common ground,[127] and on 25 May 1997, a disgruntled group of soldiers arrested their officers and attacked a prison in Freetown, freeing a number of officers and soldiers charged with treason against the government, including Major Johnny Paul Koroma. At the time of the coup, Sankoh was in detention in Nigeria, but Koroma was able to contact him and get the RUF's support for the coup. The government was overthrown, and a new military regime formed.

The coup led to heavy fighting in Freetown, during which soldiers went on a rampage of raping, killing and looting. A new government, the Armed Forces Revolutionary Council (AFRC), was formed with Koroma at its head, and Kabbah was forced to flee. The AFRC banned the *kamajors* and the RUF accepted posts in the new government, but the AFRC reckoned without the Nigerian forces in Freetown, which were reinforced by air and fought both the army and RUF. More mercenaries, this time brought in by the British company Sandline International, were deployed with the knowledge of the British government (though this was denied when the UK held an official inquiry) and worked with the Nigerian ECOMOG forces. Michael Grunberg of Sandline has since said the company's personnel played key planning roles in the ECOMOG offensive that retook Freetown from the AFRC and RUF in February 1998.[128] After this was done, Kabbah was able to return to Freetown and restore a recognised government.

With Kabbah back in office, Foday Sankoh was flown from detention in Nigeria to Freetown to stand trial for treason, and in October 1998 he was found guilty and sentenced to death. In response, the RUF launched "Operation No Living Thing", killing civilians and increasing its use of mutilation as a punishment and a warning to opponents.[129] Assistance from Liberia and Burkina Faso helped the movement regain lost territory and then seize control of the capital once again, upon which the RUF launched a reign of terror, killing over 5,000 civilians and destroying much of the city. The Nigerians fought back and regained control, but the offensive forced Kabbah to agree to peace talks in Lomé, where an agreement was signed in July 1999. It gave Sankoh and the RUF immunity from prosecution, and appointed the RUF leader as vice-president of the country and head of a mineral resources commission. UN forces would join ECOMOG and control the disarmament of the RUF forces.

The deal failed to end the division of the country between government and RUF-controlled areas, and the RUF concentrated on exploiting the diamond fields it controlled. As the UN force arrived, RUF units attacked ECOMOG troops, and in early 2000, the group abducted fifty UN peace-keepers. The UN force was weak and poorly supported, and when the RUF resumed operations it was in no position to resist. A force of 800 British paratroopers, ostensibly sent to evacuate foreign nationals, helped the UN retain control of the airport. The British force was supported by attack helicopters and special forces units and established order in Freetown, while a combination of SLA troops and the remaining *kamajor* forces stopped the RUF advance. Sankoh was captured, and the UN Security Council agreed to expand the UN force to 17,000, but the security situation remained poor, with renegade former army units such as the West Side Boys killing and looting in and around Freetown. At one stage they kid-napped eleven British troops, who were freed in a British special forces operation that killed one British hostage and sixty of the rebels.

Kabbah's SLPP won a convincing victory in elections in 2002, and later in the year British troops were withdrawn. Sankoh was put on trial, but died in detention before proceedings started. UN troops left at the end of 2005, and the following year the IMF and creditors wrote off Sierra Leone's debt of $1 billion. But although peace has prevailed since, with no sign of an RUF revival, Sierra Leone is still split between the SLPP and APC with their regional/ethnic constituencies. Little of the growth that has been generated by reconstruction and aid has trickled down to raise living standards.

Ethiopia and Eritrea: statehood, conflict and the democratic deficit

The overthrow of the Derg in May 1991 was expected to open the way for a less centralised and more democratic form of government in Ethiopia—though the Stalinist version of Marxism espoused by the leaders of the TPLF, which masterminded the military victory over the Derg, should have given pause for thought.

When Mengistu fled, the Ethiopian People's Revolutionary Democratic Front (EPRDF), dominated by the TPLF, took power in Addis Ababa.[130] The EPRDF was led by Meles Zenawi, head of the TPLF, and included the Ethiopian People's Democratic Movement, the Oromo People's Democratic Organisation (OPDO), and representatives of other regional groups. Its stated aim was to establish a democratic federation of ethnic regions enjoying equal rights. Going against all previous African political practice, the EPRDF emphasised ethnic identity rather than trying to diminish it. After the capture of Addis Ababa, the new leadership called a conference of all Ethiopia's major ethnic groups, which drafted a charter for a transitional government. This established that Ethiopia would follow "a path of reconciliation between ethnic groups and pursue peace and democratic cooperation in a federal state" whose government, in the future, would be made up of the representatives of ethnic/regional movements rather than national ones.[131] It proclaimed the protection of human rights and the right to self-determination of peoples and nationalities within the Ethiopian federation.

The conference established a transitional government with a Council of Ministers and Zenawi as president, but relatively few of the EPRDF's ethnic movements took part in national government, which remained dominated by the TPLF. Most of the alliance members had power locally or regionally and were kept in power by the TPLF army. Dissent was treated as subversion, and the new charter's human rights provisions were not implemented. Elections were organised in May 1992, with the EPRDF dominating the administration and validation of the vote. In some areas of the country where the support for its constituent members was not strong, the EPRDF required elections to be held two or three times until "the right result" was achieved, while in other areas results were simply disallowed, with EPRDF members appointed to the posts up for election.[132] There was no chance for Ethiopians to exercise their vote freely, and critics accused the TPLF of using the devolved system of government as a means of ensuring that Tigrayans could rule nationally by using divide and rule tactics locally.[133]

In 1994, the transitional government and parliament drew up and enacted a new constitution that enshrined the recognition of different nationalities with a nine region federal structure. Political representation would be through the regions and their ethnic movements. There would not be specific *national* parties, only coalitions like the EPRDF. To this day, the EPRDF has used this state structure and the new political institutions to retain power, with Zenawi in charge until his death through illness in August 2012. He acquired an international reputation for being intellectual and engaging, but in fact his approach to governing Ethiopia was "severe and dogmatic".[134] The Ethiopia he created was arguably more democratic than its predecessors, since opposition parties could and did exist; there was a freer media, but it was always threatened by harassment, the closure of papers or the arrest of journalists. Regionally, Zenawi's Ethiopia behaved like a hegemonic power, going to war with Eritrea in 1998–2000 and intervening repeatedly in Somalia. In areas of conflict, such as the Ogaden, groups like Human Rights Watch have criticised the government consistently for human rights abuses and the denial of basic rights to the Somali-speaking population.[135]

His government was less overtly authoritarian than its predecessors, and it did hold elections of a sort; it was more responsive than the monarchy or the Derg had been to food shortages, but it harassed opponents and used all the instruments at its disposal to retain power and weaken opponents. Famines weren't totally prevented, but they weren't ignored, and the government would request help and assist in the supply of food aid during severe droughts. In 2003, one in five Ethiopians, fourteen million people, were threatened by famine after a drought, but appeals and international aid in co-operation with the government meant that somewhere between 300 and several thousand people died, rather than the tens or hundreds of thousands who would have done so under previous regimes.

In political terms, the developments since 1991 have enabled Zenawi and his successor, Hailemariam Desalegn, to retain power and manipulate the federal system. Ethiopia's first-past-the-post electoral process has meant the EPRDF constituent movements have been able to use national government power, local incumbency, access to funds and the support of the security forces to retain power often with under 40 per cent of the overall vote. This is especially easy in local and regional elections, with a multiplicity of small, weak and often harassed opposition parties. The EPRDF won national elections in 1995, 2000, 2005 and 2010, but in all cases it was clear that its control of power, patronage and selective restrictions on the media, along with harassment of opponents, had made for a less than fair competition.

What the EPRDF did do, however, was negotiate the secession of Eritrea. The EPLF had captured Asmara on 24 May 1991 and established an autonomous state, and talks between the EPRDF and EPLF recognised the Eritreans' right to secede and provided for a referendum on independence. In April 1993, Eritreans voted overwhelmingly to form their own state—meaning that for the first time, the OAU's binding principle of integrity and sovereignty of states had been breached.

With huge popular support, Eritrea's *de jure* independence began on 24 May 1993. But independence did not bring about the new era of peace, freedom and democracy that most Eritreans had hoped for. At first, relations with Ethiopia were good, and Eritrea's right to self-determination was respected. The EPLF formed the government, using its reputation as "one of the most durable and successful liberation movements in the Third World" as a key selling point to its people.[136] Although the OAU was against the redrawing of borders and secessionism, the EPLF's enjoyed prestige in Africa and Ethiopia's acceptance of independence smoothed the way to widespread acceptance of an independent Eritrea. It helped that Eritrea had been a separate Italian colony joined to Ethiopia after the Italian withdrawal.

Under the leadership of Isaias Afewerki, the EPLF started to transform itself from a guerrilla movement into a political party. The People's Front for Democracy and Justice (PFDJ). The new government was recognised internationally, and Eritrea became a full member of the OAU and the UN. Having appeared to have developed an egalitarian structure and an inclusiveness that made it a national movement, the PFDJ was expected to garner wide support in an independent Eritrea and to develop a participatory style of government—but it soon became clear that like many liberation movements, it assumed that its role in the struggle gave it the automatic right to rule.

The old Eritrean Liberation Front (ELF), which had more support than the PFDJ among Muslims and people of the southern lowlands, was not allowed to operate, and any opponents of the government were dealt with harshly.[137] Far from being inclusive and encouraging plurality, the PFDJ moved against civil society organisations and local NGOs and clamped down hard on foreign NGOs, which it saw as encouraging dissent. In contrast to Ethiopia's highly ethnicised system, the Afewerki government repressed parties that could be seen as regional, religious or ethnic. The writing of a new constitution and the holding of elections were constantly put off, the war with Ethiopia being used as an excuse for delay.

A minor border skirmish with Ethiopia in May 1998 resulted in the deaths of several Eritrean soldiers. In response, Eritrean forces invaded a contested area around Badme, where the border had not been clearly defined. The war over this area lasted for two years, and killed 70,000 soldiers and civilians. In 1999, Ethiopian forces recaptured Badme, pushing 30 km into Eritrean territory, it became clear that Eritrea was losing. OAU and UN mediation efforts established a ceasefire in June 2000. Eritrea was forced to withdraw from all the areas it had seized; a UN peacekeeping force was deployed and a border demarcation operation established. By mid-2001, both the Ethiopians and Eritreans said they had withdrawn from territory seized during the war, and they agreed on a clear demarcation of the border. However when the boundary commission awarded Badme to Eritrea, Ethiopia said that it accepted it in "principle" but still maintained its claim. Tension on the border remains high.

During the conflict, Eritrean opposition groups criticised Afewerki and the government for getting involved in a costly war. This led to the arrest of hundreds of opposition activists and increasingly tight government control over any groups like student movements and civil society or human rights groups. In 2002, the national assembly voted to refuse to permit the formation of political parties other than the ruling PFDJ. The country soon moved down the road of authoritarianism with little respect for freedom of speech, a tightly-controlled media, and the arrest or forcing into exile of any dissenting individuals or groups.

After more than two decades of independence, Eritrea has developed a reputation as one of the most repressive governments in Africa, and is seen as a destabilising force in an already conflict-prone region. The border area remains tense, as relations between Ethiopia and Eritrea have been further marred by Eritrea's support for al-Shabaab in Somalia.[138] In 2007, the US State Department said it had added Eritrea to the list of countries it had identified as sponsoring terrorism. Eritrea routinely refuses to co-operate with UN mediation or human rights missions, and repeatedly refused the UN's human rights rapporteur access to the country. Nevertheless, in May 2013, UN Special Rapporteur Sheila Keetharuth issued a report detailing the excessive militarisation of Eritrean society, which she said was "affecting the very fabric of Eritrean society, and its core unit, the family" and was forcing people into exile. The UN report added that there was no rule of law to provide citizens with protection against state actions, and criticised the "pervasive human rights violations committed on a daily basis in Eritrea... [including] Extrajudicial killings, enforced disappearances, indefinite incommunicado detention, torture, cruel, inhuman or degrading treatment."[139] Eritreans have reacted to this authoritarian and repressive system by leaving, preferring the dangers of migration as refugees and the perilous routes to reach Europe—hundreds or perhaps even thousands drowning in the process. But the Eritrean government has remained intransigently blind to the opposition and aspirations of much of its population.

6

THE NEW MILLENNIUM

African history continued its uneven development in the new millennium. There were major advances that improved the quality of life for some, but without sufficiently addressing the causes of widespread poverty and inequality; there was greater freedom of speech and of political activity, but little real empowerment of ordinary citizens; there was a burst of strong economic growth and renewed international interest in African economies, but no end to the dependence on primary exports, and the curse of the gatekeeping elites and their clients persisted in evolving forms.

More accountable systems developed in some states, but in many others, elections and multiparty politics were a front for continued rule via hegemonic and unaccountable networks of power and wealth. Political parties continued to develop along personalised or community/ethnic lines rather than issue-based national ones, and remained top-down movements based on powerful people or groups. Elections were frequently marked by violence, though citizens still took them seriously even if they had little chance of changing policy and were often rendered worthless by fraud. Political change was still retarded by the lingering legacies of patrimonialism, external influence and the heavy concentration of individual or group power in places with weak state, civil and judicial institutions.

The Cold War was a thing of the past, but African states remained peripheral, weak and subject to the policies of major powers, which now centred on resource acquisition and then combating Islamist movements with a real or imagined potential to threaten Western security. The West's strategic approach to the continent had little to do with mutual interest and was instead pre-occupied with security, particularly once the US-led 'War on Terror' began after the 9/11 attacks. The other important external factor in Africa's international political and economic relations during the period was the growing economic power and reach of the Chinese, who became trading partners, investors and ever-hungry consumers of Africa's raw materials. China offered an alternative to dependence on the West and gave states a new bargaining chip, but its economic engagement with Africa was controversial and far from altruistic.

The period also saw the rise and fall of NEPAD, the creation of the African Union, and the birth of South Sudan—undermining further the principle that Africa's inherited borders were set in stone.

Sudan splits, but conflict continues

The 1990s saw the rise of a more militantly Islamic but essentially military-based regime in Sudan, built on the enduring political power of the riverine Arab elite. The new government had to cope with regional conflicts in South Kordofan, Southern Blue Nile and particularly in Darfur, all fuelled by the political and economic exclusion and marginalisation of those outside the dominant Nile Valley groups. Khartoum also faced the resurgence of SPLA/M in the south, which finally forced it to accept that the south would inevitably secede at some point. But when the South's secession came, it was anything but the start of peaceful coexistence between Khartoum and Juba. Nor did it to give birth to a united, peaceful South Sudan, or a government committed to meeting the expectations of its newly independent people. Instead, the right-to-rule syndrome of liberation movements held sway once again.[1]

The path towards first ceasefire, and then secession, was marked by conflict and uneasy compromises between the Sudanese government and the SPLA/M. All other political groups, parties and ethnic/regional movements in Sudan were excluded from the peace process at the behest of the warring sides, and with the acquiescence of African and international mediators, notably the United States. In their attempts to bring the SPLA and Khartoum together, it became clear that the parties accepted that a lasting solution to the conflict would only come when South Sudan's right to self-determination was accepted.

A complex web of factors finally made agreement preferable to stalemate: the disintegration of the ruling National Islamic Front (NIF) alliance between the Islamist leader Hassan al-Turabi and President Omar al-Bashir; the SPLA/M's ability to continually bounce back from disunity and near-defeat; on-off support for the SPLA/M from Uganda, Ethiopia and Eritrea; American sanctions against Sudan in 1998 for its suspected role in the Kenya and Tanzania embassy bombings; the international consequences of the 9/11 attacks on America (including Sudan's provision of intelligence about Osama bin-Laden and al-Qaeda); and both sides' need to come to an agreement over the all-important oil revenues. Under the pressure of these circumstances, Sudan's factions were forced into a series of meetings at Machakos and Naivasha in Kenya.

At the Machakos talks, a protocol was agreed that included Khartoum's recognition of the South's right to secede and set out vaguely worded commitments to the development of democracy. The US, IGAD and the African Union put pressure on the two principals to agree a peace deal, but excluded all other parties and failed to address the related conflicts in South Kordofan, Blue Nile and Abyei (the Three Territories) or to deal with the war in Darfur. By giving them sole representation, bilateral, internationally mediated talks only entrenched the political power of both the Bashir government and the SPLA/M.

Even the strong opposition of the SPLA/M's Garang could not keep southern self-determination out of the final agreement. Garang was still firmly wedded to the idea of a reformed and unified Sudan in which he would play a major role;[2] he wanted a formula that would maintain Sudan's integrity, but change the political balance of power and end the hegemony of the riverine political network. But his movement, as was demonstrated after he died in a helicopter crash in July 2005, did not share this vision and was in favour of secession. At the same time, Bashir and his NCP movement (the National Congress Party, which replaced the NIF after the split with Turabi, who formed the Popular Congress Party, PCP) were beginning to see a split with the South as the lesser of two evils, and as a way of preserving power in the north and retain a share of oil revenues.

After the signing of the Comprehensive Peace Agreement in January 2005, most of the southern militias that had originally formed to resist SPLA/M dominance joined with it, including many Nuer from the SSDF. Riek Machar rejoined the SPLA/M and became vice-president of South Sudan until he was sacked by President Salva Kiir, Garang's successor as leader of the SPLM, in July 2013. The reintegration of Nuer, Murle and other ethnic groups into the SPLA did not end local rivalries; the Dinka resented being integrated with those who had fought against them, while the Nuer and Murle were no happier to be footsoldiers in a Dinka-commanded army. This would cause conflict and disorder both before and after the South's independence. The availability of arms, the establishment of local, community militias for self-protection, and the resentment of the SPLA/M's supremacist approach, along with Sudanese support for rebel groups, ensured that localised and regional conflicts did not disappear from the South.

The CPA established a timetable for elections across Sudan in July 2009 and a referendum in the South on self-determination, to be held in 2011; prior to the votes, a unity government would be formed including SPLA/M leaders. The NCP was to have a majority of posts in the north and the SPLA/M in the south, with no voice for other parties. This was an imposed peace, with international mediators perfectly willing to narrow participation for the sake of reaching a deal and ending the north-south war. Neither the NCP and SPLA/M was committed to real democratisation and the detail of the CPA, and mutual accusations of failure to implement its provisions persist to this day. There is also still conflict over the Three Territories,[3] especially Abyei, a key oil producing area and scene of conflict between the Ngok Dinka and the nomadic Misseriya Arabs, who had fought in Khartoum-sponsored militias against the SPLA/M in South Kordofan.

While vital issues like land ownership and use, water resources, and the position of nomadic peoples were ignored or dealt with as peripheral matters, continuing the pattern of marginalisation that had dominated Sudanese history since before independence, the CPA concentrated on the future of Sudan's oil industry and revenues. This was Sudan's chief source of revenue, and provided 98 per cent of South Sudan's income.[4] The oil was mainly in South Sudan, with a smaller percentage in the north, and the imperative to protect it had always been at the core of the north-south conflict, since the discovery of exploitable oil deposits. As with the overall political negotiations—which established structures of governance, military power and economic management that marginalised other political forces and communities—the oil provisions in the CPA shored up the hegemony of the two signatories, splitting the oil revenues between them.

Sudan's oil industry had helped internationalise a conflict that had a strong and lingering regional involvement and impact. Exploration and exploitation had originally been in the hands of the US Chevron company, but it pulled out when the war escalated, leaving the way clear for China, Malaysia and others to move in. China's National Petroleum Corporation was the key player, and China supplemented its role in the oil industry by selling large quantities of arms to Sudan and providing loans for infrastructure projects. As was the case in Nigeria's Delta region, few of those most directly affected by the oil industry benefited from its revenues. As much as 75 per cent of the oil-producing areas' population was displaced, and there were very high livestock losses for local communities dependent on cattle.[5]

Under the division of territory in the CPA, South Sudan would have 78 per cent of the oil producing areas, but would be dependent on the pipelines controlled by Khartoum to export the oil. There was no definitive agreement on division of revenues, an issue that would bedevil the transition period and then the fractious relationship between the Sudans after secession, as Sudan periodically blocked the shipment of oil through its pipelines and South Sudan ceased oil production when it accused Sudan of stealing oil to sell to the Chinese.

The period between the signing of the CPA and the southern referendum of January 2011 was beset by mutual recriminations, the continuation of the war in Darfur, an insurgency fought by SPLA/M groups in South Kordofan and southern Blue Nile, continual rows over oil revenues, and deadlock over the future of Abyei. The one area of agreement between the two main rivals was that they should dominate their areas and exclude other parties from power. The CPA did not address the major problem in Sudan: as John Young put it, "The crux of the problem remained the structural inequities of the Sudanese state, which the international community, the SPLM, and the NCP could not agree to resolve,"[6] largely because they didn't have an overriding interest in doing so. The division of oil resources (and the disputes surrounding them) were also bound up with the "concerns and interests of elites, especially in and around the NCP and the SPLM, rather than the majority of the population."[7]

The elections established under the CPA were due to take place in 2009, but were delayed until 2010. Just before the vote, the SPLM made its pro-secession turn clear by withdrawing most of its candidates for the National Assembly and its candidate for the national presidency, leaving Salva Kiir as its candidate for the Southern presidency. Despite residual support for al-Mahdi's Umma Party and the Khatmiyya sect's DUP, Bashir won the national presidency in the first round of voting, and his NCP took 323 of 450 parliamentary seats. In the South, Kiir won the presidency with 92.99 per cent of the vote and the SPLM took 160 out of 170 assembly seats. The SPLM's Southern dominance was now superficially legitimate, but few other parties had the resources to compete and the movement was able to use its position in government to ensure its massive victory.

Kiir used the momentum from his huge win to prepare for the independence referendum, and to negotiate from a position of strength to integrate the most important of the armed groups into the ruling movement. Paulino Madeep, the head of the rump of the SSDF, was brought into the SPLM and his forces began to be integrated into the SPLA. In the period between the CPA and the elections, the UN estimated that fighting in the South between the SPLA and local militias or dissident SPLA units had killed over 2,500 people and displaced 350,000. There was also an endemic problem of cattle raiding and land disputes among the different Nuer communities, the Murle and the Dinka groups.[8]

After the CPA, the SPLA/M had made little effort to develop the civilian side of the movement beyond basic administration or to improve service provision and popular participation. When it took over government in the South, the SPLA/M remained very much a military organisation with a small political leadership drawn mainly from Dinka military commanders. The death of Garang had shifted power away from the Bor Dinka, but not from the Dinka overall; groups from Equatoria, the Murle, the various Nuer communities and the Shilluk did not have much share in power despite the South's huge ethnic and cultural diversity. Dinka dominance and Garang's autocratic style, maintained in a more understated but still authoritarian manner under Kiir and his army support network, had led to the Nuer revolt and to the bitter Nuer civil war in the early 1990s,[9] and had left a legacy of both SPLA/M hegemony and armed resistance by more marginalised or dissident groups.

This legacy has outlasted independence, with continuing armed conflict between the SPLA and rebel groups—among them former SSDF fighters, those of Murle militia leader David Yau Yau in Jonglei, and the Nuer dissidents. SPLM in-fighting and Kiir's determination to keep his power undiluted came to a head in July 2013 with the sacking of the vice-president, Nuer leader Riek Machar, and the SPLM secretary-general, Shilluk leader Pagan Amum. This in turn led to a civil war, which began in December 2013 with attempts to disarm Nuer soldiers in the Presidential Guard. At the time of writing there was continuing fighting, particularly in Unity State, despite attempts to achieve a workable ceasefire. Regular rounds of talks mediated by the Ethiopian government failed to bring peace or any real meeting of minds between the Kiir government and Machar's supporters. Machar's rebels and groups loyal to other militia leaders opposed to Kiir still control large areas of Upper Nile and Unity states, with mutual accusations of ethnic massacres against both Nuer and Dinka forces in the government and rebel forces.[10] At the time of writing the prospects of an early end to the war and a lasting political solution seem very distant. Over one million people have been displaced, 3.8 million are severely short of food and dependent on aid from international NGOs and the economy and oil industry are in tatters.

Long before the north-south peace agreement, another conflict had developed that grabbed international media attention and resulted in the International Criminal Court indicting President Bashir and a number of senior officials and militia leaders for crimes against humanity. The Darfur conflict was not a new one, but when it flared into a major revolt against Khartoum in 2003 it became a focus of world attention. The origins of the conflicts there are complex, and there are several, involve interlocking factors that on their own might not have led to such an intractable war, but which together defied the powers of traditional communal negotiating customs—even though the main combatants were local rather than national groups and communities.

Darfur is home to a diverse group of linguistic, ethnic and self-proclaimed communities. The name Darfur derives from the sultanate of the Fur people; it was inhabited by the Fur, the Tunjur, the Meidob and the Zaghawa in the north, and the Berti, Birgid and Masalit along the western part of the border with Chad. These groups came to be seen as African communities, especially after the early Darfur conflicts in the 1980s and 1990s. The Arab presence in the region goes back centuries; its most important groups were the Baggara cattle herders and the Abbala camel herders. The Baggara were divided into separate communities such as the Beni Halba and the Rizeigat. Like the Zaghawa and Masalit, the Rizeigat community was spread between Darfur and Chad.[11] With such an array of groups, there is no simple division of peoples into 'African' and 'Arab' or settled farmer and pastoralist. Conflicts between farmers and nomadic pastoralists have been part of the region's heritage, but do not alone explain the descent into war any more than ethnic factors do. The labels African and Arab encompass a range of identities that are not always obvious to outsiders; many of those seen as Africans are Arabic speakers, and there are few differences in appearance, with Rizeigat looking very 'African' and 'African' Zaghawa more 'Arabic' in appearance.[12] In such a complicated context, identities become blurred and can be manipulated to meet the political ends of ambitious elites.

A frontier region whose communities straddle the Chad-Sudan border or migrate between them, Darfur was vulnerable to the effects of the decades-old war in Chad. Chadian factions—particularly those connected with the Zaghawa community and Arabic-speaking militias or movements who received Libyan support—came and went from Darfur, bringing in weapons and exporting their conflicts to the region's divided and vulnerable communities. Chadian refugees, often armed and used to combat, fled into Darfur or migrated there looking for grazing for their animals. These incursions or migrations coincided with the environmental degradation of the Sahel and the shrinking of seasonal grazing lands and arable farmlands, and competition for land and resources soon boiled over into sharper conflicts. The intrusion of the power struggles in Sudan and the policies of Khartoum and the SPLA all helped turn Darfur's localised disputes into ethnic wars, where identity became highly politicised. Links between Darfur communities and their Chadian relatives meant weapons supplied by Libya to Chadian factions, who then took refuge in Darfur or used it as a rear base, became more widely available and were used to protect land and solve disputes. Local conflicts between farmers and nomads which once caused few fatalities escalated beyond chiefs' and elders' ability to solve with compromises and blood money in the case of deaths.

The conflict in Darfur is extraordinarily complex, and revolves around a number of interlinked issues. It's part of the broader conflict between marginalised Sudanese communities and the dominant central riverine Arabs, but also involves complex local tensions and competition for resources. It is not simply a periphery-centre conflict. The local factors include conflict between settled communities broadly identified as African—such as the Fur, Zaghawa and Masalit—and the various tribes and communities who make up the Baggara Arabs. The local conflicts have been further complicated by assorted political and military struggles in Chad and Darfur. National Sudanese politics, meanwhile, have intruded through the split in the NIF, which resulted in Turabi becoming a fierce opponent of Bashir's government and winning support among groups in Darfur which were developing into enemies of Khartoum because of the region's marginalisation and the divisive policies of the Khartoum government there. Many NIF members who were supporters of Turabi became members of his PCP movement, which gained strength in Darfur—notably among the Zaghawa community, which spreads across the Darfur-Chad border and is a major player in Chadian politics and conflicts. Zaghawi militants influenced by Turabi became key members of the rebel Justice and Equality Movement (JEM). The whole situation was made worse by Libyan meddling, with Gaddafi arming different factions according to his own constantly shifting alliances—leading to the creation of armed groups with agendas linked to Libya's periodically changing priorities.

The conflict involved rebellion against the rule by Khartoum and conflict with its local clients by Fur and Zaghawa groups united in the Sudanese Liberation Army/Movement (SLA/M). This was followed by the JEM when personal and political ambitions of some Fur and Zaghawa leaders led to splits in the SLA/M, and fighting between the factions, and shifting alliances or agreements between those factions, the SPLA and the government in Khartoum. The complexity of the conflict and the blurring of loyalties were not helped by Sudan's attempts to fight cheap local wars from a distance by using local militias supported by government forces and aircraft; local disputes were manipulated to tie militias to Khartoum and increase local enmities, thereby weakening opposition to Khartoum.[13] In Darfur, these militias were based on the Baggara communities, and they became known as the Janjaweed. They were used to fight the Darfur rebels, and were encouraged to push 'Africans' off land that the 'Arabs' wanted for grazing. The Janjaweed militias were paid with arms and money from Khartoum. These forces gained a reputation for extreme brutality, summary killings, rape and the destruction of entire villages suspected of supporting the rebels. The Janjaweed and the government were accused of atrocities and of failing to deal with the massive humanitarian consequences of both conflict and drought, which affected over two million people in Darfur. Bombing raids by the Sudanese armed forces would be followed up by horse-borne Janjaweed fighters who attacked villages and settlements suspected of harbouring rebels.

International horror at the humanitarian consequences of the Darfur war—even though the war in the South was longer and more costly in life and suffering—and the simplistic 'good Africans, bad Arabs' reporting of the conflict led the US and UN to pressure Sudan for an end to the conflict.[14] In March 2004, the UN co-ordinator in Darfur, Mukesh Kapila, called the conflict a genocide and blamed the Sudanese government and Janjaweed for mass killings.[15] After intensive lobbying by human rights and evangelical Christian groups, the US Congress condemned the government and militia killings as genocide. Similar condemnation was coming from within Africa, and the recently formed African Union sent a monitoring mission to Darfur and stepped in to assist Nigerian and Chadian efforts to broker a ceasefire. US pressure led to a UN Security Council resolution in July 2004 demanding that the Sudanese government disarm the Janjaweed within thirty days and facilitate the delivery of humanitarian aid to the two million displaced people starving in camps in Darfur and adjoining areas. The UN Security Council set up a commission to investigate the genocide, which resulted in a referral to the International Criminal Court (ICC). The ICC indicted both the JEM and SLA and seven Sudanese politicians and militia leaders—including President Bashir. While proceedings are active against those indicted, they have not been brought to trial, and Bashir remains president. The indictment against Bashir has created huge problems for the AU, as he is subject to arrest when he travels abroad. Most AU states have ignored this, but Malawi declined to hold the AU summit in 2012 as Joyce Banda refused to allow Bashir into the country. In 2015, Bashir attended the AU summit in South Africa and there was an outcry there when the Zuma government failed to detain him and allowed him to leave the country covertly through a South African military airfield.

A peace deal between the government and some of the rebels was eventually signed in May 2006. One faction of the SLA, SLA-Minnawi was a party to the deal, but another main SLA faction and the main JEM faction refused to take part. As a result of the deal, SLA-Minnawi became part of the Sudanese government, while the JEM and other SLA factions continued the war (around this time, the JEM was helping Idris Deby in Chad fight off a coup attempt). Despite the peace agreement and UN ultimatums, the Janjaweed continued to operate; they became part of the wider Central African insurgency, banditry and poaching problem through their mobility and traditional trading/smuggling role in the region. Under the peace deal, an Africa Union force, AMIS, was deployed in Darfur, but was replaced in 2008 by the UN-African Union Mission in Darfur (UNAMID). UNAMID is still there and has suffered numerous casualties during its deployment, without definitively curbing attacks by either rebel factions or the government-backed militias. The UN has estimated that the Darfur conflict has killed around 300,000 people to date (most from disease or starvation) and displaced 2.7 million, of whom 1.7 million remain displaced to this day. Despite the peace deal, conflict continues on a localised basis in areas of Darfur, as communities fight for resources, with water and grazing still competed over fiercely.

Uganda: Museveni takes root and northern rebellion spreads to Central Africa

When the Ugandan National Resistance Army/Movement (NRA/M) seized power in 1986, overthrowing the northern-based military government that had toppled Milton Obote the year before, Ugandans hoped it would end decades of conflict driven by political and military leaders who used ethnic and regional grievances to entrench their power. Museveni's movement adopted a radical and inventive approach to political reconstruction. It was convinced that old-style party politics and the divisive policies of civilian and military leaders had been to blame for the years of bloodshed, the widening of divisions between north and south and between the country's ethnic groups. Eschewing party politics and the one-party state approach, Museveni and the NRM tried to build a 'no-party' system from the grass-roots that would encourage and enable popular participation without the potentially schismatic effects of party organisations. Existing parties like the old UPC of Obote and Ssemogerere's DP were allowed to exist, but not to compete in elections or hold conventions and congresses.

Many Ugandans and donors were prepared to accept the curb on political parties. Museveni described the old parties as "sectarian and divisive", and people were at first willing to accept his different approach. They believed his promises to end the rigging of elections and elite manipulation of politics, which he said were "an insult to the people....[and] a sure recipe for instability, conflict and upheavals."[16] Alongside the need for viable new political structures, there was also an urgent need to rebuild an economy shattered by war and corruption. The NRM was initially committed to a socialist approach, but it proved to be empty rhetoric; the movement quickly dropped any socialist leanings in the face of the massive need for financial and development aid. This forced the new government to become another poster boy for the neo-liberal, capitalist, free market reforms being demanded by the IMF, World Bank and donors in return for aid. Just as he would later agree to a return to multiparty politics, Museveni opted for this change in direction purely because he deemed it expedient. This tendency to change key policies seemingly on impulse and with little consultation became one of the defining themes of his tenure. As former minister and then Supreme Court judge George Kanyeihamba put it, Museveni became exactly the type of leader that Museveni the guerrilla leader would have fought against,[17] deriding African leaders who clung on to power only to do it himself, and referring the rebel LRA and Joseph Kony to the ICC only to attack the court for indicting too many Africans.

The NRM was faced with the task of governing a country in which over 300,000 civilians were killed in Obote's campaign to crush southern resistance in the Luwero Triangle. The army under Obote and Okello had been dominated by Langi and Acholi soldiers, with Acholi troops blamed for atrocities in the fight against the NRA. The NRM had a more diverse ethnic base than the army it defeated, but it was primarily southern, with a strong contingent of Museveni's Bahima and a large number of Rwandan Tutsi exiles in senior positions. The NRM at first followed a policy of inclusiveness, and co-opted UPC and DP politicians into its government. As it sought reconciliation and reconstruction from the ground up, it still had to fight against remnants of the military government's Ugandan National Liberation Army (UNLA), which had retreated to the north.

The NRM initially announced a four-year transition to the no-party system, and set about transforming the local resistance councils (RCs) set up during the bush war into the basis for a five-tiered council structure from village to district level. It sought to increase participation but also to mobilise, and was committed to increasing the role of women in political life.[18] The constitution-making process lasted from 1988, when the constitutional reform process was formally launched, to 1995, with the resistance councils legalised and revolutionary councils set up in every village, becoming local councils under the new administrative system. This was proclaimed as a grassroots approach to building a new political structure, one that would give space for Ugandans to exercise their agency without the divisive intervention of parties. It was very much a top-down process instituted by the NRM leadership. It did generate considerable interest and mobilized substantial involvement across much of southern and western Uganda (the north was more problematic, as will be seen), but very much according to a central agenda. Parties could not put up candidates for election even at village level, but the NRM had a central role at all levels, presenting itself as a renewal movement of the Ugandan people rather than a party.[19]

This approach was at first viewed in Uganda and among Western donor nations as a brave and innovative attempt to overcome the bitter divisions of the past. It went hand-in-hand with Museveni's 1987 acceptance of massive international financial aid in return for adopting economic policies in line with IMF/World Bank adjustment formulas. Ugandans were desperate to avoid a return to conflict, and were willing to give Museveni and the NRM time to develop their system. International and donor tolerance reflected the feeling that the new, post-Cold War governments coming into being in Africa (Uganda, Ethiopia and post-genocide Rwanda being the core three) were a positive development, especially as they followed regional and international policies consonant with Western priorities. This would become even more important after the 1998 East African embassy bombings, 9/11, and the rise of Islamic groups in Somalia. Uganda was a key Western ally along with Ethiopia in combating what, in 'War on Terror' terms, were thought of as African al-Qaeda franchises in Somalia. Uganda is key to US military surveillance and support operations in Africa.

Although directed from the top with the NRM playing a guiding role in the commission that was established to hold meetings around the country to discuss the future shape of the no-party system (which was non-negotiable at this stage), the process did involve massive popular participation and consultation. Its principal opponents were the main parties and the Buganda hierarchy.[20] People were involved in discussing the country's political future at parish, village, country and district level, but on NRM terms and according to its timetable, which stretched out longer than most Ugandans had expected. The 1995 constitution that emerged from this process was a product of consultation, but nonetheless followed a preconceived model. Rather than establishing a plural new order, "a close examination of the available evidence suggests that far from being based on the people's views, the people's constitution is a product of the country's elites: it was designed, written and promulgated by them."[21] But this was still a more inclusive process than anything that had gone before, and had the particularly positive effect of involving women and establishing constitutional guarantees for their status and political role. The political and economic reform process included credit schemes aimed at providing finance for women involved in agriculture (where they make up 80 per cent of the workforce). But as with the wider political process, there was a huge gap between the technical legal position and actual practice. Women have certainly taken a greater role in Uganda's civil society and politics, but their decision-making role remains limited, and deep cultural and religious factors still constrain them—paternal traditions, kinship systems and an education system that inhibits their opportunities.[22]

The 1995 no-party constitution set out plans for presidential and parliamentary elections in 1996, and for a referendum on the future of parties in 2000. The first election, though ostensibly non-party, was really a competition between Museveni's NRM and the combined forces of the DP and UPC, led by Paul Ssemogerere. Museveni was able to use all the benefits of incumbency, the resources of the state, the institutions of the NRM, the army and police to ensure a substantial victory; though the stability the NRM had brought to the south and ordinary Ugandans' fear that the DP and UPC would return them to the violent past clearly played a strong role in the result. The opposition only gained substantial support in the north, where the NRM's conflict with both Teso and Acholi groups had made it unpopular among most of the population.[23]

Alongside the political process and the IMF-influenced economic reforms, the NRM had to cope with the HIV/AIDS crisis, which began to hit Uganda hard in the mid-1980s. Between the initial emergence of the disease and the late 1990s, an estimated 1.5 million of Uganda's seventeen million people had been infected—the majority of them in the working-age population, between fifteen and forty-five years of age. In the early 1990s, AIDS became the leading cause of death among Uganda's young adults, with over 60,000 people dying from it each year. While the NRM government's programme to combat the disease cut the infection rate in the 1990s and 2000s and provided better care and treatment for those who were infected and developed AIDS, UN figures indicate that in 2011, Uganda still had a massive problem; 1.4m people had HIV, 6.7 per cent of working age adults were affected, and 1.1m children had been orphaned by HIV/AIDS.[24] This put a huge strain on a weak and underfunded health system and cost Uganda over $2.2m dollars annually in treatment costs; it was also a massive drain on the economically active population, and lowered productivity in agriculture and industry.

The NRA had fought a successful war and made up the backbone of the NRM, with senior officers holding major political positions. But the cost of the armed forces was a serious economic problem, and the guerrilla movement needed to be converted into an apolitical national army. Under pressure from donors who were unwilling to fund a massive army and a bloated civil service, the NRM worked to reduce the size of the army and the number of public servants. Between 1990 and 1996, the army (renamed the Ugandan People's Defence Force, UPDF) was reduced from 100,000 to 40,000, while the civil service was cut from 320,000 to 156,000. The personnel reductions kept the donors happy and they seemed willing to overlook the increase in the defence budget from $44m in 1991 to $200m in 2004[25]—money eaten up by violent rebellion in the north, Uganda's intervention in the DRC, and massive corruption, with senior officers claiming the salaries of ghost soldiers.

Serving and retired officers were among the chief beneficiaries of the government's privatisation process, and they used their new assets to support the NRM's political campaigns in the 2001 and 2006 elections. The UPDF's officer corps also used the involvement in the DRC's civil war to gain access to that country's mineral wealth. There is increasing evidence that the UPDF has used regional agreements to carry out counter-insurgency operations in South Sudan, CAR and the DRC to engage in ivory poaching and smuggling.[26] Museveni has continued to turn a blind eye to the army's corruption and other illegal forms of enrichment so as to ensure its loyalty, especially given that his only major competition in elections and most vocal critics have been former officers—notably former regimental commander Kizza Besigye and General David Sejusa. The latter fled to London in May 2013 after accusing Museveni of grooming his own son to succeed him as president.

During the 1990s a major privatisation campaign helped endear Museveni to his donors, even though it was implemented slowly and with considerable corruption. International financial institutions and donors gave Uganda over $500m a year between 1992 and 1996 and over $800m a year after 1996, all on condition that it implement an SAP with emphasis on reducing the size of the government sector and privatising parastatals. Donors have not seriously monitored the implementation of the programme or the way that economic reform has been used to help bolster the position of the NRM and enrich key clients through new networks; this has allowed Museveni and the NRM to reproduce "a corrupt and patronage-based government, and also helped that government to remain in political power."[27] The number of central government posts has been cut, but what is now a multi-layered local government system with a proliferation of councils dominated by the NRM has not led to a blossoming of grassroots democracy.

Uganda now has a massive and diffused system of patronage and client relationships, all effectively funded by foreign aid. The Ugandan *Monitor* newspaper wrote on 18 May 2001 that budget support, loans and donor aid had become a vast subsidy for Museveni to turn government agencies, semi-autonomous bodies supported by aid and local government administrations into "a long gravy train". Far from developing a new, accountable, grassroots-based system of government, Museveni has established a massive network of patron-client relationships that undermine the integrity of government and distort the political process to the advantage of the ruling movement. The economic reforms have brought growth, but with heightened dependence on exports and little real development or poverty alleviation. According to one researcher, most Ugandans in rural areas react to the notion that Uganda is an economic success story with surprise; development has benefited those in the ruling patron-client networks but not the ordinary people, and little development has trickled down to the mass of the Ugandan peasantry.[28]

Although Ugandans voted to keep the no-party system in a referendum in 2000—after a huge and costly NRM campaign to defeat those in the old parties who wanted a return to multiparty politics—another referendum was held in 2005 and this time the NRM advocated a return to party politics, which Ugandans strongly endorsed. This change of heart seems to have been brought about by growing opposition to Museveni within the NRM, evidenced by Colonel Kizza Besigye's strong challenge to him in the 2001 election, and a desire to head off donors' unease at the restrictive nature of the Ugandan political system.

Although Museveni has been at pains, particularly in recent years, to ward off Western pressure for change, the NRM's executive supported the return to plural politics by saying that Uganda "can ill afford to detach herself from the rest of the world."[29] Museveni won fiercely contested elections in 2006 and 2011, partly by jailing and constantly harassing opponents (notably Besigye), journalists and opponents, and by using government resources, the police and the army. What has resulted is undeniably better for most Ugandans than Obote and Amin's periods in power, and the principle of regular elections has been established. But the system of government is far from fully democratic; it has only the trappings of democracy, while the government continues to subvert real accountability and political competition through patronage and the use of state power.[30] Decentralised administrative structures and local government bodies act as supports for the ruling movement, rather than democratic institutions resting on popular consent. The dominant feature of the system is the power of the president and his ability to preserve his power by using patronage and the backing of the security forces.

The military's power derived not only from the guerrilla origins of the NRA/M, but from the problems of insurgency in northern Uganda. Insurgencies among the Teso, Acholi and groups along the western border with the DRC have required major military operations, and in turn the maintenance of a large army and substantial defence spending—creating a class of senior officers with substantial political and economic clout. The insurgencies arose when the north suddenly lost power after years of dominance under Obote, Amin and Okello (even though the Amin period saw massacres of Acholi and Langi by Kakwa troops), and the breakdown of traditional structures of power and social control among northern communities, especially the Acholi. Museveni was able to use the insurgencies to maintain international support thanks to his own and the international media's one-sided depiction of the conflict; he also used the conflicts as an excuse to limit political activity in a potentially anti-NRM region.

Because seizing power through military means was the only viable way for the NRM to end the repression by Obote and then Okello, it was inevitable that the government would be confronted with continuing military challenges both from the remnants of the previous regime and from armed groups who still felt marginalised, or who held grievances incubated during decades of violence and corruption. In the twenty-eight years since the NRM took power, there have been rebellions or insurgent campaigns by twelve different groups operating from the north, inside Sudan, in the West Nile area, from the DRC, in Buganda and in the west in the Ruwenzori Mountains and Bwindi Forest. These groups included former soldiers loyal to Idi Amin, the rump of Okello's UNLA, a Baganda uprising in 1994–5, and fighting involving the Karamojong and other local communities near the north-eastern border with Kenya.[31] Most of these were short-lived and were no major threat to the NRA nationally or locally. The most serious and lasting insurgencies occurred in the north, involving the Teso and Acholi, and in the west, where the Allied Democratic Forces fought a five-year war between 1996 and 2001 before retreating into the DRC, from which they still periodically launch attacks into Uganda—continuing to destabilise a turbulent region of Central Africa.[32] These forces were not just reacting to the NRM victory; they had longer histories dating back to the violence of the Amin and Obote regimes, and even to the era of resistance to colonial rule.

The Teso insurgency in the north lasted from 1986 to 1996. Teso grievances arose from fears that the north would be marginalised by the southern hegemony in the NRA/M, and in response to the very direct problem of cattle raiding by the Karamojong. The raiding became an overwhelming problem for the Teso between 1986 and 1988, when the NRA had other priorities besides combating rustling. The Teso lost half a million head of cattle; this caused severe want and badly disrupted cultural and social identity, interfering with societal practices inextricably tied to cattle ownership, among them marriage and the transition to manhood.[33] Teso leaders set up the Force Obote Back Movement and the Uganda People's Army (UPA) to fight the NRA, but in the end, they achieved little more than the further impoverishment and insecurity of the region. The rebellion started petering out in 1993, and it was over by 1996.

The war in the Acholi areas of the north, on the other hand, was the most serious in terms of its humanitarian consequences and its effects on Uganda's political system. It started after the UNLA retreated north from Kampala and the NRA took control. Acholi troops in the UNLA were blamed in the south for atrocities in the Luwero Triangle, and when many former soldiers returned home to Acholi areas in the north, they were seen as tainted by the atrocities. Elders demanded that they undergo purification rituals to purge them of the spiritual effects of the killings. Strong spiritual beliefs were part of the Acholi culture and leaders exploited them to feed on the grievances of the defeated northerners. As Museveni consolidated his power and became a supporter of the SPLA in South Sudan, Khartoum used support for the UNLA and a new northern-based rebel movement, the Uganda People's Democratic Army (UPDA), to create a buffer between the SPLA and Uganda and to punish the Museveni government for supporting its enemies. In August 1986, the UPDA raided Gulu, Kitgum and Lira in the north.[34] The NRA beat off the attacks, and the UPDA was dispersed into the bush around Gulu; it posed little threat to NRA control of major towns, but continued to kill Acholi leaders who worked with the NRM, burning and looting villages and stealing cattle. The NRA forces that moved into Acholi areas benefited from the support or at least acquiescence of local people and their leaders, but the deployment of forces from the Luwero area and Baganda units led to revenge attacks on innocent Acholi civilians. These attacks and counter-insurgency operations had a brutalising effect,[35] with the Acholi civilian population caught between the rebels and the army while supporting neither. The conflict became a desperate fight by Acholi fighters fiercely opposed to rule by southerners, but alienated from their own people by their previous involvement in atrocities and tactics of forcible recruitment, plunder and rape.

The cleavages between Acholi soldiers and their elders and the defeat of the UPDA incursions made room for an Acholi spirit medium, Alice Auma, and her father, Severino Lokoya, to gain a following among former soldiers. Auma took on the name of Alice Lakwena (the Messenger) and used a fusion of traditional Acholi spiritualism and evangelical Christianity to establish a cult. She claimed that spirits had told her to recruit soldiers, cleanse them of sin and use them to fight the government.[36] Within a few months she recruited 18,000 followers to what became known as the Holy Spirit Movement. She led this horde of former soldiers, civilian men and women to attack the NRA across Acholiland and then led them south towards Kampala, picking up support among the Langi and Teso. The movement reached Jinja, 50 km north of Kampala, in October 1987—where it was crushed by the NRA. Lakwena fled, but a substantial group of her followers gave their support to Joseph Kony, a Holy Spirit follower who claimed to have been possessed by the Lakwena spirit.[37] By recruiting disenchanted UPDA fighters who refused to surrender when their leaders signed a peace agreement with the government in May 1988, Kony was able to build a new movement called the Lord's Resistance Army (LRA), which again blended Acholi and Christian beliefs.

The LRA never became a large guerrilla force capable of holding large areas of territory or seriously threatening NRA control of Acholi areas, but its attacks meant security was limited to the main towns and some protected villages. The LRA fought a brutal hit-and-run insurgency until 2008, when it was pushed completely out of Uganda into the DRC, CAR and South Sudan. This was a war of grievance and marginalisation; villages were looted, boys forced to serve as porters or fighters, and girls as cooks or sex slaves. For the LRA, this nomadic raiding became a way of life rather than a path to providing a political alternative to the NRA or defeating it militarily. Like Lakwena before him, Kony claimed that his campaign was needed to purify the Acholi through violence. The LRA's fighters mutilated, tortured and raped as a routine part of their war not just against the NRA, but against anyone seen as failing to adhere to their strictures, including the bizarre ban on the use of bicycles. The amputation of limbs and cutting off of lips, ears and noses were all ways of terrorising the population and punishing those accused of collaboration or cycling[38]

The Museveni government wanted to defeat the LRA militarily, and paid little attention to the plight of the Acholi population, even though by 1996, over two million northerners had been displaced from their homes. One of the overlooked aspects of the conflict is that as brutal and inhuman as Kony and the LRA have proved to be, the Ugandan army has been far from innocent of killing, rape and looting. But the LRA grabbed world headlines because of its bizarre beliefs and practices; journalists covering the conflict invariably did so from the government side and were briefed by the army, which was keen to dehumanise the LRA and present itself as simply out to protect civilians. The LRA's reputation for brutality towards civilians was not false, though, and was reinforced by its massacres of unarmed civilians and displaced people.[39]

In 1999, the counter-insurgency campaign received a boost when Museveni and Sudan's President Bashir pledged to stop aiding rebels in each other's countries, and in 2002, Sudan agreed to allow Ugandan troops to enter southern Sudan to crush the LRA between converging Ugandan army units. The offensive was bloody, but it failed to kill or capture Kony or eliminate many of his soldiers, and they were able to launch new offensives almost immediately. The government tried to negotiate with the LRA after this, but the referral of Kony and the LRA to the International Criminal Court and the court's indictment of Kony and other LRA leaders in 2005 meant they had little incentive to negotiate an end to the fight, since this would only put them on trial. The Ugandans could not offer Kony immunity from prosecution once he had been indicted, and have always refused to consider offering him an official post as part of a peace agreement. The Ugandan government was never fully committed to pursuing a peace deal instead of defeating Kony, and there has always been a suspicion that the military accepted the low level insurgency in the north because it justified the huge defence budget and perpetuated senior officers' accumulation of wealth through corrupt defence contracts. Perhaps more importantly, "The continuation of the war allowed the government to justify its adoption of unacceptable methods of repression under the guise of increasing security."[40]

By 2008, the Ugandan army, with the support of the autonomous Government of South Sudan, had pushed the LRA out of Uganda and most of South Sudan. Most LRA fighters fled to the Garamba National Park in the northern DRC and to southern areas of the CAR. A joint military effort to finally defeat the LRA and kill or capture Kony was launched under African Union auspices in 2011 with intelligence, logistical and other support from the US military using UN bases in the DRC. The offensive involved troops from Uganda, South Sudan, the DRC and, until the overthrow of President Bozize in March 2013, the CAR army. Bozize's overthrow began an era of chaos and lack of government in the CAR, and there are suspicions that some groups in the rebel alliance that toppled him had links with Kony. The CAR's collapse has given the LRA greater freedom to operate in areas of the country that border the DRC and South Sudan, impeding the efforts to capture him and end the insurgency.

In May 2014, the LRA was down to about 250 combatants and a similar number of civilian dependents, and was believed to be operating in an area straddling the borders of the south-eastern CAR, the DRC and South Sudan, and the UN Secretary-General Ban Ki-Moon reported that Kony was thought to be taking refuge in Sudan's Kafia Kingi enclave, near the South Sudanese border.[41] This was denied by the Sudanese government, but history suggests that Khartoum has no compunction about using groups like the LRA to undermine security in neighbouring states. The conflicts in the CAR and South Sudan have impeded efforts, supported by US military surveillance specialists, to capture or kill the remaining LRA groups or Kony himself.

The interplay of conflicts in Uganda, Sudan, the CAR, Chad and the DRC made the region one in which none of the governments could claim to exert full control over their borders or the territories along them. There are alliances of convenience between governments fighting rebels and between rebel movements from Chad, CAR, DRC, Sudan, South Sudan and Uganda. Armed groups such as the Sudanese Janjaweed, parts of the CAR Séléka rebel group and the LRA, are to this day involved in raiding villages in the DRC and CAR and in ivory poaching in national parks in Chad, the DRC, the CAR and as far west as Cameroon. The ivory is smuggled out through traditional trade routes to Khartoum via Darfur (controlled by the Janjaweed); Uganda and the DRC's armed forces have also been accused of taking advantage of insurgencies to poach ivory on an industrial scale, exporting it via Kampala. The final destination for most of Africa's poached ivory is China, which has a seemingly insatiable appetite for wildlife products such as ivory and rhino horn (most of the latter being poached in South Africa by criminal gangs with suspected political connections).[42] China's moratorium on ivory imports and pledges to combat the illegal ivory trade have yet to be seen to be anything more than promises to keep the international community quiet.

All these shifting conflicts and rebel linkages are a threat to the security of borders and bring fear, violence and insecurity to rural populations. Across Central Africa, West-Central Africa, and Central-East Africa there are large areas of territory beyond the control of national governments. This is particularly so in the DRC, the southern and eastern CAR, South Sudan and Darfur. In these areas, borders cannot be policed even when it comes to fighting anti-government insurgencies and rebel movements. The mutual suspicions between governments and the tit-for-tat relationships among rebel and insurgent movements mean that even if the LRA is beaten in Uganda, for example, it can spring up in South Sudan, the CAR or the DRC. Meanwhile, the levels of political and military corruption are so high, and impunity for senior politicians and military officers so entrenched, that conflicts have become sources of enrichment not just for rebel movements but for the politicians and militaries purportedly seeking to end them. This is not a case of primitive, irrational conflict or the symptom of ethnic or tribal hatreds, but of politicians and military commanders taking rational decisions to exploit grievances, prolong conflicts and use them to produce wealth or maintain patron-client networks through which political and economic agency is exercised by powerful groups. It's hard to argue with Chabal and Daloz that, "Political action operates rationally, but largely in the realm of the informal, uncodified and unpoliced" in these areas, and that political and military actors "maximise their return on the disorder generated."[43]

Oil and diamonds: boon or bane? The cases of Nigeria, Angola and Botswana

It is usual to celebrate the discovery of natural resources that could be mined or extracted to add to the wealth of a country and its population. You would expect people in an area where gold, diamonds or oil are discovered to welcome the prospect of jobs, income and improvements in living standards. But in extraverted economies, where elite gatekeepers use the rents or revenues from export of natural resources for their own benefit rather than for the benefit people in the mineral-producing areas or for the overall development of their countries, mineral resources have often been a bane and not a boon.

People may be forced from their land, lose access to safe water and suffer repression from the security operations that surround mining, the conflict that frequently accompanies the exploitation of resources or the pollution that results from oil spills. People in the Niger Delta are still fighting for compensation for the massive pollution of their home area and the negative effects of decades of oil exploitation, and for a fair share of the wealth generated. In July 2006, the UNDP released a report showing that wealth generated in the Niger Delta "has barely touched people's lives" other than to subject them to the violence of the security forces and the effects of pollution. In the same month in northern Burkina Faso local people armed themselves with pangas, clubs and other weapons to try to stop a local council allowing the continuation of gold mining on a local hill sacred to the community.[44] At the end of October 2013, Tullow had to suspend oil exploration in the Turkana region of northern Kenya as local people demonstrated over the lack of employment of locals. Diamonds have been a resource used to fund conflicts in Liberia, Sierra Leone, Ivory Coast, the DRC and Angola. Just a few of the many examples of how local people often see mining as a curse and feel they do not benefit. All too often local communities have little say in how their land is used, or what happens to the wealth generated. Land rights are a major problem in much of rural Africa with local communities having use, but not ownership, of land which may be vested in local chieftaincy systems or in the state.

Nigeria's post-independence history has been marked by regional conflict, attempted secession and astounding levels of corruption, and oil wealth has not been used to develop a modern and integrated economy or to alleviate the crushing poverty in which the majority of Nigerians still live. Political and economic management is dysfunctional and overburdened with pointless public offices, which not only offer their holders salaries but brings them into the extensive patron-client system that still oils the wheels of politics and business. Attempts at decentralisation haven't dented the power of the patrons who dominate the political process and distribute oil wealth; malfeasance has simply been devolved. As Nigeria's federal institutions have proliferated from three to thirty-six constituent states, the country has established state governments and public bodies that perform identical functions to those in the preceding larger states but at greater cost, and with total dependence on the allocation of resources from the central, oil-dependent budget. This has only extended and multiplied the networks of power that developed in the old north, west and east, and served to use up vital revenues that could have funded broader and deeper economic development.

The federal political system means that to succeed nationally, politicians emerging from state or regional political networks have to forge coalitions across states to garner enough support across the federation. Victory in elections is not just a matter of getting the most votes, but of getting the most votes with a consistently high number of votes across the country—to win in the first round, a presidential candidate must win either an absolute majority or at least 25% in two-thirds of the states. But the distorting effects of patronage mean that those with access to wealth and resources can effectively buy support through direct payments to clients or through promises of lucrative public office or government tenders. In a system where accountability is weak, administrative and legal institutions dominated by politics rather than delivering public good, informal political, military and business networks control access to power, and the overwhelmingly dominant source of revenue is the extraverted export sector. Oil is the source of over 90 per cent of government revenue, and provides ample resources to support a top-heavy and wasteful administrative structure; transparency is sorely wanting, and the opportunities for rent-seeking and corruption are huge.

Such an institutionally weak system, where informal structures are more powerful than formal ones, is doomed to suffer from what has been termed the Dutch disease, where major resource booms and increases in revenue inflate exchange rates, raise living costs and damage agriculture and industry making them unprofitable.[45] Along with the gatekeeping/rent-seeking phenomenon, this means the massive increase in resource output and income accrues to the few and serves to damage growth and development elsewhere in the economy.[46] Nigeria is a textbook victim. Its oil boom period coincided with the decline of the non-oil economy; oil revenues were never used to promote broad and integrated economic development, and were instead mortgaged as revenue and loans or wasted and embezzled, increasing indebtedness and income inequality. As rural people sought better lives in oil-funded urban areas, the agricultural labour force shrank drastically, handicapping the labour-intensive and poorly mechanised agricultural system, this in turn drove down food output and deepened the country's dependence on imports. Between 1965 and 1981, as the oil boom accelerated, agriculture's share of GDP declined from 68 to 35 per cent, and production of cash crops like palm oil, cocoa and rubber by 75 per cent.

It might have been expected that the flood of revenue into Nigeria and the massive expansion of public sector and the maintenance of a large army would have increased incomes and employment, thereby reducing poverty, but statistics from the IMF and the African Development Bank show otherwise. In the early years of Nigeria's oil boom in 1970, nineteen million Nigerians were estimated to be living below the poverty line; in 2000, despite the influx of $400bn in oil revenues over thirty years, the number had increased to over ninety million.[47] There has also been a huge increase in wealth inequality: in 1970 the top 2 per cent of Nigerians earned as much in aggregate as the bottom 17 per cent, but by 1990 they earned as much as the bottom 55 per cent. Per capita GDP declined from $1,113 in 1970 to $1,084 in 2000. By the early 2000s, around 50 per cent of the population lived on less than 30 US cents a day, and a fifth of children died before their fifth birthdays from preventable diseases connected with lack of clean water, malnutrition and poor health provision. Despite a bloated rural public sector workforce (many of whom, as in the army, were ghost workers whose salaries accrued to corrupt senior officials or officers), basic amenities like water, sewerage and rubbish disposal are in many places almost non-existent.[48]

Poverty persists alongside the extravagant wealth of the elite and the staggering level of resource theft. It is no joke to say, as Richard Dowden does, that politics in Nigeria is a business career, with politicians ending up multi-millionaires. According to a Nigerian commission of inquiry in 1996, $12 billion in surplus oil earnings made during the Gulf War was simply missing from government revenues, and was thought to be in foreign bank accounts controlled by former President Ibrahim Babangida. His successor, Sani Abacha, stole between $2–4 billion during his period in his office.[49]

Decades of corruption combined with abysmal basic services left a volatile political inheritance for the civilian government that took over in

May 1999. The failure of central and state governments to be accountable or meet basic needs had created alternative channels for political agency. Borno State and other areas of northern Nigeria had Boko Haram and Ansaru, both militant Islamist movements appealing to the poor and marginalised and blaming their condition on modernity and westernisation; the Delta gave birth to Ogoni and Ijaw rebel groups, such as the Movement for the Emancipation of the Niger Delta (MEND). MEND was a more organised and better-armed version of the previous Delta-based rebel groups and drew its support from the Ijaw people, who were livid at being deprived of any benefit from oil production. The group began attacking oil installations and pipelines, and kidnapped oil workers. An amnesty was offered in August 2009 to end MEND's insurgency, and the Delta region was promised ten per cent of oil revenues. But the deal was never fully implemented and the promised jobs for local people never materialised, while funds pledged for the region disappeared before reaching the people they were supposed to benefit.

The Delta violence and Islamist insurgency are dire threats to security, the oil industry and stability in key areas of the country. The major security response demands significant forces and weaponry, and ballooning portions of revenues are now allocated to the military, which sits at the heart of the power networks underpinning the political and economic system. The stream of funding to the military and for what are termed "security votes" allows revenues to be misappropriated on a massive scale and intertwines informal but powerful political and military networks, subverting attempts to develop truly democratic and accountable political and economic management structures that would enable Nigerians to hold their government to account. Studies have demonstrated that "it is indisputable that the widespread practice of stealing and diverting public funds which has been fuelled by the country's enormous oil rents, is extensively intertwined with the concept of national security."[50] This stolen wealth is used to control the political process through bribery, patronage and what has been termed prebendalism,[51] a system of patronage in which elite groups or networks feel they have the right to the revenues of the state. Elected office-holders, government employees, and members of ethnic and religious groups enmeshed in informal networks receive a share of government revenues, but in an unearned and unaccountable way that distorts the whole system of politics, service delivery and resource allocation. This is simply a variation on the old gatekeeper model. The return from military to civilian rule may have lasted fourteen years and at last seen peaceful changes of power, but the nature of the federal system has not spread power down to ordinary people; it has merely widened the scope of patronage and prebendalism.[52]

The other side of this coin, as Okri has said, is that the marginalisation and continuing impoverishment of the majority,

> have been eating away at the nation's heart. In a country rich with oil revenues, where billions vanish from the national coffers with no one held to account, where going into politics means acquiring vast and sudden wealth, where slums breed in larger numbers every day, where the national revenue does not improve people's lives across the whole country, it is unsurprising that violent sects grow from such a festering condition.[53]

Corruption feeds the elite patronage networks, and the resulting poverty and despair provide a breeding ground for violence.

The militant groups that spring up in turn justify further security allocations and greater misuse of funds. Political leaders and their networks can rig the system and argue the case to ensure that accountability and democratic control are "subordinated to the desire for improved security, and, in the absence of accountability and transparency, it is not difficult for rulers to exploit the concept of national security in order to steal from the public purse."[54] That magic word, 'security', is used to ward off investigations by journalists and human rights organisations of the abuses committed by the security forces while fighting the Delta rebels or Boko Haram. A recent example is the destruction of much of the town of Baga in Borno State during counter-insurgency by the Nigerian army's Joint Task Force (JTF) in 2013. Soldiers ransacked the town after Boko Haram attacked a military patrol, killing one soldier. Community leaders said that after the army attack, they counted 2,000 burned homes and 183 bodies; satellite images of the town show 2,275 buildings were destroyed, the vast majority of them civilian residences.[55]

These are the obstacles that have impeded democratic development in Nigeria since the end of military rule. With impunity and freedom to treat state resources as their own, informal networks have maintained Nigeria's reputation as one of the most politically and economically corrupt countries in the world. This has kept it from being the African leader it should be. Its size, economic potential and military strength should have made it a regionally dominant state and one of the key African actors on the world stage, but its reputation, the suspicion of its neighbours and its competition for continental influence with South Africa have hobbled it both in Africa and globally. But bleak as this history is, there is still hope: sustained civilian rule, peaceful (if corrupt) transitions from one civilian government to another, an ever freer media and a new generation of well-educated young Nigerians all offer a better chance than ever before to seize the initiative. Nigerians are accumulating the means to resist and change the system, which still perpetuates corruption, mismanagement, and an almost total lack of accountability or responsible state control over national territory.[56]

> Angola presents a terrible, shocking paradox. One of the best resource endowments in Africa has been associated not with development and relative prosperity, but with years of conflict, economic decline and human misery on a massive scale. Few countries present such a stark contrast between economic potential and the state of their populace.[57]

That bleak assessment came in 2001, just a year before the death of Jonas Savimbi and the end of the decades-old civil war. But despite nearly fifteen years of peace and of Chinese and other foreign investment in the economy and expansion of oil production, the majority of Angolans still live in poverty. The 1990s and the opening years of the 21st century have been dominated by policies that serve narrow interests of those in power, with political players happy to be bought off with a share of the wealth that flows from power. Angolans have remained powerless in the face of a richly-endowed but mismanaged and corrupt state that rules in the interests of those who control it rather than those who live in it, while the ruling MPLA and opposition politicians alike seem unable to look beyond their own self-interest.

The end of the Cold War coincided with the dismantling of apartheid, providing an opportunity to move beyond war and the knock-on effects of external conflicts and start rebuilding. But the fierce hatred between UNITA and the MPLA did not end, and nor did the flow of external support to both sides. With oil wealth paying for the government's weapons and plundered diamonds and timber paying for UNITA's, both sides could afford to keep fighting. In the 1990s, UNITA received between $2 billion and $3.7 billion from the illegal sale of what became known as blood diamonds.[58] The MPLA proved unable to snuff out UNITA, which in turn could not defeat the MPLA, and between 1988 and 1991 fighting escalated, rather than declining.

It took four years of negotiations involving the MPLA, UNITA, regional states, Portugal, Cuba, the Soviet Union (then Russia) and the USA for a ceasefire to be agreed. This was followed by a timetable for elections. UNITA was legalised as a party; it set up offices in Luanda, and tried to establish a presence and support beyond the areas it had controlled as a guerrilla army. The UN provided a verification and monitoring force (UNAVEM), but it was tiny, with only 350 observers, ninety UN police and 400 election monitors. Their task was made almost impossible by two protagonists, who were utterly unwilling to share power. Neither the MPLA nor UNITA had experience of plural politics and elections, and had never grappled with the concept of conceding and becoming a functioning opposition; their experience against the Portuguese and each other had been based on the principles of kill or be killed, win or be destroyed. The guarantors of the peace deal and international community wanted a quick and cheap fix,[59] but the bitterness of the civil war and the regional and ethnic divisions it had entrenched meant there was little hope for free political activity, or that parties could campaign safely in what had previously been enemy territory. There were serious problems of implementation and mutual accusations of violence and harassment, but the international guarantors wrote them off as teething troubles.[60] They were more than that. Both sides retained their military forces, and both were preparing to seize power if the election results did not go their way. Despite overwhelming evidence that the people outside UNITA areas were scared of it, and that non-Ovimbundu people (who made up nearly two-thirds of the population) feared UNITA would establish an ethnic hegemony, Savimbi was convinced that the Angolan people would reject the MPLA.[61]

Despite the two sides' reluctance to demobilise, the elections were held as planned at the end of September 1992. Only 45 per cent of government troops and 24 per cent of UNITA's guerrillas (mainly the old or very young, as UNAVEM officials told me in 1992) had been disarmed, but the voting was peaceful and 91 per cent of the electorate voted.[62] The UN head in Angola, Margaret Anstee, and US chief representative, Jeffrey Millington, both praised the Angolans for the conduct of the vote—but before the release of the results, Savimbi said that UNITA would not accept any result other than a clear victory. On 5 October, the UNITA army commander in the military integration programme, General Ben-Ben, announced that UNITA was pulling out of the process. The USA, the UN, Portugal and South Africa all pressured UNITA to drop its accusations of election-rigging and resume the process, but UNITA refused and prepared to go back to the bush. As the political process broke down, there was evidence that South African military intelligence was flying in weapons for Savimbi and that former South African soldiers were being recruited to fight for UNITA.[63]

The official results gave the MPLA 53.74 per cent of the vote and UNITA 34.10, and put MPLA leader Jose Eduardo dos Santos 9 per cent ahead of

Savimbi in the presidential election. UNITA rejected the results and fighting resumed, with no clear indication of who started it. UNITA tried to seize Luanda airport, but then failed to defend its positions in the capital; it was forced out of Luanda, and many of its leaders killed or captured, but it nonetheless went on the offensive and quickly captured 60–70 per cent of the country. Attempts to get the peace talks back on track failed, and civil war continued until 2002. The US, aghast at UNITA's reversion to war and keen to get a share of the Angolan oil industry, dropped its opposition to the MPLA and threw its diplomatic weight behind the Angolan government, leaving only Zaire, Ivory Coast and, until 1994, South Africa helping UNITA. UNITA used revenues from ivory poaching and alluvial diamond deposits to buy weapons and hire mercenaries from the South African Executive Outcomes group (recruited from former members of the SADF's 32 battalion, which had fought alongside UNITA in the 1980s), but it was gradually forced back. A peace agreement signed in Lusaka in November 1994 produced a shaky ceasefire that lasted (with periodic skirmishes) for four years, during which UNITA's hired mercenaries left the country.

But in 1998, the MPLA lost patience with UNITA's unwillingness to properly implement the peace agreement and take part in a national unity government, as it instead obstructed the extension of government control to its territories; the government renounced the peace deal, and launched a military offensive in the Angolan central highlands. Without South African or mercenary support, UNITA was unable to defend its territory and had to revert to guerrilla warfare. It lost control of the diamond areas, and the fall of the Mobutu autocracy and UN sanctions imposed in 1998 cut off its crucial income streams. Government forces, meanwhile, were strengthened when the state oil company Sonangol hired the very same Executive Outcomes mercenaries who had fought for Savimbi. They were used to protect onshore oilfields from UNITA's guerrilla attacks.

The war continued for four years, with UNITA steadily losing ground. It ended when Jonas Savimbi was killed during an army offensive in February 2002. Proving how personalised the conflict had become, his death brought a rapid end to fighting and the MPLA-led government and UNITA soon agreed a peace deal. This deal was the result of a domestic process rather than an internationally imposed or mediated one, and it ended the war for good. 50,000 UNITA troops were demobilised. Some were integrated into the national armed forces, but most returned to civilian life. For many thousands of them, the war was all they had known as adults and they had little or no education or even basic agricultural skills. UNITA was transformed into a political party and jumped on the political gravy train, fed by oil and diamond revenues.

The size of Angola's army was cut, but the military budget still devoured a large portion of government income from oil and diamond exports. Army generals and other senior officials in the security structure were a key part of the ruling network of political, military and economic power that centred on President dos Santos and his extended family; they all benefited from access to oil contracts and diamond concessions.

One product of the end of the Cold War, the oil economy and the end of the Angolan-Cuban-Soviet relationship was that the MPLA's commitment to Marxism was formally renounced at a party congress in 1990. It began to restructure itself as a capitalist party that embraced market forces, though it remained highly militarised and hierarchical well after the end of the war. The move away from Marxism was not only a product of the end of the Cold War and the Soviet Union, but also a recognition that the party's elite members had spent years enriching themselves by exploiting the oil industry with little role for socialist policies. The MPLA's Marxist-Leninist programme, though an efficient tool for organising anti-colonial insurgency and a useful ideology for explaining the history of colonialism, had never been adapted (as Cabral had tried to do in Guinea-Bissau) to local conditions and needs. It had a rather mechanistic feel, and its pronouncements and prescriptions for Angolan political and economic development bore little relation to the realities of class in the country. Leading party members were intellectuals and military leaders, with few real workers involved, and the alliance with the peasantry was a fiction. Angola's peasants remained marginalised, despite making up the bulk of the warring armies. As a result, The MPLA became just another ruling party committed to maintaining the personal power and client networks of the president, his family and their close associates. Its Marxist-Leninist political discourse was never much more than rhetoric, and there was never any serious attempt to actually implement socialist rather than just state-centred policies—or any evidence of a developed understanding of how the ideology could be applied to Angolan conditions.

The violent suppression of the Nito Alves group and the death of President Agostinho Neto had ended any real enthusiasm among the core leadership for socialism, but an abiding and more realistic discourse of the party during the civil war, and its claim to legitimacy afterwards, was that it defended the population against UNITA and external aggression. By the time of the ideological shift in 1990, the party's socialist rhetoric was strongly at odds with the class interest of the wealthy elite at the top of the hierarchy in party, government, army and the economy, and having jettisoned socialism, the MPLA presented its role as developmental and defensive. There was no essential change in policies, and national interest continued to be conflated with the interests of the network of party, state and the military leaders.[64] Political and economic power was confined to the dos Santos clan and the Bermuda Triangle of the treasury, the state oil company (SONANGOL) and the National Bank, into which oil and diamond revenues and external loans disappeared never to be seen or heard of again.[65]

With massive oil and increasing diamond revenues and, in the 2000s, significant investment and infrastructural assistance from China, one might have expected a concerted effort to rebuild shattered infrastructure, invest heavily in health, education and poverty alleviation, and reintegrate former soldiers and UNITA guerrillas into society. Agricultural production had been decimated by the war and the country relied heavily on imported food, while coffee exports had dwindled. But this did not happen, instead the elite enriched itself further and Chinese aid went into prestige infrastructural projects rather than the development of agriculture and industry. Angola remains heavily import dependent.

China is now a major investor and has provided several multi-billion dollar oil-backed loans to fund the infrastructural developments. The China Petroleum & Chemical Corporation (Sinopec) and China National Offshore Oil Corporation (CNOOC) are among the national oil companies increasing their presence in Angola's oil sector, and Angola is now the second largest supplier of oil to China after Saudi Arabia. Crude oil is estimated to make up around 40 per cent of economic production and over 70 per cent of government revenue. Just after the war, Angola was producing 1.1 million barrels of oil per day, but with considerable investment and the exploitation of new off-shore fields, this had risen to over 1.85 million per day by 2011 and continues to expand, with significant reserves still to be exploited. Similarly, since regaining control of the diamond areas of Lunda Norte, Angola has tried to increase production and bring in investment from companies like De Beers. Exact income from the oil and diamond sectors is hard to assess, as accountability and accounting for the sectors is opaque in the extreme and both are tightly controlled by SONANGOL and ENDIAMA—state companies run by the president's network of allies and clients.

SONANGOL's primacy was proven when President dos Santos apparently anointed its former head, Manuel Vicente, as his successor—a choice not welcomed enthusiastically at the MPLA congress in April 2012, where Vincente was seen as having neither a party nor military background. While many Angolans would welcome a change from dos Santos, a handover to Vicente is unlikely to appease the growing numbers of people protesting against the government, and could also lead to further factionalism within the MPLA. What this would do is strengthen the economic and political elite connected with the dos Santos family. Under Vicente, SONANGOL has diverted billions of dollars of oil revenue from the public treasury into private pockets.[66] As Jon Schubert put it, "Far from marking the start of a necessary generation change, Vicente would in fact signify the reproduction of the 'System dos Santos', safeguarding him and his family from scrutiny over their ill-gotten gains".[67]

Angolans are still waiting for the government to meet its promises to combat poverty and improve living standards, and in particular to build new homes to replace the shantytowns that grew up around Luanda and other major towns when rural peoples fled the war and sought employment. Despite burgeoning revenues, little is being done to repair or replace Angola's crumbling Chinese-built hospitals, which are both falling apart and empty of patients because of the lack of trained staff. This contrasts with the expensive private health care, foreign treatment and fabulously rich lifestyle enjoyed by the small, well-connected elite.

There is growing anger at the wealth of the dos Santos family and its allies, as evidenced by growing protests by youth groups, military veterans who have not been paid pensions, and the growth of critical civil society groups and media outlets—all of which are met with police harassment and the regular arrests of investigative journalists. The problem for them and the embryonic political parties seeking to transcend the old rivalries and corrupt practices is that the dos Santos/MPLA grip on the export economy means the regime can deploy "near limitless resources in order to create dependencies which in turn help perpetuate its existence...poverty is not a 'problem' for the government; it is an instrument used in order to create more dependencies, raise the stakes for those who offer resistance, and thus to perpetuate the existing situation."[68] Wealth maintains power, which is used to generate more power, while poverty increases marginalisation and disempowers the majority.

Botswana's political and economic trajectory since independence has been very different to Nigeria's and Angola's, despite remarkable mineral wealth and a perilous position in the centre of southern Africa's zone of conflict. A thinly populated country with South Africa, Namibia, Zambia and Zimbabwe for its neighbours, Botswana could have become an archetypal gatekeeper state, and could easily have been drawn disastrously into regional violence. This has not come to pass; and while it would be an exaggeration to depict Botswana as a democratic paradise, with total accountability and equal participation for all, or as an unqualified economic success, it would be inaccurate and unfair not to recognise that in the context of the region and other post-colonial states, what Botswana has achieved since independence is remarkable.[69] It has achieved sustained economic growth and maintained a liberal democratic political system, albeit one with strong elite group hegemony, a strong strain of traditional paternalism and weak opposition movements. Elections have been held every five years without fail, and while the ruling Botswana Democratic Party (BDP), founded by the first president, Seretse Khama, has never lost an election, its share of the vote has declined. Presidents have not clung endlessly to power, but since the early 1990s have adopted a pattern of serving for two terms.

In the first thirty-five years of independence, Botswana has recorded the greatest progress of any Sub-Saharan African country in terms of overall human development, according to the UNDP's Human Development Reports. There are still vast gaps between the income and living standards of rich and poor, and access to education, healthcare and economic opportunity is highly unequal, but the progress in major areas of service delivery to the population is impressive. Between the mid-1960s and 2000, while other African economies declined and their governments failed to provide education and health services, Botswana made significant progress: infant mortality was brought down from 108 per thousand in 1966 to thirty-eight in 1999, and malnutrition among children fell five down from 25 per cent in 1978 to 13 per cent in 1996; primary healthcare is now available to 80 per cent of the rural population; 83 per cent of households have access to potable water; primary school enrolment rose from 50 per cent at independence to 97 per cent at the turn of the millennium; adult literacy was up to 79 per cent.[70] The country annually tops Transparency International's ranking of African countries according to their freedom from corruption.

Botswana has an international reputation for being well governed, with a responsive and honest civil service and government and a high level of popular support for the basic system of government and economics—even though there has been limited redistribution of the benefits of economic growth based on diamond revenue. The exception to the basic acceptance of the social, political and economic structures is among the San people—known to

Batswana as Basarwa, and internationally as Bushmen—who make up three per cent of the population. They have at best been marginalised and neglected, or at worst progressively deprived of land, economic and political rights (the view of NGOs like Survival International).[71] They have been forcibly moved from their traditional hunting lands in areas of the Kalahari on the grounds that they could not stay within a conservation area in the Central Kalahari Game Reserve, and also to enable mineral prospecting.

The San's traditions and their linguistic and ethnic origins set them apart from the Tswana majority and other groups in the country, and the government has portrayed their nomadic lifestyle as backward. But the basic independence and impartiality of Botswana's judicial structures has been proven by the San's legal victories against government attempts to permanently remove them. Nevertheless the initial removal and obstacles put in the way of their return from their traditional areas of habitation forced many into inadequate resettlement areas, leading to impoverishment and severe social problems, notably with alcohol.[72] Other minority groups in Botswana, notably the Kalanga, have at times complained of Tswana dominance, but this is not entirely borne out by what has happened in practice. The third president of the country, Festus Mogae, was of Kalanga origin, and that he was not Tswana did not prevent him serving two terms as president following a period as vice-president.

Even some of the most trenchant critics of Botswana's political and economic development have been unable to ignore the successes achieved in terms of health, education and planned uses of diamond revenue. One critic, rather in the fashion of the discussion of "What have the Romans done for us" in Monty Python's *Life of Brian*, has had to admit that since 1966, BDP governments have built roads, railways, airlines, an education system, health facilities, modern communications, foreign exchange reserves and achieved a balanced budget—and yet still characterises these as "the limited fruits of an undiversified, high growth economy" which has "promoted injustice, potential instability and restricted democracy."[73] But this potential instability has never been realised in terms of political violence or the development or incitement of serious ethnic or community strife; as the San case proves, it does not cancel out the judiciary's ability to overrule government decisions. Similarly, the discovery of diamonds has not turned Botswana into a rapacious gatekeeping state as some have suggested; that judgment focuses on an admitted failure to successfully diversify the economy away from a heavy dependence on diamonds, a failure to industrialise, and the strong connection between the government bureaucracy and what is described as "the cattle-keeping elite".[74] While Botswana has some of the characteristics (a strong elite structure, dependence on diamonds, inequality in distribution of wealth) that have defined gatekeeping states, its prudent and planned use of economic resources sets it outside the accepted application of the term. Those who use it to describe Botswana miss the point, since the term was originally coined to describe a divorce between the gatekeeping state's elite and its society. There has been inequality in Botswana, but also "state-society cohesion, and the class relations within Botswana which underpinned this, lie at the heart of any explanation of the country's path."[75]

Since independence, Botswana has sought to make efficient use of its resources in economic terms, and while the elite has indeed perpetuated social and economic inequalities, the provision of basic services has been effective and sustained. Starting in 1966, this was achieved with extensive foreign aid (especially from Britain) and assistance from NGOs. At independence, Botswana had a small mineral sector based on salt and soda ash but was overwhelmingly dependent on the cattle industry. The country had just twenty-two university graduates, 100 secondary school graduates, 22km of paved roads, no national army, and British or expatriate-staffed civil service; it relied on British budget support for 50 per cent of its spending.[76] Seretse Khama's government was aware of its limited financial and human resources and gave priority to managing economic development, establishing an Economic Planning Unit and a Central Statistics Office. The lack of Batswana graduates and the ability to resist the limited pressure for Africanisation resulting from this, allowed for a gradual promotion of indigenous staff, and many key economic posts in government departments responsible for the economy, financial management and agriculture were held by expatriates until fully qualified Batswana were available. Nonetheless, between 1966 and 1976 public sector employment expanded fast, reaching 21,675 in 1976. This expansion was not just a means of employing elites through community, ethnic or political networks, but was closely linked to the aid-funded expansion of infrastructure and services.[77]

To this day, cattle remain at the heart of rural society, power structures and the non-diamond economy; the cattle sector still provides employment for 80 per cent of Batswana in rural areas, and is at the heart of Tswana culture and local institutions. Using foreign assistance, the government built abattoirs, boreholes and veterinary centres. Through planned development of veterinary services and disease eradication/prevention, Botswana's Meat Commission was able to get to lucrative export markets in the European Union and South Africa. Water provision and health services were developed in rural areas alongside services for the cattle industry, and cattle-owning elites and rural people had a common interest in this process. The elite that has ruled the country since independence and continues to do so today is based on the establishment of consensus among political leaders, traditional chiefs, major land and cattle owners, the business sector and the carefully developed civil service.[78] Cattle exports brought in income to supplement aid and enriched rural elites, chiefs and many senior BDP politicians—but not to the total exclusion of rural people, who were employed in the cattle industry and used the government services that were developed with its revenues. Traditional chiefs were made part of the local administrative systems and their social hierarchies maintained, but the chiefs represented in national legislative and local structures had advisory rather than executive power. They were effectively co-opted into a broad-based elite that was committed to development and modernisation, all while accommodating but limiting traditional sources of authority.

In the process of developing the economy, the BDP governments have encouraged the education and the employment of women, but for a democratic system Botswana has relatively few women in positions of authority: as of the last elections, only four of its fifty-seven directly elected MPs are women,[79] well below the numbers for most African states.[80] Women are not barred from politics, but there clearly is a glass ceiling, and studies of the local traditional consultative bodies, the *kgotlas*, show that while women attend, they do not speak much and do not have the influence that men retain in the system. The *kgotlas* are a traditional form of consultation, which the government uses to explain policies and mobilise support locally through traditional chief and headman structures. They are convened and chaired by chiefs but enable all adult Batswana to express their views. They are, taken sufficiently seriously that concerted opposition to government policies at *kgotlas* can lead to policies being changed or dropped. This was the case in 1992, when *kgotlas* in the southern Okavango region successfully opposed government plans to divert waters from the Okavango Delta for mining and other commercial uses.[81]

Tradition is important in Botswana, but not immutable; it is subject to the judicial system, and has been affected in particular by the growing clamour for gender equality. In September 2013, the court of appeal overturned customary practices barring women from inheriting land. According to Priti Patel, deputy director of the Southern Africa Litigation Centre (SALC), which supported women's right to inherit, the judgment:

> made it clear that women are not second class citizens in Botswana...Some people had feared that the Court of Appeal would set the fight for women's

> rights back yet again. But instead they ruled unanimously in favour of equality and against gender discrimination. It is a hugely important decision not only for Botswana but for women across southern Africa.[82]

The decision again demonstrated the independence of the courts from the male-dominated Tswana elites who dominate public life, politics and government.

Economically, Botswana still relies on diamond income, but the government has tried to use that income for service provision and attempts at planned economic development. As a result, Botswana has yet to develop a strong, diversified industrial or non-cattle agricultural base. The country's small population, just over two million in 2013, means that its domestic market is small; it has to compete in manufacturing with its giant neighbour, South Africa, and with the growing trading power of China. This has stunted industrialisation beyond some food processing and a small textile industry. Still, diamond income has supported planned growth and the government has moved beyond just taking rents from the diamond industry. Diamond mining, which started under De Beers at Orapa in 1972, now accounts for 70 per cent of export revenue, 50 per cent of government income, and 35 per cent of GDP; in 2013, diamond exports were only a little below $5 billion. The industry is run by Debswana, 50 per cent of which is owned by the Botswana government and 50 per cent by De Beers. Through Debswana, Botswana owns a 15 per cent share in De Beers and has a seat on the board. In 2013, Botswana moved towards a greater role in processing, sales and marketing of De Beers's diamond output, beginning with the cutting, polishing and sales of diamonds. It is anticipated that De Beers will move as much as $6 billion worth of sales operations to Gaborone from London, leading to the growth of diamond-related industries such as jewellery manufacturing.

Unemployment remains high; official figures put it at 20 per cent at the end of 2014,[83] but the real figure is probably much higher, with youth unemployment a serious and growing problem. The funding of infrastructural development and government services has meant that despite elitism in politics, a tendency towards a more tightly managed democracy, a powerful executive president and signs of a less tolerant attitude towards opposition and the free media,[84] Botswana has been able to maintain a strong consensus about the advantages of the system. While many Batswana outside elite circles may have no political participation beyond attendance at *kgotlas* or voting every five years, most still appear to buy into the developmental character of the state and the political system. Corruption remains low, politics has avoided the violence and outright authoritarianism of neighbouring states (notably Zimbabwe and Angola), and despite government pressure the courts remain willing to give verdicts that go against the BDP. The ruling party, meanwhile, has been able to defend and maintain the dominance of its class alliance without resort to force and through the co-option of key social groups;[85] with the benefit of incumbency and a weak and divided opposition, the BDP has stressed inclusiveness projected an image of stability and growth. The elite may prosper the most and enjoy a strong hold on power, but it does so in a system that involves some distribution of wealth and "not inconsiderable attention to the welfare of the masses".[86] Compared to Botswana in 1966, today's Botswana is a success story by any standards, and a remarkable one in the southern African context.

Kenya and Zimbabwe: patrimonialism rules

If Botswana showed that patrimonialism could still leave space for accountability and grassroots political influence, Kenya and Zimbabwe showed how patrimonial elite networks could be used to avoid accountability and encourage impunity and corruption—though with very different outcomes for those at the apex of power.

Kenya was for decades held up as a model of stability, with a pro-Western government, no successful military interventions or civil war, a safari and beach paradise for tourists, and a developing capitalist economy. This image masked the corrupt and patrimonial nature of politics under Kenyatta and Moi and the poor majority's simmering grievances over land, unemployment, inadequate healthcare and education, and the elite's barely-disguised looting of national resources. But even despite outbreaks of election violence since the re-introduction of a plural political system in 1992, it came as a major shock when the December 2007 elections were followed by widespread violence, with politicians inciting hatred in areas such as the Rift Valley and the slums of Nairobi.

The political and communal violence was triggered when the incumbent president, Mwai Kibaki, had himself sworn in as president after a clearly fraudulent vote count. The conflict that followed displaced hundreds of thousands of people in the Rift Valley and led to at least 1,200 deaths. It started with angry political demonstrations over the election result, but soon developed an ethnic edge as Orange Democratic Movement (ODM) leaders in the Rift Valley used grievances over land and wealth to incite the

Kalenjin-speaking peoples against the Kikuyu living there. The president's Party of National Unity (PNU) struck back, with members of the Kikuyu Mungiki sect used as the ruling party's private army.

The election was a contest between Kibaki's PNU alliance and Raila Odinga's ODM, the latter supported by an alliance of Luo, Kalenjin and Maasai politicians. Kenya's parties are formed around personalities who exploit patronage networks based on their own linguistic, ethnic and regional origins. By the 2007 elections, alliances between these political networks had become the key to success, since no single party could hope to win enough seats nationally to gain a majority in parliament or win the presidency outright. In 1992 and 1997, Moi had used his access to state power and the media, as well as the development of informal militias loyal to leading politicians, to ensure that his coalition was the strongest. He built a strong organisation that allowed him to intimidate potential challengers or win them over with promises of political office, government contracts or other forms of patronage. In 2002, by which time there was enough political opposition to stop Moi running for a third term in office, a strong coalition including Kibaki, Odinga and other leading opposition figures defeated his chosen candidate for the ruling KANU party, Uhuru Kenyatta. Odinga expected to be prime minister and to have a large share of cabinet, civil service and parastatal positions with which to repay his supporters, but the victorious alliance fell apart amid bitter recriminations, which were carried through into a violent and politically divisive constitutional referendum campaign in 2005.

During the referendum campaign, Odinga forged an alliance of Luo, Luahya and Kalenjin politicians in opposition to Kibaki and his allies in the Kikuyu, Meru and Kamba political networks. In a foretaste of things to come, Kibaki lost the vote amid a violent campaign. This turned the opposing parties into bitter enemies, and Kenyan politics became polarised, with key personalities like Kibaki and Kenyatta on one side and Odinga and William Ruto (the most influential Kalenjin politician) on the other.

Kibaki's incumbency saw none of the redistribution of land, wealth or solving of historical land and other grievances that Odinga's supporters had hoped for when they joined him in the National Rainbow Coalition to defeat Uhuru Kenyatta. Many Kenyans saw President Kibaki as ruling for the benefit of a small group of politicians and businessmen, known as the Mount Kenya Mafia, drawn from the Kikuyu/Kamba elite supporting Kibaki who gained access to government contracts and other forms of patronage.[87] In the 2007 campaign, Odinga's coalition put forward a populist agenda based on poverty reduction, the settlement of land and economic grievances dating back to colonial land seizures, and reviving ideas of federalism and devolution of power, something which particularly appealed to Kalenjin and Maasai leaders. For once, the election was not only about personality but also serious political and economic differences.[88]

Anger at Kibaki's economic policies even extended to his own Kikuyu community, and manifested itself in the rise of a Kikuyu criminal gang/sect known as Mungiki, which carried out violent extortion in slums, recruited poor, badly educated and unemployed Kikuyu youths, and used oathing ceremonies reminiscent of the Kikuyu-based Mau Mau movement. It came into conflict with the government, and in the years before election there were outbreaks of violence in slum areas between the police and sect members. Despite their violent struggle with the government, the Mungiki, like other criminal or youth gangs in other communities, provided paid thugs for Kikuyu politicians during the elections. As the one-party system broke down and the ruling party lost its monopoly on coercive power, political violence became more informal, as politicians used hired thugs and local community networks to bolster their power and intimidate opponents. These weren't permanent alliances, but shifting relationships based on money, mutual benefit for gangs and patrons, and common community/ethnic identity—the latter not specifically a result of ethnic animosities, but because gangs were recruited in the political strongholds and heartlands of powerbrokers and politicians.[89]

Odinga, meanwhile, had the support of the Luo and younger, poorer Kenyans, particularly in Nairobi slums like Kibera. His alliance-building efforts were helped by a power struggle within the Rift Valley political elite, which he exploited to win over the most powerful Kalenjin and Masaai political factions. The Kalenjin have usually voted as a bloc in every election, but have not consistently supported the same candidate or alliance in every election. Their 2007 dispute was the result of a number of factors, including a generational struggle between Moi, who in 2007 was supporting Kibaki, and a younger politician, William Ruto. Ruto won the struggle and threw Kalenjin support behind Odinga and the ODM.[90] He wanted an Odinga-led government to settle land issues in the Rift Valley and move towards devolution of power to the provinces.

Devolution became a central plank of the ODM's 2007 campaign, though Odinga worked hard to avoid simplistic provincialism, with its connotations of ethnic separatism and ethnic cleansing. Moi's Kalenjin supporters had been accused of ethnic cleansing in the Rift Valley in the 1990s, when over 2,000 were killed and 500,000 displaced in land conflicts there.[91] Land disputes and other grievances among the Maasai and Kalenjin became rallying points for politicians allied with Moi against what were seen as Kikuyu-led or influenced parties/coalitions, and were exploited repeatedly during the 1992, 1997 and 2002 elections and the 2005 referendum. This was done with varying degrees of success, but always with elements of whipped up anti-outsider feeling and the threat or use of violence.

During the 2007 election campaign, politicians intent on maintaining power or trying to challenge incumbents deployed violence and hate propaganda against opponents.[92] There was a substantial escalation after votes were counted, when Odinga charged that the presidential election had been fraudulent—accusations backed up by the findings of international election monitors. Initial protests by ODM supporters in the Kibera slum near Nairobi, the Rift Valley and Nyanza province drew a swift and brutal response from the police, with scores of fatalities when they used live ammunition against demonstrators. The unrest generated by the ODM, the police response and the reaction by PNU supporters took on a life of its own, and rapidly came to resemble ethnic warfare, with Luo/Kalenjin ODM supporters on one side and Kikuyu supporters of the PNU on the other. Some of this was spontaneous violence resulting from anger and fear, but much of it was organised by politicians connected with the ODM and PNU.[93] The extensive violence was widely interpreted by politicians in Kenya (for their own mercenary purposes) and by the Kenyan and international media as spontaneous ethnic or tribal violence that had its roots in primordial hatreds. Powerful politicians—whether ODM leaders using violent protest to force a recount or rerun of the election, or PNU leaders protecting their rigged victory and hitting back at the ODM—wanted the violence to be seen this way to mask their own roles in it, and to use the tribal accusation as a stick with which to beat their opponents. As with most African conflicts framed this way, there are major problems with the simple ethnic hatred explanation.

The Kalenjin, for example, shifted their political allegiances many times, by turns supporting Moi and his allies, Kibaki, or Odinga. The name Kalenjin, which was first used to describe the community in the late 1950s, was developed by political leaders from within the Nandi, Kipsigis, Tugen and other communities that now make up the group to bring together those communities in the Rift with common linguistic and cultural roots to increase their political influence as independence approached.[94] There is no history of sustained ethnic conflict between the Kalenjin and Kikuyu. The grievances of non-Kikuyu communities in the Rift Valley and surrounding areas revolved principally around the loss of land during the colonial period, and then the failure of politically motivated post-independence land redistribution schemes to return it to its original occupiers. There soon arose a perception, especially among the Kalenjin and Maasai, that "outsiders" had gained at the expense of indigenous communities, creating a level of suspicion and political competition that had not previously existed. Competitive elections became opportunities to seek redress, making poor, rural communities vulnerable to politicians keen to exploit their grievances for political and electoral support. Major issues like land and personal political rivalries combined with huge economic inequality and specific community grievances to provide plenty of combustible material; only a spark was needed to ignite conflict.

There was a well of deprivation and anger among poor Kenyans of all communities who had not benefited from decades of independence, a well from which politicians could draw to bolster their ambitions and thwart those of political opponents. That is exactly what happened, with Kenyan politicians and their propagandists using ethnicity, culture and genuine grievances to incite fear, hatred and violence. It was just such incitement that got the current president, Uhuru Kenyatta, his now vice-president, William Ruto, and a Kalenjin politician and radio presenter, Joshua arap Sang, indicted by the International Criminal Court in the Hague on charges of crimes against humanity,[95] after Kenyan courts failed to take action to end political leaders' impunity. Kenyatta's case has since been dropped as witnesses have withdrawn testimony, been killed or simply disappeared. Ruto's and Sang's case continues.

After the 2007–8 violence, a unity government was formed with Kibaki as president and Odinga as prime minister. This shaky coalition was riven by defections, crises and rampant corruption, but it survived until the elections in 2013, which were won by Kenyatta and Ruto. There was surprisingly little violence during the campaign. What was most interesting about the election was that former bitter enemies Ruto and Kenyatta could form an alliance based on Kikuyu and Kalenjin constituencies, proving there was in fact no insurmountable ethnic animosity and demonstrating the importance of shifting alliances in Kenyan politics. After his victory, President Kenyatta stirred up strong support at African Union summits for an anti-ICC position and demands for the termination of the indictments—his own being overturned in December 2014 after the prosecution failed to garner enough witnesses to proceed.

In Zimbabwe, one man supported by a well-organised political and security network has managed to cling to power since independence in 1980. But Robert Mugabe has not done this alone. While he remains the overwhelmingly dominant political figure, that dominance depends on the ZANU-PF establishment and a military-security alliance that benefits directly from his rule.

Mugabe had to compete with ZAPU and other parties to be elected to office in 1980, but by the end of the decade, there was little real political opposition left in Zimbabwe. Ian Smith's Rhodesian Front had become the Conservative Alliance of Zimbabwe, but had little role once the reserved parliamentary seats for whites were abolished in 1987. ZAPU, emasculated after the brutal Matabeleland campaign, had been forced into a marriage of convenience with ZANU. Small parties existed, but they were unable to challenge ZANU-PF's primacy. The ruling party had built up a strong base in rural areas, first by its years of guerrilla infiltration and political campaigning during the liberation war and then in the 1980s through subsidised inputs for agriculture and the provision of basic social services. It began to set up rural ZANU branches, offering greater access to economic resources for 'loyal' areas through preferential treatment for party supporters.[96] The party also shored up its local power by undermining local chiefs, who it accused of siding with the white minority regime, though it later revived relationships with chiefs, using them to undermine support for opposition parties. Rural people, rather than educated or skilled urban dwellers, became the party's main constituency and a reliable voting resource during elections. The expansion of the civil service after independence was used both to reward ZANU supporters and to keep administration in party hands.

The combination of rural service provision and Africanisation of the civil service built up serious support for ZANU-PF, which spent the first decade of independence delivering benefits to core supporters in rural areas, the party and the military. It also fostered rural networks of mutual benefit controlled by the party, and the merging of party and state functions. While this approach did not entail major land redistribution or the wholesale sacking of experienced white civil servants, it ensured that commercial agricultural output was maintained and that administration continued to run smoothly.

Thanks to increased government support for small-scale black farmers in communal areas and the few who were resettled on land willingly sold by white farmers, the first decade of ZANU government saw a substantial increase in the output of maize and other food crops. Britain had pledged £20m for land redistribution on a 'willing seller' basis at Lancaster House, but the government made relatively little use of these funds and only 52,000 families had been resettled by 1989, with about 2.7 million hectares redistributed or 16.9 per cent of commercial farmland purchased from willing sellers. This was well below the target the Mugabe government had set itself in 1984 of resettling 162,000 black farmers on purchased land. Another million hectares of white farmland had been purchased by the new black elite connected with the party or the military.[97] Those who benefited from resettlement at this stage were a mix of poor farmers from over-crowded communal areas, some war veterans, and families displaced by the war.

Resettlement was seen not as the path to the restructuring of agriculture but as more of a social welfare programme, one that could have political advantages in the right context.[98] This meant that despite demands from veterans and many in the poorest communal areas, resettlement was not an economic or political priority. Resources in agriculture could be concentrated on the new black commercial farmers, part of the growing client base of the developing ZANU-PF patronage network, and on those communal areas with increasing productivity. The British government, which had promised funds for resettlement, was in no hurry to encourage mass resettlement and gave every sign of wanting to see the Lancaster House willing-seller provisions retained after the ten year period provided for in the peace deal.[99]

Resettlement and land distribution briefly became an issue during the 1990 elections when Mugabe and his restored ZANU-PF partner Joshua Nkomo called for land reform and redistribution of land owned by the small number of rich white farmers. The tenor of the election speeches was anti-white and strongly anti-British, distancing ZANU-PF from the slow speed of reform and using the issue to distract from economic decline, low incomes and corruption scandals like Willowgate, an affair involving senior ministers importing cars illegally for profit; it ended the career of one of Mugabe's right-hand men, Maurice Nyagumbo, credited with being one of the few who would tell Mugabe when policies weren't working. He was sacked from the government, charged with perjury and then committed suicide.[100]

In the first decade of independence, the ground had been laid for the total hegemony of ZANU-PF and the military elite with Mugabe at the apex of a pyramid of patronage. ZANU-PF rather than parliament was politically dominant, and the freedom of the press was progressively reduced. Through the Nigerian-funded Mass Media Trust, the government gained control of most national newspapers and used the Zimbabwe Broadcasting Corporation (ZBC) as its mouthpiece. The police and the Central Intelligence Organisation were used to harass independent-minded journalists, who were frequently detained for publishing critical stories. Civil society and independent organisations were also treated as potential enemies rather than as part of a plural, open political system. The trades unions too were always viewed with suspicion by ZANU-PF, despite being headed at one stage by Mugabe's brother.

Zimbabwe's Economic Structural Adjustment Programme (ESAP, nicknamed Extreme Suffering for African People by critics) really began to bite in the 1990s, eroding the advances in social service provision achieved in the 1980s.[101] Improved health provision and reductions in child mortality had helped reduce overall mortality rates, with the population rising by nearly 300,000 per year in the late 1980s and early 1990s (about 2.7 per cent per annum), before the effects of AIDS reduced the growth rate. In the 1990s, GDP growth slowed to only 0.9 per cent, and per capita income fell by 9 per cent between 1990–96. Spending on public sector employment was kept high as ESAP policies reduced service delivery without cutting public service jobs for ZANU-PF supporters. Along with allocations to maintain the military and security services even as revenue declined, partly because of lower income from export crops, this meant the budget deficit remained at around 13 per cent of GDP in 1995. Zimbabwe's debt soared from 16 per cent of GDP in 1980 to over 50 per cent in the 1990s, and in 1993 debt servicing was 33 per cent of export revenue. Provision deteriorated in areas like health, education, welfare and aid for poor farmers, and yet members of the ruling patron-client network still enjoyed public employment and the opportunities for wealth creation it entailed. The result was an ever-increasing gap between the politically connected rich and the marginalised poor.

Between 20,000 and 30,000 workers lost their jobs in industry, services or low-ranking civil service sectors in the first half of the 1990s, with unemployment reaching 44 per cent in 1994. Falling employment, low incomes and rising prices hit urban workers particularly hard. Opposition to the government was growing among young, educated urban people and the urban jobless, fuelled partly by the increased provision of education, a rise in the number of black pupils completing their schooling, and the large increase in the number of black college and university graduates. Their expectations of jobs and higher living standards, like those of a majority of Zimbabweans, were not being met; and while the elite was prospering amid widespread hardship, there was now an articulate black educated class emerging in the towns, where harassment had not entirely silenced critics in the media, human rights or civil society groups.

ESAP did not tackle corruption and the use of public office for enrichment. During the 1990s details emerged of major financial irregularities and missing funds in the Grain Marketing Board and Air Zimbabwe, both run by ZANU-PF nominees,[102] and there was growing evidence of senior ZANU-PF figures and military leaders enriching themselves as the country became poorer. To maintain thc power of the party and military/security structures on which he relied, Mugabe allowed senior officers to acquire land and businesses. A good example is Solomon Mujuru, an army commander and ZANU-PF powerbroker and a chief representative of Mugabe's Zezuru community within the leadership. Mujuru was Mugabe's key man in the military chain of command and a vital part of his patronage network. While still army chief, he built up an empire of farms, hotels, a chain of supermarkets and other property; he benefited substantially from defence procurement contracts, and was one of the wealthiest men in Zimbabwe. Mujuru also helped bring in the key votes of women through his wife, Joice Mujuru, who would later become vice-president—before falling foul of Mugabe's wife Grace and being sacked as vice-president and then forced out of the ruling party.[103] When Mujuru retired as army commander he still remained a link with the former guerrilla leaders and younger officers running the army, and helped maintain a network of senior Zezuru officers in the army, air force and police—a core part of Mugabe's strategy for retaining power and rewarding trusted supporters. The other main Shona groups—Karanga and Manyika—were well-represented in the party and the military, but with the exception of Emmerson Mnangagwa (a Karanga and a key part of the security and intelligence system), they had second-rank positions.

Mnangagwa, who aside from his cabinet position and key role in security still has an important role in running ZANU-PF's large business empire, is the favourite to succeed Mugabe since the sacking of Joice Mujuru, whose political power declined rapidly after the unexplained and highly suspicious death of Solomon Mujuru in a fire on his farm in August 2011. The only obvious competition to succeed Mugabe could come from the president's wife, Grace, whose entry into politics and carefully contrived election as head of the ZANU-PF Women's League in 2014 have put her in a strong position. She is a growing power in the land and could be a decisive influence on the succession.

Lower public spending in rural areas on health, schools, roads and support for small farmers hit living standards, and in the long term threatened the early improvements in output and rural incomes that made ZANU-PF the politically dominant force across rural Zimbabwe. In the tighter economic climate of the late 1990s, patronage networks became more and more important as access to economic resources and employment relied heavily on political connections. This only got worse as the government developed an 'indigenisation' programme to reduce white and foreign economic control and award lucrative government contracts to black businesses with the right contacts.[104] But it was financially impossible to maintain services developed in rural areas, and state capacity was weakened across the country. Although ZANU-PF still had its own structures in rural areas, its powers of patronage were badly undercut by economic decline.

The rise in political conflict towards the end of the 1990s had multiple causes: economic decline and widespread poverty; an unaccountable government whose members brazenly enriched themselves while everyone else got poorer; frustration over the lack of land and wealth redistribution; and ESAP-induced pressures on workers, low-ranking public servants and smaller businesses. Some of the first stirrings of discontent came from one of the groups expected to be particularly loyal to ZANU-PF: war veterans. In the mid-1990s, they began to protest at the small payments from a compensation fund set up for them. A former ZANU activist, Margaret Dongo, exposed the theft of money from the compensation funds. Her campaign over the theft, payments for veterans and outspoken criticism of the government saw her elected as an independent MP in Harare in 1995. This demonstrated not only the power of the veterans, but also growing anger at ZANU-PF in urban areas. Dongo used her victory to publicise the cause of the War Veterans' Association.[105]

The late 1990s were a period of crisis both for Zimbabweans and for ZANU-PF, but the latter was able to rebuild its power, forge new networks and use them and its control of the security apparatus to stay in power, harassing and intimidating opponents while executing a fast, violent and messy programme of land reform. This enabled it to ride out political challenges, build new alliances, ignore defeat in an election and survive international sanctions. The use of land seizures to bolster the flagging ZANU-PF structures in rural areas, the rebuilding of relations with traditional chiefs, and the symbolic and economic effects of the rapid land reform all ensured that even when the opposition Movement for Democratic Change (MDC) began to make inroads in some areas and garner support from educated people and urban dwellers, ZANU-PF could still call on the peasantry to turn out on its behalf.

Nonetheless, Mugabe and his party faced a political crisis. Student demonstrations, pressure from the black business sector, a public sector strike in June 1996, a general strike by the ZCTU and the growth in civil society groups all put pressure on the government over the economy, corruption and accountability. But it was the campaign by war veterans that tipped the balance, culminating as it did in demonstrations that forced the government into actions that in turn led to economic disintegration and then the seizure of white-owned farmland.

The war veterans could mobilise thousands to protest while also counting on support from serving soldiers. After Dongo uncovered the compensation scandal, a senior officer, Brigadier Gibson Mashingaidze, used the funeral of a war veteran to attack ZANU-PF and military leaders who,

> Have ten farms to their names and luxury yachts and have developed fat stomachs when ex-combatants...live in abject poverty. Is this the ZANU-PF I trusted with my life...To the majority of Zimbabweans I say our party, which I believe is still a great party, has abandoned us."[106]

Veterans took to the streets in Harare in July and August 1997; they harassed ministers, besieged Mugabe's office and demonstrated outside an investors' conference he addressed. But on 11 August, Heroes' Day, they chanted over Mugabe's speech—something previously inconceivable. Despite the country's dire economic straits, Mugabe tried to buy them off, promising compensation of Z$50,000 for each veteran and a monthly pension of Z$2000. The government did not have the resources to pay this, so it just printed money and promised the veterans land.[107] A war veterans' levy was added to taxes and higher sales and petrol taxes were announced, along with plans to seize 800 white-owned farms.

In November 1997, the value of the Zimbabwe dollar fell through the floor. Deteriorating relations with Britain and the US over human rights issues meant that aid was not forthcoming from them or the World Bank. Food prices rose rapidly, maize meal increasing by 26.7 per cent in 1997 and a further 21 per cent in 1998 at a time of high unemployment, falling wages and declining rural incomes. The ZCTU, now allying itself with civil society groups, had strong support from workers suffering from the meltdown of industry and services. Manufacturing was down to 17 per cent of GDP, a fall of over 25 per cent in eight years due to a lack of demand, low investment and South Africa's re-emergence as a competitor in the textile and small industry sector. The ZCTU's growing political role and alliance with pressure groups led to the founding of the MDC, led by ZCTU head Morgan Tsvangirai.

The MDC sought to mobilise opposition to ZANU-PF and to oppose a mooted new constitution, which would legalise the seizure of farmland without compensation while strengthening the powers of the presidency. It also attacked the decision to send troops to the DRC to support President Kabila. While senior officers and ZANU-PF leaders gained financially from this intervention thanks to mining and other lucrative concessions in the DRC, the IMF estimated it cost Zimbabwe $1.3 million a day. The DRC intervention became another means of enrichment for the political-military network, whose use of national resources for personal gain was becoming ever more apparent. Around this time, it emerged that among those who benefited from the looting of the war veterans' fund were commissioner of police Augustine Chihuri, air force commander (and former 5th Brigade head) Perence Shiri, and defence force head Vitalis Zvinavashe.[108]

The government's new constitution was put to a referendum in February 2000, ahead of that year's legislative elections and the 2002 presidential vote. The referendum proceeded amid preparations for a programme of rapid land redistribution, an attempt to restore ZANU-PF's flagging rural support and outflank the MDC. But despite a vigorous campaign, accusations of intimidation and violence, and blanket media coverage by the ZANU-PF controlled press, the opponents of the government won: the new constitution was rejected by 54 per cent of voters. Mugabe denounced the result as a conspiracy between the urban middle class, the unions and the whites,[109] and accelerated the land seizure plans.

The land invasions started on 26 February 2000, spearheaded by war veterans and gangs of youths ferried to white farms in government and army vehicles. There was considerable violence; farmers and their workers were attacked, farm buildings destroyed and livestock killed. Much of the violence was spontaneous, but the campaign as a whole was organised with the clear aims of seizing land, portraying it as justice, using it to regain ZANU-PF hegemony in rural areas, and portraying the MDC as allies of the rich white farmers. By the July elections, 1,000 farms (about a quarter of the total commercial farms) had been seized.[110] The seizures reduced 200,000 black farmworkers to destitution; twenty-six people, mainly black farm workers and a majority of them MDC supporters, were killed during the invasions. After the land occupation, the outgoing parliament amended the constitution to allow for rapid land reform, and then the announcement of the Fast Track Land Reform Programme in July 2000—which Mugabe named the Third Chimurenga (revolutionary struggle).[111]

The campaign was a major political issue inside Zimbabwe and internationally, with Britain, the European Union and the US all major critics.

They imposed targeted sanctions against Zimbabwean leaders and ZANU-PF officials linked with human rights abuses. The sanctions had some economic effect, but by the early 2000s, Zimbabwe had an alternative trading partner, source of arms supplies and investor in China, which took a non-political approach to its economic relations and had no qualms about supporting its old liberation struggle ally whatever the nature of his government.

In the countryside, most people supported the occupations, even though they caused a 70.4 per cent fall in maize production the next year; four years later it was still 45.6 per cent below previous levels. About 6,000 white farmers had lost land, but they had been replaced on that land by 245,000 black farmers. Output was disrupted for several years, though drought was also partly to blame. Although senior politicians and military officers took substantial farms for themselves, most of the land went to small-scale farmers, who have gradually increased their productivity and now grow almost 50 per cent of the country's maize and 40 per cent of its tobacco crop.[112] There is still considerable controversy over the results of the land reform in the short and long term, but there is growing evidence that the acquisition of land was not simply dominated by the elite, that agriculture has not been irreparably damaged by the seizures, and that however brutal the process, fourteen years on they cannot be seen as the total failure many expected them to be.[113]

The violence and disruption of the occupations set the scene for a bitterly fought election campaign in 2000, in which violence and intimidation that prevented the MDC could safely campaign in only twenty-five constituencies, was attacked or harassed in forty-six others and was totally excluded from the other forty-nine because of the levels of violence. Despite this, the MDC ran ZANU-PF very close: ZANU-PF won sixty-two seats but fell just below half the total vote, while the MDC had fify-seven seats with 47 per cent of the vote. Seven ZANU-PF ministers were voted out of office.[114] In the 2002 presidential election, massive intimidation and electoral malpractices could not prevent Tsvangirai from running Mugabe closer than he had ever been run before, and this challenge pushed ZANU-PF to rely heavily on violence, intimidation and vote-rigging during subsequent elections. The party and state became ever more militarised.[115]

Between the 2000 land occupations and the 2013 elections, which reaffirmed ZANU-PF and Mugabe's dominance, Zimbabwe was dominated by the political struggle between the governing party and the MDC, the splintering of the MDC, two contested and highly questionable elections, and the continuing crisis in the economy. In 2006, GDP per capita was only 53 per cent of its 1980 level, inflation was out of control at 230 per cent, and formal sector employment was down to under one million. Politics was dominated by continual harassment of the MDC and its activists by ZANU-PF and the security forces, while journalists working outside government media were detained, beaten or forced into exile.

Zimbabwe was becoming an embarrassment for South Africa's Thabo Mbeki, who had spearheaded the adoption of the New Partnership for Africa's Development (NEPAD) at the OAU summit in July 2001; part of his African Renaissance initiative, it aimed to achieve sustainable growth alongside good governance across Africa. Zimbabwe was in deficit on both counts, and resisted Mbeki's rather too gentle and diplomatic approach as he tried to rein in ZANU-PF and stop Zimbabwe's meltdown from damaging the economies of South Africa and the wider region. South African pressure was exerted bilaterally and through the SADC, but was not matched by any sanctions; Mbeki failed to use his country's economic power to bring pressure to bear on the increasingly violent and authoritarian Mugabe government.

The 2005 elections were dominated by ZANU-PF's campaign of violence and intimidation. The MDC remained strong in urban areas and a few rural ones, winning forty-two seats, but ZANU-PF's dominance in rural areas, blatant rigging of voting rolls and strong-arm tactics brought it seventy-two seats. Two months after the elections, the government launched Operation Murambatsvina, a massive and violent onslaught against the informal urban trade system and the large numbers of people who had moved from rural areas to informal or squatter settlements around Harare and other towns. Carried out by the police and ZANU-PF cadres, it was aimed at cracking down on the black market and forcing people back from urban shantytowns to the rural areas. This might have been an attempt to punish MDC supporters, but it was just as likely to have been aimed at reducing the urban population in areas where high food prices and poor availability had created a vast informal economy beyond government control, serving swelling urban populations that ZANU-PF could not control as easily as it could rural ones.[116] About 650–700,000 people were made homeless by the destruction of informal settlements. Among the beneficiaries of the destruction were Chinese traders, who began to gain a share of the small-scale retail market as Sino-Zimbabwean economic co-operation grew.

The MDC's political fortunes after the election were not helped by growing personality conflicts in the party. In October 2005, the party split, with

MDC-T led by Tsvangirai and MDC-M by Arthur Mutambara, and another faction led by Welshman Ncube, which accused Tsvangirai of authoritarianism. The weakening of the MDC as an opposition party was part of the familiar and "depressing pattern of divisions around personalities, perceived 'intelligence' differences within party leadership, and the ever-present ethnic solidarities that at times seem exaggerated yet over time become self-fulfilling" within Zimbabwean and many other African political parties.[117]

The splits did not stop the MDC mounting a serious challenge in the March 2008 elections, in which ZANU-PF was also opposed by a former SADC head, Simba Makoni, and a former government minister and ZANU-PF propagandist, Jonathan Moyo. Mugabe and ZANU-PF were beaten in the elections, but supported by the army, they refused to accept defeat, and there was a huge delay in announcing the results. When they were released, they showed MDC-T with ninety-nine seats and ZANU-PF lagging with ninety-seven. The MDC-M had ten seats, and Moyo was elected as an independent. In the presidential vote, Tsvangirai got 47.9 per cent, Mugabe 43.2 and Makoni 8.3. Most people believed that Tsvangirai had won outright and that the count had been rigged to force a second round. Some estimates put the 'real' Tsvangirai vote at 57 per cent.[118]

What was most worrying for ZANU-PF was that for the first time, there was serious opposition to it in rural areas. But despite losing, Mugabe still had a majority in parliament through his power to nominate thirty MPs. The inconclusive presidential vote triggered a second round, and ZANU-PF used the time between the rounds to launch a campaign of violence against those who had voted against it and warn them not to dare do so again. It was the worst [violence] seen in the country since the Gukurahundi massacres of the 1980s, and was directed by the joint operations command of the armed forces with the participation of party militants as well as the security forces, centring on Mashonaland regions that had defected to the opposition. The violence forced Tsvangirai to withdraw from the second round of voting, giving Mugabe victory by default.

This hardly defused the political crisis and did nothing to stave off international criticism. The SADC and South Africa tried to find a political solution amid much criticism that their softly-softly approach to Mugabe and ZANU-PF had allowed the mass use of violence and intimidation in the face of a clear electoral defeat. Botswana's President Festus Mogae was particularly critical from within the SADC, but he was a lone voice. The upshot was that the SADC and South Africa had few options, but Mbeki ultimately facilitated the Global Political Agreement (GPA) of early 2009, which set up a unity government with Tsvangirai as prime minister and several cabinet posts for the MDC. ZANU-PF retained control of the security services, police, army and therefore a monopoly of force, but the MDC was in charge of trying to fix the broken economy. The MDC-T's agreement to take part was heavily criticised by many of its allies in the civic movements;[119] Tsvangirai's answer was that he was trying to continue the fight for democracy in a new arena, and that the GPA was a milestone on the journey.

The GPA turned into a millstone round the neck of the MDC-T. Its attempts to work from the inside to increase its political clout and prepare for the 2013 elections failed. Those elections, following a complex and fractious process of drafting a new constitution, saw less violence but extensive rigging of the voters' rolls (which remained under ZANU-PF's control) but also a resurgence of ZANU-PF's hold over rural areas and considerable disenchantment with the MDC-T and Tsvangirai for having collaborated but not delivered. Mugabe's victory was achieved through a monopoly over coercive force, the army's open statements that it wouldn't accept an MDC government and the very obvious buying of votes by ZANU-PF in rural areas. The SADC tried to play a role in keeping the elections free and fair, but Mugabe attacked a South African member of the SADC election facilitation team, Lindiwe Zulu, calling her a 'street woman' when she criticised the process. She received no support from President Zuma, who effectively disowned her and gave Mugabe carte blanche to ensure a ZANU-PF victory. ZANU-PF is believed to have funded its campaign largely through access to the massive revenues from the lucrative Marange diamond fields, which have remained under the control of the party, the Ministry of Mines and the army. One of ZANU-PF's most crucial tools was its role in drawing up the voters' rolls, which allowed it to disenfranchise many urban voters and keep huge numbers of dead voters on rolls in rural areas—meaning ZANU-PF supporters could vote multiple times.

The Johannesburg-based Solidarity Peace Trust's report on the election found no direct evidence of vote-rigging, but raised serious questions over the accuracy of voters' lists; it found evidence of intimidation and promises of gifts and rewards if ZANU-PF was elected. Written by a leading expert on contemporary Zimbabwe, Brian Raftopoulos, it draws on information collected from the rural areas, and features some telling testimony from a range of voters. These examples are a reflection of the general tenor:

> I voted for ZANU-PF even though I do not support them. The war veterans told us that there would be war if MDC won. [Old man, Nkayi].

> The other thing was the rice; the rice issue was a problem. You see food was used in campaigning and people had no choice. They ended up giving that bucket of rice an exaggerated value, maybe because it could have found them without mealie meal at home...When election time comes they have no choice but to vote for that bucket of rice. [Middle aged man, Insiza]
>
> I am glad that ZANU PF has won—they have promised us that we can own factories now, so I am waiting to be given part of a factory. [Young man, Tsholotsho][120]

The report describes how ZANU-PF managed to keep the MDC-T focused on the GPA and the new constitution while it rebuilt its support in rural areas and prepared for the elections. It also points out that the changes in the rural areas resulting from the fast land redistribution of 2000 and the gradual recovery of the rural economy certainly helped ZANU-PF's campaign, and that Mugabe and the party "have retained a substantial social base in the country... the maintenance of this social base has not been based solely on violence and coercion but on a combination of the ideological legacies of the liberation struggle, the persistent memories of colonial dispossession, and the land reform process."[121] In the end, the election revived ZANU-PF's power; even allowing for fixing of voters' lists and the effects of bribery and intimidation, this was a considerable resurgence in rural support for the party. In the presidential contest, Mugabe received 61 per cent compared to the 44 per cent he garnered in 2008; Tsvangirai's vote plunged from 48 per cent to 33. ZANU-PF increased its parliamentary seats from 99 seats in 2008 to 159 in 2013; MDC-T's number dropped from 99 seats to 49.

MDC-T failed to use the GPA period to its advantage, and it was politically outmanoeuvred by ZANU-PF. Fundamentally, during the GPA period and since the elections,

> The ZANU-PF strategy, consistent with its hegemonic political culture, has been to engage in cosmetic political and economic reforms that will not result in further democracy or result in a loss of its historic monopoly over power. ... ZANU-PF has kept the strategic doors to its power, such as the security sector and the mining and agricultural industries, firmly closed.[122]

There is little prospect of this changing in the coming years. The main focus is shifting from the challenge from the MDC to ZANU-PF's succession battle, and the upcoming fight by Mugabe's successor to entrench his or her power.

7

AFRICA AND THE WORLD

A NEW UNITY, THE CHINA SYNDROME, AND AFRICA RISING

The final chapter of Africa's story in the post-independence era focuses on new attempts to find unity and integration across the continent with the replacement of the stale, old OAU with a more pro-active African Union (AU). Alongside the quest for unity, there was a renewed search for African answers to economic development and good governance through the New Partnership for Africa's development (NEPAD), spearheaded by President Thabo Mbeki of South Africa. In terms of international relations, the rise of China as a major economic player and role model for Africa was a major development with implications both economic and political, and it dovetailed with the growing discourse of Africa Rising, which built on improved growth rates and export earnings to posit a new dawn for African development and living standards.

African unity in the new millennium: The AU and the rise and fall of NEPAD

The problems the SADC encountered in its attempted mediation in Zimbabwe mirrored ECOWAS's difficulties in Liberia, Sierra Leone and later Mali, and the IGAD and OAU's in Sudan. Taken together, they demonstrated the limits of collective state action in Africa. The OAU had been a talking shop and, in the words of Julius Nyerere, a trades union of heads of state that protected their interests.[1] It worked fitfully for unity, and had little success in averting or ending conflicts. The OAU and regional organisations like ECOWAS, SADCC/SADC, IGAD and the host of eastern and southern free trade areas had made little progress towards breaking down trade and travel barriers, let alone advancing realistic economic integration. The OAU in particular played little or no role in encouraging democracy, establishing viable continental institutions, funding itself or aggregating African states' global influence. It was infamous for "turning a blind eye to bad governance" and accepting the endless cycle of coups and corruption.[2]

As Thabo Mbeki built on South Africa's international image as the champion of democracy and reconciliation in the late 1990s, he was acutely aware of the need for Africa to take its proper place on the global stage, and developed his idea of an 'African renaissance' to meet the challenge. Supported by other relatively new leaders like Zenawi, Museveni, and Kagame and later Obasanjo, his approach created the impetus for transforming the OAU into the AU, the launching of NEPAD, and the creation of the African Peer Review Mechanism (APRM). The latter projects were meant to integrate Africa's economies, expand and strengthen their participation in the global economy, and encourage growth and development. The new institutions aimed to improve governance and democracy, and to support peace and stability; this was to be done at the expense of ditching the OAU's cast-iron law of non-intervention in member states' affairs. The AU declared its intent to play a more pro-active role in preventing or ending conflict in Africa.

While Mbeki and his allies clearly wanted a new, well-functioning body that would strive for peace and development and for greater African clout internationally, many leaders quite clearly saw the AU's pledges to development, democracy and good governance as window dressing, a sop to maintain Western development aid by appearing to accept good governance strictures while making few substantive changes. Others saw the transformation of the OAU as an opportunity to push for a United States of Africa—notably Libya's Colonel Gaddafi, whose vision naturally included him as the dominant force. This complicated the creation of the new Union, and wasted time at a series of OAU and then AU summits. Libya had allies within Africa (including South Africa's ANC) to whom it still gave economic and military help, or who were indebted for past support for liberation or election campaigns and this meant that despite suspicion over

Libya's intentions, they couldn't be rejected out of hand. Instead, they were argued over, committees were formed—and in true OAU fashion, nothing was done.

Once they had circumvented Gaddafi's bombastic ambitions, African leaders spent the late 1990s and early 2000s working out the AU's charter and key objectives. Their aim was not just to create a revitalised and strengthened OAU, but to make plans for economic regeneration; those plans ultimately created a new development body in NEPAD and support for democracy in the APRM. Mbeki, Nigeria's President Obasanjo, Ethiopia's President Zenawi, Senegal's President Wade and Algeria's President Bouteflika were the key movers. The OAU summits in Libya and Togo in 1999 and 2000 discussed and agreed the Constitutive Act and charter of the AU. This created a strong Commission in place of the weak OAU secretariat and established the Peace and Security Council (PSC), a standing decision-making body for the resolution of conflicts made up of fifteen of the fifty-three member states, representing North, East, West, Central and Southern Africa.[3] The AU was officially constituted in Addis Ababa, which remained its headquarters, and existed alongside the OAU until it was formally launched at the 2002 Durban summit by Thabo Mbeki, who said that:

> The time has come that Africa must take its rightful place in global affairs. The time has come to end the marginalisation of Africa...Through our actions let us proclaim to the world that this is a continent of democracy, a continent of democratic institutions and culture. Indeed, a continent of good governance, where the people participate and the rule of law is upheld.[4]

The AU has not been totally effective in pursuing these ambitious objectives, but democracy is on the march; as one stern Kenyan critic of the record of African governments put it, "Democratic space is significantly broader in many countries while free elections are far more common, and coups far less so, than at any time since the continent's independence."[5]

The AU adopted NEPAD to provide a vision and policy framework for accelerating economic co-operation, integration and growth. Endorsed by the leaders of the economically dominant G8 countries in 2001, its policies were really an extension of the neoliberal economic strategies that had underpinned SAPs and the good governance agenda. There was no implicit or explicit challenge to the structure of global economic power, trade relations or the hegemony of the economically powerful as exerted through trade policy, the WTO, the IMF and the World Bank. Instead, NEPAD formalised the hegemony of Western economies and economic doctrines. Far from mounting any challenge or demand for restructuring, NEPAD's framework and its adherence to G8 policies served "to legitimise instead of aiming to restructure the existing global power relations" of which African countries have so long been victims.[6]

Through NEPAD, African countries pledged themselves to fight corruption and further develop good governance, even though the detail of the NEPAD policy framework directly contradicted the political practices of the majority of AU members, even those which had embraced competitive elections. NEPAD and the APRM looked good on paper, but they had no mechanisms for sustained monitoring, and lacked the resources to achieve their laudable but unrealistic aims. Far from heralding a new era of effective governance, they were another cosmetic device that contained no real commitment.[7] When neither NEPAD or any sort of peer review exercise stopped Mugabe's blatant vote-rigging and resort to election violence or improved Zimbabwe's ever-deepening corruption and economic mismanagement, any hope there might have been for the initiatives abruptly dissipated. In May 2010, while still lauding its objectives and his own role in its foundation, Mbeki admitted that NEPAD had failed to achieve economic change or good governance, remarking in a public lecture that, "The tragedy is that in practical terms this action plan has fallen by the wayside." He blamed it on the G8 becoming the G20, which had not adopted the NEPAD Africa Action Plan and which had failed to "place the challenge of Africa's development at the centre of the global agenda," leaving Africa on the periphery of global economic decision-making and power.[8] One might add that NEPAD's chief architect was hardly a model leader, given the growing evidence of high-level corruption in South Africa and the use of the intelligence services to smear Mbeki's challengers within the ANC.

If NEPAD and the APRM have become increasingly irrelevant, the AU has had a more mixed record, with distinct successes and abiding weaknesses, the latter being the lack of funds and physical resources, and the difficulty in reaching African consensus for action in cases where conflicts or other threats to peace and stability might involve a number of member states. The AU has nonetheless been far more decisive than the OAU in reacting to military coups and civil conflict, and has a far better peacebuilding record. It has been free to play this role since its Constitutive Act broke with the OAU's core principle of non-intervention, instead enshrining the concept of intervention against the will of a member state in certain "grave circumstances...namely war crimes, genocide and crimes against humanity."[9] In 2003, the AU summit added that the Peace and Security

Council could act to prevent "a serious threat to legitimate order to restore peace and security to a Member State"; this gave it the right to intervene through the PSC, a standing body with more clout than the OAU ever had.

Consensus among a majority of states is still required to fund and authorise action, but the AU has been better equipped and more willing to intervene than the OAU. It has suspended states from membership in cases of coups or violent changes of government: Madagascar was suspended in 2009 (and the SADC played a major role in mediating and creating conditions for elections in October 2013), Guinea-Bissau in 2012, Egypt in 2013 (after the overthrow of President Morsi) and the CAR after the 2013 overthrow of President Bozize by the Séléka rebel alliance—though in that case, the AU and neighbouring states failed to provide sufficient troops or strong enough leadership to stop a descent into communal violence.

Rather like Africa's process of democratisation and political change, the AU's record has been uneven, but it's a clear improvement on what went before. It has been willing to get involved, to aggregate African opinion and to commit troops. And even if policy does not always match principle, it has established the idea that the furtherance of democracy and better standards of governance are things for which Africa should strive as a continent. The organisation and its leading members have demonstrated a clear opposition to coups and other forms of violent seizure of power. Its biggest drawback is its dependence on international funds, unlike ECOWAS, which draws 5 per cent of customs duties from its member states and so has its own funding. The AU has managed to work with bodies like ECOWAS, the SADC and IGAD, though the relationships are not well defined and are often slow and cumbersome. ECOWAS and AU were late to respond to the 2011 Mali crisis, when their sluggishness meant Mali was ultimately left to rely on its former coloniser, France.

The crisis began with a combined revolt in late 2011 by the Tuareg National Movement for the Liberation of Azawad (MNLA) and Islamist groups with Tuareg and extra-territorial support. The MNLA wanted independence for areas of northern Mali. The revolt grew out of long-standing grievances, and President Traore's failure to honour agreements with Tuareg groups. After the overthrow of Gaddafi in Libya, Tuareg fighters in Libya's Islamic Legion fled Libya and returned for Mali with their weapons. This ignited a new revolt, and then an army coup that overthrew Traore. It was joined in its revolt by Islamist groups, among them al-Qaeda in the Islamic Mahgrib (AQIM) and Ansar el-Dine. The Islamists hijacked the Tuareg revolt and involved it in a wider Islamist and pro-al-Qaeda movement in the Sahel. The groups' combined forces rapidly captured areas of northern Mali, and began to advance south. In November 2011, with AU and UN backing, ECOWAS decided to send a military force, but was slow to assemble it, forcing Mali to rely on French troops. The French intervention was supported by the AU because of the slowness of the African response. In January 2013 the outgoing AU chairman, President Thomas Boni Yayi of Benin, told AU leaders their response to conflict in Mali had been too slow, and thanked France for taking the lead in the military intervention.

In the spring of 2013 the UN Security Council adopted resolution 2100 authorising the UN Multidimensional Integrated Stabilisation Mission in Mali (MINUSMA), which replaced the African force, AMISMA, which had eventually arrived to support the French operations. By November 2013, some stability had been achieved and elections held, but 3,000 French troops remained in the country in addition to the UN force, many of whose troops were in fact ECOWAS/AU military units transferred to UN control. France, its allies in the region, and Britain and the USA (who provided support for the military intervention) saw the Mali conflict not in terms of a long-standing political and cultural conflict but as part of the 'War on Terror,' the prism through which the West has viewed African security throughout the 2000s and 2010s. Accordingly, the response in Mali was followed by growing backing for Nigeria against Boko Haram in 2014, just as the USA's intelligence and other involvement greatly expanded in Central Africa between 2012 and 2014.[10]

The AU was much more effective in its intervention in Burundi. During the 1980s and 1990s, the OAU had failed to negotiate an end to the conflict between the country's Tutsi military and political elite and Hutu rebel groups. A little progress was made by former Tanzanian President Julius Nyerere and then Nelson Mandela, but the Tutsi army consistently refused to allow an African peacekeeping force to be deployed. In 2000, under pressure from Mandela, Tanzania and other regional states, a partial peace agreement was signed, followed by a ceasefire among most of the warring groups in October 2002. South Africa had deployed a well-armed 700-strong force in Burundi to protect politicians involved in the negotiations, and in 2003, the addition of Ethiopian and Mozambican troops transformed this into a 3,335-strong force to supervise the ceasefire and support the demobilisation, disarmament and reintegration of former fighters, as well as to provide some guarantee of basic security and political stability. While the disarmament and demobilisation targets were not met, the intervention was broadly successful; it set the scene for power-sharing and then for the deployment of a UN-funded force, ONUB, when the AU's funding ran out. Many of the ONUB troops were re-hatted members of the AU force, AMIB.[11] The AU and east African regional leaders are proving less successful, though, in defusing the crisis around President Nkurunziza's decision to run for a third term in office.

The AU's military operation in Somalia, AMISOM, has been more problematic, with Ugandan, Burundian and other troops (joined by the Kenyans in 2011 after their invasion of Jubaland) helping support the transitional government and trying to rid Somalia of Al-Shabaab. While areas around Mogadishu and in Jubaland were liberated, security remains uncertain, Al-Shabaab has never been decisively defeated, and bombings and other insurgent attacks continue, including in the Somali capital. The African Union intervention in Darfur, AMIS, was even less successful; poorly equipped and badly underfunded, it suffered major casualties and generally failed to police or properly monitor the conflict, proving unable to prevent attacks on civilians. Its UN successor, UNAMID, incorporated many of the AU contingents. It is better funded, but is still struggling with limited resources, too few troops and a mandate that allows it to do little more than protect itself and monitor any violations of the peace agreements. Lasting peace in Darfur still seems a long way off.

The AU still has a long way to go to establish itself both as a strong and effective African voice internationally, and to successfully prevent or reverse violent changes of government. One area where it has singularly failed has been its pledge to reach out to and involve civil society groups and empower citizens beyond the formal structures of government. The Union has barely paid lip service to this, and has played no discernible role in "empowering African citizens to engage and influence their states".[12] This inability to look beyond heads of state and governments was also apparent in the AU's increasing criticism of the ICC's cases against President Kenyatta of Kenya and his vice-president, as well as the older case against President Bashir of Sudan. At the AU summit in May 2013 the then-chairman, Ethiopian Prime Minister Hailemariam Desalegn, said the ICC was "hunting" Africans because of their race. A special summit of the AU in October 2013 called on the ICC to defer cases against incumbent leaders; a diplomatic effort was started at the UN, with the support of China, to have the Kenyatta and Ruto cases deferred until they stepped down from office. This was unsuccessful, as eight of the Security Council's fifteen members—including the US, Britain and France—abstained, and thereby stopped the resolution being passed. The AU's anti-ICC push spoke of a tolerance for the impunity of political leaders, though some governments dissented: Malawi's President Joyce Banda refused to allow Bashir into Malawi for a planned AU summit, and Botswana opposed the deferral of the cases.

Archbishop Desmond Tutu of South Africa, a consistent voice in favour of human rights and democracy, pointed out that the ICC's chief prosecutor Fatou Bensouda was African and that many of the African cases had been referred by African governments. He dismissed the accusations of a witch-hunt and called on African leaders to support the court, urging heads of states at the Union to stand up against their "least democratic" counterparts and defend the ICC, which he argued Africa had helped found, initiate cases at, and staff; "So while the rhetoric of leaders at the AU may play both the race and colonial cards, the facts are clear. Far from being a so-called 'white man's witch hunt', the ICC could not be more African if it tried."[13]

There is one area in which the AU has played an important symbolic role, though not a hugely effective institutional or policy one: the role of women. In 2012, former South African Foreign Minister Nkosazana Dlamini-Zuma became the AU's chairperson. Hot on the heels of Africa's first two women presidents, Ellen Johnson-Sirleaf in Liberia and Joyce Banda in Malawi, this was a symbolic rather than substantive step forward in the empowerment of women, but it was a clear acknowledgment of women's ability to take on major political roles. Prior to the 1990s there were a few women in cabinet posts across Africa, but they were token appointments and tended to be limited to areas such as community affairs, education and health. Women attracted little attention and held little power, despite their central economic role in basic agriculture and small-scale commerce. The appointment of women to senior political or economic positions—such as Nigeria's powerful and effective finance minister, Ngozi Okonjo-Iweala—has been matched by a slow but steady expansion in the number of women elected to legislatures, especially in South Africa, Mozambique and Namibia. Rwanda, still struggling to balance the needs of stability, security and democracy, has one of the world's largest proportion of women parliamentarians, at 64 per cent. Courageous women campaigners, like Margaret Dongo in Zimababwe and the late Wangari Maathai in Kenya, have played increasingly important roles in challenging governments and traditional practices. Women are increasingly able to exercise their agency politically and economically, though they are still struggling for equality in law and socially. Where women play a strong role and have the greatest agency is where "the national culture and religion are not overly hostile to women in positions of power."[14]

Progress is also particularly poor when it comes to gay and lesbian rights, and also to the support and empowerment rather than total marginalisation of the disabled. Africa lags strongly behind the rest of the world in these fields, with many constitutions denying gay rights and criminalising homosexual activity. Conservative politicians and traditional church bodies and leaders continue to resist attempts to liberalise laws or local and international demands for recognition of gay rights and the protection of law. Attacks on gay men and women, and particularly those campaigning for their rights, are frequent and often encouraged by powerful politicians.[15]

Africa and the world: the 'War on Terror' and the China syndrome

If African history from independence to the 1990s was dominated by the Cold War, Africa's new millennium has been dominated by three forces: the US-led War on Terror following 9/11, the global hegemony of neo-liberal economics, and the rise of China as an economic power and its growing role in Africa, which once more gave African leaders choices in terms of sources of investment, trade, aid and weapons without political strings—but at a cost. These were tectonic shifts of world politics and economics, and while they would not govern events in Africa, they would influence them by changing the global environment in which the African river flows.

The War on Terror became, and to an extent remains, Western leaders' primary narrative to make sense and find simplistic explanations for Africa's diversity and complexity, replacing the rather unstable and unsure New World Order and Humanitarian Intervention themes that had briefly replaced the Manichaean terms of the Cold War. Just as the fight against an imagined Soviet threat gave an impetus to broad Western diplomatic and military strategies during the Cold War, so the exclusion or destruction of Islamist movements adhering to Jihadist beliefs or thought to be linked with al-Qaeda became a preoccupation of the United States and its allies after September 2001, along with a renewed interest in African oil resources as an alternative to vulnerable Middle Eastern supplies. Before this era, the US's involvement in Africa had been patchy; the Reagan Administration was perhaps the most active one, largely for Cold War reasons, with Chester Crocker (for good or ill) playing a major role in Southern African regional politics. George Bush Sr., flexing American muscle in the New World Order, began the clumsy intervention in Somalia, an action continued disastrously by his successor Bill Clinton. That failure led Clinton to pull back from Africa, and he avoided involvement in Rwanda in 1994, despite being aware of the developing crisis. The US State Department refused to call the mass killings genocide while they were in progress, and its inaction undermined international efforts to deal with the crisis.

After 9/11, many Africans had feared that Africa would be totally sidelined as US and Western policy as a whole concentrated on the Middle East and Afghanistan. But instead, the War on Terror would become the dominant strategic issue and "subsume all other currents, democracy and human rights included."[16]

In 2002, Colin Powell, the first African-American to serve as Secretary of State, visited Africa. He concentrated on oil-producing nations like Angola and Gabon, trying to ensure continuity of supply. By the time of his visit, the USA was already buying 20 per cent of its oil from sub-Saharan Africa.[17] Africa's crucial position in the wider War on Terror picture was made clear by American backing and encouragement for Ethiopia's intervention in Somalia to destroy the Islamic Courts movement, which had the most marginal of connections with jihadist groups elsewhere but which was replaced by the overtly jihadist and pro-al Qaeda Al-Shabaab. With backing at the UN (where none of the permanent members of the UNSC had any interest in sympathising with Islamist movements), the USA also supported and encouraged the AU's AMISOM operation to combat Al-Shabaab, though it was less keen on Kenya's ambitions in Jubaland. America's backing for French intervention in Mali after the Islamist groups hijacked the Tuareg uprising, itself partly caused by the Western-assisted overthrow of Gaddafi and the ensuing exodus of Tuareg fighters from Libya, was yet another indication that the West's Africa security policy was now a War on Terror project above all else.

In the wake of the Mali intervention, US forces carried out drone attacks in Somalia, and in February 2013 they established a drone base in Niger. They also expanded the use of airstrips in both Burkina Faso and Ethiopia to facilitate surveillance, drone attacks and other forms of intervention in areas of Africa where the rise of Islamist movements was most likely and where the majority of populations followed Islam. And in May 2014, the Chibok schoolgirl abductions revealed just how vulnerable northern Nigeria was to Boko Haram. The British, French and US governments all hurried to pledge support and send intelligence teams to Nigeria, concerned not only about the country's stability, but also about the danger of Islamist insurgency spreading to Niger and Cameroon.

The major US effort to monitor and prevent the spread of jihadist groups in Africa was led by AFRICOM, the US military command group concerned with Africa that was established in 2007. Aid was also directed towards regions most affected by Islamist movements and to those key regional powers seen as the major obstacles to the movements: Ethiopia, Kenya, Nigeria and Sudan. The latter was a self-proclaimed Islamic state, but had co-operated closely with the US after 9/11 in providing intelligence, particularly on al-Qaeda. Despite calling the Janjaweed and Sudanese army killings in Darfur genocide, US administrations have continued to work with Sudan and the Bashir government, putting the fight against al-Qaeda before issues of human rights. This is also evident in the US and international disinterest in the growing crisis in the Central African Republic in 2013. The seizure of power by the Séléka rebel alliance, although it involved a mainly-Muslim rebel group ousting President Bozize by force, was not seen in War on Terror terms and little attention was given to the killings and mass displacement of people by Western governments or the UN.[18] A major problem for US military policy on the continent was that African states were unwilling to serve as hosts for AFRICOM, which was forced to work out of a command and operational centre in Germany. The US did secure the use of naval and air facilities in Djibouti, which already hosted substantial French forces; it based 1,800 troops there, with the option of increasing the deployment to 18,000 in times of crisis. Uganda also provided some facilities for surveillance and for the coordination of efforts to track down Kony and the LRA.

The US has also become ever more involved in the Sahel since 2001, providing arms and military training to a region not previously of particular strategic or political interest.[19] But the change there is not just military. The West's imperatives in the War on Terror have also registered in the levels of international aid pledged to the Sahel region in the wake of the Mali conflict. After decades struggling to get substantial aid for food security projects or development, things suddenly changed for the Sahel in November 2013 when the international community, through the UN, pledged over $8 billion to boost economic growth there. The announcement pointed to the joint problems of poverty, hunger and instability, and as UN Secretary-General Ban Ki-Moon said, "The challenges in the Sahel respect no borders—neither should our solutions. The cycle of crises can be broken." UN reports of the aid commitment stressed the importance of overcoming political instability at a time when, "Terrorist acts, as well as organised crime, have threatened the region's stability."[20] While it did address poverty and the lack of development, the aid package was clearly driven not by an intrinsic interest in the region's people but in ensuring that social and economic problems did not provide fertile ground for instability and groups linked with "terrorism". This pattern was played out across the continent in the opening decade of the new century. US aid to African countries increased from $2.5bn to $7.5bn, but it concentrated on those keen to present themselves as allies in the new global war, and arms deliveries and military training doubled between 2002 and 2005 to $597m in answer to requests for aid from allied African states.[21]

The fight against security threats was a key determinant of France and Britain's policies in the Sahel, Horn of Africa and wider West African region. Often competitors in Africa between the 1960s and 1990s, by the new millennium the two states were co-operating closely across the continent. The British government provided logistical support for the French military intervention in Mali, and both states were involved in capacity-building projects with ECOWAS and its member states. France maintained military bases in a number of west and central African states, and was more inclined to intervene militarily at the request of regional allies, while Britain (the brief Sierra Leone intervention aside) was more concerned with trade and development, but policies were increasingly dove-tailed—even as in other areas both states pursued their individual interests.[22]

Many African governments were willing actors in the War on Terror drama. They were no keener than Western governments to let Islamist movements threaten state and regional security, or to see jihadist movements exploit local grievances in the service of largely extra-territorial objectives. At times, though, there was a suggestion that some states deployed 'War on Terror' vocabulary to bring in outside help for crushing internal dissent, cynically using the label 'terrorist' or 'Islamist' to attract Western support and sympathy and provide a pretext for human rights abuses.[23] Those states keen to garner support against internal movements could latch on to the US's concern that Islamist movements were spreading to Africa, and that they could use its vast remote areas as a base from which to launch attacks on the West. Once again, the focus was not on Islamist gains in Africa per se, but potential threats to Western security. Despite the endless ICC row, countries like Kenya strengthened their military and security ties with the West, and were able to use attacks like the 2013 Westgate Mall massacre to make their case for support in the fight against terror. Kenya remained a target for attacks by Al-Shabaab in 2014 and 2015, with bombings in Nairobi, Mombasa and near the tourist resort of Lamu, and a massacre at Garissa University in which 147 people were killed.

The other new defining factor in Africa's international relations, and an influence on the West's evolving Africa policy, is the growing economic role of China. While not as openly conflictual, the competition between the West and China has come to feel like a less ideological and less militarised version of the Cold War. Western media representations of China's developing economic relations with Africa and its rapidly growing levels of trade and investment there are reminiscent of the uniformly bad press given to Soviet involvement in Africa. But this time, the stress is on economic exploitation and hegemony rather than ideological or military ambition. During the 1990s, Western trade, aid and financial policies had set the tone for Africa's international economic relations. There was no alternative model, and states unwilling to accept IMF/World Bank or donor strictures were left out in the cold. When China arrived as a major economic player on the African scene, it restored some agency and choice, revolutionising economic development and trade relations for many states.

From the 1960s to the end of the 1980s, China's Africa policy had been a mixture of political and military support for liberation movements such as Frelimo and ZANU, strategic competition with the Soviet Union (as in Angola, which even meant siding with movements supported by the US and South Africa), and attempts to coax African states away from ties with Taiwan. Major infrastructural projects like the TanZam Railway had been built, and the Chinese remained committed to assisting the repair and rehabilitation of the line, despite massive technical and managerial problems. But as China moved away from the Maoist model towards state-driven capitalism, the search for allies in Africa fell away. Although trade and some economic assistance continued, Africa was not a priority area for China, which was more concerned with domestic politics after the Tiananmen Square events, economic reform and growth, and relations with the US.

But by the end of the 1990s, China had gained much greater political and economic confidence. It also needed raw materials to fuel its economic growth and markets for its manufactured goods, and that led to a renewed interest in Africa. Beijing still wanted to exclude Taiwan from diplomatic ties there and steer African states away from it—something aided by the death or political demise of leaders like Banda, who had been a key Taiwanese ally, and the demise of apartheid South Africa. African votes were important at the UN to ward off formal condemnation of Chinese human rights violations,[24] and with strategic competition against the Soviet Union a thing of the past, trade and economic relations became the main sphere of competition.

From the point of view of African states, China is a very attractive economic partner. It offers trade and investment without the political or economic strings the West attaches. States such as Sudan and Zimbabwe, whose human rights records have made them pariahs, are welcomed with open arms. They have not only developed trade and investment deals that benefit both the Chinese and their own ruling elites, but are also able to purchase arms and other military hardware that Western states deny them. China's attraction also stems from the way it has reconstructed its own economy and achieved very high levels of growth, infrastructural development and diversification, all through state-led reforms. It is an increasingly attractive role model, one that has not undergone major changes of political leadership but instead adapted the existing hierarchy to meet the needs for economic reform and expansion. Its precise model can hardly be applied to African conditions since its size, human and material resources and massive domestic market are unlike anything in Africa, but to many African leaders China is a far more enticing role model than more plural and open societies.

Unlike Western donors or institutions, China had the capital and the manpower to make major, long-term investments after the financial crisis of 2008, and it was willing to offer the sort of inducements that appealed to African elites—building presidential palaces, parliament buildings, sports stadia and other prestige projects as well as more practical infrastructural ones like roads, railways and hospitals. Along with substantial investments of capital in previously failing industries (such as mining in Zambia), this enabled China to develop lucrative trade and investment deals to feed its growing need for oil and other raw materials and open up markets for Chinese-manufactured goods and expertise.[25]

China has been avid in its search for supplies of oil, copper, platinum, cotton, palm oil, cocoa and other raw materials for its continuing economic growth. It also found a ready market for cheap manufactured goods, though often to the detriment of African states' struggling industries. By 2011, China's total two-way trade with Africa exceeded $160bn, with a heavy emphasis on importing oil from Sudan and Angola along with minerals like manganese from Gabon, copper and iron ore from Zambia, platinum from Zimbabwe, and diamonds, copper and iron ore from Angola.[26] As with Western states and companies before them, the Chinese imported the raw minerals rather than processed supplies.

By the end of 2011 China accounted for 18 per cent of Africa's total trade, with imports from Africa marginally outstripping exports to Africa. Large Chinese parastatals with a global reach (such as the China National Offshore Oil Corporation) and state or provincial Chinese construction and mining companies became major players in Africa as a whole, and developed particularly large presences in individual states, such as in the mining sector in Zambia.

Chinese offers of long-term investment, construction assistance and loans in return for resources are highly attractive to African governments seeking to develop their inadequate and dilapidated infrastructure, especially given the failure of Western companies or donors to invest in it. Western financial institutions and governments have criticised China's resource-for-loans deals mortgaging future mineral or raw material earnings—yet African states hardly have an alternative. As one Africa specialist at the IMF has been quoted as saying, citing the example of Chinese minerals-for-infrastructure deals with the DRC, "No one else is lining up to provide funding for developments in the Democratic Republic of Congo. A country like the DRC needs infrastructure. It can't attract much donor aid. Given these limitations, the Chinese are filling a huge gap."[27]

For states in this sort of urgent need, China offers a lifeline, albeit with policy or political strings replaced with long-term resource supply consequences and the effects of Chinese penetration of African markets. This penetration includes migration. Exports of low-cost manufactured goods ranging from radios to bicycles to capital goods were accompanied by workers and traders migrating to Africa in large numbers. There were over 350,000 Chinese residents in Africa at the end of the first decade of the twenty-first century, compared with less than a quarter of that number twenty years before. Most were unskilled or semi-skilled workers employed on Chinese-funded construction projects or small traders, who set up shops in urban and rural areas and imported cheap consumer goods under preferential deals with Chinese companies. The availability of such goods at low prices was welcomed by poor African consumers, but not by the ailing African manufacturing sector or small Africans traders who could not compete with Chinese migrants. In Senegal, for example, "the Chinese swiftly put Senegalese retailers out of business by selling affordable and locally adapted products,"[28] and similar grievances have been heard in South Africa and Zambia.[29]

In 2013, the Ghanaian government had to take measures to stop illegal Chinese gold miners forcing out small-scale Ghanaian miners in the alluvial mining sector. In areas where major Chinese construction of mining projects have been established there is also often anger that managerial, skilled and even unskilled posts are given to Chinese workers brought in for the purpose, rather than Africans to whom skills could be passed on. So even in Africa's oldest state, Ethiopia, it is not unusual to see building sites where the, "Hammering, grinding and showers of glittering acetylene sparks proclaim the arrival of armies of Chinese workers and the rise of mighty steel and glass constructions,"[30] with Ethiopian workers only employed on lesser projects. There have also been questions raised about the quality of Chinese-built structures—when I flew out of Botswana in July 2015, I noticed the very new Chinese-constructed airport in Gaborone was rather tatty around the edges, with automatic doors that didn't work and peeling plaster. One Batswana worker there said to me, "what is built here by Chinamen go up fast and fall down fast".

On the positive side of the balance sheet, China is playing an important role in training African agricultural workers, with training centres built and staffed by Chinese agricultural institutes in Mozambique, Zimbabwe and Senegal, and the development of jointly-owned agribusinesses. The Koba joint rice venture in Guinea is a good example, using Chinese methods and improved seed varieties to increase grain output and improve food security.[31] These ventures are trying to develop more commercially driven approaches to small-scale agriculture as well as agri-businesses. But there is also a worrying side to the Chinese involvement in African agriculture, one that involves not just China but also Western companies and agri-businesses from Malaysia, Singapore, Saudi Arabia and South Korea (to name but a few). It is the leasing or sale of large areas of fertile land to foreign companies who use them to grow food, bio-fuel crops or cash crops. China has leased land in Zambia, and by 2009 there were over twenty state or privately owned Chinese farms operating there; Singapore and Malaysia have set up large oil palm plantations in Liberia, and the London-based Lonrho company owns 200,000 hectares of prime farming land across Africa.[32] The head of the UN Food and Agriculture Organisation, Jacques Diouf of Senegal, has warned of a new colonialism developing as foreign companies or countries seek to use African farmland to improve their own food or bio-fuel security.

Particularly in countries like Zambia, where past government support for farmers has been poor and there is a growing Chinese presence, African farmers fear they will progressively lose land to migrants, agri-businesses and Chinese control, taking away what little agency they have. As China and other states seek both raw materials and land for food or bio-fuels, the weakness of land tenure for African farmers is a serious long-term threat to rural populations, and could exacerbate ordinary Africans' growing resentment of Chinese-driven development. This resentment runs alongside the concerns of some governments (including Ghana and Cameroon) of illegal Chinese mining and logging. There is evidence that up to half the timber that China imported from Africa was illegally obtained.[33]

African resentment of the Chinese has been most evident in Chinese-managed or -owned mining and other raw materials projects. Michael Sata, president of Zambia until, his death in 2014, based his 2006, 2008 and 2011 election campaigns on criticism of the government's deals with China, the lack of control over Chinese companies and their flouting of labour laws. More than 300 Chinese companies operate in Zambia, with over 25,000 employees. The most prominent and controversial has been the China Non-Ferrous Metals Corporation (CNMC), which owns 85 per cent of the Chambishi copper mine. Safety records at the mine have been poor, with fifty-one workers killed at the explosives factory at the mine in 2005 and one worker shot by a Chinese manager the following year during a wage dispute. Sata warned that unchecked Chinese involvement in and migration to Zambia would damage the country, saying, "China is sucking from us. We are becoming poorer because they are getting our wealth."[34]

Countries like Zambia have a major problem. They need investment and infrastructure for development and markets for their raw resources, but the deals struck with China and Chinese trade and business practices may in the long-term be just as structurally damaging as past relations with the dominant Western economic powers. African governments need to develop greater control over their relationships with China and must avoid signing over large tracts of land, and ensure that imports of manufactured goods and permission for Chinese companies and traders to operate do not destroy Africa's weak manufacturing sector. That threat is particularly serious in Africa's textile sector. Kenya, Lesotho, Swaziland and South Africa have lost 48,000 textile sector jobs between them, and have suffered major declines in production thanks to competition from cheap Chinese imports. In Nigeria, "Chinese imports undercut local-manufactured products so that by 2005 more than 80 per cent of the country's textile factories had been forced to shut down and an estimated 250,000 workers were laid off."[35]

In the short term, the future of Sino-African relations will be more of the same, with China's resource hunger the driving force and African leaders keen to garner what investment and infrastructural development they can as a quid pro quo for guaranteed oil, metal and other raw material supplies. But the growing signs of resentment at the grassroots level, Chinese enterprises' labour and management problems, and the dangers of land loss and the destruction of manufacturing mean that change is inevitable. As with so many other spheres of Africa's global relationships, African governments must manage the relationships more effectively to ensure mutual benefit. That means developing national economies and improving living standards, not just funnelling the benefits to elites, gatekeeper fashion. China's involvement in Africa will continue as long it's in China's perceived interest—otherwise, it will simply withdraw. But its evolution should be shaped by the needs and interests of Africa's people, not just those of the gatekeepers.

Africa Rising: a false dawn, or palpable progress?

Living standards and benefits for African peoples, rather than just elite networks, are at the heart of the debate over the Africa Rising discourse, which has been growing in volume over recent years. The thesis that Africa is 'Rising' or 'Emergent' points to the growth achieved in African economies over the last decade, signs of emerging democracy, evidence of improvements in educational provision, and falling child mortality rates. The most vocal proponents of this view believe that Africa has turned a corner, and that fast economic growth rates mean that Africa is experiencing the rise of what has been called 'the fastest billion'—the "last phase of a global economic transformation that began a little over 200 years ago."[36] Rising growth rates and increasing commodity revenues are interpreted to mean that Africa is moving away from "the growth destroying uncertainty of bouts of currency weakness and very high inflation, towards a confidence-inducing environment of low inflation and high investment."[37]

These high growth rates and increasing revenue from commodities such as oil, metals, diamonds and other primary products are undeniable. And it is certainly true that Africa is more democratic now than it was twenty years ago, that child mortality rates are falling, and education is better provided. Key communications systems such as mobile phones and phone banking are improving, and urbanisation continues at a fast rate—all important aspects of social, political and economic development. But has Africa really turned a corner? Are its social, political and economic structures really undergoing a transformation that will ensure the continent can "begin rapidly catching up with progress and modernity in the rest of the developing world and, soon, with advances everywhere"?[38] And is it really the case that the incomes of Africans have increased by 30 per cent in the last ten years?[39]

As ever, there are no simple answers to these questions. Many African countries (Angola, Chad, Ethiopia, Ghana, Uganda and Zambia among them) have seen soaring growth, huge increases in commodity incomes as well as a rise in foreign direct investment (mainly from China, and mainly tied to resource exports); they have seen rising average per capita incomes; huge improvements in communications; and since 2000, a rise of nearly 50 per cent in secondary school enrolment. These advances cannot be ignored. They may well help provide a foundation for more sustained economic growth, diversification and transformations in industry and agriculture—but then again, they may not. There was a commodity demand and price boom in the 1950s, and there have been many more over the last six decades. But the booms were short-lived, and were frequently followed by bust. This could happen again when the massive demand for oil, metals, minerals and primary agricultural produce peaks or falls away, which it will if and when the new engines of global trade and growth in China and India start to stutter and slow. The lustre of Africa's gems could fade, and with them the foreign direct investment, infrastructure development and high growth, which could again slow or go into reverse.

The current boom is just that, a boom. There have not been substantial structural changes in African economies, which are still built on a narrow range of unprocessed mineral or agricultural exports—leaving them very dependent on foreign markets. More worryingly, manufacturing has not been growing. As the preceding account of China's economic role in Africa demonstrated, manufacturing sectors even in the economic giants of Nigeria and South Africa have in fact been damaged by Chinese influence. This is not covered in the major expositions of the Africa Rising thesis. Under structural adjustment programmes and ever since, the thrust of economic policy in much of Africa and the weight of Western pressure to reform has concentrated on free trade, and the strategies adopted were based on continued dependence on primary agricultural products, oil, minerals and the extraverted economy.[40] Most African countries:

> Are either stagnating or moving backwards when it comes to industrialisation. The share of MVA [manufacturing value added] in Africa's GDP fell from 12.8 percent in 2000 to 10.5 percent in 2008, while in developing Asia it rose from 22 percent to 35 percent over the same period...In terms of manufacturing growth, while most have stagnated, twenty-three African countries had negative MVA per capita growth during the period 1990—2010, and only five countries achieved an MVA per capita growth above 4 percent.[41]

Commodity income, service sector growth and average per capita incomes have risen, but this has not led to a growth in industry or the transformation of small-scale agriculture, and nor has it provided employment for the mass of unemployed or under-employed young, urban Africans. Urbanisation has been rapid—especially in countries like Angola, where failing agriculture and conflict led to a massive increase in urban populations, or Nigeria, where the lure of oil-fuelled wealth caused migration to the cities—but has not been accompanied by a corresponding increase in employment. This has created a mass of unemployed humanity living in poverty and only surviving through the operation of informal and often illegal economic systems, which exist outside the formal structures of the economy and which contribute only to survival, not to economic growth or improved living standards. Nigeria provides a sobering example. As even some proponents of the Africa Rising thesis have had to admit, the African Development Bank and even Nigeria's own statistics show that despite Nigeria's ever-increasing oil revenues and newly claimed ranking as sub-Saharan Africa's biggest economy, more of its people were living in absolute poverty in 2013 (61 per cent) than in 2004 (55 per cent), and that this was vastly worse than the figures before the oil boom. Between 1970 and 2000, the number of Nigerians in poverty increased from 19m to 90m.[42]

The gap between the very wealthy and the mass of poor people has increased rather than decreased, and even the growing, educated middle classes would be classed as very poor in Asian and more developed countries. The African Development Bank said in a 2013 study that those labelled middle class in Africa subsist on $2–20 a day—way below European or Asian levels. The 30 per cent average growth in incomes has not been evenly spread but instead concentrated among the elite. This has limited the purchasing power of the middle and poorer classes and impeded the development of strong internal markets, as well as continuing to depress living standards.

African school enrolment has certainly increased, but literacy rates still lag behind the rest of the world and are only improving slowly; 62 per cent of Africans were literate by the end of the first decade of the new millennium, compared with 82 per cent in Asia, and the fourteen least literate countries in the world are all African. A similar picture is emerging with child mortality. Africa Rising proponents are right that levels in Africa are falling and the improvements are encouraging, which in countries like Rwanda they are. But they are still falling at a slower rate than the rest of the world, and Africa has fallen well short of the 2015 UN Millennium Development Goals agreed to by African countries. Sub-Saharan Africa still has the worst rate of child mortality in the world, with ninety-two deaths per thousand live births.[43] This is an improvement, down from 177 per thousand in 1990, but it is still below all other areas of the world and the rate of improvement is lower than any other region. All the worst performing countries on this measure are in Africa, and all the countries in the world bottom fifteen for under-five mortality rates are African.[44] Improvements in child mortality rates alongside high GDP growth have to be taken in the "context of a sobering reality of continual deprivation, and with evidence of a wide and persistent gap between Africa and the rest of the world."[45]

Another important aspect of the Africa Rising narrative is the move of countries like Ghana into global classifications such as 'middle-income'. This was set as a goal by Ghanaian President John Atta Mills, and when Ghana was designated as such he was able to proclaim it a national success; but there is increasing evidence that the move up in statistical status was achieved through a recalculation of national statistics in 2010, which 'increased' GDP by 60 per cent in one go. This had nothing to do with economic growth or broad national development, but was a matter of using a different statistical base. In the same way, Liberia can be classed as Africa's second poorest country or one of its richest according to which data set you use. African statistics are notoriously unreliable, and basing projections of transformation and sustained growth on them is highly questionable.[46]

As health and education gradually improve, what is needed is employment for young people and the modernisation of industry and small-scale agriculture, not just the leasing of land for agri-businesses. This approach would change structures and increase the scope for the exercise of human agency—first economic, and ultimately social and political. At present, growth is restricted to the export and export-related infrastructure sectors and to unproductive prestige projects. High growth and increased income has not led to foreign or domestic investment, and 'rising' countries like Ethiopia and Malawi still rely on foreign aid to fund their budgets—almost 90 per cent in the case of Ethiopia and 40 per cent in Malawi, little different from in preceding decades.[47] The African Progress Panel at the World Economic Forum on Africa in Cape Town in 2013 was told that Africa is still losing more in illicit financial outflows than it gains in direct investment and aid. Despite some advances in democracy and accountability, increased export income still accrues mainly to the gatekeepers, who continue to dominate politics and the economy and use the income they receive as rents for personal wealth accumulation rather than productive investment. Value is not being added to African products and the income from those products does not provide investment capital for industrial or agricultural development.

Africa also needs to empower its people to play a full role in political life and to let them hold their leaders and economic managers accountable. That is slowly progressing, but there is a long way to go. It is a work in progress, with variable results across the continent. Elections are held, issues raised and grievances aired, but do things actually change, and are people able to seriously challenge their elites? So far, not really. Governments are voted out in elections, but generally as a result of shifting coalitions around politicians and political networks rather than because of grassroots pressure or serious differences over policy. Kibaki's replacement by the ICC-indicted Kenyatta is no great victory for the agency or prospects of ordinary Kenyans. Next door in Uganda, one of the radical hopes for the continent in the late 1980s and early 1990s, Yoweri Museveni, has turned into another limpet-like incumbent. He recently banned political gatherings of more than three people and has increasingly harassed the press for reporting corruption and his evident plans to create a dynasty, with his son primed to succeed him—an echo of Togo, Gabon and the DRC. Formal political structures have changed and some space has been created for popular participation, but the underlying informal structures of power remain strong. The past forty years in Africa has shown that these are capable of evolving to ensure the hegemony of the gatekeeping elite—which continues, albeit with slightly diminished power and freedom of action, to rule and reap the benefits of power.

POSTSCRIPT

STRUCTURE AND AGENCY IN AFRICA

Men make their own history, but they do not make it as they please; they do not make it under self-selected circumstances, but under circumstances existing already, given and transmitted from the past...

Karl Marx, *The 18th Brumaire of Louis Napoleon*

Africans have not selected the structural circumstances of their history. The continent's geography, its climate, its soils, and global political and economic forces that are largely beyond their control have all had a strong influence on Africa's historical development. External forces have played a strong role in moulding aspects of Africa's structures and history: the mechanisms of world trade, which themselves have evolved both externally and with some African agency, still hold Africa in a subordinate, dependent and essentially peripheral position; the intrusion and lasting effects of colonialism on pre-colonial structures and their forms of agency; and the continuing effects of international intrusion into African development, whether in the form of the Cold War, Western humanitarian interventions, structural economic programmes and neo–liberal agendas imposed from outside, or the effects of the War on Terror.

These external forces have had a role in shaping the contours of structure and agency across the continent, as well as their interplay. But at the heart of African history are Africans and their agency, their shaping of cultural, social, and economic structures and their interaction with global structures and international forces. To take Marx's quote, they have taken the circumstances of Africa, and of Africa in the world and have developed their own responses and therefore their own history. No state or region develops in glorious isolation or enforced seclusion, but nor is Africa a blank page on which external forces have written its history for its people to endure.

Africa is essentially no different to any other region of the world. It has adopted or at times had foisted upon it various structures, institutions, economic systems and political norms, variously taken on, adapted, discarded or grafted on to the African rootstock. To use Davidson and Braudel's river analogy, global events and forces might have helped shape the African riverbed, but so did Africa's own forces, and Africa's rivers and flow have in their turn affected the global environment. The social, cultural, political and economic structures that are vital to understanding the contemporary history of Africa have not evolved in isolation; as in any region of the world, they have blended indigenous and exogenous influences and experienced the distorting effects of unequal trade, slavery and colonialism, but not to the extent that Africans have been excluded from a role in their own history.

There was African agency even in the slave trade. African structures and agency are at the heart of its history, a history nonetheless bound up with globalisation and external pressures and the African responses to them. African history has had its own dynamics that are not identical to Western or East Asian ones, and which cannot be measured precisely against them. Much analysis of African history and development has been a project of working out whether African systems have succeeded or failed in terms of criteria drawn ahistorically from comparisons with the systems of the Northern/Western hemisphere or Asia, which have implicitly provided some sort of "universally valid prescription for economic transformation and social advance." But this prescription is *not* universally applicable, and while Africa's history of economic transformation and social advance is not divorced from global history, it is distinct from it. Attempts to hammer Africa into other historical frameworks and timeframes are therefore profoundly ahistorical.[1]

Following this line of argument, it is ahistorical to measure Africa's process of nation- and state-building against Eurocentric, Weberian, post-Westphalian ideals with their concept of the nation state. These are not helpful in examining how and why African states have developed as they have. This doesn't mean Africa has lacked structures or institutions or that its nations are formless or primitive; they are different in form, and in the way agency is exercised through them or even despite them. The historian or political scientist must be careful not to examine historical development, political, social, cultural and economic structures and agency in Africa through a normative lens calibrated to view Western-style development as the ideal, or in a teleological mindset, which holds that states have to develop towards a Western model—and that if they don't they are failed states or even a failed continent. As Chabal and Daloz observed, "The model of the modern Western European state, itself the outcome of a most singular historical development, cannot be simply transported to a wholly different socio-cultural setting."[2] African states may have European elements grafted on to them, but they have become something genetically different.

The grafting of Western institutions on to the African rootstock during the colonial period has given rise to organisms that may look familiar to Western eyes, but which are growing in a very different political, economic and cultural soil, and developing in different ways from a Western ideal type, despite the addition of Western-prescribed weed killers or fertilisers ill-adapted to African soils—foisted political institutions, structural adjustments, Western-inspired development models. Some of these grafted institutions have been pruned away over time or have evolved out of all recognition, but they are nonetheless a part of the way that structures and institutions have developed and affect the exercise of agency.

In any society there is interplay between formal and informal structures and actors. These are especially important in Africa, where much of society was relatively untouched first by colonialism and then by the process of modernisation since independence. Important structures remain informal, and the agency exercised through these structures is hidden beneath the surface of more formal institutions and structures. The state or formal structures and their manifest forms of agency appear disordered or irrational not only because are they different to Western models, but also because many of their key aspects are not formalised, or operate outside what would be considered the public sphere.

To extend the root analogy, using Bayart's analysis, the African state has aspects of the plant structure, the rhizome, about it. Much of the dynamic core of the system is buried and is made up of informal networks, which entrench forms of state power "through the agencies of family, alliance and friendship"—but also of culture, religion, belief systems, community, region and language,[3] as well as through formal, if weak, state institutions. Bayart also emphasises the extraordinary vitality of the cross-fertilisation of African precolonial, colonial and postcolonial history.[4]

This organic way of viewing historical development of states in Africa is easily translatable back into the analogy of the river. Much of the flow of the rivers is at a depth that is not easily observable, fed by underground springs, aquifers and other subterranean sources that strengthen, weaken, divert or otherwise change the nature of the flow, and so erode or undermine the structure of the riverbeds. In terms of historical or political science analysis, these do not easily fit into Western approaches. The developmental approach, with its normative concept of how an economy and its political institutions should develop, generally excludes, ignores or downplays informal networks, be they in cross-border trade, unrecorded and untaxed domestic exchange, or the workings of patronage and gatekeeping. Neo-colonial or Western-centric Marxist analyses may also misinterpret or fail to take account of socio-economic forces and structures that differ from those of Europe and North America. Class analysis may be applied rigidly, and without real understanding of the shifting and very different formations in Africa; this does not rule out forms of Marxist analysis, but demands greater rigour in identifying the relationship between classes and to modes of production, formal and informal institutions and the relationship between economic development and political power.

Whatever approach one adopts, African history must be regarded on its own terms and in light of its own dynamics and structures, not viewed from an arbitrary Western perspective. One could take Amilcar Cabral's view that, "Man is part of reality, reality exists independently of man's will," but that when man "acquires consciousness of reality, to the extent that reality influences his consciousness or creates his consciousness" then there can be a greater understanding, and consciousness can be applied to reality—that is, man can take action.[5] So we must not confuse the reality of Africa with ideas that have been used to categorise it, slipping into narratives of the failure of its nation-states or the basket case continent.[6] We must always ask ourselves according to whose criteria or measure Africa or a particular African state has 'failed', appreciating that no state in societal development is an end state, just a location on a continuing journey. Think of Somaliland's development—starved of diplomatic recognition and international aid, it was also spared the swarm of external players trying to direct its reconstruction. From being part of what was labelled a failed state, It has built a new political system from the ground up and started developing its economy free from the diktat of the IMF or World Bank. It has developed forms of civil society and conflict resolution that are working to achieve stability and accountability, and to foster an indigenous democracy.[7] Somalis there have taken local ownership of their development, and are not part of a system of extraversion or gatekeeping.

One should also avoid the structuralist and quite narrow approach that colonialism alone is responsible for Africa's problems. Colonialism played its role and still does but not to the exclusion of African agency and it developed with the collaboration of African elites, willlingly or unwillingly, with the colonisers. There is also the utopian Africanist approach, that African genius will rescue the continent from the mess left by colonialism. That view, grounded in a desire to ditch ideas of failure to make Western-style democracy and economic development work and stress African agency fighting a poisoned inheritance, tends to ignore or explain away the failures of African elites, instead adopting the well-intentioned but misplaced view that the African genius will always eventually prevail and that Western analysis has simply failed to appreciate it and has sought to underplay the distortions of colonialism.[8]

All these approaches distort the way that Africa is viewed. They prevent the description and analysis of a system that is developing in a different way to Europe, a fusion of structures, agency and experience that has its own dynamics and forces and not just a backward version of some other existing societal type.

Africa has always been part of the global system—from the point that man migrated from Africa to people the world. Africa does not have a 'relationship' with the world, it is an integral part of it. But as Bayart wrote, its unequal political and economic position in "international systems has been for several centuries a major and dynamic mode of the historicity of African societies"[9] and continues today, giving it a subordinate and marginalised position in the international economic system—despite its pivotal role as a source of raw materials and an exporter of capital. This position has engendered dependence on outside markets, sources of finance, aid and expertise. This is not a simple, structurally ordained dependence devoid of human agency; instead, "African governments exploit, occasionally skilfully, the resources of a dependence which is, it cannot ever be sufficiently stressed, astutely fabricated as much as it is predetermined"[10]—and that fabrication depends on the agency of African leaders. Acting as gatekeepers to the external world and international economy, they derive wealth and political power from control of the gate for trade, finance, aid and, at times, external military support.

Even in the current period of African growth and advances in democracy, the dominant elites and their patronage networks "continue to live chiefly off the income they derive from their position as intermediaries *vis-à-vis* the international system."[11] Growth through exports has not so far led to wider or deeper economic development and the formation of a modern, productive system of agriculture that enriches and empowers rural people or sustainable and developing industrial and commercial systems. These are prerequisites for balanced and sustainable economic development and rising living standards, but are still held back by systems in which "politics is a more lucrative and reliable source of livelihood than productive investment [and in which] multiparty political competition strengthens the tendency for policy-making to be driven by the needs of constructing and maintaining a supportive client base."[12]

From my narrative, it is clear that conflict has played and will continue to play a major role in shaping social structures, states and the Sub-Saharan region as a whole. But conflict is not something peculiarly African. As Scott Straus writes, "Africa is not uniquely prone to violence," and given the history of colonial invasion, liberation struggles, arbitrarily imposed borders and the exploitation of African resources by powerful external forces, one might have reasonably expected even more violence.[13] Some have argued that it is amazing that Nigeria, for example, has not been more violent, and that, "If Africans fought back sooner against theft and oppression instead of allowing themselves to be slaves to the rich and powerful, Africa would be a much more peaceful place."[14] There have not been the equivalents of the French, Russian or Chinese Revolutions or the overthrow of Soviet and East European communism from within; leaders have been overthrown through popular protest, as with Blaise Compaoré in Burkina Faso in November 2014, but the systems they led have persisted. There has been conflict, but it has been primarily elite-generated or localised reactions to oppression or exploitation. Rural or urban grievances have been harnessed by elites to challenge their opponents or create new networks of patrons and clients.

Africa's political, economic and social systems are constantly evolving. These are sometimes referred to as 'hybrid systems', which to me implies some sort of established and permanent state or a stage on the way to achieving Western-style statehood.[15] It is more accurate to see them as continually evolving systems that are eroding away some inherited structures, shedding or reshaping some forms of agency and gradually replacing them (Somaliland being an example of this) with systems that seek to emulate or adapt aspects of other models, such as versions of parliamentary government within structures provided by local, customary practices. This would seem the most appropriate way forward, as opposed to forcing political and economic systems on states through aid conditionality and good governance strictures.

Africa is still facing conflict, corruption, incompetent government and massive social inequality, but so is much of the rest of the world. Historical accounts of analyses of 20th century Europe or East Asia are not written around themes of conflict and corruption, though both were abundantly present—whereas it is often the dominant theme in analyses of Africa. Look at the history and the major changes that have formed modern Europe over the last century and you will see that for much of the period, they have more than their fair share of war, greed, dictatorship, political and economic corruption and attempted genocide or ethnic cleansing. The future of the Balkans is by no means set in stone, and it remains a whisker away from war; the conflict in Ukraine is another example of the way Europe's contours are still evolving, and doing so through conflict. The same can be said of much of Asia and certainly of the Middle East, as ISIS/Islamic state eats away at the post World War I state systems in Syria and Iraq. But it is Africa that is portrayed as the continent of war, ethnic or religious violence, corruption and poverty. These things are present, and they are too prevalent, but they are not the sole defining characteristics of Africa's history.

Nor is ethnicity. In much analysis, particularly in the media, tribe or ethnicity are used "as a ready-made explanation for the eruption of civil wars", for the operation of networks of power and for the marginalisation of peoples.[16] Ethnicity is an easy explanation that makes complex historical, social and political processes more understandable, but this mistakes it for the determinant rather than the product of those processes and of elite agency—it is a symptom not a cause. Ethnicity is too often discussed as an immutable force that moulds agency, rather than a product of agency, playing on shifting and multiple identities and using local grievances for political and economic advantage. Ethnicity is shaped by societal and economic factors and human action, it is not an identity set in stone. Questions around identity and conflict between communities have in part been created by the artificial borders first imposed by colonials and then accepted and utilised by the new gatekeeping elite. Ethnic antagonism is not inevitable and ethnic competition is more a symptom than a cause of political and economic conflict.

African history is the output of the dynamic effects of structure and agency, the interplay of internal and external forces, of the operation of formal institutions and informal networks. The combination is not the same for every country in Africa, but the elements involved frequently are. Africa is ultimately characterised by diversity, and its history is an aggregation of many histories, not a single, indivisible history. You can write a history of the continent, as you can of Asia, Europe or North America—but it can only be built from the histories of each constituent part. African history is the history of Africans and their societies—plural not singular, but singularly African.

HISTORIOGRAPHICAL NOTE

My narrative and analysis have sought to identify the warp and weft of structure and agency in the fabric of Africa's contemporary history and to offer some understanding of the diverse forces at work in African history. This theme of structure and agency takes inspiration from Basil Davidson's approach to their interplay in his study of the modern history of Africa, itself an adaptation of Fernand Braudel's idea of depicting history as a river with structure (the riverbed) and contingency or human actions (the flow of the river). Davidson's assertion that trying to understand the modern history of Africa the historian has to try to keep afloat, and moving forward "upon a torrent of first-hand information, second-hand interpretation, gusts of opinion, tempests of disagreement and baffling calms of doubt or sheer bewilderment" is just as relevant to the historian today.[1] He goes on to ask which parts of the torrent of events and information:

> ...belong merely to the confused and often chaotic river of events, and which to the shaping bed of the river? Where does the bed of the river decide the flow of history, and where does the flow itself wearing and eroding by its sheer unceasing power, shift the bed into a new direction? For there are two histories, the contingent and the structural...deeper structural features build the river...It would be possible to make a list of ephemeral or contingent features. The personalities of history would stand near the head of these. ...Or were these vivid personalities decisive and structural, rather than ephemeral and contingent... the difference between the river's flow and the bed of the river is sometimes hard to tell.[2]

My task has been to follow, describe and explain the extent to which the journey of this metaphorical river combines structure and agency, and how their interaction governs its flow.

Having adopted the concept of structure and agency, further development is necessary to identify the key historical themes to which their interplay has given birth. In his analysis of African politics, Alex Thomson, identifies six core problem areas which African states inherited from colonialism:

1. **Arbitrary borders**—Illogical territorial units, divided communities, irredentist movements, internal ethnic competition, inappropriate economic units (landlocked, under-resourced).
2. **Non-hegemonic states**—inability to project power into hinterland, state power concentrated only on strategic and profitable regions.
3. **Weak links between state and society**—no shared political culture between state and society; legitimacy deficit; unaccountable states; distant civil societies; society disengaging from the state.
4. **Formation of a state elite**—strong links between political office and personal wealth; social mobility dominated by access to the state, corruption, an exploitative bureaucratic bourgeoisie.
5. **The economic inheritance**—disadvantaged in the international economy, underdevelopment of human resources, economies over-reliant on primary sector, over-reliance on exports, bias towards European and not local or regional markets.
6. **Weak political institutions**—fragile liberal democratic institutions without historical moorings, return to colonial-style authoritarian and bureaucratic state.[3]

These inherited problems were a consequence of the way that colonialism changed pre-colonial structures and of the exercise of agency in the political, social and economic spheres. The process of achieving independence led to the evolution of states in which one can detect continuity as well as change and the embedding of these problems as major factors in the history of African states over the first half century of independence from colonial rule. The six areas overlap to a great extent, and I refine them down to four key themes that shape my narrative and analysis: boundaries and the shape of states; weak states and institutions; the formation of dominant elites and informal networks of power; and extraverted economic systems.

1. **Boundaries and the shape of states**: African states' borders were not designed with their populations or future needs in mind, and yet they were retained unchanged by new governments. Peoples were thrown together against their will; communities were divided, fuelling irredentism, splitting loyalties and providing the possibility of cross-border

interference by one state in another. The lack of any basic legitimacy or logic means the new borders have been obstacles to the development of markets and have made states porous, reducing their ability to monitor and manage the movement of people, goods and money. Most state borders throughout the world are to some extent arbitrary, splitting communities or throwing together people who would not choose to share the same state, but Africa's borders were established at the stroke of a pen by imperial rulers in Berlin in 1884–5 and were an exercise in colonial competition and aggrandisement, with no African input whatsoever. The aspiring leaders of independent Africa accepted these borders both to speed colonial withdrawal but also for reasons of political and economic expediency, and the result is a complex and often contradictory set of problems for African states and their peoples.

2. **Weak states and institutions**: African states have all too frequently been inherently weak, unable to exert sovereignty over borders and resources or to resist intervention and interference by external actors. They have often been unable to project state power in all aspects of government and administration and across the whole of their territories. They frequently fail to meet the requirements deemed essential to states in the international system: to make rules for the functioning of the state and its institutions that are broadly accepted and viewed as legitimate, to communicate those rules, and if necessary, to enforce them as laws through the use of law-sanctioned force and through sanctions imposed by force.[4] Crucially, they also fail to achieve the level of legitimacy among their subjects that derives from "a sense of *common interests* in the elementary goals of social life."[5]
3. **Formation of dominant elites and informal networks of power**, which are able to exploit state and institutional weakness to retain power and so avoid accountability or adherence to the rule of law, while controlling political and economic transactions with the rest of the world. Africa's elites have varying levels of control over state resources and instruments of coercion and develop informal networks of patronage and power to reinforce their ability to maintain power. The elites came to fulfil the role of gatekeepers (for a fuller exposition of this concept, see below), utilising informal networks of wealth, power and patronage in the face of weak formal state institutions and civil society. Informal structures of power allowed leaders and clients to retain power in the face of the state's inability to establish full hegemony. Elite formation has not been accompanied by investment in the development of work-

able political systems, which would command legitimacy, accommodate change and coexist with viable civil society institutions. As noted in the previous point, they fail to represent the aggregated interests of their populations or to instil sets of rules or institutions that confer legitimacy or establish consensus over rules and the rule of law.

4. **Extraverted economic systems** remain dependent on export revenues and are marked by a failure to translate growth into development. They have a vulnerable revenue base and are unable to break away from the dominance of global economic forces and institutions; domestic agricultural and manufacturing sectors are weak and starved of investment. This duality of the economies reinforces the power of gatekeepers and fails to deal with key developmental issues such as food insecurity, inequality and widespread poverty. At the core of the system of extraversion "is the creation and capture of a rent generated by dependency and which functions as a historical matrix of inequality, political centralisation and social struggle."[6] Such an approach reinforces Annan's point about the mutually reinforcing nature of Africa's worst ills.

The idea of the gatekeeper state was developed by Frederick Cooper,[7] who argues that governments in newly independent African states:

> Inherited both the narrow, export-oriented infrastructure which developmentalist colonialism had not yet transcended and the limited markets for producers of raw material... Colonial states had been gatekeeper states. They had weak instruments for entering into the social and cultural realm over which they presided, but they stood astride the intersection of the colonial territory and the outside world.[8]

The new African governments took over this role, first relying on revenues from exports and duties on goods entering and leaving their territory, and then becoming the gatekeepers for the influx of aid and loans. This was not a simplistic matter of a system being foisted on the new rulers, but something they saw as in their interests. Pre-colonial rulers had likewise exercised the power of gatekeepers in early trade with the outside world, a period in which the seeds of unequal relations and economic dependence were sown—through the slave trade, for example, both inhuman and damaging to the economic development of the regions from which the slaves were taken, but "also advantageous for those who managed to monopolise the position of gatekeeper to the external world."[9] The pre-colonial gatekeeping function, in which rulers of powerful polities and particularly coastal communities increased their economic and military power through control of trade with Europe or the Arab world and the/Persian Gulf, was succeeded first by the colonial occupation of Africa by foreign rulers, and then by, "A domestic ruling elite, both distant from the population it governed, exercising control over a narrow range of resources focused on the juncture of domestic and world economies, fearful of threats to its domination."[10]

The use of concepts of extraversion and the gatekeeper state is not to deny that European colonialism in Africa was exploitative, or to dismiss the continuing power of the global capitalist order and the dominant states within it (now including China) to influence events in and the evolution of Africa. But it restores a crucial theme to the argument: African elites have been active agents in the process of underdevelopment and the creation and maintenance of dependency. As gatekeepers, they have turned the extraversion of economies, the subordination and dependence of their states, and the weakness of formal state structures and institutions to their own advantage—but not to the advantage of their own peoples.

NOTES

INTRODUCTION

1. Sithole, Ndabaningi, *African Nationalism*, London: Oxford University Press, 1968.
2. Ellis, Stephen, 'Writing Histories of Contemporary Africa', *The Journal of African History*, 43, 1 (2002), pp. 1–26, p. 6.
3. Hobsbawm, Eric, *The Age of Extremes: The Short Twentieth Century 1914–1991*, London: Abacus, 1994, p. 6.
4. See Arnold, Guy, *Africa: A Modern History*, London: Atlantic, 2005. This is an excellent, immensely detailed but non-theoretical journalistic study of the main events, states and leaders in contemporary African history.
5. The underdevelopment and neo-colonialist approach is best represented in Rodney, Walter, *How Europe Underdeveloped Africa*, Cape Town: Pambazuka, 2012.
6. An example of the modernisation approach stressing party formation in Africa and charting a path to American or European-style state and economic development, and one which was part of my study of African political science in the 1970s, is Apter, David, *The Gold Coast in Transition*, Princeton: Princeton University Press, 1955. For a good discussion of these approaches see Leys, Colin, *The Rise and fall of Development Theory*, London: James Currey, 1996.
7. Marx, Karl, 'The Eighteenth Brumaire of Louis Bonaparte', in Marx, K. and Frederick Engels, *Selected Works Volume 1*, Moscow: Foreign Languages Publishing House, 1950, p. 225.
8. Annan, Kofi, *Interventions: A Life in War and Peace*, London: Allen Lane, 2012, p. 17.
9. Ibid., p. 170.
10. For examples of this discourse see Richardson, Charles, *The Fastest Billion: The Story Behind Africa's Economic Revolution*, London: Renaissance Capital, 2012; or Rotberg, Robert I., *Africa Emerges: Consummate Challenges, Abundant Opportunities*, Cambridge: Polity, 2013.

1. CONTINUITY AND CHANGE: FROM PRE-COLONIAL SOCIETIES THROUGH COLONIAL OCCUPATION TO INDEPENDENT STATES

1. Ellis, Stephen, 'Writing Histories of Contemporary Africa', *The Journal of African History*, 43, 1 (2002), pp. 1–26, p. 2
2. Iliffe, John, *Africans: the history of a continent*, Cambridge: Cambridge University Press, 2nd edition, 2007, p. 1.
3. See Thomson, Alex, *An Introduction to African Politics*, Abingdon: Routledge, 3rd edition, 2010, p. 9.
4. For a detailed account of the nature of ethnicity and identity see Waller, Richard, 'Ethnicity and Identity' in Parker, John and Richard Reid, *The Oxford Handbook of Modern African History*, Oxford: Oxford University Press, 2013, pp. 94–113, p. 94.
5. For a more substantial account of this region's role in the trans-Saharan slave trade see Azevedo, Mario, *Roots of Violence: A History of War in Chad*, London: Routledge, 1998, pp. 22–44.
6. Iliffe, op. cit., pp. 50–1, 77.
7. A detailed account of the trade and its effects is provided in Larson, Pier M., 'African Slave Trade in Global Perspective', in Parker and Reid, op. cit., pp. 56–76, p. 60.
8. Bayart. Jean-François, *The State in Africa: The Politics of the Belly*, London: Longman, 1993, p. 25.
9. For a more detailed development of this theme see Davidson, Basil, *West Africa Before the Colonial Era: A History to 1850*, London: Longman, 1998, p. 189.
10. Larson, op. cit., p. 61.
11. Cited by Thomson, op. cit., p. 14.
12. For a comparative approach to colonial occupation, the drawing of borders and issues of decolonisation, see Martin Shipway, *Decolonisation and its Impact: A Comparative Approach to the End of the Colonial Empires*, Malden, MA and Oxford: Blackwell, 2008, p. 20.
13. Prior, Christopher, *Exporting Empire: Africa, Colonial Officials and the Construction of the Colonial State, 1900–39*, Manchester: University of Manchester Press, 2013, pp. 13.
14. The idea of the creation of the concept of tribe and its application to Africa is covered well in Mamdani, Mahmood, *Citizen and Suibject: Contemporary Africa and the Legacy of Late Colonialism*, Princeton: Princeton University Press, 1996, p. 41; see also Waller, op. cit., p. 95.
15. For a development of this approach to explaining the nature of colonial indirect and direct rule see Hawthorne, Walter, 'States and Statelessness', in Parker and Reid, op. cit., pp. 77–93, p. 89.
16. See Nugent, Paul, *Africa Since Independence: A Comparative History*, Basingstoke: Palgrave Macmillan, 2nd edition, 2012, pp. 13–4.
17. For more extensive discussion of the French and Portuguese approaches see Sharkey, Heather J., 'African Colonial States', in Parker and Reid, op. cit., pp. 151–170; Chafer, Tony, *The End of Empire in French West Africa: France's Successful*

Decolonisation?, Oxford: Berg, 2002, pp. 27–33; and Bender, Gerald, *Angola Under the Portuguese: The Myth and Reality*, London: Heinemann, 1978.

18. Cooper, op. cit., October 2005, p. 11, http://m.einaudi.cornell.edu/sites/default/files/04-2005.pdf, last accessed 6 July 2015.
19. Reid, Richard, *A History of Modern Africa: 1800 to the Present*, Oxford: Wiley-Blackwell, 2nd edition, 2012, p. 303.
20. There were many different approaches to the anti-colonial struggle, but they are aggregated together under the heading of African nationalism. For an influential exposition of this broad approach see Mazrui, Ali A. and Michael Tidy, *Nationalism and New States in Africa*, Nairobi and London: Heinemann, 1984, pp. 15–18.
21. Cited by Davidson, Basil, *Africa in Modern History: The Search for a New Society*, Harmondsworth: Penguin, 1978, p. 197.
22. Howe, Stephen, *Afrocentrism: Mythical Pasts and Imagined Homes*, London, Verso, 1998, p. 4.
23. Ibid.
24. Cited by Davidson, Basil, op. cit. 1978, p. 199.
25. Central Intelligence Agency, *The Break-Up of the Colonial Empires and Implications for US Security*, ORE 25–48, 3 September 1948, http://www.foia.cia.gov/sites/default/files/document_conversions/89801/DOC_0001166383.pdf, last accessed 6 July 2015.
26. See Woodward, Peter, *Condominium and Sudanese Nationalism*, London: Rex Collings, 1979 and *Sudan 1898–1989: The Unstable State*, London: Lester Crook, 1990, for a detailed history and analysis of the condominium and the development of British control of Sudan.
27. Woodward, op. cit., 1990, p. 43.
28. Madut Jok, Jok, *Sudan: Race, Religion and Violence*, Oxford: One World, 2012, p. 52.
29. Young, John, *The Fate of Sudan: The Origins and Consequences of a Flawed Peace Process*, London: Sed, 2012, pp. 2–3.
30. Crook, Richard C., 'Decolonisation, the Colonial State, and Chieftaincy in the Gold Coast', *African Affairs*, 85, 330, 1986, pp. 76–106, p. 78.
31. Sherwood, Marika, 'Pan-African Conferences, 1900–1953: What Did 'Pan-Africanism' Mean?, *The Journal of Pan African Studies*, 4, 10, 2012, pp. 108 and 113.
32. Rathbone, Richard, *Nkrumah and the Chiefs: The Politics of Chieftaincy in Ghana 1951–60*, London: James Currey, 2000, p. 19.
33. Jeff Crisp, *The Story of an African Working Class: Ghanaian Miners' Struggles 1870–1980*, London: Sed, 1984, p. 128.
34. Nugent, op. cit., p. 29.
35. Thomson, op. cit., p. 75.
36. For a detailed account of the role of women in Tanganyika/Tanzania, see Geiger, Susan, *TANU Women: Gender and Culture in the Making of Tanzanian Nationalism, 1955–1965*, Portsmouth, NH and London: Heinemann, 1998.
37. See Branch, Daniel, *Defeating Mau Mau and Creating Kenya: Counter-Insurgency,*

Civil War and Decolonisation, Cambridge: CUP, 2009; and Anderson, David, *Histories of the Hanged: Britain's Dirty War in Kenya and the End of Empire*, London: Phoenix, 2005.

38. Manyak, Terrell G. and Isaac Wasswa Katono, 'Decentralisation and Conflict in Uganda: Governance Adrift', *African Studies Quarterly*, 11, 4, p. 3, http://asq.africa.ufl.edu/manyak_katono_summer10/, accessed 6 July 2015.
39. Somerville, Keith, *Foreign Military Intervention in Africa*, London: Pinter, 1990, pp. 2–3.
40. Thompson, Leonard, *A History of South Africa*, New Haven: Yale University Press, 3rd Edition, 2001, p. 185.
41. Welsh, David and J.E. Spence, *Ending Apartheid*, London: Longman, 2011, p. 13.
42. See Welsh and Spence, op. cit., p. 66–72; and Ellis, Stephen, *External Mission: The ANC in Exile 1960–1990*, London: Hurst, 2012, pp. 3–11.
43. See Somerville, Keith, *Southern Africa and the Soviet Union: From Communist International to Commonwealth of Independent States*, Basingstoke: Macmillan, 1993, pp. 12–35.
44. Cruise O'Brien, Donal B. and Richard Rathbone, 'Introduction' in Cruise O'Brien, Donal B., John Dunn and Richard Rathbone (eds.), *Contemporary West African States*, Cambridge: Cambridge University Press, 1989, p. 3.
45. See Chafer, op. cit., pp. 86–91, and Cooper, Frederick, *Decolonisation and African Society*, Cambridge: Cambridge University Press, pp. 16–18, on the unions and emerging political elites in Francophone Africa.
46. See Markovitz, Irving Leonard, *Léopold Sédar Senghor and the Politics of Negritude*, New York: Athenaeum, 1969.
47. Nugent, op. cit., p. 7.
48. Chafer, op. cit., p. 4.
49. Somerville, Keith, *Angola: Politics, Economics and Society*, London: Pinter, 1986, pp. 24–5; for a detailed account of the rise of Angolan nationalism, see Marcum, John, *The Angolan Revolution, Vol 1: the Anatomy of an Explosion (1950–1962)*, Cambridge, MA: MIT Press, 1969.
50. Marcum, op. cit., pp. 123–5.
51. For further discussion of the origins of the insurgency and US-Soviet competition in Angola, see John Marcum, *The Angolan Revolution, Vol II: Exile Politics and Guerrilla Warfare, 1962–1976*, Cambridge, MA: MIT Press, 1978, pp. 16–8; and Somerville, op. cit., 1986, pp. 25–35.
52. See Nzongola-Ntalaja, Georges, *The Congo from Leopold to Kabila: A People's History*, London: Zed, 2007, pp. 52–3.
53. For more details see Somerville, op. cit. 1990, pp. 12–3.
54. See Lemarchand, René, *Rwanda and Burundi*, New York: Praeger, 1970; and Mamdani, Mahmood, *When Victims Become Killers: Colonialism, Nativism, and the Genocide in Rwanda*, Princeton, NJ: Princeton University Press, 2002.
55. Lemarchand, op. cit. pp. 79–80.
56. Mamdani, op. cit., pp. 103–4.
57. Gerard Prunier, *The Rwandan Crisis: History of a Genocide*, London: Hurst, 1997, p. 49.

58. See for more detail, Rene Lemarchand, *Burundi: Ethnic Conflict and Genocide.* Cambridge: Cambridge University Press, 1996.
59. Crawford Young, 'The African colonial state and its political legacy', in Rotchild, Donald and Naomi Chazan (eds), *The Precarious Balance: State and Society in Africa*, Boulder, CO: Westview, 1988, pp. 25–66, p. 45.

2. THE TRIALS OF STATEHOOD: DISILLUSIONMENT, DICTATORS, COUPS AND CONFLICT

1. Ellis, Stephen, *Season of Rains: Africa in the World*, London: Hurst, 2011, p. 23.
2. Thomas Kanza, *Conflict in the Congo*, Harmondsworth: Penguin, 1972, p. 179; and Somerville, Keith, *Foreign Military Intervention in Africa*, London: Pinter, 1990, pp. 15–6.
3. Meredith, Martin, *The State of Africa: A History of Fifty Years of Independence*, Free Press, 2006, p. 104.
4. See Dayal, Rajeshwar, *Mission for Hammarskjöld: The Congo Crisis*, Oxford: Oxford University Press, 1976.
5. Cited by Arnold, Guy, *Africa: A Modern History*, London: Atlantic, 2005, p. 82.
6. Young, Crawford, 'Zaire and Cameroon' in Duignan, Peter and Robert Jackson (eds), *Politics and Government in African States*, London: Croom Helm, 1986, p. 135. See also, Somerville, op. cit. 1990, pp. 19–21.
7. Parker, John and Richard Rathbone, *African History: A Very Short Introduction*, Oxford: Oxford University Press, 2007, pp. 4–5.
8. Nkrumah, Kwame, *Africa Must Unite*, London: PANAF, 1963, p. 136.
9. Nkrumah, op. cit., pp. 85–6.
10. Nugent, Paul, *Africa since Independence: a Comparative History*, Basingstoke: Palgrave Macmillan, 2nd edition, 2012, p. 103.
11. *The OAU Charter*, http://www.au.int/en/sites/default/files/OAU_Charter_1963_0.pdf, accessed 6 July 2015.
12. Mohammed Sahnoun, 'Nyerere, the Organisation of African Unity and liberation', *Pambazuka News*, http://www.pambazuka.org/en/category/features/59501, accessed 6 July 2015.
13. Diamond, Larry, *Class, Ethnicity and Democracy in Nigeria: The Failure of the First Republic*, Basingstoke: Palgrave Macmillan, 1988, p. 108.
14. Falola, Toyin, A. Ajayi, A. Alao and B. Babawale, *The Military factor in Nigeria, 1966–1985*, Lewiston, New York: Edwin Mellen Press, 1994, pp. 4–5, and Dudley, B. J., *Instability and Political Order: Politics and Crisis in Nigeria*, Ibadan: University of Ibadan Press, 1973, p. 92.
15. Falola et al, op. cit., pp. 22–3.
16. Somerville, op. cit. 1990, pp. 58–9.
17. Falola et al, op. cit., p. 30.
18. Cooper, op. cit., p. 9.
19. Cooper, op. cit., pp. 5–6, 157–8.
20. Kenneth Kaunda, interview with the author, Lusaka, 22 February 1991.
21. See Jackson, Robert H. and Carl G. Rosberg, *Personal Rule in Black Africa: Prince,*

Autocrat, Prophet, Tyrant, Berkeley: University of California Press, 1982; and Utas, Mats (ed), *African Conflict and Informal Power: Big Men and Networks*, London: Zed, 2012.

22. See Mapanje, Jack, *And Crocodiles are Hungry at Night*, London: Ayebia Clarke Publishing, 2011.
23. For a detailed account of the development of politics under Kenyatta and the demonisation of *majimboism* see Haugerud, Angelique, *The Culture of Politics in Modern Kenya*, Cambridge: Cambridge University Press, 1993, p. 41; and Ogot, B. A. "Transition from Single to Multiparty Political System 1989–93', in Ogot, B. A. and W. R. Ochieng' (eds), *Decolonization & Independence in Kenya*, Columbus: Ohio State University Press, 1995, and B. A. Ogot and W.R. Ochieng', *Decolonisation and Independence in Kenya 1940–93*, London: James Currey, 1995, pp. 239–61, p. 258.
24. Nkrumah, op. cit., p. 99.
25. Douglas Rimmer, *Staying Poor: Ghana's Political Economy, 1950–1990*, Oxford: Pergamon Press, 1992, p. 86.
26. Dr Nii Moi Thompson in Agyeman-Duah, Baffour, *Ghana Governance in the Fourth Republic*, 2008, Sakumono: Digibooks Ghana Limited, pp. 58–9.
27. Rimmer, Douglas, *Ghana's Political Economy, 1950–1990*, Oxford: Pergamon, 1992, p. 103.
28. Jackson and Rosberg, op. cit., p. 140.
29. Le Vine, Victor T., *Politics in Francophone Africa*, Boulder, CO: Lynne Reiner, 2004, p. 209.
30. Diouf, Mamadou, 'The Public Role of "Good Islam": Sufi Islam and the Administration of Pluralism' in Diouf, Mamadou (ed), *Tolerance, Democracy, and Sufis in Senegal*, New York: Columbia University Press, 2013, pp. 1–35, p. 18.
31. Nugent, op. cit., pp. 198–99; see also Schumacher, Edward J., *Politics, Burueacracy and Rural Development in Senegal*, Berkeley: University of California Press, 1975, pp. 63–5.
32. Schumacher, op. cit., pp. 71–2; see also Jackson and Rosberg, op. cit., p. 90.
33. Nyerere, Julius K., *Ujamaa: Essays on Socialism*, Dar es Salaam: Oxford University Press, 1968, pp. 3–4.
34. Thomson, Alex, *An Introduction to African Politics*, Abingdon: Routledge, 3rd edition, 2010, p. 50. Also see Andrew Ivaska, *Cultured States: Youth, Gender, and Modern Style in 1960s Dar es Salaam*, Durham and London: Duke University Press, 2011, pp. 3–15, for a more detailed discussion of the attempt to build a national culture while not demeaning or sweeping away traditional cultures or diversity.
35. Hyden, Goran, *Beyond Ujamaa in Tanzania: Underdevelopment and an Uncaptured Peasantry*, London: Heinemann, 1980, p. 13.
36. Ibid., p. 103; and Ibhawoh Dibua, 2003, p. 67.
37. Hyden, op. cit., p. 18.
38. Nugent, op. cit., p. 150.
39. Hyden, op. cit., p. 99.
40. Eckert, Andreas, 'Useful Instruments of Participation? Local Government and

Co-operatives in Tanzania, 1940s to 1970s', *International Journal of African Historical Studies*, 40, 1 (2007), pp. 97–118, p. 97. See also Hunter, Emma, 'The History and Affairs of TANU: Intellectual History, Nationalism, and the Postcolonial State in Tanzania', *International Journal of African Historical Studies* 45, 3 (2012), pp. 365–83, p. 367.

41. McGowan, Pat and Thomas H. Johnson, 'African Military Coups d'État and Underdevelopment: A Quantitative Historical Analysis', *Journal of Modern African Studies*, 22, 4 (1984), pp. 633–666, pp. 633–4.
42. Young, John, *The Fate of Sudan: The Origins and Consequences of a Flawed Peace Process*, London: Sed, 2012, p. 21.
43. S. E. Finer, *The Man on Horseback: The Role of the Military in Politics*, Harmondsworth: Penguin, revised edition, 1976, p. 18.
44. Reno, William, *Warfare in Independent Africa*, Cambridge: Cambridge University Press, 2011, p. 2.
45. Somerville, op. cit., 1990, p. 36; see also Johnson, Douglas H., *The Root Causes of Sudan's Civil Wars: Peace or Truce*, London and Kampala: James Currey and Fountain Publishers, revised edition, 2011, p. 28.
46. Madut Jok, Jok, *Sudan: Race, Religion and Violence*, Oxford: Oneworld, 2007, p. 54.
47. Ibid., pp. 58–9.
48. Johnson, op. cit., p. 30
49. Adefuye, Ade, 'The Kakwa of Uganda and the Sudan: The Ethnic Factor in national and International Factors' in Asiwaju, A.I. (ed), *Partitioned Africans: Ethnic Relations Across Africa's International Boundaries, 1884–1984*, London: Hurst, 1987, p. 61.
50. Somerville, op. cit., 1990, p. 39 and Beshir, Mohammed Omar, *The Southern Sudan from Conflict to Peace*, Khartoum: The Khartoum Booksop, 1975, pp. 91–2.
51. Keller, Edmond J., *Revolutionary Ethiopia: From Empire to People's Republic*, Bloomington: Indiana University Press, 1991, pp. 152–3.
52. Selassie, Bereket Habte, *Conflict and Intervention in the Horn of Africa*, New York: Monthly Review Press, 1980, pp. 51–3 and 62–3.
53. Markakis, John, 'The Nationalist revolution in Eritrea', *Journal of Modern African Studies*, 26, 1 (1988), pp. 51–70, p. 55.
54. Keller, op. cit., p. 153.
55. Somerville, op. cit., 1990, p. 47.
56. Markakis, op. cit., p. 59.
57. Schwab, Peter, *Ethiopia: Politics, Economics and Society*, London: Pinter, 1985, p. 10.
58. Harper, Mary, *Getting Somalia Wrong? Faith, War and Hope in a Shattered State*, London: Zed, 2012, p. 36.
59. Lewis, Ioan, *Understanding Somalia and Somaliland*, London: Hurst, 1993.
60. Barrington, Lowell W., *After Independence: Making and Protecting the Nation in Postcolonial and Postcommunist States*, Ann Arbor: University of Michigan Press, 2006, p. 115.
61. Ndulu, Benno J. and Stephen A. O'Connell, 'Policy Plus: African growth

Performance 1960–2000', p. 2, http://www.swarthmore.edu/Documents/faculty/oconnell/Chap1_BNSOC.pdf, accessed 6 July 2015.

62. Collier, Paul and Jan Willem Gunning, 'Explaining African economic performance', *Journal of Economic Literature*, 37, 1 (1999), pp. 64–111, p. 10.
63. Green, Reginald H. and Ann Seidman, *Unity or Poverty: The Economics of Pan-Africanism*, Harmondsworth: Penguin, 1968, p. 31.
64. Collier and Gunning, op. cit, p. 5.
65. Nugent, op. cit., p. 71.
66. Mkandawire, Thandika and Charles C. Soludo, *Our continent, Our future: African Perspectives on Structural Adjustment*, Trenton, NJ: Africa World Press, 1999, p. 25.
67. Collier and Gunning, op. cit., p. 15.
68. Ndulua and O'Connell, op. cit., p. 36.
69. Akonor, Kwame, *African Economic Institutions*, London: Routledge, 2010, p. 21.
70. For an account of Zaire's economic development and the absence of a class that sought to invest, create growth and profit and reinvest to grow further, see McGaffey, Janet, 'Economic Disengagement and Class Formation in Zaire', in Rothschild, Donald and Naomi Chazan (eds), *The Precarious Balance: State and Society in Africa*, Boulder, CO: Westview, 1998, p. 172.

3. REVOLUTION, LIBERATION WARS AND ECONOMIC CRISIS

1. Tiruneh, Andargachew, *The Ethiopian Revolution 1976–1987: A Transformation From an Aristocratic to a Totalitarian Society*, Cambridge: Cambridge University Press, 1993, p. 15.
2. Zewde, Bahru, *A History of Modern Ethiopia, 1855–1991*, Oxford: James Currey, 1991, p. 178.
3. Ibid., p. 214.
4. For an in-depth account of the development and ideology of the EPLF and its war against Ethiopia, see Pool, David, 'The Eritrean People's Liberation Front' in Clapham, Christopher (ed.), *African Guerrillas*, Oxford: James Currey, 1998, pp. 19–35.
5. Somerville, Keith, *Foreign Military Intervention in Africa*, London: Pinter, 1990, pp. 138–9.
6. de Waal, Alex, *Famine Crimes: Politics and the Disaster Relief Industry in Africa*, London: James Currey, 1997, p. 107.
7. Ibid., p. 108.
8. Arnold, Guy, *Africa: A Modern History*, London: Atlantic, 2005, pp. 484–5.
9. Zewde, op. cit., p. 235.
10. Tiruneh, op. cit., p. 103.
11. Cited by Tiruneh, op.cit., p. 211.
12. Arms details from the International Institute of Strategic Studies, *Military Balance*, London: ISS/Brassey's, 1975–76 and 1977–78.
13. Somerville, op. cit., pp. 131–2.
14. *Africa Contemporary Record 1977–78*, New York: Africana Publishing, 1979, p. 374.

15. Henze, Paul B. 'Communism and Ethiopia', *Problems of Communism*, May–June 1981, p. 63; see also US Congress, Senate Committee on Foreign Relations, *Ethiopia and the Horn of Africa*, 94th Congress, 2nd Session, 4–6 August 1976, *Senate Report*, Washington: US Congress, 1976, p. 121.
16. Somerville, op. cit., pp. 132–4.
17. *Pravda*, 5 May 1977.
18. Patman, Robert, *The Soviet Union in the Horn of Africa: The diplomacy of intervention and disengagement*, Cambridge: Cambridge University Press, 1990, pp. 206–7.
19. Legum, Colin and Bill Lee, *Conflict in the Horn of Africa*, London: Rex Collings, 1977, p. 7.
20. Patman, op. cit., p. 222.
21. *Africa Contemporary Record*, op. cit, p. B 228–9; and Somerville, op. cit., pp. 136–7.
22. Fearon, James and David Laitin, *Portugal*, Stanford University, 2005, http://www.stanford.edu/group/ethnic/Random%20Narratives/PortugalRN1.3.pdf accessed 6 July 2015.
23. Gil Ferreira, Hugo and Michael W. Marshall, *Portugal's Revolution: Ten Years On*, Cambridge: Cambridge University Press, 1986, p. 190.
24. See Cabral, Amilcar, *Unity and Struggle: Speeches and Writings*, New York: Monthly Review Press, 1979.
25. Quoted in Adi, Hakim and Marika Sherwood, *Pan-African History: Political Figures from Africa and the Diaspora Since 1787*, London: Routledge, 2003, p. 18.
26. Munslow, 1983, pp. 79–82; see, also, David Birmingham, *Frontline Nationalism in Angola and Mozambique*, London: James Currey1992, pp. 65–6.
27. Somerville, Keith, *Angola: Politics, Economics and Society*, London: Pinter, 1986, p. 29; and Marcum, John, *The Angolan Revolution, Vol. 2: Exile Politics and Guerrilla Warfare*, Cambridge, MA: MIT press, 1978, p. 45. For in-depth accounts of the guerrilla war in Angola see Somerville, pp. 23–45, and Marcum pp. 9–16.
28. Marcum, op. cit., p. 17; see Stockwell, John, *In Search of Enemies*, London: Andre Deitsch, 1978, for a CIA insider's account of US support for the FNLA and UNITA to prevent the MPLA from taking power.
29. Hodges, Tony, *Angola: From Afro-Stalinism to Petro-Diamond Capitalism*, Oxford: James Currey, 2001, p. 9.
30. Ibid., pp. 9–13; Somerville, op. cit., 1990, pp. 49–63.
31. Stockwell, op. cit., p. 78; Marcum, op. cit., p. 257.
32. Col. Breytenbach gave the author information about the force's activities in a series of telephone interviews in 1990.
33. Mason, Philip, *Year of Decision: Rhodesia and Nyasaland in 1960*, London:Institute of Race Relations/Oxford University Press, 1960, p. 267.
34. Nkomo, Joshua, *The Story of My Life*, London: Methuen, 1984, p. 102; this was confirmed to the author by Ndabaningi Sithole, former ZAPU member and then founder of ZANU, in Harare in April 1982 and by ZAPU member and former guerrilla, Joshua Mpofu, Harare, April 1982.
35. Author's interviews with Sithole, Harare, April 1982; Nathan Shamuyarira

(a leading ZANU member and Zimbabwe Minister of Information), Harare April 1982; Emmerson Mnangagwa, (ZANU guerrilla and later Zimbabwean Minister of Defence), Harare, March 1991. See also Nyagumbo, Maurice, *With the People*, London: Allison and Busby, 1980, p. 165.

36. Martin, David and Phyllis Johnson, *The Struggle for Zimbabwe: The Chimurenga War*, Harare: Zimbabwe Publishing House, 1981, p. 24. This account was confirmed to the author by Emmerson Mnangagwa in an interview in Harare in March 1991.
37. For more on South Africa's unhappiness over UDI, its official policy of neutrality but its material support for the Smith government, see Flower, Ken, *Serving Secretly: An Intelligence Chief on Record. Rhodesia into Zimbabwe 1964 to 1981*, London: John Murray, 1987, p. 32; and Meredith, Martin, *The Past is Another Country: Rhodesia 1890–1979*, London: Andre Deutsch, 1979, p. 145.
38. In an interview with the author in February 1991 in Lusaka, President Kaunda said that assisting liberation was not just a moral choice for his government but a political and economic necessity.
39. Confirmed to the author in Harare, April 1982, by Mayor Urimbo and by ZANLA's Chief of Operations, William Ndangana. See also, Martin and Johnson, op. cit., pp. 11–34.
40. Ranger, Terence, *Peasant Consciousness and Guerrilla war in Zimbabwe*, London: James Currey, 1985, pp. 177–8.
41. Ibid., pp. 185–216.
42. Hanlon, Joseph, *Mozambique: The Revolution Under Fire*, London, Zed, 1984, pp. 220–1.
43. As a monitor and then editor with the BBC Monitoring Service, the author monitored African radio stations and edited their output for publication in the BBC's *Summary of World Broadcasts* throughout the 1980s.
44. For a more detailed and fascinating account of the development of African musical culture, see Bender, Wolfgang, *Sweet Mother: Modern African Music*, Chicago: University of Chicago Press, 1991.
45. Hodges, Tony, 'Mozambique', in Gwendolen M. Carter and Patrick O'Meara (ed), *Southern Africa: The Continuing Crisis*, London: Macmillan, 1979, pp. 57–92, p. 77.
46. Cited in Bridgland, Fred, *Jonas Savimbi: A Key to Africa*, Edinburgh: Mainstream, 1986, p. 239.
47. Somerville, Keith, *Southern Africa and the Soviet Union: From Communist International to Commonwealth of Independent States*, Basingstoke: Macmillan, 1993, p. 71.
48. For a full and fascinating account of the May 1977 events, see Pawson, Lara, *In the Name of the People: Angola's Forgotten Massacre*, London: I. B. Tauris, 2014.
49. Information given to the author by senior De Beers employees. De Beers later championed the Kimberley Process to identify so-called blood diamonds from conflict zones and stopped the purchase of UNITA gems.
50. Landis, Elizabeth S. and Michael I. Davis, 'Namibia: Impending Independence?', in Carter, Gwendolen M. and Patrick O'Meara, op. cit., pp. 141–174, p. 146.

51. Ellis, Stephen, *External Mission: The ANC in Exile 1960–1990*, London, Hurst, 2012, p. 7.
52. Somerville, op. cit. 1993, p. 207. The alliance was effectively cemented at an Afro-Asian Solidarity conference in Khartoum in 1968, attended by the liberation movements and Soviet representatives.
53. For differing accounts see Ellis, op. cit.; Somerville, op. cit., 1993, pp 204–72; and Somerville, Keith, 'South Africa—the ANC and SACP in exile, which tail wags which dog?', *Africa—News and Analysis*, *http://africajournalismtheworld.com/2012/12/27/south-africa-the-anc-and-sacp-in-exile-which-tail-wags-which-dog/*, 27 December 2012, accessed 6 July 2015.
54. Welsh, David and J.E. Spence, *Ending Apartheid*, London: Longman, 2011, p. 82.
55. Buthelezi stressed this in an interview with the author in London in 1991.
56. For a more detailed account see Somerville, Keith, 'Radio Wars', *Index on Censorship*, 43, 1, (2014), pp. 66–73.
57. See Lipton, Merle, *Capitalism and Apartheid, South Africa 1910–1984*, London: Wildwood, 1986; Nattrass, Jill, *The South African Economy: its Growth and Change*, Cape Town: Ewell Books, 1981; and Thompson, Leonard, *A History of South Africa*, New Haven: Yale University Press, 3rd Edition, 2001, pp. 261–8.
58. Biko, Steve, 'The Quest for True Humanity', in *I Write What I Like*, London: Bowerdean Press, 1979, p. 49.
59. Author's interview with Donald Woods, London 1990.
60. Welsh and Spence, op. cit., pp. 41 and 91.
61. Author's interview with Sexwale in London, 17 June 1992.
62. Mandela, Nelson, *Long Walk to Freedom*, London: Abacus, 1995, pp. 576 and
63. Young, Crawford and Thomas Turner, *The Rise and Decline of the Zairian State*, Madison, WI: University of Wisconsin Press, 2012, p. 175.
64. Meredith, 2005, pp. 203–308.
65. Ndikumana, Léonce, and James K. Boyce, *Africa's Odious Debts: How Foreign Loans and Capital Flight Bled a Continent*, London: Zed, 2011, p. 1.
66. Ibid., p. 4.
67. *African Contemporary Record, 1977–8*, p. B77.
68. Somerville, op. cit. 1990, p. 126.
69. Chabal, Patrick and Jean-Pascal Daloz, *Africa Works: Disorder as Political Instrument*, Oxford: James Currey, 1999, pp. 14–5.
70. Ellis, Stephen, *Season of Rains: Africa in the World*, London: Hurst, 2011, p. 7.
71. Ndikumana and Boyce, op. cit., p. 20.
72. Moyo, Dambisa, *Dead Aid: Why Aid is Not Working and How There is Another Way for Africa*, London: Penguin 2010, p. 15.
73. Mkandawire, Thandika and Charles C. Soludo, *Our Continent Our Future: African Prespectives on Structural Adjustment*, Dakar: Codesria, 1999, pp. 11–13.
74. Mkandawire, Thandika, 'The State and Agriculture in Africa: Introductory Remarks', in Mkandawire, Thandika and Naceur Bourenane (eds), *The State and Agriculture in Africa*, London: Cosdresia Book Series, 1987, pp. 1–25, p. 1.
75. Bates, Robert H., 'Agricultural Policy and the Study of Politics in Post-

Independence Africa', in Rimmer, Douglas (ed), *Africa Thirty Years On*, London: James Currey/Royal African Society, 1991, pp. 115–29, p. 118.
76. World Bank, *World Development Report, 1981*, Washington: World Bank, 1981, pp. 136–7.
77. Cooper, Frederick, *Africa Since 1940: The Past of the Present*, Cambridge: Cambridge University Press, 2002, p. 103.
78. Mkandaqwire and Soludo, op. cit., p. 13. See also Collier, Paul and Jan Willem Gunning, 'Explaining African Economic performance', *Journal of Economic Literature*, 37, 1 (1999), 64–111.

4. STRUCTURAL ADJUSTMENT, FAMINE, ENVIRONMENTAL DEGRADATION AND AIDS

1. Riddell, J. Barry, 'Things fall Apart Again: Structural Adjustment Programmes in sub-Saharan Africa', *Journal of Modern African Studies*, 30, 1 (1992), pp. 53–68, p. 53.
2. Somerville, Keith, *Southern Africa and the Soviet Union: From Communist International to Commonwealth of Independent States*, Basingstoke: Macmillan, 1993, p. 288.
3. Mkandawire, Thandika and Charles C. Soludo, *Our Continent Our Future: African Prespectives on Structural Adjustment*, Dakar: Codesria, 1999, p. 41.
4. Van der Walle, Nicolas, *African Economies and the Politics of Permanent Crisis, 1979–1999*, Cambridge: Cambridge University Press, 2001, p. 1.
5. International Monetary Fund, *Survey*, Washington, DC: IMF, 9 April 1979, p. 111.
6. Loxley, John, 'Structural Adjustment in Africa: Reflections on Ghana and Zambia', *Review of African Political Economy*, 17, 47 (1990), 8–27, p. 8.
7. Foreword to Mkandawire and Soludo, op. cit., p. vii.
8. Carl Lopes, 'Are Structural Adjustment Programmes an adequate response to globalisation?' *UNESCO 1999*, Oxford: Blackwell, 1999, pp. 511–19.
9. Loxley, op. cit., pp. 10 and 16.
10. Riddell, op. cit., p. 54.
11. Hibou, Béatrice, 'The "Social Capital" of the state as an agent of deception or the ruses of economic intelligence', in Bayart, Jean François, Stephen Ellis and Béatrice Hibou, *The Criminalisation of the State in Africa*, Oxford: The International African Institute/James Currey, 1999, pp. 69–113, p. 71.
12. Riddell, op. cit., p. 80.
13. Loxley, op. cit., p. 15.
14. Van der Walle, op. cit., p. 6.
15. Loxley, op. cit., p. 20.
16. Cited by Nugent, Paul, *Africa Since Independence: A Comparative History*, Basingstoke: Palgrave Macmillan, 2nd edition, 2012, p. 330.
17. Killick, Tony, *Economic Inflexibility in Africa: Evidence and Causes*, London: Overseas Development Institute, 1993, p. 8.
18. Binns, Tony, Alan Dixon and Etienne Nel, *Africa: Diversity and Development*, London: Routledge, 2012, p. 61.

19. Timberlake, Lloyd, 'The Sahel: Drought, Desertification and Famine', *Draper Fund Report*, 14, September 1985, pp. 17–9.
20. Loxley, op. cit., p. 18.
21. See, for example, World Food Programme, *Niger Overview*, http://www.wfp.org/countries/niger/overview# accessed 6 July 2015; World Food Programme, *Niger: Special Focus*, http://documents.wfp.org/stellent/groups/public/documents/ena/wfp257181.pdf accessed 6 July 2015; USAID, 'Niger: Food Insecurity', http://reliefweb.int/sites/reliefweb.int/files/resources/09.30.11%20-%20USAID-DCHA%20Niger%20Food%20Insecurity%20Fact%20Sheet%20%231%20-%20FY%202011.pdf, accessed 15 May 2013.
22. UNEP, 'Climate Change and Variability in the Sahel Region: Impacts and Adaptation Strategies in the Agricultural Sector', UNEP, http://www.unep.org/Themes/Freshwater/Documents/pdf/ClimateChangeSahelCombine.pdf, accessed 6 July 2015.
23. FAO, 'Funds for the Sahel are needed now, Raúl says', http://www.fao.org/news/story/en/item/143403/icode/ accessed 6 July 2015.
24. Baynham, Simon, *The Military and Politics in Nkrumah's Ghana*, Boulder, CO: Westview Press, 1988, pp. 185–94.
25. Herbst, Jeffrey, *The Politics of Reform in Ghana, 1982–1991*, Berkeley, CA: University of California Press, 1993, p. 15.
26. Ibid., p. 24.
27. Ibid., p. 64.
28. Talk on the 2012 Ghanaian elections at King's College, London, 7 May 2013 by Michael Amoah. See also Amoah, Michael, *Nationalism, Globalisation, and Africa*, Basingstoke: Palgrave Macmillan, 2011, pp. 189–99.
29. World Bank, *African Economic and Financial Data*, Washington, DC: World Bank, 1989, p. 196 and Herbst, op. cit., p 27.
30. Herbst, op. cit., p. 66.
31. Moses Agaga, Deputy Finance Minister under Rawlings in the 1990s, interviewed in Agyeman-Duah, Ivor (ed), *An Economic History of Ghana: Reflections on a Half-Century of Challenges and Progress*, Banbury, Ofordshire: Ayebia Clarke Publishing Ltd., 2008, p. 109.
32. Thomson, Alex, *An Introduction to African Politics*, London: Routledge, 3rd Edition 2010, p. 207.
33. Dudley, Billy J., *An Introduction to Nigerian Government and Politics*, London: Macmillan, 1982, p. 81.
34. Arnold, Guy, *Africa: A Modern History*, London: Atlantic, 2005, pp. 399–401.
35. Ogubadejo, Oye, 'Nigeria and the Economic Community of West African States', in *African Contemporary Record 1986–1987*, pp. A124–A140, p. 124.
36. Arnold, op. cit., p. 401; Nugent, op. cit., p. 220.
37. Dudley, op. cit., p. 81.
38. Meier, Karl, *This House Has Fallen: Nigeria in Crisis*, Boulder, CO: Westview Press, 2000, p. 15.
39. Cited by Arnold, op. cit., p. 401.
40. Thomson, op. cit., p. 77.

41. Cunliffe-Jones, Peter, *My Nigeria: Five Decades of Independence*, Basingstoke: Palgrave Macmillan, 2010, p. 105.
42. Osaghae, Eghosa, *Crippled Giant: Nigeria Since Independence*, London: Hurst, 1998, pp. 130–2.
43. Ibid., p. 70.
44. Meier, op. cit., p. 16.
45. Cunliffe-Jones, op. cit., p. 106.
46. Dowden, Richard, *Africa: Altered States, Ordinary Miracles*, London: Portobello Books, 2008, p. 462.
47. Ndikumana, Leonce and James K. Boyce, *Africa's Odious Debts: how Foreign Loans and Capital Flight Bled a Continent*, London: Zed, 2011, pp. 15 and 48.
48. Meier, op. cit., p. 16.
49. Cunliffe-Jones, op. cit., p. 107.
50. Osaghae, op. cit., p221.
51. Dowden, op. cit., p. 470.
52. See Cunliffe-Jones, op. cit., p. 109; Meier, op. cit., p. 17; Dowden, op. cit., p. 470.
53. Welsh, David and J.E. Spence, *Ending Apartheid*, London: Longman, 2011, p. 48.
54. Geldenhuys, Deon, 'The Constellation of Southern African States and the Southern African Development Co-Ordination Council: Towards a new regional stalemate?', *South African Institute of International Affairs*, 1981, p. 2, http://www.africaportal.org/dspace/articles/constellation-southern-african-states-and-southern-african-development-co-ordination, accessed 6 July 2015.
55. Hodges, Tony, *Angola: From Afro-Stalinism to Petro-Diamond Capitalism*, Oxford: The Fridtjof Nansen Institute and The International African Institute/James Currey, 2001, p. 11.
56. Hanlon, Joseph, *Beggar Your Neighbours: Apartheid Power in Southern Africa*, London: James Currey, 1986, p. 159.
57. Interviews with the author in Dar es Salaam in October 1986 and Abidjan in November 1987.
58. Shubin, Vladimir, *The Hot "Cold War": The USSR in Southern Africa*, London: Pluto, 2008, pp. 94–5. Shubin, who was involved in Soviet policy in Angola, reveals differences between Angola, Moscow and Havana over strategy and suggests the Cubans were reluctant to get involved in combat with the South Africans.
59. Crocker, Chester, *High Noon in Southern Africa: Making Peace in a Rough Neighbourhood*, New York: W.W. Norton, 1992, p. 187.
60. Somerville, Keith, *Foreign Military Intervention in Africa*, London: Pinter, 1990, p. 180. This was confirmed to the author by Col. Jan Breytenbach, who commanded 32 Battalion of the SADF in Angola.
61. Ibid., p. 153.
62. Shubin, op. cit., pp. 97–8.
63. Crocker, op. cit., p. 354.
64. Crocker, op. cit., p. 367.
65. For more details of the origins of the war and Renamo's formation, see Hanlon, Joseph, *Mozambique: The Revolution Under Fire*, London: Zed, 1984; and Vines,

Alex, *Renamo: From Terrorism to Democracy in Mozambique*, York: Centre for Southern African Studies and Eduardo Mondalen Foundation, 1996.

66. Khadiagala, Gilbert M., 'The SADCC and its approaches to African regionalism', in Saunders, Chris, Gwinayi A. Dzinesa and Dawn Nagar (eds), *Region-Building in Southern Africa: Progress, Problems and Prospects*, London: Zed, 2012, pp. 25–38, pp. 25 and 27.
67. Conveyed in off-the-record discussions with the author in Malawi between late 1981 and April 1982, and in an interview the author conducted with Zimbabwean Foreign Minister Witness Mangwende in Harare in April 1982.
68. Confirmed to the author by Zimbabwean Vice-President Simon Muzenda and Information Minister Nathan Shamuyarira in Harare in February 1992.
69. BBC News, 12 December 2012, http://www.bbc.co.uk/news/world-africa-20694109, accessed 6 July 2015.
70. Hanlon, Joseph, *Mozambique: Who Calls the Shots?*, London: James Currey, 1991, p. 19.
71. World Bank, *World Development Report 1990*, Washington DC: World Bank, 1990.
72. Hanlon, op. cit. 1991, pp. 259–63.
73. Martin, David and Phyllis Johnson, *Frontline Southern Africa*, Peterborough: Ryan Publishers, 1989, p. 65.
74. See Alexander, J., J. McGregor and T. Ranger, *Violence and Memory: One Hundred Years in the 'Dark Forests' of Matabeleland*, Oxford: James Currey, 2000, pp. 180–196; Alao, Abiodun, *Mugabe and the Politics of Security in Zimbabwe*, Montreal and Kingston, ON: McGill-Queen's University Press, 2012, pp. 78 and 82–4.
75. Alao, op. cit., pp. 84–5.
76. Muzondidya, James, 'From Buouyancy to Crisis: 1980–1997', in Raftopoulos, Brian and A.S. Mlambo, *Becoming Zimbabwe: A History from the Pre-Colonial Period to 2008*, Harare: Weaver Press, 2009, pp. 167–200, p. 179.
77. Catholic Commission for Justice and Peace, *Gukurahundi in Zimbabwe: A Report on the Disturbance in Matabeleland and the Midlands, 1980–1988*, Harare: CCJP/LRF, 2008; Catholic Commission for Justice and Peace, *Breaking the Silence, Building True Peace: A Report on the Disturbances in Matabeleland and the Midlands, 1980–1988*, Harare: CCJP/LRF, 1997.
78. Ibid.
79. Khadiagala, op. cit., p. 29.
80. Mandela, Nelson, *Long Walk to Freedom*, London: Abacus, 1994, p. 605. Mandela details how while he was on Robben Island the government allowed traditional leaders to visit him, as they were keen to promote traditional leaders as a counterweight to the ANC and later the UDF—but also hoped that "the more I was involved in tribal and Transkei matters, the less I would be committed to the struggle."
81. The South African Minister of Law and Order, Adriaan Vlok, a key member of the security establishment, told the author in Johannesburg in March 1990 that the core belief of the NP leadership was that the future of white South Africa could only be protected by using the security apparatus to prevent the spread of communism and radical nationalism.

82. Welsh and Spence, op. cit., pp. 50–1.
83. Arnold, op. cit., p. 730.
84. Feinstein, Andrew, *After the Party: Corruption, the ANC and South Africa's Uncertain Future*, London: Verson, 2009, p. 9.
85. This was recounted to the author by Raymond Suttner, a UDF and later ANC/SACP activist, in correspondence in 2013, and by Popo Molefe of the UDF in an interview in Johannesburg in March 1990.
86. Thompson, Leonard, *A History of South Africa*, New Haven, CT: Yale University Press, Third Edition, 2000, p. 229.
87. Feinstein, 2009, p. 9.
88. Welsh and Spence, op. cit., p. 103.
89. Sir Robin Renwick, the British Ambassador in South Africa in 1990, told the author that Margaret Thatcher was furious with this speech and with later intransigence as it made her desire to help South Africa and to resist sanctions all the more difficult to achieve.
90. From author's discussion in South Africa in March 1990 with Renwick, South African Constitutional Affairs Minister Gerrit Vijoen and Glenn Babb, former South African diplomat and NP MP.
91. This view was put to the author by Walter Sisulu in a telephone interview in November 1989 and by Thabo Mbeki in an interview in the same month in London.
92. Binns et al, op. cit., p. 220.
93. *The Guardian*, 14 March 2000, http://www.guardian.co.uk/world/2000/mar/14/unitednations, accessed 6 July 2015.
94. UNAIDS, World Aids Day Report 2011, New York: UN, 2011, p. 7, http://www.unaids.org/en/media/unaids/contentassets/documents/unaidspublication/2011/JC2216_WorldAIDSday_report_2011_en.pdf, accessed 6 July 2015.
95. Ibid., pp. 6–7.
96. Furman, Katherine, 'Mbeki's AIDS Denialism', *Think Africa Press*, 17 November 2011, http://thinkafricapress.com/south-africa/mbeki-aids-denialism accessed 14 June 2013.
97. 'African President Warns of Extinction from Aids', *Daily Telegraph*, http://www.telegraph.co.uk/news/worldnews/africaandindianocean/botswana/1347791/African-president-warns-of-extinction-from-Aids.html, accessed 6 July 2015.
98. Avert, 'HIV/AIDS in Botswana', http://www.avert.org/aids-botswana.htm accessed 6 July 2015.
99. Nana K. Poku, *AIDS in Africa: How the Poor are Dying*, Cambridge: Polity Press, 2005, p. 11.
100. UNAIDS, *Swaziland Country Report on Monitoring the Political Declaration on HIV and AIDS*, 2012, http://www.unaids.org/en/dataanalysis/knowyourresponse/countryprogressreports/2012countries/ce_SZ_Narrative_Report[1].pdf, accessed 6 July 2015.
101. AVERT, 'HIV and AIDS in Swaziland', http://www.avert.org/aids-swaziland.htm, accessed 6 July 2015.
102. Anup Shah, 2009.

103. World Health Organisation, *World Malaria Report 2013*, Geneva: WHO, 2013. See also *Mail and Guardian*, 1 June 2014. http://africajournalismtheworld.com/2014/06/01/africa-and-malaria-success-in-bringing-down-death-rates-in-10-states/, accessed 6 July 2015.
104. WHO, op. cit. 2013.
105. Somerville, 'Africa and Ebola—the IMF's Ebola-Friendly Reforms', *Africa News and Analysis*, 2 December 2014, http://africajournalismtheworld.com/tag/tom-somerville/

5. THE RAINBOW NATION, RWANDA'S GENOCIDE, AND THE GOOD GOVERNANCE BALANCE SHEET

1. Somerville, Keith, 'Africa After the Cold War: Frozen Out or Frozen in Time?' In Fawcett, Louise and Yezid Sayigh, *The Third World Beyond the Cold War: Continuity and Change*, Oxford: OUP, 1999, pp. 134–69, p. 134.
2. Crocker, Chester A., *High Noon in Southern Africa: Making Peace in a Rough Neighbourhood*, New York: W. W. Norton and Co, 1992, p. 17.
3. Ake, Claude, 'Rethinking African Democracy', in Diamond, Larry and Marc F. Plattner (eds), *The Global Resurgence of Democracy*, Baltimore: Johns Hopkins University Press, 1996, p. 63–75, p. 64.
4. Bayart, Jean-François, *The State in Africa: The Politics of the Belly*, London: Longman, 1993. p.x.
5. Harbeson, John W., 'Civil Society and Political Renaissance in Africa', in Harbeson, John W., Donald Rothchild and Naomi Chazan, *Civil Society and the State in Africa*, Boulder, CO: Lynne Rienner, 1994, p. 2.
6. See the Kenya and Rwanda chapters of Somerville, Keith, *Radio Propaganda and the Broadcasting of Hate: Historical Development and Definitions*, London: Palgrave, 2012.
7. Wrong, Michela, *It's Our Turn to Eat: The Story of a Kenyan Whistleblower*, London: Fourth Estate, 2010. This is a masterful investigation into the networks of political and economic corruption in Kenya.
8. I was staying with Mike Hall and Melinda Ham, Western journalists who worked with M'membe on the setting up of the *Post*, at the time of the newspaper's birth, and witnessed at first hand politically active Zambians increasingly free to criticise, and journalists increasingly free to investigate stories without being bound by working for state or party-controlled media.
9. My website, Africa—News and Analysis, http://africajournalismtheworld.com/2014/06/10/how-many-nigerians-does-it-to-take-to-change-a-light-bulb/ covers the African media's reporting of major stories on a daily basis, and is a good way of seeing the growth of a critical and investigative media.
10. Lancaster, Carol, 'Democratisation in Sub-Saharan Africa', *Survival*, 35, 3 (1993), pp, 38–51, p. 41.
11. In interviews with the author in Harare in March 1991, democracy campaigners Mabere Marando, James Mapalala and Christopher Mtikila, as well as Prime Minister John Malacela, told the author in Dar es Salaam in February 1991 that

events elsewhere in Africa, rather than in Eastern Europe, had encouraged moves towards plurality. Raphael Hamadziripi of the Zimbabwe Unity Movement, Michael Auret of the Catholic Commission for Justice and Peace and Professor John Makumbe all believed that Zimbabwean opposition in to one-party rule was influenced by events elsewhere in Africa more than those in Eastern Europe.

12. The author was informed of these a day after Chiluba became MMD leader by former Zambia foreign minister and MMD fixer Vernon Mwaanga in an interview in Lusaka in March 1991.
13. BBC News, 'Zambia's Chiluba guilty of graft', 4 May 2007, http://news.bbc.co.uk/1/hi/world/africa/6624547.stm accessed 6 July 2015.
14. Somerville, Keith, 'Malawi Votes for Reform', *The World Today*, RIIA, London, 49, 8–8, August–September 1993, pp. 150–1.
15. Africa—News and Analysis, 'Malawi: Banda brings Malawi back from the brink', http://africajournalismtheworld.com/2012/05/22/malawi-banda-brings-malawi-back-from-the-brink/, accessed 6 July 2015.
16. Ogot, B.A. 'The Politics of Populism', in Ogot, B.A. and W.R. Ochieng', *Decolonisation and Independence in Kenya 1940–93*, London: James Currey, 1995, pp. 187–213, pp. 200–1.
17. The latter tactic even involved arresting and deporting foreign journalists seeking to investigate the strength of the pro-democracy camp. In March 1991, I was arrested and briefly detained at Nairobi airport and then deported while seeking to make a documentary on the democracy movement. The British minister then responsible for Africa, Lynda Chalker, told me she would give the Kenyan government a "slap on the wrist" for this.
18. Branch, Daniel and Nic Cheeseman, 'Democratisation, sequencing, and state failure in Africa: lessons from Kenya', *African Affairs*, 108, 430, (2009), pp. 1–26, p. 4.
19. Somerville, Keith, 'British media coverage of the post-election violence in Kenya, 2007–8', *Journal of Eastern African Studies*, 3, 3 (2009), pp. 526–542.
20. Mueller, Susanne D., 'The Political Economy of Kenya's Crisis', *Journal of Eastern African Studies*, 2, 2 (2008), pp. 185–210.
21. Somerville, Keith, op. cit., 2012, p. 164–7.
22. Lemarchand, Réne, *Rwanda and Burundi*, New York: Praeger, 1970, pp. 216–9; see also Mamdani, Mahmood, *When Victims Become Killers: Colonialism, Nativism, and the Genocide in Rwanda*, Princeton, NJ: Princeton University Press, 2002, p. 130–1.
23. Ndayambaje, Damascene and Jean Mutabarika, 'Colonialism and the Churches as Agents of Ethnic Division', in Berry, John A. and Carol Pott Berry, *Genocide in Rwanda: A Collective Memory*, Washington D.C.: Howard University Press, 2001, pp. 42–3.
24. Straus, Scott, *The Order of Genocide: Race, Power, and War in Rwanda*, Ithaca: Cornell University Press, 2006, p. 23.
25. Mamdani, op. cit., p. 144.
26. See Prunier, op. cit., 2008, pp. 61–74 and 90–2 for a detailed account of the rise of the RPF/RPA.

27. Gérard Prunier, *Africa's World War: Congo, the Rwandan genocide, and the Making of a Continental Catastrophe*, Oxford: OUP, 2009, p. 14.
28. BBC, *Summary of World Broadcasts, Part 4, Middle East and Africa*, Caversham: BBC Monitoring Service, 9 October 1990.
29. Philip Gourevitch, *We Wish to Inform You That Tomorrow We Will Be Killed With Our Families*, New York: Acado, 1998, p. 84.
30. Article XIX, *Broadcasting Genocide: Censorship, Propaganda and State-Sponsored Violence in Rwanda 1990–1994*, London: Article XIX, 1996 p. 101.
31. See report by BBC News, http://www.bbc.co.uk/news/world-africa-16472013; accessed 10 January 2013.
32. Gourevitch, 1998, p. 111.
33. Dallaire, 2004, pp. 231, 234–5.
34. See Prunier, op. cit., pp. 281–99 for an insider's account of Operation Turquoise by the French and the anti-RPF stance of the French government and military. The French had 2,500 well-armed troops in Rwanda, but did nothing to stop the genocide or capture those responsible. Rather, they helped them first to a safe haven and then out of the country as French troops were withdrawn.
35. Polman, Linda, *War Games*, London: Viking, 2010, pp. 24–5.
36. Lemarchand, René, *The Dynamics of Violence in Central Africa*, Philadelphia: University of Philadelphia Press, 2009, p. 7.
37. Polman, op. cit., p. 25.
38. Melvern op. cit., p. 251.
39. Prunier, op. cit., pp. 27–8.
40. Kabemba, Claude, 'The Democratic Republic of Congo', in Clapham, Christopher, Feffrey Berbst and Greg Mills (eds), *Big African States*, Johannesburg: Wits University Press, 2001, pp. 104–5.
41. Cited by Ndikumana, Léonce, and James K. Boyce, *Africa's Odious Debts: How Foreign Loans and Capital Flight Bled a Continent*, London: Zed, 2011, p. 8.
42. Georges Nzongola-Ntalaja, *The Congo From Leopold to Kabila: A People's History*, London: Zed, 2007, pp. 185–6.
43. Prunier, op. cit., p. 69.
44. Reed, 1998, p. 147
45. Polman, op. cit., p. 32.
46. See Lemarchand, op. cit., pp 3–19 and Prunier, op. cit., pp. 358–64 on the complexity of the causes and effects of conflict in the region.
47. M23 appeared to have been defeated by the Congolese and UN forces in late 2013, but then re-emerged in the Ituri region in 2014.
48. Good examples are Lemarchand, op. cit., pp. 5–7, and Keen, David, *Complex Emergencies*, London: Polity, 2008, pp. 25–31.
49. Paul Collier, 'Doing well out of war: an economic perspective', in Mats Berdal and David M. Malone (eds), *Greed and Grievance: Economic agendas in Civil Wars*, Boulder, CO: Lynne Rienner (2000) pp. 91–112, pp. 100–1.
50. For a detailed and incisive account of the process see Devon Curtis, *The Peace Process in Burundi: Successful African Intervention?* http://www.igd.org.za/jdownloads/Global%20Insight/gi_24.pdf, accessed 25 June 2015.

51. Harper, Mary, *Getting Somalia Wrong? Faith, War and Hope in a Shattered State*, London: Zed, 2012, pp. 1–6.
52. Schmidt, Elizabeth, *Foreign Intervention in Africa: From Cold War to the War on Terror*, Cambridge: Cambridge University Press, 2013, p. 203.
53. Cited by Harper, op. cit., p. 57.
54. Ibid.
55. Verhoeven, Harry, 'The self-fulfilling prophecy of failed states: Somalia, state collapse and the Global War on Terror', *Journal of Eastern African Studies*, 3, 3 (2009), pp. 405–25, p. 411.
56. Marchal, 2009, p. 387.
57. Harper, op. cit., pp. 81–2.
58. Harper, op. cit., p. 127.
59. Mark Bradbury, *Becoming Somaliland*, London: Progressio, 2008, p. 242.
60. Harper, op. cit., p. 134.
61. Edward Paice, 'Somalia, remittances and unintended consequences: in conversation with Abdirashid Duale, chief executive of Dahabshiil', *Africa Research Institute*, 31 July 2013, http://www.africaresearchinstitute.org/blog/somalia-remittances-and-unintended-consequences-in-conversation-with-abdirashid-duale/ accessed *6 July 2015*.
62. Harper, op. cit., p. 132.
63. Marchal, op. cit., p. 394.
64. Rob Wise of the Centre for International and Strategic Studies, Georgetown University, cited by Jonathan Masters, *Al-Shabaab*, Council on Foreign Relations, 9 July 2013, http://www.cfr.org/somalia/al-shabaab/p18650 accessed 6 July 2015.
65. Harper, op. cit., p. 86.
66. Plaut, Martin, 'Ethiopia and Kenya help dismember Somalia', *New Statesman*, 3 September 2013, http://www.newstatesman.com/africa/2013/09/ethiopia-and-kenya-help-dismember–somalia, accessed 6 July 2015.
67. Ibid.
68. Nelson Mandela's address to a rally in Cape Town, 11 February 1990, http://www.anc.org.za/show.php?id=4520, accessed 6 July 2015.
69. Welsh, David and J.E. Spence, *Ending Apartheid*, London: Longman, 2011, p. 124.
70. Personal communication with former National Intelligence Service agent, professor Anthony Turton, in April and May 2015.
71. The NP Minister of Constitutional Development, Gerrit Viljoen, and Law and Order Minister, Adriaan Vlok, both told the author in interviews in Johannesburg in March 1990 that group rights were vital for them as was the protection of property against confiscation.
72. Meredith, Martin, *Nelson Mandela A Biography*, London: Hamish Hamilton, 1997, p. 474.
73. This was emphasised to me by leading ANC member Tokyo Sexwale in London on the day of the Boipatong killings. Sexwale said the killers were incited to do it by Buthelezi and by the security forces, and that they had been driven to the scene of the killing in police vehicles. On the same day, Frank Mdlalose, chairman of the IFP, said to me that the ANC was inciting violence and the IFP was not involved. A number of IFP supporters were later convicted of the killings.

74. Barber, 1999, p. 294.
75. Derby-Lewis was on the lunatic fringe of white politics, and when I interviewed him in Klerksdorp in March 1990, he denounced de Klerk, George Bush and Margaret Thatcher as lackeys of the world Bolshevik-Jewish-banking conspiracy.
76. Welsh and Spence, op. cit., p. 132.
77. A few months after the World Cup victory, I was in the Western Cape making radio documentaries on the process of integration in sport. In August 1995, Western Cape Finance Minister and National Party heavyweight Kobus Meiring told me it was hard to overestimate the importance of being accepted back into the world of sport and of Mandela acknowledging the importance of that win with his presence at the rugby final. Conservative white rugby club members and executives told me repeatedly that Mandela's gesture had been deeply felt even by whites still profoundly suspicious of the ANC and hankering after the old days.
78. Welsh and Spence, op. cit., p. 201.
79. For a detailed study of the corruption, the arms deal and Zuma's diverse business, intelligence and political network see Plaut, Martin and Paul Holden, *Who Rules South Africa?*, London: Biteback, 2012.
80. Kasrils, Ronnie, 'How the ANC's Faustian pact sold out South Africa's poorest', *The Guardian*, 24 June 2013, http://www.guardian.co.uk/commentisfree/2013/jun/24/anc-faustian-pact-mandela-fatal-error accessed 5 July 2015.
81. Ibid.
82. Terreblanche, 2002, pp. 95 and 100.
83. Terreblanche, op. cit., pp. 135–7
84. Thomson, Alex, *An Introduction to African Politics*, London: Routledge, 2000, p. 209.
85. Cited by Nugent, Paul, *Big Men, Small Boys and Politics in Ghana: Power, Ideology and the Burden of History, 1982–1994*, London: Pinter, 1996, p. 118.
86. Gilbert, Guy, Réjane Hugounenq and François Vaillancourt, 'Local Public Finances in Ghana', in Dafflon, Bernard and Thierry Madiès (eds), *The Political Economy of Decentralisation in Sub-Saharan Africa*, Washington DC: International bank for Reconstruction and Development/World Bank, 2013, pp. 107–160, p. 109.
87. Ayee, Joseph R. A., 'A Decade of Political Leadership in Ghana, 1993–2004', in Boafo-Arthur, Kwame (ed), *Ghana: One decade of the liberal state*, Dakar, Codesria Books, 2007, pp. 165–87, p. 168.
88. Thomson, op. cit., 3rd edition, 2010, p. 126.
89. Crook, Richard C. and James Manor, *Democracy and Decentralisation in South Asia and West Africa: Participation, Accountability and Performance*, Cambridge: Cambridge University Press, 1998, p. 183.
90. Le Vine, Victor T., *Politics in Francophone Africa*, Boulder, CO: Lynne Reiner, 2004, p. 213.
91. Global Security, 'Ivory Coast Conflict 2002', http://www.globalsecurity.org/military/world/war/ivory-coast-2002.htm accessed 28 June 2015.

92. William Reno, *Warfare in Independent Africa*, Cambridge: Cambridge University Press, 2011.
93. Ellis, Stephen, 'Liberia 1989–1994: A study of ethnic and spiritual violence', *African Affairs*, 94, 375 (1995), pp. 165–197, p. 175.
94. Harris, David, *Civil War and Democracy in West Africa: Conflict Resolution, Elections and Justice in Sierra Leone and Liberia*, London: I.B. Tauris, 2012, pp. 47–8.
95. Ibid., p. 49.
96. Stephen Ellis, *The Mask of Anarchy: The Destruction of Liberia and the Religious Dimension of an African Civil War*, New York: New York University Press, 1999, p. 33.
97. Ibid., pp. 223–50.
98. Ibid., p. 53.
99. Ibid. The author is grateful to Stephen Ellis for advice on the relationships of Houphouët-Boigny's female entourage members and their roles in West African politics.
100. Harris, op. cit., p. 67.
101. Berkeley, Bill, *Liberia: A Promise Beyond*, New York: Lawyers Committee for Human Rights, 1986, p. 117.
102. Ellen Johnson-Sirleaf told the author in telephone interviews in the early 1990s that she feared for her life if she stayed politically active in Liberia under Doe.
103. Richards, Paul 'Rebellion in Liberia and Sierra Leone: A Crisis of Youth?' In Furley, Oliver (ed), *Conflict in Africa*, London: I. B. Tauris, 1995, p. 142.
104. The author spoke to Taylor and his lieutenants on a number of occasions when he phoned the *Newshour* programme to get on air.
105. Richards, op. cit. 1995, p. 143.
106. Ellis, 199, p. 77.
107. Ibid. pp. 79–80
108. See Keen, op. cit., pp. 25–49 for the counter argument to the Paul Collier dominance of greed approach—Collier, Paul, 'Doing Well Out of War: An Economic Perspective', in Mats Berdal and David M. Malone (ed), *Greed and Grievance: Economic Agendas in Civil Wars*, Boulder, CO: 2000, pp. 91–112.
109. Meredith, op. cit., 2011, p. 572.
110. Personal correspondence with former BBC African Service journalist and current UN official, Max Bankole Jarrett. The quotation is from his unpublished dissertation on the Liberian civil war.
111. Ellis, op. cit. 1995, p. 183.
112. Keen, David, *Conflict and Collusion in Sierra Leone*, Oxford, James Currey, 2005, p. 14.
113. For a detailed history of the development of Sierra Leone's political system, parties and conflicts see, Harris, David, *Sierra Leone: A Political History*, London: Hurst and Company, 2013.
114. Richards, Paul, *Fighting for the Rain Forest: War, Youth & Resources in Sierra Leone*, Oxford: James Currey/The International African Institute, 1998, p. 40; and Keen, op. cit. 2005, p. 15.

115. Harris, op. cit., pp. 63–6.
116. Harris, op. cit., p. 57.
117. Keen, op. cit. 2005, p. 17.
118. Koroma, Abdul K., *Sierra Leone: The Agony of a Nation*, Freetown: Andromeda, 1996, p. 83; Zack-Williams, Alfred, 'Crisis, Structural Adjustment and Creative Survival in Sierra Leone', *Africa Development*, 18, 1 (1993), pp. 51–65, p. 58; and Keen, op. cit. 2005, pp. 26–7.
119. Richards, op. cit. 1998, p. 5.
120. This view was strongly put by Professor Paul Richards in my correspondence with him.
121. Author's conversations in London in April 1991 with West African diplomats and telephone interview with Nigeria's Olusegun Obasanjo.
122. Keen, op. cit. 2005, p. 87.
123. Bamford, David, 'Foday Sankoh: Rebel Leader,' BBC News, 12 May 2000, http://news.bbc.co.uk/1/hi/world/africa/737268.stm, accessed 6 July 2015.
124. Richards, op. cit. 1998, p. 10.
125. Eeben Barlow of Executive Outcomes told the author that his group played a major role in directing SLA and militia forces and its deployment of combat helicopters and rapid response units made up mainly of South Africans and Angolan mercenaries in helicopters turned the tide against the RUF in several areas.
126. Harris, op. cit., p. 95.
127. Keen, op. cit. 2005, p. 203.
128. This was communicated to me by Michael Grunberg of Sandline and confirmed by the former British High Commissioner to Sierra Leone, Peter Penfold.
129. Meredith, 2011, p. 570.
130. Young, John, 'The Tigray People's Liberation Front', in Clapham, Christopher (ed), *African Guerrillas*, Oxford: James Curry, 1998, pp. 36–52, p. 49.
131. Pauswang, Siegfried, Kjetil Tronvoll and Lovise Aalen, 'A process of Democratisation of Control: The Historical and Politicfal Context', in Pauswang, Siegfried, Kjetil Tronvoll and Lovise Aalen (ed), *Ethiopia Since the Derg: A Decade of Democratic Pretension and Performance*, London: Zed, 2002, pp. 26–44.
132. Ibid. p. 31.
133. Woodward, Peter, *Crisis in the Horn of Africa: Politics, Piracy and the Threat of Terror*, London: I. B. Tauris, 2013, p. 53.
134. Dowde, Richard, 'How Meles Rules Ethiopia', *African Arguments*, 21 May 2012, http://africanarguments.org/2012/05/21/how-meles-rules-ethiopia-by-richard-dowden/, accessed 6 July 2015. My impression when I interviewed him in London in early 1991, just before the EPRDF took power, was that he was dour and had little time for the opinions of others or for frivolity like celebrating his movement's victory.
135. Human Rights Watch, *Ogaden: War Crimes*, http://www.hrw.org/features/ogaden-war-crimes-ethiopia-0 accessed 6 July 2015.
136. Pool, David, 'The Eritrean People's Liberation Front', in Clapham, op. cit. 1998, pp. 19–35, p. 19

137. Woodward, op. cit., p. 146.
138. Woodward, op. cit., p. 167.
139. UN General Assembly, *Report of the Special Rapporteur on the Situation of Human Rights in Eritrea, Sheila B. Keetharuth*, http://www.ohchr.org/Documents/HRBodies/HRCouncil/RegularSession/Session23/A.HRC.23.53_ENG.pdf accessed 6 July 2015.

6. THE NEW MILLENNIUM

1. For a very detailed first-hand account of the secession and post-independence struggles in South Sudan, see Copnall, James, *A Poisonous Thorn in Our Hearts: Sudan and South Sudan's Bitter and Incomplete Divorce*, London: Hurst, 2014.
2. Young, John, *The Fate of Sudan*, London: Zed, 2012, pp. 94–5 and 102.
3. Woodward, Peter, *Crisis in the Horn of Africa: Politics, Piracy and the Threat of Terror*, London: I. B. Tauris, 2013, p. 118.
4. The crucial role of oil in the South's secession and post-secession conflict, as well as the development of the oil industry in both Sudans and the crucial role of the Chinese are detailed superbly in Patey, Luke, *The New Kings of Crude: China, India and the Global Struggle for Oil in Sudan and South Sudan*, London: Hurst and Company, 2014. Copnall, op. cit., pp. 77–84 and 93–12 also sets the political scene for the importance of oil.
5. Maduk Jok, Jok, *Sudan: Race Religion, and Violence*, Oxford: One World, 2007, p. 194.
6. Young, op. cit., p. 133.
7. Woodward, op. cit., p. 119.
8. Copnall, 2014, pp. 168–76, and Woodward, 2013, p. 129.
9. Douglas H. Johnson, *The Root Causes of Sudan's Civil Wars: Peace or Truce*, Kampala: Fountain Publishwers, revised edition 2011, p. 117.
10. Copnall, op. cit., p. 255–60.
11. For a detailed account of the origins of the different communities, see Flint, Julie & Alex de Waal, *Darfur: A New History of a Long War*, London: Zed, 2008, pp. 6–9.
12. Prunier, Gérard, *Darfur: The Ambiguous Genocide*, London, Hurst, 2005, pp. 4–5.
13. Flint and de Waal, op. cit. 2008; and 2005.
14. For a journalistic analysis of the simplistic reporting of Darfur see Crilly, Rob, *Saving Darfur: Everyone's Favourite African War*, Rob Crilly, Kindle edition, 2010, Location 174.
15. Flint and de Waal, op. cit. 2008, p. 278.
16. Furley, Oliver and James Katalikawe, 'Constitutional Reform in Uganda: The New Approach', *African Affairs*, 96, 383 (1997) pp. 243–60, p. 245.
17. The author is indebted to Dr Michael Twaddle for this key observation.
18. Tripp, Aili Mari, *Museveni's Uganda: Paradoxes of Power in a Hybrid Regime*, Boulder, CO: Lynne Rienner, 2010, p. 2.
19. Makara, Sabiti, Lise Rakner and Lars Svasand, 'Turnaround: The National Resistance Movement and the Reintroduction of a Multiparty System in Uganda', *International Political Science Review*, 30, 185, (2009) pp. 185–204, pp. 187–9.

20. In 1993 the NRM restored the Buganda monarchy, but on an equal basis with other traditional hierarchies among the main ethnic groups and with no overt political role. Museveni was willing to provide a cultural role for the Kabaka, but not a political one.
21. Furley and Katalikawe, op. cit., pp. 252–3.
22. Mugyenyi, Mary M., 'Towards the Empowerment of Women: A Critique of NRM Policies and Programmes', in Hansen, Holger Bernt and Michael Twaddle (eds), *Developing Uganda*, Oxford: James Currey, 1998, pp. 133–44, pp. 137.
23. Twaddle, Michael and Holger Bernt Hansen, 'The changing state of Uganda', in Holger Bernt Hansen and Michael Twaddle, op. cit., pp. 1–18, p. 5.
24. Uganda AIDS Commission, *Global AIDS Response Progress Report: Country Progress Report Uganda*, Kampala: Uganda AIDS Commission, April 2012, p. 1. http://www.unaids.org/en/dataanalysis/knowyourresponse/countryprogressreports/2012countries/ce_UG_Narrative_Report[1].pdf, accessed 18 September 2013.
25. Andrew M. Mwandi and Roger Tangri, 'Patronage Politics, Donor Reforms and Regime Consolidation in Uganda', *African Affairs*, 2005, 104, 416, pp. 449–676, p. 456.
26. Somerville, Keith, 'African Wars and the Politics of Ivory', *e-International relations*, April 2013, http://www.e-ir.info/2013/04/09/african-wars-and-the-politics-of-ivory/ accessed 6 July 2015.
27. Mwandi and Tangri, 2005, p. 452.
28. Ibid., p. 157.
29. Makara et al, op. cit., p. 188–9.
30. Tripp, op. cit., p. 1.
31. Tripp, op. cit., p. 153, has a clear table setting out the time span, location and leaders of the various rebellions.
32. See, for example, Titeca, Kristof, 'The spiritual order of the LRA', in Allen, Tim and Koen Vlassenroot (ed), *The Lord's Resistance Army: Myth and Reality*, London: Zed, 2010, pp. 59–73; and Behrend, Heike, 'The Holy Spirit Movement's New World: discourse and development in the North of Uganda', in Hansen and Twaddle, op. cit., pp. 245–53.
33. Jones, Ben, *Beyond the State in Rural Uganda*, Edinburgh: Edinburgh University Press, 2009, p. 48.
34. Tripp, op. cit., p. 152.
35. Kustenbauder, Matthew, 'Northern Uganda: Protracted Conflict and Structures of Violence', in Falola, Toyin and Raphael Chijioke Njoku (eds), *War and Peace in Africa*, Durham, NC: Carolina Academic Press, 2010, pp. 451–81, p. 457.
36. Allen, Tim and Koen Vlassenroot, 'Introduction', in Allen and Vlassenroot, op. cit., London: Zed, 2010, pp. 1–21, p. 8.
37. Behrend, op. cit., p. 247.
38. Allen and Vlassenroot, op. cit., p. 10.
39. Tripp, op. cit., p. 161.
40. Tripp, op. cit., p. 170.
41. Sudan Tribune, 14 May 2014, http://www.sudantribune.com/spip.php?article51012, accessed 6 July 2015.

42. See Somerville, op. cit. April 2013; Somerville, Keith, 'Rhino Poaching in South Africa: Organised Crime and Economic Opportunity Driving Trade', African Arguments, 29 October 2012, http://africanarguments.org/2012/10/29/rhino-poaching-in-south-africa-organised-crime-and-economic-opportunity-driving-trade-%E2%80%93-by-keith-somerville/ accessed 6 July 2015; and Titeca, Kristof, 'Ivory Beyond the LRA: Why a Broader Focus is Needed in Studying Poaching', African Arguments, http://africanarguments.org/2013/09/17/ivory-beyond-the-lra-why-a-broader-focus-is-needed-in-studying-poaching-by-kristof-titeca/ accessed 6 July 2015.
43. Chabal, Patrick and Jean-Pascal Daloz, *Africa Works: Disorder as Political Instrument*, Oxford: James Currey, 1999, p. xisx.
44. Africa Renewal, 'Conflict Resources: From 'Curse' to Blessing', www.UN.org/africarenewal/magazine/january–2007/conflict-resources-%E2%80 accessed 6 July 2015.
45. Sala-i-Martin, X. and A. Subramanian, *Addressing the Natural Resource Curse: An Illustration from Nigeria*, Washington, D.C.: IMF, IMF Working Paper WP 03/139, 2003, p. 5.
46. Leite, Carlos and Jens Weidmann, *Does Mother Nature Corrupt? Natural resources, Corruption, and Economic Growth*, Washington D.C.: IMF, IMF Working Paper WP 99/85, 1999, p. 3.
47. Sala-i-Martin and Subramanian, op. cit., p. 4.
48. Meredith, op. cit., 2011, p. 580.
49. Dowden, Richard, *Africa: Altered States, Ordinary Miracles*, London: Portobello, 2008, p. 445.
50. Egbo, Obiamaka, Ifeomana Wakoby, Josephat Onwumere and Chibuike Uche, 'Security Votes in Nigeria: Disguising Stealing from the Public Purse', *African Affairs*, 111, 445 (2012), pp. 597–614, p. 597.
51. See Joseph, Richard A., *Democracy and Prebendal Politics in Nigeria: The Rise and Fall of the Second Republic*, Cambridge: Cambridge University Press, 1987.
52. Bach, 2006, p. 73.
53. Okri, 2014.
54. Egbo et al, op. cit., p. 599.
55. *Human Rights Watch*, 'Satellite Images, Witness Accounts Raise Concerns of Cover-Up', *1 May 2013, http://africajournalismtheworld.com/2013/05/01/satellite-images-reveal-massive-damage-to-civilian-areas-of-baga-in-northern-nigeria/ accessed 6 July 2015.*
56. Cunliffe-Jones, op. cit., p. 217. Bach, op. cit., p. 86 says this situation of a lack of state control or accountability demonstrates Nigeria's development into a country without a functioning state.
57. Hodges, Tony, *Angola from Afro-Stalinism to Petro-Diamond Capitalism*, Oxford: James Currey, 2001, p. 1.
58. Ibid., p. 152.
59. This was conveyed strongly to the author in 1992 and later in 1996 by Margaret Anstee, the UN Secertary-General's chief representative in Angola during the 1991–2 peace process and effective head of UNAVEM. See, Anstee, Margaret

Joan, *Orphan of the Cold War: The Inside Story of the Collapse of the Angoloan Peace Process, 1992–3*, Basingsatoke: Macmillan, 1996, pp. 532–544.

60. Somerville, Keith, 'The Failure of Democratic Reform in Angola and Zaire', *Survival*, 35, 3 (1993), pp. 51–77, p. 61. During the peace process and then after the breakdown of the deal when UNITA lost the elections, the chief US representative in Luanda, Jeffrey Millington, and US Deputy Assistant Secretary of State for Africa Jeffrey Davidow both told the author that mutual accusations were inevitable and would not affect the final success of the accord.
61. This was Davidow's view of Savimbi's outlook and was confirmed to me by Isias Samakuva, the UNITA London representative in 1992. Samakuva is now UNITA's leader.
62. Nohlen, D., Krennerich, M. & Thibaut, B. (1999) *Elections in Africa: A Data Handbook*, Oxford: Oxford University Press, 1999, pp. 71–74.
63. Somerville, op. cit. 1993, p. 65.
64. Pearce, Justin, 'Control, Politics and Identity in the Angolan Civil War', *African Affairs*, July 2012, 111, 444, pp. 442–65, pp. 456–7.
65. Mills, Greg, 'From *confusão* to *estamos juntos?* Bigness, Development and State Dysfunction in Angola', in Clapham, Christopher, 2006, pp. 121–54, p. 129.
66. Pearce, Justin, 'Angola: Demonstrations and Presidential succession (things start to get interesting...)', African Arguments, 5 December 2011, http://africanarguments.org/2011/12/05/angola-demonstrations-and-presidential-succession-things-start-to-get-interesting%e2%80%a6-%e2%80%93-by-justin-pearce/, accessed 6 July 2015
67. Schubert, Jon, 'Angola Elections 2012: Dos Santos Victory Likely to Bring More Protests and Violent Repression', *African Arguments*, 28 August 2012, http://africanarguments.org/2012/08/28/angola-elections-2012-dos-santos-victory-likely-to-bring-more-protests-and-violent-repression-%E2%80%93-by-jon-schubert/ accessed July 6 2015.
68. Faria, Paulo C., *The Post-War Angola: Public Sphere, Political Regime and Democracy*, Newcastle: Cambridge Scholars Publishing, 2013, p. 177.
69. Thomson, op. cit., p. 101.
70. Taylor, Ian, *Botswana's 'Developmental State' and the Politics of Legitimacy*, paper prepared for international conference co-sponsored by the Political Economy Research Centre at the University of Sheffield and the Centre for the Study of Globalisation and Regionalisation. University of Warwick, 'Towards a New Political Economy of Development: Globalisation and Governance', University of Sheffield, United Kingdom, July 4–6, 2002, p. 4.
71. See Survival International, *Boycott Botswana Tourism*, http://www.survivalinternational.org/emails/boycott-botswana, accessed 6 July 2015.
72. Survival International, *The Bushmen*, http://www.survivalinternational.org/tribes/bushmen, accessed 6 July 2015.
73. Good, Kenneth, 'Resource Dependency and its Consequences: The Costs of Botswana's Shining Gems', *Journal of Contemporary Africa Studies*, 23, 1 (2005) pp. 25–50, pp. 25, 28–9.
74. Hillbom, Ellen, 'Botswana: "A Development-Oriented Gate-Keeping State"', *African Affairs*, 111, 442 (2012), pp. 67–89, p. 67.

75. Taylor, Ian, 'Botswana as a "Development-Oriented Gate-Keeping State": a Response', *African Affairs*, July 2012, 111, 444 (2012) pp. 466–76, p. 469.
76. For accounts of Botswana's early years and development path see, Molutsi, Patrick, The ruling class and democracy in Botswana', in Holm, John and Patrick Molutsi (eds), *Democracy in Botswana*, Gaborone: Macmillan, 1989; and Abdi Ismail Samatar, *An African Miracle: State and Class Leadership and Colonial Legacy in Botswana*, Portsmouth, NJ: 1999.
77. Eriksen, Stein Sundstøl, 'Regimes, constituencies and the politics of state formation: Zimbabwe and Botswana Compared', *International Political Science Review*, 33, 3 (2011) pp. 261–78, p. 267.
78. Somerville, Keith, 'Botswana at the Crossroads', *World Today*, February 1994, 50, 2, 22–4, p. 22; and Molutsi, op. cit., p. 105.
79. http://www.thevoicebw.com/2014/10/31/political-analysis/, accessed 4 July 2015.
80. UN Economic Commission for Africa, *African Governance Report III: Elections and the Management of Diversity*, Oxford: UNCA/Oxford Univeristy Press, 2013, p. 99.
81. Then-Vice-President Festus Mogae told me in October 1993 in Gaborone that the government was taken aback by the level of opposition and so changed the water plans; he lauded it, though, as an example of Botswana's accountability. See also UNECA, *Democratic Governance in Botswana*, 1998, http://www.uneca.org/unsia/cluster/govern/botswana.htm#5.%20SUMMARY, accessed 3 October 2013.
82. AlertNet, 'Botswana Women Win Landmark Right to Inherit Under Customary Law', http://allafrica.com/stories/201309040672.html?aa_source=mf-hdlns, accessed 7 July 2015.
83. http://www.tradingeconomics.com/botswana/unemployment-rate, accessed 4 July 2015.
84. Good, Kenneth and Ian Taylor, 'Mounting Repression in Botswana', *The Round Table*, 96, 390 (2007), pp. 275–8, p. 275.
85. Taylor, op. cit., pp. 472–3.
86. Thomson, op. cit., p. 105.
87. Anderson, David, *Kenya's Agony*, Royal African Society, 2008, http://mail.royalafricansociety.org/ras-publications-and-reports/443.html, accessed 7 July 2015.
88. Cheeseman, Nic, 'The Kenyan Elections of 2007: An Introduction,' *Journal of Eastern African Studies*, 2, 2 (2008), pp. 166–84, p. 167.
89. Branch, Daniel and Nic Cheeseman, 'Democratization, Sequencing and State Failure in Africa: Lessons from Kenya', *African Affairs*, 108, 430 (2009), pp. 1–26, p. 15.
90. Lynch, Gabrielle 'Courting the Kalenjin: The Failure of Dynasticism and the Strength of the ODM Wave in Kenya's Rift Valley Province', *African Affairs*, 2008, 107, 429, pp. 541–568, pp. 542–3.
91. Mueller, Susanne D., 'The Political Economy of Kenya's Crisis', *Journal of Eastern African Studies*, 2, 2 (2008), pp. 185–210, p. 191.
92. See Human Rights Watch (2008), *Kenya: Ballots to Bullets*, https://www.hrw.org/report/2008/03/16/ballots-bullets/organized-political-violence-and-kenyas-crisis-governance, accessed 7 July 2015.

93. Ibid.
94. Lynch, Ganrielle, *Kenyan Politics and the Ethnic Factor: The Case of the Kalenjin*, PhD dissertation, Univeristy of Oxford, 2007, Chapter 1.
95. For more details see the Kenya chapter in Somerville, Keith, *Radio Propaganda and the Broadcasting of Hatred*, Basingstoke: Palgrave Macmillan, 2012. The author was used by the ICC to provide expert opinion on the use of hate propaganda.
96. Eriksen, op. cit., p. 264
97. Scoones, Ian, Nelson Marongwe, Blasio Mavedzenge, Jacob Mahenehene, Felix Murimbarimba and Crispen Sukume, *Zimbabwe's Land Reform: Myths and Realities*, Woodbridge, Suffolk: James Currey, 2010, p. 15.
98. Scoones et al, op. cit., pp. 15–6.
99. Palmer, Robin, 'Land Reforms in Zimbabwe, 1980–1990', *African Affairs*, 89, 335 (1990), pp. 163–81, pp. 163–4.
100. Bourne, Richard, *Catastrophe:What Went Wrong in Zimbabwe*, London: Zed, 2011, p. 122.
101. James Muzondidya, 'From Buoyancy to Crisis, 1980–1997', in Raftopoulos, Brian and Alois Mlambo (eds), *Becoming Zimbabwe: A History from the Pre-Colonial Period to 2008*, Harare: Weaver Press, 2009, pp. 167–200, p. 189.
102. Bourne, op. cit., p. 127.
103. Meredith, Martin, *Mugabe: Power, Plunder, and the Struggle for Zimbabwe*, New York: Public Affairs, 2002, p. 82.
104. See Davies, Rob, 'Memories of Underdevelopment: a Personal Interpretation of Zimbabwe's Economic Decline', in Raftopoulos, Brian and Tyrone Savage (eds), *Zimbabwe: Injustice and Political Reconciliation*, Cape Town: Institute of Justice and Reconciliation, 2004, http://www.sarpn.org/documents/d0001154/P1273-davies_zimbabwe_2004.pdf, accessed 7 July 2015.
105. Bourne, op. cit., p. 127.
106. Cited by Meredith, Martin, op. cit., 2002, p. 133.
107. Bourne, op. cit., p. 128; and Meredith, op. cit., 2002, pp. 135–6.
108. Bourne, op. cit., p. 146.
109. Southall, Roger, *Liberation Movements in Power: Party and State in Southern Africa*, Pietermaritzburg: University of KwaZulu-Natal Press/James Currey, 2013, p. 113.
110. Scoones et al, op. cit., p. 23.
111. Alexander, Jocelyn, *The Unsettled Land: State-making and the Politics of Land in Zimbabwe, 1893–2003*, Oxford: James Currey, 2006, p. 185.
112. Hanlon, Joseph, Jeanette Manjengwa, and Teresa Smart, *Zimbabwe Takes Back Its Land*, Sterling, Vrginia: Kumarian Press, 2013, p. 209.
113. Scoones et al, op. cit., pp. 236–40. For a critical approach see Plaut, Martin, 'Zimbabwe takes back its land—a review by Martin Plaut', *African Arguments*, 21 March 2013, http://africanarguments.org/2013/03/21/zimbabwe-takes-back-its-land-%E2%80%93-a-review-by-martin-plaut/, accessed 7 July 2015.
114. Bourne, op. cit., p. 176.
115. Raftopoulos, Brian, 'The Crisis in Zimbabwe, 1998–2008', in Raftopoulos and Mlambo (eds), op. cit., pp. 201–32, p. 215.

116. Bourne, op. cit., pp. 194–5 and Raftopoulos, op. cit., 2008, pp. 220–1.
117. Scarnecchia, Timothy, '*The Hard Road to Reform: the Politics of Zimbabwe's Global Political Agreement*—reviewed by Timothy Scarnecchia', *African Arguments*, 15 July 2013, http://africanarguments.org/2013/07/15/review-the-hard-road-to-reform-the-politics-of-zimbabwe%E2%80%99s-global-political-agreement-reviewed-by-timothy-scarnecchia/, accessed 7 July 2015.
118. Bourne, op. cit., p. 204.
119. Raftopoulos, op. cit., 2009, p. 230.
120. Solidarity Peace Trust, 'The End of A Road: The 2013 Elections in Zimbabwe', *Solidarity Peace Trust Johannesburg*, October 2013, http://www.solidaritypeace-trust.org/download/The%20End%20of%20A%20Road%20final%20version.pdf accessed 7 July 2015, p. 3.
121. Ibid., p. 16.
122. Muzondidya, James, 'The opposition dilemma in Zimbabwe: A Critical Review of the Politics of the Movement for Democratic Change Parties under the GPA Government Framework, 2009–2012,' in Raftopoulos, Brian (ed), *The Hard Road to Reform: the Politics of Zimbabwe's Global Political Agreement*, Harare: Weaver Press/Solidarity Peace Trust, 2013, p. 50.

7. AFRICA AND THE WORLD: A NEW UNITY, THE CHINA SYNDROME, AND AFRICA RISING

1. Nugent, Paul, *Africa Since Independence: A Comparative History*, Basingstoke: Palgrave Macmillan, 2nd edition, 2012, p. 107.
2. Makinda, Samuel M. and F. Wafula Okumu, *The African Union: Challenges of Globalisation, Security and Governance*, Abingdon, Oxon.: Routledge, 2008, p. 2.
3. Rodt, Annemarie Peen, *The African Mission in Burundi: The Successful Management of Violent Ethno-Political Conflict?* Exeter: Ethnopolitics Papers, no. 10, May 2011, pp. 4–5; http://centres.exeter.ac.uk/exceps/downloads/Ethnopolitics%20papers_No10_peen%20rodt%20-%20african%20union.pdf accessed 7 July 2015.
4. Cited by Meredith, Martin, *The Fate of Africa: A History of the Continent Since Independence*, New York: Public Affairs, 2011, p. 690.
5. Maathai, Wangari, *The Challenge for Africa*, London: Arrow Books, 2010, p. 127.
6. Melber, Henning, *South Africa and NEPAD—quo vadis?* Centre for Policy Studies, Policy Brief 31, http://www.cps.org.za/cps%20pdf/polbrief31.pdf, accessed 7 July 2015.
7. For a development of this argument see Taylor, Ian, *NEPAD: Towards Africa's Development or Another False Start*?, Boulder, CO: Lynn Rienner, 2005.
8. Ocnus.net, 'China is Filling the Gap Left by Nepad's Failure', June 2010, http://www.ocnus.net/artman2/publish/Africa_8/China-is-Filling-the-Gap-Left-by-Nepad-s-Failure.shtml, accessed 7 July 2015.
9. AU Constitutive Act, http://www.au.int/en/about/constitutive_act, accessed 7 July 2015.
10. See Washington Post, 'MAP: The U.S. Military Currently Has Troops in These African Countries', 21 May 2014, http://www.washingtonpost.com/blogs/world-

views/wp/2014/05/21/map-the-u-s-currently-has-troops-in-these-african-countries/, accessed 7 July 2015.

11. Rodt, op. cit., p. 11.
12. Murithi, Tim, 'Briefing—The African Union at Ten: An Appraisal', *African Affairs*, 111, 445 (2012), pp. 662–9, p. 668.
13. Tutu, Desmond, 'Pulling out of the ICC Would be Tragic For Africa', *The East African*, 11 October 2013, http://www.theeastafrican.co.ke/OpEd/comment/Pulling-out-of-the-ICC-would-be-tragic-for-Africa/-/434750/2029008/-/4d5ljez/-/index.html, accessed 7 July 2013.
14. Hyden, Goran, *African Politics in Comparative Perspective*, Camrbidge: Cambridge University Press, 2nd edition, 2013, p. 177.
15. For an excellent analysis of these issues, see Epprecht, Marc, *Sexuality and Social Justice in Africa: Rethinking Homophobia and Forging Resistance*, London: Zed, 2013.
16. Hentz James J., 'The Contending Currents in United States Involvement in Sub-Saharan Africa', in Taylor, Ian and Paul Williams, *Africa in International Politics External Involvement on the Continent*, London: Routledge, 2004, pp. 23–40, p. 38.
17. Van de Walle, Nicolas, 'US Policy Towards Africa: The Bush legacy and the Obama administration', *African Affairs*, 109, 434 (2010), pp. 1–22, p. 8.
18. Bell, Martin, 'Disaster on a Colossal Scale—But as Far as the Media is Concerned, it isn't News', *The Independent*, 14 November 2013, http://www.independent.co.uk/voices/commentators, accessed 7 July 2015; and Plaut, Martin, 'Why the Threat of Genocide Hangs Over the Central African Republic', http://martinplaut.wordpress.com/2013/11/04/why-the-threat-of-genocide-hangs-over-the-central-african-republic/ accessed 7 July 2015.
19. See Lyman, Princeton N., *The War on Terrorism in Africa*, available at http://www.cfr.org/content/thinktank/Lyman_chapter_Terrorism.pdf, accessed 7 July 2015.
20. Africa—News and Analysis, 'Global Leaders Pledge Over $8bn for Sahel Growth Projects', http://africajournalismtheworld.com/2013/11/05/global-leaders-pledge-over-8bn-for-sahel-growth-projects/ accessed 7 July 2015.
21. Francis M. Deng, 'Reconciling Sovereignty with Responsibility: A Basis for International Humanitarian Action', in John W. Harbeson and Donald Rothchild (eds), *Africa in World Politics*, Boulder, CO, Westview Press, 2013, pp. 234–5.
22. This was set out very clearly by Tony Chafer at his seminar, 'The UK and France in West Africa: towards convergence?' at the Africa Research Group, War Studies, King's College London, 30 October 2013.
23. Deng, op. cit., p. 333.
24. Taylor, Ian, 'The 'All-Weather Friend'? Sino-African Interaction in the Twenty-First Century', in Taylor, Ian and Paul Williams (eds), *Africa in International Politics External Involvement on the Continent*, London: Routledge, 2004, pp. 83–101, p. 83.
25. Alden, Chris, 'China and Africa: from Engagement to Partnership', in Power, Marcus and Ana Cristina Alves (eds), *China and Angola: A Marriage of Convenience*, Cape Town: Pambazuka Press, 2012, pp. 10–25, p. 11. See also Alden, Chris, *China in Africa*, London: Zed, 2007.

26. Ibid., p. 15.
27. Cited by Brautigam, Deborah, *The Dragon's Gift: The Real Story of China in Africa*, Oxford: Oxford University Press, 2009, p. 146.
28. Dittigen, Romain, 'From Isolation to Integration? A Study of Chinese Retailers in Dakar', *SAIIA Occasional Papers*, 57, March 2010, p. 12.
29. Alden, op. cit., p. 20.
30. Dowden, Richard, 'Extraordinary Ethiopia—Ancient, Booming but Undemocratic', *African Arguments*, 19 November 2013, http://africanarguments.org/2013/11/19/extraordinary-ethiopia-ancient-booming-but-undemocratic-by-richard-dowden/ accessed 7 July 2015.
31. Brautigam, op. cit., p. 248.
32. Cotula, Lorenzo, *The Great African Land Grab? Agricultural Investments and the Global Food System*, London: Zed, 2013, p. 63; and Brautigam, op. cit., p. 253.
33. Bond, Patrick, *Looting Africa: the Economics of Exploitation*, Scottsville: University of KwaZulu Natal Press/Zed, 2006, p. 74.
34. Cited by Brautigam, op. cit., pp. 5–6.
35. Alden, 2007, pp. 80–1.
36. Robertson, Charles et al, *The Fastest Billion: The Story Behind Africa's Economic Revolution*, London: Renaissance Capital Securities Ltd, 2012, p. 4.
37. Ibid., p. 7.
38. Rotberg, Robert I., *Africa Emerges: Consummate Challenges, Abundant Opportunities*, Cambridge: Polity, 2013, p. 5.
39. August, Oliver, 'A Hopeful Continent', *The Economist*, 2 March 2013, http://www.economist.com/news/special-report/21572377-african-lives-have-already-greatly-improved-over-past-decade-says-oliver-august, accessed 7 July 2015.
40. Rowden, Richard, 'The Myth of Africa's rise', *Third World Economics*, 536 (2013), pp. 5–6.
41. Ibid.
42. Rotberg, op. cit., p. 13.
43. United Nation's Children's Fund, *Levels and Trends in Child Mortality, Report 2014: Estimates Developed by the UN Inter-Agency Group for Child Mortality Estimation*, http://www.unicef.org/media/files/Levels_and_Trends_in_Child_Mortality_2014.pdf, accessed 5 July 2015.
44. World Bank, 'Mortality rate under five (per 1,000 live births)', http://data.worldbank.org/indicator/SH.DYN.MORT?order=wbapi_data_value_2013+wbapi_data_value+wbapi_data_value-last&sort=asc, accessed 5 July 2015.
45. African Child Policy Forum, *The African Report on Child Well-being 2013*, Executive Summary, http://www.africanchildforum.org/africanreport/, 2013, p. xiv, accessed 7 July 2015.
46. See Jerven, Morten, *Poor Numbers: How we are Misled by African Development Statistics and What to Do About It*, Ithaca: Cornell University Press, 2013; and The Globe and Mail, 'B.C. professor ruffles feathers by spotlighting Africa's data problems', 14 November 2013, http://www.theglobeandmail.com/news/world/bc-professor-ruffles-feathers-by-spotlighting-africas-data-problems/article15434240/, accessed 7 July 2015.
47. Muchayi, William, 'Where Africa's New Narratives Go Wrong', *Think Africa*

Press, 6 July 2013, available at http://www.albanyassociates.com/notebook/2013/07/where-africas-new-narratives-go-wrong/, accessed 7 July 2015.

POSTSCRIPT: STRUCTURE AND AGENCY IN AFRICA

1. Booth, David and Diana Cammack, *Governance for Development in Africa: Solving Collective Actions Problems*, London: Zed, 2013, p. 1.
2. Chabal, Patrick and Jean-Pascal Daloz, *Africa Works: Disorder as Political Instrument*, Oxford: James Currey, 1999, p. 10.
3. Bayart, Jean-François, *The State in Africa: The Politics of the Belly*, London: Longman, 1993, p. 261.
4. Ibid. p. 32.
5. Cabral, Amilcar, *Unity and Struggle: Speeches and Writings*, New York: Monthly Review, 1979, pp. 44–5.
6. This approach has rather been taken by a number of political scientists examining Africa in recent years. A good example is Rotberg, Robert, *Africa Emerges*, London: Polity, 2013, pp. 71–7.
7. Mills, Greg, *Why States Recover: Changing Walking Societies into Winning Nations, from Afghanistan to Zimbabwe*, London: Hurst, 2014, pp. 471–80.
8. This tendency has been critiqued well by Chabal and Daloz, op. cit., p. 125.
9. Bayart, op. cit., p. 27.
10. Ibid., p. 26.
11. Ibid., p. 25.
12. Booth and Cammack, op. cit., p. 130.
13. Straus, Scott, 'Wars Do End! Changing Patterns of Political Violence in Sub-Saharan Africa', *African Affairs*, 111, 443 (2012), pp. 179–202, p. 200.
14. Richard Dowden, *Africa: Altered States, Ordinary Miracles*, London: Portobello, 2008, p. 454.
15. See Tripp, 2010, pp. 2–4.
16. Azam, J. P., 'The Redistributive State and Conflict in Africa', *Journal of Peace Research*, 38, 4 (2001), pp. 429–44, p. 429.

HISTORIOGRAPHICAL NOTE

1. Davidson, Basil, *Africa in Modern History: The Search for a New Society*, Harmondsworth: Penguin, 1978, p. 23.
2. Ibid., pp. 23–5.
3. Thomson, Alex, *An Introduction to African Politics*, Abingdon: Routledge, Third Edition 2010, p. 22.
4. For a detailed argument on the role of states and their constitution within the international system, see Bull, Hedley, *The Anarchical Society*, London: Macmillan, 1977, p. 58.
5. Ibid., p. 53.
6. Bayart, Jean-François, 'Africa in the *World: A History of Extraversion*', *African Affairs*, 99, 395 (2000), pp. 217–67, p. 222.

7. Cooper, op. cit., 2002.
8. Ibid. pp. 4–5.
9. Nugent, Paul, *Africa Since Independence: A Comparative History*, Basingstoke: Palgrave Macmillan, 2nd edition, 2012, p. 3.
10. Cooper, Frederick, 'From Colonial State to Gatekeeper State in Africa', The Mario Einaudi Centre for International Studies, Working Paper Series, Paper 04–05, (2005), p. 8.

INDEX

INDEX

INDEX

UNIVERSITIES AT MEDWAY LIBRARY